The COMPLETE ILLUSTRATED ENCYCLOPEDIA *of*
Horses
& Ponies

Publisher and Creative Director: Nick Wells
Project Editor: Cat Emslie
Assistant Project Editor: Victoria Lyle
Picture Research: Victoria Lyle and Gemma Walters
Art Director: Mike Spender
Layout Design: Dave Jones and Mike Spender
Illustrator: Ann Biggs
Digital Design and Production: Chris Herbert
Copy Editor: Siobhan O'Connor
Proofreader: Amanda Leigh
Indexer: Penny Brown

Special thanks to: Claire Walker, Carmen Herbert,
Fiana Muhlberger and Tamsin Pickeral

18 20 21 19

3 5 7 9 10 8 6 4

This edition first published 2016 by
FLAME TREE PUBLISHING
6 Melbray Mews, Fulham,
London SW6 3NS, United Kingdom

www.flametreepublishing.com

Printed in China

The COMPLETE ILLUSTRATED ENCYCLOPEDIA of Horses & Ponies

Sarah Gorrie, Pippa Roome,
Catherine Austen, Nicola Jane Swinney

FLAME TREE
PUBLISHING

Contents

History, Culture & Anatomy

Care, Management & Riding

The Breeds

How to Use This Book

This book is divided into three main chapters, each designed to enhance an understanding of horses, their practical care, enjoyment of horses, and the various breeds that exist.

History, Culture, & Anatomy

This is an introduction to horses—their many roles throughout history and their involvement in human culture, such as art and literature, alongside their physical characteristics and behavior.

Care, Management, & Riding

This chapter offers a practical guide to horses, taking you on a journey from deciding whether and how to buy a horse, through taking care of it, to even breeding horses. If you are ready to get into the saddle, you will learn everything from the basics of tack and riding through to competing with horses.

The Breeds

This chapter begins with a closer look at the evolution of horses into the breeds we know today. It discusses wild and feral horses, and the close relatives of horses, the Equus family—such as zebras and donkeys. It then explains what a "breed" is and how they evolve and develop, as well as the different "types" that horses can be classified under. This is followed by a hefty section that details almost all known breeds of horses that exist today, divided into ponies, light horses, and heavy horses, organized within those sections by geographical origin and size.

Average height

Color variations

Basic personality type

Typical uses

Similar breeds (with similar origins)

Rough geographical origin

Typical temperament

LUNDY

HEIGHT: 13.2 hh
COLOR: all/solid colors
PERSONALITY TYPE: warm-blooded
TYPICAL USE: riding, competition

TEMPERAMENT: gentle, hardy
ORIGIN: England
SIMILAR BREEDS: Welsh, New Forest

Contrary to popular belief, the ponies of the island of Lundy, situated off the southwest coast of England, are not closely related to the area's Dartmoor and Exmoor ponies. A comparatively new equine breed, the Lundy Pony was developed in 1928 using New Forest and Welsh Section B bloodlines. The island's then owner, Martin Coles Harman, imported 34 New Forest mares and let them run with a Welsh stallion. The stallion died after only one year, having produced just a single offspring.

Height and Substance

Coles Harman's vision was a pony of style and height, a good-looking equine with quality and substance. The one colt the deceased stallion left behind proved his breeder's vision: he was a creamy dun with black points named Pepper and was to be the foundation of the herd. Allowed to breed unchecked, the herd on the island grew, until in the 1930s around 50 were rounded up and sent to the mainland to be

sold. During the Second World War, when the shipping lanes were closed, the herd increased to around 100 ponies.

The herd was moved to the mainland in 1980, but the

breed society formed in 1984 returned some of the ponies to the island later in the same decade. Connemara and Welsh Mountain Pony blood have been introduced, but otherwise the breed has had no outside influence.

Good Doer

Still a rare breed, the Lundy Pony is attractive and hardy, with a wide, deep chest, sloping shoulders, and hard, sound legs. It has a neat head and short, muscular neck. Common colors are

LEFT
The Lundy, of which there are sadly only a small number, is a well-conformed pony with a natural aptitude for jumping and a quiet temperament.

dun, roan, palomino, bay, and liver chestnut. It is a good doer and strong but is gentle enough to be a suitable child's mount. It has natural jumping ability and would make a good hunting or competition pony.

HACKNEY PONY

TEMPERAMENT: intelligent, spirited
ORIGIN: England
SIMILAR BREEDS: Fell, Hackney Horse, Thoroughbred

HEIGHT: 12–14 hh
COLOR: bay, black, brown, chestnut
PERSONALITY TYPE: warm-blooded
TYPICAL USE: driving, show

High-stepping, elegant, and spirited, the Hackney Pony is a breed in its own right and not a scaled-down version of the Hackney Horse. It owes its existence to one man, Christopher Wilson, who bred the Hackney Horse St. George to a Fell mare in 1866 and then interbred the resulting offspring to make a fixed type—for some years they were known as Wilson Ponies. Left out on the inhospitable Fells with little food or care, the breed became hardy and resilient.

withers. Its back is compact, and it has fine legs with good joints. The feet are small and hard and often allowed to grow long in the toe to accentuate the action. Ponies are usually bay, black, and brown, with the occasional chestnut, with some white markings.

The high-stepping gait is exaggerated in the Hackney Pony—it lifts its knees almost to its chest and brings its hocks right under its body. This action is not just for show; it can move at good speed with minimum bounce on a cart or carriage.

speed—head and tail carried high and proud—appearing suspended in the air for a moment at the highest point.

Exaggerated Action

By 1880 the Hackney Pony was an established breed and in high demand for its stamina and good looks. The pony has a fine head with tapering muzzle and large eyes, small, neat ears, elegantly arched neck on powerful shoulders, and low

Fascinating Facts

The Hackney Horse gets its name from the French *haquenée*, a language commonly spoken in the country in Medieval times, meaning a riding horse with an especially comfortable gait.

ABOVE LEFT
The Hackney is one of the most elegant and refined pony breeds. It has a naturally extravagant, high-stepping movement and is athletically built.

Fluid and Energetic

Its showy good looks make the Hackney Pony popular, and its fluid and energetic gait is spectacular. While the breed has a tendency to pugnaciousness, its spirit and intelligence make it a joy to watch. It is the king of the show ring, exploding across the arena with pistonlike

Height

Gives the approximate height or height range of the adult horse. Most horses are measured in "hands," which are equal to 4 in. (10 cm). If a horse is 14¾ hands high ("hh") it is written as "14.3"—this is not a decimal point.

Very Small (< 12.3 hh/ 51 in./1.28 m)

Small (13 hh/ 52 in./ 1.30m–14.3 hh/ 59 in./1.48 m)

Medium (15 hh/ 60 in./ 1.50m–15.3 hh/ 63 in./1.58 m)

Large (16 hh/ 64 in./ 1.6m–16.3 hh/ 67 in./1.68 m)

Very Large (17 hh/ 68 in./ 1.7m <)

Color

This gives the various possible color and pattern combinations that the horse is known in.

Dun, Palomino or **Gold**

Gray

White, Cremello, or **Grullo**

Black

Bay, Brown, or **Dark brown**

Chestnut or **Sorrel**

Roan (a white-flecked coat with any various possible base colors)

Patched (various, including pinto—piebald, skewbald, "colored;" tobiano, overo, sabino, tovero)

Spotted (such as Appaloosa)

Dual colored (can be any mix)

All dark, solid colors

All colors (can be found in any or most colors)

Personality Type

This does not indicate the actual body temperature of the horse (which of course is a warm-blooded animal), but rather the generalized character type that the horse fits into—for example, is it a quick, high-spirited horse that originated in the warmer regions of the world, such as the hot-blooded Arabian? Is it a half-bred or part-bred horse or the result of mixing hot-blooded and cold-blooded breeds; one of a more "solid" or "tempered" nature, and thus "warm-blooded"? Or is it a heavy horse, known as "cold-blooded" arguably because they often originated in colder, northern regions or because of their gentle, easygoing nature and stocky strength?

Cold-blooded   **Warm-blooded**   **Hot-blooded**

Typical Use

Horses can be used for many things. These icons indicate some of the uses that the breed in question is put to.

All-rounder

Driving Harness

Herding Ranching Stockhorse

All-round utility

Military Police Parade

Farm Agriculture Draft

Dressage Show Competition

Riding Leisure

Meat

Polo

Tourism Trekking Trail

Donkey/mule production

Racing

Feral

Child's pony Mounted games

Rodeo Bullfighting

Pack Stalking

Temperament

This gives a more detailed summary of the typical temperament of the breed—which may be helpful when choosing what horse to buy.

Origins

Gives the rough geographical origin of the breed, if known. Sometimes this issue can be debated.

Similar Breeds

These are examples of breeds that have similar origins—such as the Fell and Dales having Friesian influences—and are often likely to be similar in appearance.

This information is followed by a more in-depth discussion of the breed, including a look at its origins, history, development, and status today; its physical characteristics, temperament, and behavior; and its common uses.

Reference Section

At the end of the encyclopedia is a list of useful addresses and contacts, from riding schools to veterinary associations; there is also a list of titles suggested for further reading. A glossary explains any terms that might be unfamiliar or sums up what you have already learned, and a thorough index will allow you to quickly locate a specific topic.

Introduction

"Wherever man has left his footprint in the long ascent from barbarism to civilization we will find the hoof print of the horse beside it," wrote John Trotwood Moore.

The first section of this book will give readers an insight into this claim, and the book as a whole demonstrates the different ways in which horses have enriched the lives of human beings. Horses have been human companions for millions of years, and it is questionable whether civilization would have developed in the same way, or at the same speed, without them. Horses can be given significant credit for the development of civilization, as you will find as you read on in this book.

An Ever-expanding Importance

Initially, horses were hunted for meat like the prey of Neanderthal man, but they soon found a higher place in society, to the point that even today some societies frown upon the idea of eating horse meat.

With the invention of the wheel and the domestication of the horse, humankind was provided with a method of transportation that widened its horizons. Empires were expanded and enemies defeated from the backs of horses or chariots. War may

not be seen as a positive function of the horse, but think what more became possible with this new method of transportation. No longer reliant only on their two feet, humans could not only travel, but they could also communicate over much greater distances because of horses and their riders, who delivered news for centuries, long before the development of the telegraph or telephone.

Being a beast of burden, the horse also aided the plight of farmers, providing a swifter and more controllable alternative to the ox prior to the development of tractors and other locomotives. The horse has helped stricken humans in the simplest ways,

performing search and rescue in otherwise impassable terrain, aiding the police at riots with crowd control, and centuries ago bringing aid to soldiers and the sick—the first ambulances were, after all, pulled by horses. All these services and more that have been carried out around the world throughout history are described within the book.

Part of Human Culture
Humankind has repaid its debt to the horse by honoring this animal through art, literature, mythology, and legend. The horse's importance has not been forgotten and was recognized even thousands of years ago when humans painted horses on cave walls. The horse is still the only animal used to carry the monarch in most societies, or for example, to pay tribute to a fallen president.

Animals of Flight

Being that they are flight animals, it is a wonder that horses allow riders to mount them at all. The horse's instincts of flight have had to be conquered in order that it can carry out its roles as war horse, cart horse, police horse, and so on. This behavior and psychology is discussed in the first section of this book, too.

Understanding Horses Today

These creatures of many roles are complicated beings, a fact that is also explored within this encyclopedia. As any horse owner will be aware, there are plenty of ailments that can afflict a horse, and these are described within this resource. The complicated structure of their legs, for example, as described in Anatomy and Appearance, combined with the horse's use, makes leg injuries to working animals common.

In the twenty-first century, horses are predominantly used for recreation, although in less ind`ustrialized countries they still perform the functions in agriculture, for example, that they used to in the Western world. Private individuals increasingly keep horses for recreation, and riding is a popular sport for all ages. There are riding schools around the world where anyone can learn. In this encyclopedia, you will find an explanation of the basic principles of horse riding.

Horse riding is one of the only sports where men and women compete alongside each other, even at an Olympic level. The numbers of spectators at equestrian events are growing. Racing is by far the most popular sport, with its association with gambling, but show jumping, dressage, eventing, and other

sports have increasing levels of support and attract more and more interest.

Invaluable Information

Horses are not easy animals to take care of, and their care and maintenance is explained

in Care, Management, and Riding. This section describes how a horseman or woman should keep and take care of the animal, from possible ailments that might be witnessed, through an explanation of the breeding process, to tacking up the horse for riding.

You will also find an explanation of the different types of recreational and sporting activities horses are now involved in, from show jumping to gymkhanas.

The Breeds section of the encyclopedia explains in detail the hundreds of different breeds of horses that are seen today. Different types are more equipped for different tasks, and many have been bred for certain purposes throughout history. Readers can discover the myriad difference between breeds, and each of their strengths and unique characteristics.

History, Culture & Anatomy

A CREATURE OF MANY ROLES

No other animal has contributed to society as much and in as many different ways as the horse. Since first being domesticated around 3000–4000 B.C., horses have been utilized for transport, warfare, reconnaissance, raids, communication, hunting, logging, farming, and ranching; their meat and milk have provided sustenance. They play important roles in patrol, law enforcement, search and rescue, and ceremonial duties, and are used in sports, leisure, and even therapy. Possibly no other animal has been responsible for assisting the advancement of civilization to the same degree as the horse.

War

For thousands of years, the horse's warfare role included combat, raids, transportation, and reconnaissance. Types of warhorses developed over time. For example, with the start of armored knights in Europe, heavier horses that were able to cope with the extra weight replaced the small, swift horses chosen for their maneuverability.

Early Mounted Warfare

Homer's *Iliad* describes warriors being taken to battle in chariots and fighting on foot; however, archaeological evidence suggests that the Egyptians, for example, chose early on to fight from chariots. Armies later had no choice but to fight from horseback when encountering impassable terrain. The Greek general Xenophon (*c.* 430–355 B.C.) wrote a manual on the art of horsemanship that is still referred to in the twenty-first century. The Romans" mounted army invaded Britain, but their Empire was destroyed in turn by horsemen, including the Huns. The Mongols famously raided and fought ruthlessly from horseback.

Changing Times for Warhorses

Horses remained on the front line for centuries after the invention of firearms in the 1500s. Hundreds of horses were lost to gunfire at the Battle of Waterloo (1815) and again when Britain's Light Brigade advanced into Russian guns during the Crimean War (1853–56). Charging cavalry with lances took part in the First World War alongside artillery. Thousands of horses were lost to German guns in the Second World War. In recent conflicts—for example, in Afghanistan and Bosnia—horses have helped armies over difficult terrain and transported both goods and refugees.

Ceremonial Horses

Horses have performed ceremonial responsibilities for centuries in countries including China, Russia and India, where the President's Bodyguards perform ceremonial duties as well as being trained paratroopers. Most European royalty kept carriage horses for ceremonial occasions. The French cavalry regiment, the Garde Républicaine, carries out law enforcement and acts as the state escort.

American Ceremonial Horses

The Third United States Infantry Regiment, known as the Old Guard, escorts the president and serves at state and military full-honors funerals. Horses are extensively trained for this purpose so that they always remain calm, despite the gunfire. The regiment's horses are divided into separate groups of light and dark colors. Six horses, three of which are mounted, pull the funeral caisson. A horse without a rider, known as a caparisoned horse, is led in funeral possessions with boots placed backward in its stirrups. Black Jack was the most famous caparisoned horse, serving in presidential funerals including that of President John F. Kennedy. President Abraham Lincoln's own horse, Old Bob, performed this duty at his funeral.

British Royal Horses

The Household Cavalry is made up of two mounted regiments, the Life Guards and the Blues and Royals. Its role includes guarding the monarch and participating in ceremonial duties such as Trooping the Color. Both regiments are predominantly made up of black horses. The King's Troop Royal Horse Artillery also carries

out ceremonial duties and displays with six horses pulling heavy artillery at great speeds. The Windsor Grays, who are responsible for driving the sovereign, pulled the gold state coach that took Elizabeth II to her coronation in 1953. The Royal Canadian Mounted Police gave Queen Elizabeth II a charger named Burmese, whom she rode for nearly 20 years at Trooping the Color.

Transport

After horses were domesticated, they were the most effective form of transport for thousands of years. With the wheel already in existence, domesticated horses were immediately used to pull chariots. Horses were also ridden, but many early types were too small to carry much weight, so two would pull a chariot together. Chariots gradually became more refined—for example,

changing from solid wheels to those with spokes. The Chinese, in particular, quickly developed effective chariots and harnesses.

The Effects of Horse Transportation

Horse transportation enabled larger battles—for example, between the Hittites and Egyptians—and for empires to extend their boundaries farther than would have otherwise been possible. Transportation also improved communication. Nations, including those of the Mongols and Romans, sent horses and riders several hours" riding distance apart, so that messages could be passed quickly over great

distances by relay. Until the invention of telegraphs, postal services around the world relied on individual riders and stagecoaches for communication. The famous Pony Express in the United States is one example of this.

Later Forms of Horse Transportation

Throughout the nineteenth and twentieth centuries, even after the invention of self-propelled vehicles, tradespeople in countries including the United Kingdon and the United States made deliveries by horse and cart. Horses also pulled buses and trams, ambulances, police and fire vehicles, funeral carriages, and garbage collectors. These

animals" burdens were heavy, and they had a low life expectancy. Thousands worked as taxis in cities including New York and London. In the U.K., heavier horses pulled boats along canals and large vehicles on railroads, even after the invention of steam trains in the early 1800s. Throughout the Industrial Revolution and until the 1990s, ponies transported coal in mines. The wealthy kept horses and carriages or dogcarts for private use, or smaller vehicles such as gigs and phaetons.

Fascinating Facts

The renowned Pony Express, which carried mail from Missouri to California from 1860–61, inspired the 1950s Western *Pony Express*, starring Charlton Heston.

BELOW

Clydesdales like these are especially popular in the United States, and are associated with the brewery Budweiser, who breed them. They are used for pulling the brewery drays and tourist trolleys, as seen here.

BELOW

Hansom cabs were the "original" taxis and were widespread in Europe and the United States during the 1800s. The last horse-drawn taxi license was issued in London, England, in 1946.

Agriculture

Horses have played an essential role in agriculture around the world for thousands of years and still do so in areas of Eastern Europe, such as Romania, as well as parts of the developing world. The horse's role in farming changed over time and has now largely been filled by machinery. Many economics relied heavily on horse-powered agriculture until the invention of tractors, at which point millions of horses bred for farming became surplus to requirements.

Farm Horses

Horses worked the land in countries including the United Kingdom and the United States by pulling plows, transporting produce, and being used for logging. Other countries, such as China, used oxen and mules for farming, keeping horses for transportation and military purposes. Oxen were stronger but slower than the relatively small horses available. Countries that chose to use horses in agriculture had to breed heavier "draft" types capable of pulling heavy plows and loads. They also developed lighter plows

that the horses could cope with more easily and which were better equipped for faster movement, therefore increasing productivity. Later on in North America, teams of horses were used to pull large combine harvesters, while other horse-drawn machinery included reapers and threshing equipment. Even in the U.S., horses are still used in ranching today.

Horse Products

Before their domestication, horses were hunted for meat and are still slaughtered for food in parts of the world today. Countries including Mongolia consume horse

milk and produce *kumis*, which is fermented mare's milk. Horsehide is used to make a variety of leather goods, while horsetails can be used to make bows for string instruments. Parts of the horse, including their hooves and skin, can be turned into glue. In the United States, hormones are extracted from pregnant mares" urine to be used for hormone replacement therapy.

Police

Mounted police still operate in the twenty-first century all around the world, in countries including the United States, Japan, Canada, Australia, India, the United Kingdom, and many parts of Europe. They are mainly used for patrol and crowd control. In countries including India, they might be used to control crowds at a festival, while in the United Kingdom they are often seen outside soccer games, where they are used to intimidate potential troublemakers. Horses also form part of search-and-rescue teams in areas that are hard to reach by vehicle.

Police around the World
Mounted police form part of border patrols in countries such as India and the United States, where U.S. Customs and Border Protection monitors the border with Mexico, to prevent illegal immigration and other unlawful activities. The

Royal Canadian Mounted Police (RCMP), with their distinctive red uniforms and "Mounty" nickname, used to be solely responsible for law enforcement and keeping the peace in large areas of desolate landscape throughout Canada. Mounted police in the RCMP are still commonly seen—mostly on patrol in national parks (as are American mounted police), and they also take part in musical rides. British police horses also take part in displays, where they can be

seen jumping through hoops of fire. Police horses commonly wear protective tack, including kneepads and a clear shield across their face when attending demonstrations where riots are predicted. Police also use horses when controlling and directing traffic in busy cities around the world.

Training Police Horses
Police horses have to be trained to cope with loud and frightening situations where their instinct is to flee. They

undergo months of special training to ensure they will be unfazed by traffic, large crowds, loud noises, smoke, and other potential hazards. Some horses with nervous dispositions never adjust to this line of work and are sold out of the police force.

BELOW

The United States mounted border patrol operates primarily along the Mexican-American border to prevent illegal immigration. The horses are able to navigate difficult terrain and form an essential part of the team.

Sport

As machinery has replaced horses in agriculture, transportation, and warfare in the developed world, horses are most commonly used for leisure activities and in sports. Professional horsemen and women earn money from training, selling, breeding, and competing. The most popular horse sport—racing—with its links to gambling, has the greatest effect on the economy.

Harness Racing

The Persians used horses for racing as early as 600 B.C. Chariot racing with teams of four and two horses took place in Ancient Greece at early Olympiads, as well as racing on horseback. The Romans also held chariot

RIGHT

The British Grand National is the most famous steeplechase and one of the most challenging in the world. It attracts over 600 million viewers worldwide. See page 18.

ABOVE

The Kentucky Derby, a race for three-year old Thoroughbred horses, is one of the most famous flat races in the world. It is held annually on the first Saturday in May and is run over a 1.25-mile dirt track.

races. Harness racing is now popular in Australia, New Zealand, Russia, parts of Europe, and predominantly the United States. Horses are raced at two different paces, either trotting (with the legs moving in diagonal pairs) or pacing (where the legs move in lateral pairs). The driver sits in a lightweight carriage called a 'sulky." In Switzerland, harness races take place on snow using a sleigh instead of a wheeled vehicle.

Flat Racing

Britain is the home of racing, and from the 1600s, British breeders developed the Thoroughbred racehorse. The United Kingdom's flat racing governing body, the

Jockey Club, is located in Newmarket, which is also the most popular base for trainers. Flat races in the United Kingdom and Europe run predominantly on grass between March and October, although all-weather tracks are also used. The biggest flat races in the United Kingdom include the Derby, the Oaks, and the St. Leger. The United Kingdom's most famous flat courses include Epsom, Doncaster, and Goodwood. Despite being based on the British model, flat races in the United States commonly run on dirt tracks. Lexington, Kentucky, is the home of flat racing and of the famous Kentucky Derby. In the United States, American Quarter Horses are used for the shorter, sprinting races (of just two furlongs or 0.25 of a mile—which explains the name Quarter Horses), rather than the Thoroughbreds required in British racing. Thoroughbreds are raced in longer sprints, however.

Show Jumping

Show jumping developed from the cavalry training of horses over cross-country fences. Show-jumping competitions became more common in the late 1800s, and team events (Nations" Cups) were dominated by the military for decades. Back then, style played a part in the competition, while in the twenty-first century penalty marks are scored for time faults or jumping errors such as a knockdown or refusal. Show jumping is an Olympic sport affiliated to the international equestrian federation (Fédération Equestre Internationale, or

Jump Racing

The U.S.'s Maryland Hunt Cup is a cross-country race featuring fixed fences and is a variation of steeplechasing, which is a popular sport in the U.K. and Ireland, where horses race over obstacles built out of natural materials. Steeplechases are longer than flat races, and the jumps are large, challenging, and can feature drops, ditches, and water. The U.K.'s most famous steeplechase—the Grand National—has 30 fences and takes place in Liverpool every year.

The legendary Red Rum won the Grand National a record three times. Other great steeplechases include the Cheltenham Gold Cup, held at Cheltenham racecourse in Gloucestershire, and the Pardubice, which is held in the Czech Republic. Hurdle races are similar to steeplechases, but these run over smaller fences that give way when the horse hits them. Point-to-pointing is a form of jump racing for amateurs organized by hunts around the U.K. and also takes place in Ireland.

FEI). Competition formats vary, and classes can include several rounds. There are competitions for speed, and in puissance classes (the high jump), a wall is built up until there is only one horse remaining that can clear it. A common show-jumping track includes portable fences made out of colored poles. Popular international events include those that take place at Spruce Meadows in Alberta, Canada, and those in Aachen, Germany.

Leisure

In countries where horses are no longer required for transportation and farming, they are now rented or kept for leisure purposes. Horses are playing a larger role in tourism, too—for example, on horseback safaris and for ranching vacations. Millions of people worldwide learn horsemanship at riding schools and enjoy renting horses for trekking excursions. Millions more

Types of Leisure Riding

Horse owners also compete for leisure, often through clubs or associations. Competition formats vary in different countries, and each has their own governing body. In showing, exhibitors present their horse or pony to a judge to be assessed for conformation, movement,

keep horses and ponies for leisure either at livery yards or on their own land. Popular activities include hacking, trail riding, and hunting plus riding club and Pony Club activities.

and manners. Classes are split for different breeds and types. There are both in-hand and ridden classes, and handlers can also use lead reins on small ponies with very young riders. In hunter classes, competitors also jump a course of rustic fences.

Dressage is an Olympic sport but at lower levels is a popular leisure activity. Dressage means training a horse to the highest possible level, so that it accurately

performs a number of movements at different paces in a relaxed way in response to the rider's subtle aids. Eventing is a complete competition combining dressage, show jumping, and cross-country, which is a test of endurance and bravery over challenging natural fences. Events take place over one, two, or three days. Other sports for leisure riders include show jumping, polo, driving, and endurance.

Young Riders

Hundreds of pony clubs are active in the United Kingdom, the United States, Canada, Australia, and New Zealand, teaching riding, horse management, and teamwork through rallies and camps during vacations. Countries including the U.K. and the U.S. have schemes that young riders can join to concentrate on one discipline, such as show jumping, and train to compete against children from other regions or internationally. Some schools and universities also have their own riding clubs.

Fascinating Facts

The Annual Brooksville Raid Festival has become the largest civil war reenactment and is located in Florida, with over 3,700 reenactors and their families participating in 2007, where they also had 32 cannons and 78 horses.

Other Popular Activities

In the United States and Canada and other parts of the world such as Australia and Argentina, rodeos are popular with spectators, who witness professional riders on bucking broncos, bareback riding, and roping. The U.S. Professional Rodeo Cowboys Association governs rodeos in the United States, and competition involves prize money. Women more commonly take part in barrel racing, where riders are timed racing around barrels set at points in the arena. Western classes are also more common in the United States. In these competitions, riders have to demonstrate how responsive their horses are to their aids through a variety of movements and obstacles. The level of difficulty at such events ranges from the most straightforward pleasure classes to reining, which is an international sport featuring difficult maneuvers performed at high speeds.

Hunting

Hunting on horseback, which used to be essential for food, is now a form of pest control and a leisure activity for all ages of riders in countries including the U.K., Ireland, France, New Zealand, and the United States. Packs of hound dogs most commonly hunt foxes, boar, and stag, depending on the area. In places where hunts have been banned from hunting with hounds, they still follow a trail of scent. Hunts in the U.K. are currently seeking to reverse a hunting ban. Drag hunting, where riders and hounds follow a "line," is also a popular pastime.

Reenactments

Riders can combine an interest in horses with history by joining historical reenactments of famous battles. Horses and riders are dressed in clothing and tack appropriate for the era, adding to the authenticity. In the United States, reenactments of the Civil War are popular, and some take place on the actual battlegrounds. In the U.K., common reenactments include those of the English Civil War and battles from the Napoleonic era.

Industry and Commerce

Around the world, horses play a significant role within world economies, whether this is through farming, transportation, tourism, sports, or leisure.

The Horse's Contribution to World Economies

Ranching is still big industry in areas including North and South America, and horsemeat is a major source of income for many other farmers. Horses are used heavily in the developing world within agriculture and transportation, too. In the industrialized world, horses mainly contribute to the economy through their roles in sports and leisure. Racing has a large impact on these economies, partly due to its association with gambling. In the future, horses may play a lesser role in farming and transportation in developing countries, but leisure and sporting activities are likely to expand as these countries become wealthier. Jobs supported by the horse industry include areas such as retail, saddlery, farriery, grooming, veterinary, and farming, as well as horse breeders, trainers, and dealers.

American and British Horse Economies

In 2005, the American Horse Council commissioned Deloitte Consulting to produce a study entitled *The Economic Impact of the Horse Industry in the United States*. This study found that the U.S. horse industry made a $39 billion impact on the American economy. When including indirect and induced spending, this figure reached $102 billion. The report found there were

9.2 million horses in the United States, supporting 1.4 million jobs.

The British Equestrian Trade Association's (BETA) National Equestrian Survey 2006 concluded that horse owners and riders in the U.K. spend around £4 billion ($8 million) on their leisure activity. It stated there are around 1.35 million horses in the U.K. At least one person out of 2.1 million British households had ridden or driven a horse regularly in the past year, and at least one person out of 1 million households is responsible for a horse's maintenance.

HORSES IN HUMAN CULTURE

The tremendous impact that horses have had on the progress of civilization is reflected in the high regard in which horses have been held throughout history. This regard has been demonstrated through both literature and art over the centuries. The fact that horses were even placed up with the gods in mythology illustrates their significance in the ancient world, and many cultures have built legends and traditions based on the importance of the horse and the reverence held for it.

Ancient Significance around the World

Horses played a hugely significant role in ancient civilizations, changing the way people lived, worked, and fought. At first, horses were solely used for meat. The first paintings of horses, dated from 30,000 B.C., were found on cave walls in Chauvet, France, but bones have been found in areas where humans are known to have lived over 50,000 years ago. Thousands more bones were found at the bottom of cliffs, suggesting that horses were hunted off steep drops.

ABOVE
Horses were very important to the early nomadic cultures across the steppes of eastern Europe and Asia. The Mongolians under the formidable Genghis Khan were excellent horsemen and expanded his empire through their skilled mounted attacks.

Some scholars believe that man began keeping horses for milk and meat on the steppes of Central Asia from 4000 B.C.; others argue horses were not domesticated until 2000 B.C. Horses have been found with tack in chariot burials in northern Kazakhstan dating back to this era. Studies agree that domestication may have taken place in several areas of Eurasia around the same time.

Ride or Drive

Scholars do know that horses were being ridden before 1345 B.C., when the Hittite horse master Kikkuli wrote about how to keep and train chariot horses. (It is thought that horses were not ridden in areas of the Middle East until around 1000 B.C.)

The Hittites" power increased with their knowledge of horse warfare. They used horses for transportation and later developed cavalry; some people believe this is because they had to breed bigger horses in order to start riding.

It may have become essential for men to ride in order to herd livestock, but

ABOVE
The Emperor Qin Shi Huang (259–210 B.C.) was the first emperor of a unified China and had under his control a huge cavalry and an army of foot soldiers, replicas of which, made out of terracotta, were discovered in 1974 in his tomb.

it is not known exactly when. Early bridles were like hackamores, with no bit through the horse's mouth, and the first mouthpieces were made of soft material such as hide. Metal bits date back to *c.* 1500 B.C. As tack developed, riders had more control over the horses, whether driving or riding.

LEFT
The white chalk horse of Uffington dates back around 3,000 years to the Bronze Age and reflects the importance of the horse in early cultures. It is one of several chalk hill carvings of horses, but it is the oldest in existence.

Chinese Invention

The Chinese developed their cavalry and began using archers on horseback to defend themselves from the Huns from around 1500 B.C. China also set up advanced breeding programs, importing stallions from Southeast Asia. The Chinese are credited with developing more effective harnesses that went around the horse's chest, as well as the first metal stirrups.

Scythian and Greek Horsemen

The Scythians are thought to have started using archery in warfare from around 800 B.C. They invaded Eurasia and settled before being removed by the Persians. Wealthy Scythians have been found buried with their horses and objects bearing images of the horse, suggesting the horse's great significance to this nation.

In Greece, riders began to replace chariots with drivers some time around 700 B.C. In his writings, the Greek soldier Xenophon (*c.* 430–355 B.C.) encouraged greater sensitivity in his compatriots" riding. Alexander the Great was perhaps the most accomplished Greek horseman, having extended an empire from the back of his horse, Bucephalus.

The Roman Empire

The Roman army initially depended more on infantry, but before long there was demand for mounted troops. The Greeks began chariot racing at the Olympics from 684 B.C., but the sport was even more popular with the Romans. They built the Circus Maximus in Rome, which had a capacity of around 250,000, suggestive of the importance of this sport in their lives. With their impressive roads, the Romans were also best able to utilize horses for transportation.

Fascinating Facts

Some scholars believe that a 35,000-year-old ivory carving of a horse found in Germany had spiritual significance.

Horses in Myth and Legend

Greek and Roman Mythology

Horses feature heavily in Greek and Roman mythology, often in connection with the ruler of horses, Poseidon (Roman name: Neptune). One such example is Arion, the swift, immortal horse described in Homer's *Iliad*. Arion is said to be the offspring of Demeter, who turned herself into a mare to avoid the advances of Poseidon, only for Poseidon to turn himself into a horse as well.

Poseidon is said to have given two immortal horses—Balius and Xanthos (*see* below right, pictured)—to Peleus, whose son Achilles drove them in the Trojan War. When Patroclus, dressed as Achilles, led the Myrmidons to fight the Trojans he was killed, and Achilles reprimanded the two horses for leaving Patroclus on the battlefield. Xanthos turned to Achilles and prophesied his death in war, having been given a voice by the goddess Hera.

At the end of this war, Greek soldiers sent the wooden Trojan horse (*see* left, pictured) that is described in Virgil's *Aeneid* as a gift to Troy. The horse held Greek soldiers who opened the gates of the city for the returning army to enter and attack while Troy celebrated the end of the war.

The winged horse Pegasus is thought to be the son of Poseidon, having formed from Medusa's blood when Perseus cut off her head (Medusa was impregnated by Poseidon). Bellerophon, who rode Pegasus when killing monsters including the Chimaera, tried to ride the horse to Mount Olympus, but Zeus made him fall to the ground, crippled. Pegasus later carried the goddess of the dawn, Eos.

Heracles (Roman name: Hercules) had to capture the flesh-eating horses of Diomedes for Eurystheus as the eighth of his 12 labors. Heracles released them onto high ground and dug a trench around them. He then killed Diomedes and fed him to the horses. Having eaten, the horses were calm and allowed Heracles to capture them.

Norse Mythology

Odin, father of the Norse gods, was given an eight-legged horse called Sleipnir by the god Loki. Sleipnir was able to run over land and sea. Loki turned himself into a mare to lure the stallion Svadilfari away from the mason who was rebuilding the wall around Asgard that protected the gods from the giants. The mason had been promised the goddess Frigg if he completed the work in six months, and he would fail without the stallion's help. Sleipnir is said to be the offspring of Loki and the stallion.

Frigg, the goddess of love, had a messenger called Gna who rode the horse Hofvarpnir, who could also run over land and water.

Irish and Celtic Mythology

In Irish mythology, Niamh, the daughter of the sea god Manannan Mac Lir, rode a horse called Embarr. She rode him over the sea to Ireland, as the horse could run on water, and fell in love with Oisin, taking him back with her to Tir na n"Og. After three years he returned to

Ireland, where 300 years had passed, riding Embarr. He touched the soil, which Niamh had told him not to, and became an old man.

Kelpies are a feature of Celtic myth and were feared water horses that haunted Scottish rivers. A Kelpie could turn itself into different guises, such as a grazing horse. If a man tried to ride the horse, it would run in to the water and drown him.

Arthurian Legend

According to legend, King Arthur's horse, Llamrai, helped him to destroy the afanc, the monster of the lake Llyn Barfog. Arthur placed a chain around the lake, and he and Llamrai pulled the monster out and killed it. There is a stone near the lake known as the Stone of Arthur's Horse that is believed to carry Llamrai's hoof print.

Horses in Art

As the horse's relationship with humankind has developed, so too has the way in which it has been depicted in art. The earliest examples of horses in art are cave paintings dating back as far as 30,000 B.C., such as those discovered in France in the 1900s. There are various explanations as to why prehistoric man chose to paint horses; some believe that the images have spiritual significance, where others suggest that they formed a type of hunting map. The fact that horses were painted so frequently suggests their importance to prehistoric man, be it a spiritual or physical importance.

Horses are still a popular subject for art in the 2000s, but much less so than in the past, when they featured more heavily in human civilization. Every activity that horses have taken part in—from warfare, through to jousting, racing, and dressage, has been a key subject for artists from many different eras.

The Physical Development of the Horse in Art

The horse's appearance in art tells us something about their physical development, as well as their uses during different periods. As an example, light, fast, sport horses pulling racing chariots were a popular feature in Roman mosaics. The Egyptians painted chariot warfare on wood, with the horses appearing petite compared to the men in their chariots. The Chinese emperor Qin Shi Huang's Terracotta Army included horses of a

still small but sturdy stature (*see* page 22).

Horses in Art in Their Different Roles

Horses have been featured in art in all their roles, even down to a mare being milked in Eugene Delacroix's (1798–1863) *Ovid among the Scythians* (1859). Agricultural horses became a more popular subject for artists from the 1700s, while hunting scenes

have been produced for many centuries, from the British and French tapestries of the 1500s and 1600s to the oil-on-canvas Cornish hunting scenes of Alfred Munnings (1878–1959).

The artist George Stubbs was the leading British painter of horses in the 1700s and was an expert on equine anatomy and physiology, which is apparent in this realistic depiction of the stallion Whistlejacket.

Saint George and the Dragon Working in the 1400s, the artist Paolo Uccello painted some of the finest horses of his time, including this magnificent, powerful, gray horse that carries St. George as he battles a ferocious dragon.

The most common portrayal of horses in art is at war. Famous examples include the Bayeux Tapestry, which was commissioned in the 1070s after the Normans conquered England at the Battle of Hastings in 1066. Hundreds of horses in battle are stitched with wool into the linen. Another groundbreaking example, due to his use of perspective, is the *Rout of San Romano* (c. 1456) by Paolo Uccello (1397–1475), which depicts warfare between the cavalries of Siena and Florence. The English painter Alfred Munnings traveled to France to paint Canadian troops with their horses as well as battle scenes. War reporter and artist Richard Caton Woodville (1856–1927) most famously produced the *Charge of the Light Brigade* (1854).

The Horse as a Symbol of Greatness

Horses appeared in portraits of great kings and generals and added prestige to these works because of their significance in the development of civilization. They acted as a symbol of strength and wealth. For example, in royal artist Anthony van Dyck's (1599–1641) *Equestrian Portrait of Charles I* (c. 1637–8), the king is mounted on a huge horse, and by appearing to control the prancing beast effortlessly, symbolizes his power. British painter George Stubbs (1724–1806) was perhaps the first artist to make the horse central to a painting, rather than simply serving to add splendor to the composition. His oil on canvas *Whistlejacket* (1762) appears to be purely a tribute to the great stallion, which started a trend continued even today for immortalizing top sport horses in art.

Horses of Legend in Art

Other popular topics for artists who incorporated horses in their work include the biblical Four Horsemen of the Apocalypse, mythical creatures such as unicorns and centaurs, and the winged horse Pegasus. Pre-Raphaelite artists, among others, also depicted horses from Arthurian legend.

Fascinating Facts

Eadweard Muybridge, the inventor of the motion picture, took a series of pictures entitled *The Horse in Motion*, which answered questions about the horse's gallop, demonstrating that during mid gait all four of the horse's hooves leave the ground and tuck underneath the animal rather than extending out from the animal as previous artistic representations depicted.

The Bayeux Tapestry is 250 feet long and depicts in great detail the events that culminated in the Norman invasion of England in 1066. The horses depicted are especially fine and are examples of the powerful warhorses of the day.

Horses in Literature and Movies

Horses appear in literature and movies in the various roles they have served humankind throughout history. In addition, there is a plethora of books and movies where horses are the leading

BELOW
The iconic American hero, the Lone Ranger, rode his trusty horse Silver through endless dangers and adventures, saving the day and righting injustices.

characters. These stories often tell of the hardships faced by equines at the hands of humans from the horse's perspective. Anna Sewell's *Black Beauty*, which was first published in 1877, follows the life of a black gelding. The horse tells his own story under various owners, as well as those of his companions, including Ginger, who dies in service as a carthorse; Merrylegs, a well-behaved children's pony; and an old war horse. Through these stories, Sewell describes the often poor treatment of the workhorses of her era.

Superior Horses in Fiction
J.R.R. Tolkien, in his trilogy *The Lord of the Rings* (1954–5), which was brought to the big screen by Peter Jackson, describes a race of wild horses called Mearas that live in Middle-earth. These animals are superior to normal horses, live longer, and are more intelligent. The kings of Rohan predominantly ride them. The chief of the Mearas is Shadowfax, who is ridden by

one of the heroes of the novel, Gandalf, without a saddle or bridle. It has been suggested that Shadowfax's name derives from the horses of Norse mythology Skinfaxi and Hrinfaxi, who pulled the moon and the sun.

Jonathan Swift's *Gulliver's Travels* (1726) also features a superior race of horses called the Houyhnhnms, who are an especially rational and intelligent species.

Children's Books
Horses have been a popular topic for children's stories over the past century, one example being Mary O"Hara's trilogy that began with *My Friend Flicka*, in 1941. The book follows the lives of a rancher's son, Ken McLaughlin, and his horse Flicka. This book and its two sequels, *Thunderhead, Son of Flicka* (1943) and *Green Grass of Wyoming* (1946), were adapted for motion picture.

The Black Stallion was also published in 1941, being the first in a series of books by

Walter Farley and again was later made into a movie. The books tell the story of a wild stallion and a boy, Alec Ramsay.

The Silver Brumby (1958–2003) series of children's books by Elyne Mitchell follows the adventures of a wild stallion, Thowra, and his progeny, and are set in Australia (where wild horses are known as "brumbies"). His color, palomino, means that other horses are hostile to Thowra, while men try to capture him.

BELOW
My Friend Flicka, the story of a young boy and his horse who he tames, has touched the hearts of children (and adults) since it was written in 1941. It was adapted for the big screen in 1943 and was also made into a television series.

From Book to Movie

National Velvet (1935), by Enid Bagnold, tells the story of a girl called Velvet Brown who, disguised as a boy, enters her horse—The Pie—in the United Kingdom's Grand National steeplechase. The novel became a popular movie starring Elizabeth Taylor (1944), and in 1978 a sequel was produced called *International Velvet*, starring Tatum O"Neal.

The book *The Horse Whisperer* (1995), by Nicholas Evans, was adapted for the big screen by Robert Redford in 1998. Here a teenage girl, Grace MacLean, suffers a road accident with her horse Pilgrim. Grace loses part of one leg and the horse is scared and traumatized. Grace's mother, Annie, seeks the help of a horse whisperer, Tom Booker, to regain Pilgrim's trust and in turn aid her daughter's recovery. Nicholas Evans based the retraining of the horse in his novel on the methods of real horse trainers he met in the American West.

The story of champion American racehorse Seabiscuit (1933–1947) was made into a movie in 1949, *The Story of Seabiscuit*, and again in 2003, *Seabiscuit*, which received an Oscar nomination for best picture. The story of this racehorse, who came through to win against all odds, captured the imagination of the American people during the Great Depression.

Fascinating Facts

The "wild" mustangs that the character Tom Smith is chasing at the beginning of the movie *Seabiscuit* are shod.

ANATOMY AND APPEARANCE

Physically, horses and ponies vary as much as, if not more than, humans. The different breeds and types all have their own characteristics. Although all horses may look like similar large, four-legged animals to the untrained observer, to the expert it is obvious that each equine is an individual, with its own shape, color, and personality. Biologically, the horse is a complex system. Horses have more than 200 bones, as well as a well-developed muscular system and numerous essential organs.

POINTS OF THE HORSE

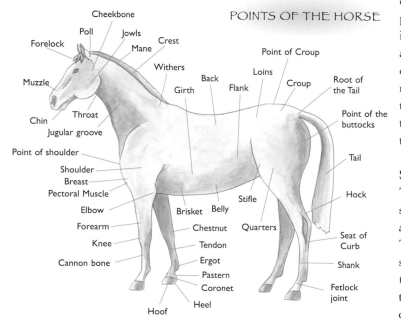

Cheekbone, Poll, Jowls, Forelock, Mane, Crest, Forelock, Withers, Muzzle, Back, Point of Croup, Loins, Croup, Root of the Tail, Girth, Flank, Point of the buttocks, Chin, Throat, Jugular groove, Point of shoulder, Shoulder, Breast, Pectoral Muscle, Elbow, Stifle, Tail, Forearm, Brisket, Belly, Hock, Knee, Chestnut, Quarters, Cannon bone, Tendon, Seat of Curb, Ergot, Shank, Pastern, Coronet, Heel, Fetlock joint, Hoof

Points, Skeleton, and Organs

Before we consider the points, skeleton, and organs of a horse, we should look at the straightforward aspects of height and weight.

Horses are measured at the highest point of the withers, the bony part at the base of the neck. Traditionally, horses are measured in hands, each hand being 4 in. (10 cm). The common abbreviation for this is "hh" (hands high), so a horse might be described as 15.2 hh (15 hands and 2 in.). Ponies measure 14.2 hh or

less. More recently, equines have started to be measured in centimeters for competitions, so, for example, some 12.2 hh classes have been replaced by 128-cm classes.

A 16.2 hh horse weighs, on average, around 1,325 lbs (600kg), depending on its type and condition.

Points of the Horse

These are the terms used to describe certain specific external parts of the horse. The "points" of the horse include the muzzle, poll, withers, stifle, hock, girth, quarters, and tail, among

others. They have several practical applications, such as in telling a vet exactly where a horse is injured or judging conformation. If used in relation to describing color, the points of the horse refer to the mane, tail, muzzle, tips of the ears, and lower legs.

Skeleton

The horse's skeleton has two separate parts—the axial and appendicular skeletons.
The **axial** skeleton is the skull, backbone, and ribcage (including the sternum and the ribs). It protects vital organs such as the brain, spinal cord, heart, and lungs

and gives the body shape. The backbone does not run all the way along the top of the horse. Behind the horse's poll it curves down toward the underside of the neck. As the shape of the crest of the neck is determined by muscle, not bone, it can be changed by exercise.

The **appendicular** skeleton consists of the bones of the horse's legs and the associated bones in the shoulders and hindquarters. The horse's muscles attach to the skeleton and work with ligaments and tendons to allow the animal to move.

SKELETON OF THE HORSE

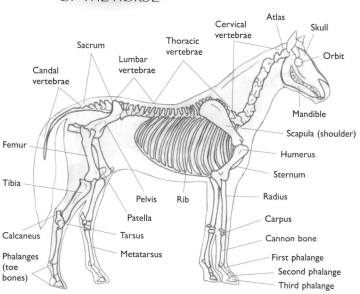

Sacrum, Candal vertebrae, Lumbar vertebrae, Thoracic vertebrae, Cervical vertebrae, Atlas, Skull, Orbit, Femur, Mandible, Scapula (shoulder), Humerus, Tibia, Sternum, Pelvis, Rib, Radius, Patella, Calcaneus, Tarsus, Carpus, Metatarsus, Cannon bone, Phalanges (toe bones), First phalange, Second phalange, Third phalange

Principal Organs and Systems

The horse's heart sits slightly to the left side of its chest and pumps blood around the body. Gaseous exchange, which sends oxygen around the body in the blood and returns carbon dioxide to the lungs to be breathed out, takes place in the lungs.

The horse's food passes from the mouth, down the esophagus, and into the stomach. The muscle at the entrance to the stomach—the cardiac sphincter—is like a one-way street: food cannot pass back through it, so horses cannot vomit.

Digestion begins in the stomach. The food gradually passes into the small intestine, which is around 72 ft. (22 m) long, then into the shorter large intestine. As food travels along the intestines, it is broken down

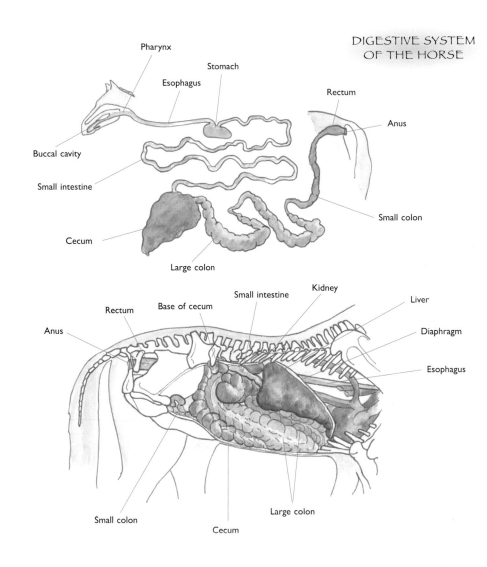

DIGESTIVE SYSTEM OF THE HORSE

Pharynx
Stomach
Esophagus
Rectum
Buccal cavity
Anus
Small intestine
Small colon
Cecum
Large colon

Rectum
Base of cecum
Small intestine
Kidney
Liver
Anus
Diaphragm
Esophagus
Small colon
Large colon
Cecum

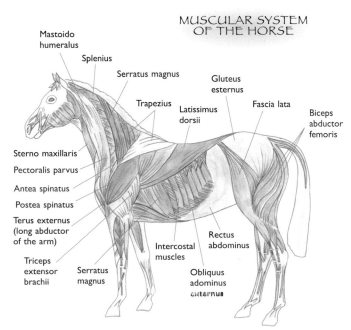

MUSCULAR SYSTEM OF THE HORSE

Mastoido humeralus
Splenius
Serratus magnus
Trapezius
Gluteus esternus
Latissimus dorsii
Fascia lata
Biceps abductor femoris
Sterno maxillaris
Pectoralis parvus
Antea spinatus
Postea spinatus
Terus externus (long abductor of the arm)
Triceps extensor brachii
Serratus magnus
Intercostal muscles
Rectus abdominus
Obliquus adominus externus

and nutrients are absorbed through the walls into the blood. By the time the food reaches the rectum, only waste is left, which leaves the horse's body as droppings through the anus.

Approximately 65 percent of the horse's body consists of water. The horse has two kidneys, which filter the blood and send the waste and excess water to the bladder, where it is held until the horse urinates.

The horse also has a complex nervous system, a reproductive system, an endocrine system for releasing hormones, and a lymphatic system, which drains excess fluid and helps the body fight infection.

Fascinating Facts

The horse's heart beats at 30 to 45 beats per minute at rest, increasing to up to around 200 beats per minute during hard work. Each beat pushes one quart of blood out of each side of the heart.

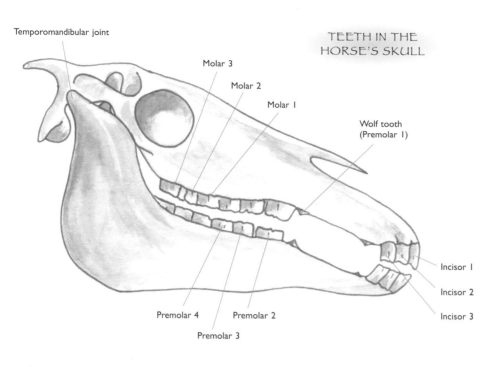

TEETH IN THE HORSE'S SKULL

Temporomandibular joint

Molar 3

Molar 2

Molar 1

Wolf tooth (Premolar 1)

Incisor 1

Incisor 2

Incisor 3

Premolar 4

Premolar 2

Premolar 3

Teeth and Age

Milk and Permanent Teeth
Foals have a full set of milk teeth, some of which may be present at birth. The milk teeth continue to develop until the horse is around one year old. From the age of two and a half, the horse sheds its milk teeth, and the permanent teeth replace them.

How Many Teeth?
Adult horses usually have 12 incisors, 12 premolars, and 12 molars. Incisors are the biting teeth at the front of the mouth, while the premolars and molars are used for chewing and are at the back. In addition, male horses (stallions or geldings, which are castrated males) generally have four canines (or tushes) in the "interdental space" between the incisors and the premolars. Females (mares) do not usually have canines,

and if they do, they are likely to be small. So most adult geldings and stallions have 40 teeth, while mares have 36.

Some horses also have one or more wolf teeth. These sit in front of the second premolar (the first tooth behind the interdental space) and are the remnants of the old, defunct, first premolar. Sometimes the wolf teeth cause pain or problems with the bit and are removed.

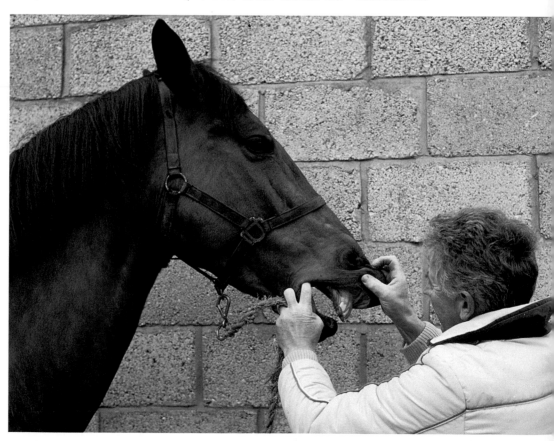

Aging

An experienced person can age younger horses with some accuracy. After the age of eight there are clues, but even an expert can be 5 to 10 years out in their estimation. The development of the incisors is the clearest aging tool.

The middle two incisors on each jaw are the central incisors. The temporary centrals are the first milk teeth to come out, at two-and-a-half years, and by three the horse will have its full, permanent centrals. At three and a half, the next two teeth back on each jaw on each side, the temporary lateral incisors, come out, replaced by the age of four by their permanent equivalents.

At four and a half, the horse sheds the temporary corner

incisors, the farthest back of these front teeth. By the age of five, their permanent replacements are fully grown. Males generally grow their tushes between the ages of four and five.

At seven, a hook appears on the corner incisors of the top jaw, hanging over the top of the lower corner incisors. This will remain for around one year. Another hook can appear later in life, often at around 13, which is generally permanent. As the horse ages, the teeth slope forward more and appear longer.

Galvayne's Groove This develops down the outside of the upper corner incisors. The groove usually appears at around the age of 10, will be halfway down the tooth at 15, and stretches to the bottom at 20. By the age of 25, the groove will have disappeared from the top half of the tooth, and at 30 it will have gone altogether.

Tables

The teeth wear down with

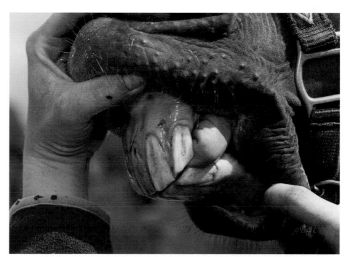

use, and more is pushed up through the gum. The top surface of the lower incisors, the "tables," can be used to help with aging, as a different cross-section is exposed.

In the younger horse, a large dark hole shows in the center of the table, called the "infundibulum." This gets smaller with age, until it disappears completely. As the infundibulum shrinks, a black mark between it and the front of the teeth grows. This is the "dental star."

The central incisors show these changes first, then the laterals, and next the corner incisors. By the time the horse is eight years old, the infundibulum is likely to be nearly gone or have disappeared completely, with the dental star showing very clearly. With continuing wear, the dental star becomes a dot in the middle of the tooth.

With increasing age, the tables also become more triangular.

TEETH IN THE HORSE'S SKULL

1 Year

3 Years

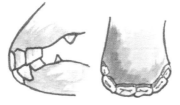

5 Years

10 Years

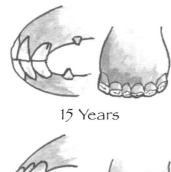

15 Years

20 Years

STRUCTURE OF THE FOOT

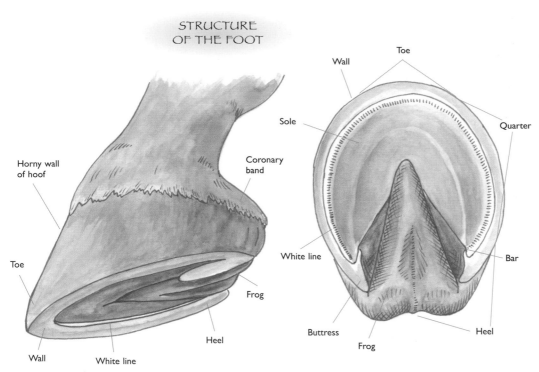

Horny wall of hoof

Toe

Wall

White line

Coronary band

Frog

Heel

Wall

Sole

Toe

Quarter

White line

Bar

Buttress

Frog

Heel

Bones

The main bone in the foot is the pedal bone. Above this, the short pastern extends from the lower leg down into the foot. The joint between the pedal bone and the short pastern is the coffin joint. Behind this is a small bone called the "navicular" bone.

Other Structures

Inside the hoof wall are the laminae, which are like leaves of tissue attaching the wall to the pedal bone. The insensitive, horny laminae are on the outside by the wall, with the sensitive laminae inside of them.

Structure of the Foot

External parts

The outside of the horse's foot, which can be seen when the foot is on the ground, is called the "hoof wall." When the foot is lifted, the sole and frog underneath are visible. The wall grows continuously, taking about one year to regenerate from top to bottom. The domesticated horse wears the foot down faster than happens in the wild, which is why most horses wear metal shoes. A farrier will trim the foot and replace the shoes approximately every six weeks.

A large percentage of lamenesses stem from the foot, either following an injury, such as a sharp object piercing the sole, or due to poor foot shape or internal problems, which can be triggered by bad conformation. Corrective shoeing can sometimes help.

Probably the largest non-bony structure in the foot is the digital or plantar cushion, a piece of tissue at the back of the foot below the bones. Below this and the

The Senses

The horse evolved as a grazing animal, and its natural defense is flight not fight, so its senses are highly developed to detect approaching danger.

Sight and Hearing

The horse's eyes are on the side of its head, giving it an excellent range of vision. With its head down grazing, the horse can see almost all around it, although it does have limited vision directly in front and behind it. It is thought that horses may have a more limited color vision than humans or see colors differently. They see better in the dark, however, and can probably see farther than humans.

Horses have finely tuned hearing. Their two large ears are highly mobile so that they can pick up sound from every direction. The brain analyzes incoming sounds from both ears and works out from where the noises are originating.

Taste, Smell, and Touch

Anyone who has tried to feed a horse medicine knows that these animals have an acute sense of smell and taste. In the wild, these senses would prevent them from eating poisonous plants, while smell would help them recognize other members of their herd and to detect predators.

Horses tasting or smelling something unusual will sometimes display the flehmen response, lifting the head and curling back the upper lip. Stallions also do this as part of sexual behavior.

Horses are also sensitive to touch. They sometimes even have an involuntary reaction to it, such as twitching the skin to remove flies. They also enjoy some touching; horses will often groom each other with their teeth, and many horses relish the feel of being brushed by their rider.

pedal bone are the sensitive sole and frog, which line their equivalent insensitive external structures. At the top of the horse's foot is the coronet band. Inside, the coronet has an excellent blood supply to carry nutrients to the wall. There are also tendons and ligaments in the foot, which allow movement.

Fascinating Facts

Horses seem to possess a 'sixth sense,' which allows them to tune into human moods and detect danger. There are plenty of stories of horses not wanting to pass places of death or danger or saving their riders by refusing to cross a bridge, which is later found to have collapsed.

LEFT
Curling the top lip back as seen is referred to as the flehmen response, or flehming, and facilitates horses to smell certain scents, especially pheromones.

GOOD CONFORMATION

Conformation

The horse's conformation describes its shape. Conformation is not just important in making a horse look attractive and move well for the show ring. A horse with good conformation is also likely to stay sound longer, be a more comfortable ride, and be able to gallop faster and jump higher.

Although broadly speaking the same conformation traits are desirable whatever sort of horse you are examining, certain points are more important for different disciplines. For example, a horse with an ewe-neck is never going to make a top dressage horse, but it may be a good jumper. And some horses do break the rules and defy average or poor conformation to stay sound and become excellent performers.

Assessing Conformation

Assessing conformation is largely a matter of experience. It is more difficult to assess the conformation of a horse in poor condition (too fat, too thin, or wrongly muscled) than that of one that is fit and well. Although some faults can be harder to recognize in the correctly muscled horse, an expert should still be able to pick out serious problems. Equally, an experienced person should be able to spot good conformation in a horse in poor condition.

When assessing a horse's conformation, start by taking an overall look at the animal. Are its different parts in proportion? Does it give an impression of kindness and good character? Next, move on to analyze its different parts.

Head and Neck

Look for a horse with a kind expression in its eye and an attractive head. Too much white showing in the eye can indicate bad temper, while small, "piggy" eyes can indicate an obstinate nature.

If the horse's profile is concave, this is known as a "dish face," and often signifies Arab or Welsh breeding. The opposite, a Roman nose, generally indicates heavy horse blood but can be a sign of a genuine horse.

Make sure that the head is well set on the neck and that the horse is not "thick through the gullet." This will make it difficult for the animal to work in an outline.

The neck should be of good length for a comfortable ride and curve naturally out of the

EWE-NECK

shoulder, with the crest well developed. An ewe-neck (well-developed muscle underneath the neck and weak topline, a condition that can sometimes be improved with correct work), bull neck (short and thick), and swan neck (long neck which is dipped in front of the withers, then arched, with the highest point farther back than the poll) will all make it hard for the horse to work correctly. If the neck is set too low on the shoulders, the horse will struggle to stay off the forehand and work "uphill."

BULL-NECK

Withers, Shoulder, and Front Leg

The withers should be higher than the croup in the mature horse or the animal will find it very difficult to work "uphill." Young horses" hindquarters are often above the withers. Very high, prominent withers may cause problems with saddle fitting. The horse should have a good angle from the wither to the point of shoulder. This angle dictates the length of its stride and should be the same as the angle of the pastern of the front legs. A horse with an upright shoulder will have a short stride and be less comfortable to ride.

The front legs should be a pair. Viewed from the front, the legs should not turn in or out. The forearms should be well muscled, and the cannon bones should be short because long cannon bones are likely to compromise the horse's soundness. The horse's "bone" is assessed by measuring the circumference of its leg just below the knee and dictates how much weight it can carry. The amount of bone will vary depending on type, but a horse with too little bone will be weedy and weak.

The knees and fetlocks should be large, flat, and well defined, not rounded. The elbow must not be "tied in," as this will restrict movement. Seen from the side, if the knee appears to be behind the cannon bone, which comes out of it at a forward angle,

HIGH WITHERS

the horse is "back at the knee" —this is a serious fault that can lead to lameness. Being mildly "over at the knee" is not usually a problem.

Chest, Body, and Back

The chest should be broad enough (and the barrel deep enough through the girth) to give adequate room for the heart and lungs. If the chest is too narrow, with "both front legs out of one hole," the horse is likely to brush (rub or knock its front legs against each other); if it is too wide, the action is likely to be rolling and uncomfortable. "Well-sprung ribs" means that the ribs come well out from the backbone, giving a comfortable platform for the rider and room for the essential organs.

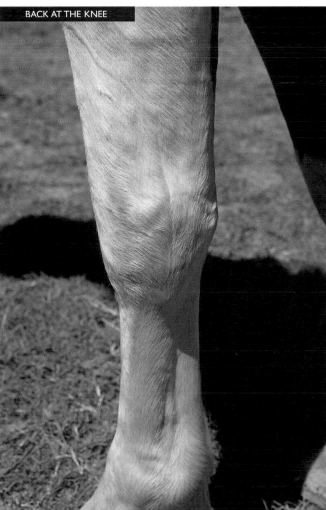

BACK AT THE KNEE

HOLLOW BACK

ABOVE

Hollow or sway backs, where the back dips behind the withers, can be seen in very elderly horses. The horse pictured is actually higher in his croup than withers, which exaggerates the condition.

wide, flat, and well muscled. From behind, the hips should be level. A horse with a pronounced croup (buttocks) has a "jumper's bump," while if the quarters slope sharply from croup to dock (top of the tail) the horse is "goose-rumped." Both indicate a good jumper.

The horse should have good length from the point of hip to the point of buttock and be "well let down" (good length from stifle to hock). From the side, the point of buttock and point of hock should form a straight line, which then follows down the back of the cannon bone to the fetlocks. If the hocks hang out behind it, the horse will find engagement difficult, and if the fetlocks are in front of the line the hocks will be too bent and weak. These are called 'sickle hocks."

An excessively long back is likely to be weak, and such a horse will be harder to collect and keep together than one which is 'short-coupled." A longer back is more common in mares, which need room to carry a foal. A dipped back is called a "hollow" or 'sway"

back and can develop with age, while a "roach" back curves up toward and over the loins.

On a "herring-gutted" horse, the underside of the body slopes steeply up toward the stifle. This is a conformation

fault that can be seen whatever condition the horse is in, but many horses will "run up light" and show this tendency to some extent after hard work.

Hindquarters and Back Leg
The hindquarters should be

POOR HINDLEG CONFORMATION

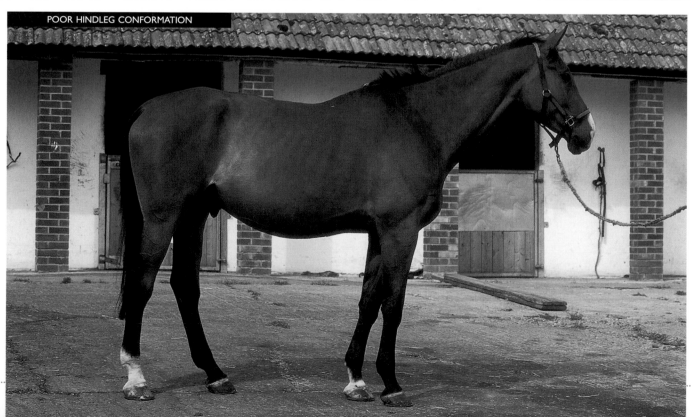

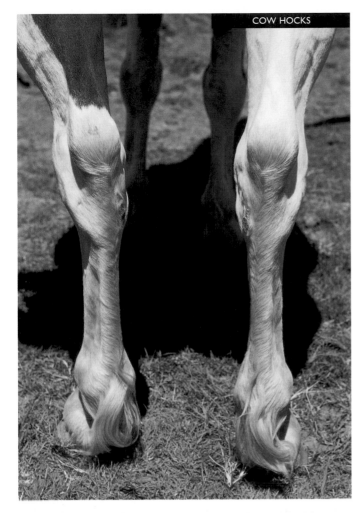

COW HOCKS

The hocks should be large and well defined. Viewed from behind, "cow hocks" describe those which are turned in with the toes turned out, while "bowed hocks" are turned out with the toes turned in. Both cause strain.

Feet

The front feet should be a pair in size, shape, and slope, as should the back feet. The front feet will be more upright than the hind, and the slope should follow the angle of the pastern for the best chance of soundness.

Wide heels, a large frog (wedge-shaped pad on the bottom of the foot), and concave sole are desirable. Small, narrow, or "boxy" feet are likely to cause soundness problems. Flat feet, which are often large, too sloping, and with low heels, are a trait seen especially in Thoroughbreds, and due to the lack of concavity in the soles they are prone to bruising. Feet which turn either outward or inward (pigeon toes) can both put strain on the limbs.

FLAT FEET

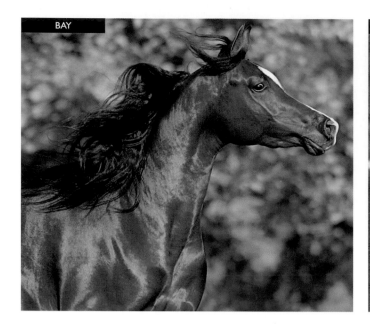

BAY

CHESTNUT

Colors

Solid Colors

Probably the most common color of horse is a bay. Bay horses are brown with black points; the points being the mane, tail, muzzle, tips of the ears, and lower legs. Bays can be "bright," "light," or "dark."

Horses can also be brown or black or gray. No horse is ever correctly described as white—even those that are pure white are known as gray. Dappled gray horses have ring-shaped markings of darker and lighter shades on their coats, while flea-bitten grays have specks of black or brown on their white coat. Iron grays are those with a steely, dark gray appearance.

Chestnut horses have a ginger or orange coat. Chestnuts come in "light" or "dark" shades, while "liver" chestnuts have a deep liver color. Some chestnuts have a pale mane and tail, known as "flaxen."

Dun horses are a yellowy brown color and vary in shade; a dun can be described as "mouse," "yellow," "silver," "blue," or "golden." Duns have black points and also have a dorsal, or "eel" stripe, which is a black line along the backbone. Some duns also have black stripes, known as zebra markings, on their legs. Palomino horses have a yellowy gold coat, with a white mane and tail.

"Colored" horses

Any horse of more than one color, or which is an unusual color, can be known as a colored horse.

BELOW
Dun horses always have black points and may have a dorsal stripe. Buckskin is a similar color to dun, but the coat has an almost metallic sheen. Buckskins can also have a dorsal stripe.

GRAY

DUN

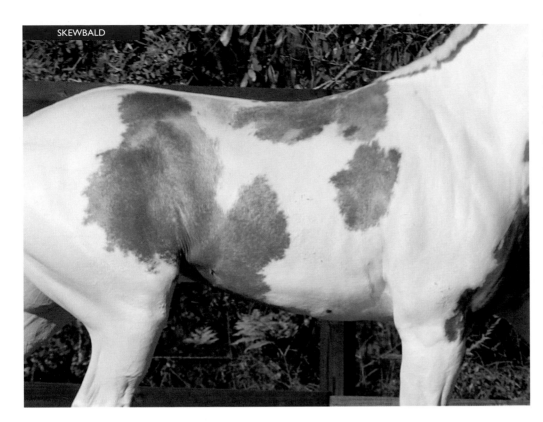

SKEWBALD

Skewbald coloring consists of patches of white coat with any other color except black. In the United States, skewbald and piebald horses are commonly referred to as Paints.

A piebald horse is black and white, while a skewbald is white and any other color. Roan horses have white hairs and another color interspersed through their coat. The most common roans are blue roans, where the hairs are white and black or brown, and strawberry roans, where the hairs are white and chestnut.

Spotted horses come in a number of common variations, including "leopard," with dark spots on a white background; "snowflake," which is the reverse; and "blanket," a white rump with dark spots on it.

In the United States, some colored horses and ponies are registered as pintos. Pintos can be a variety of breeds, but they must meet specific color requirements, while Paint horses are basically colored horses with Quarter Horse or Thoroughbred blood. There are many terms and subdivisions, used mostly in the United States, for different coat patterns. In general, however, tobianos have a white coat, white legs, and white across the back, with patches of color. Overos have a colored coat, with splashes of white that rarely go across the back.

Changing Color

Horses can change color with age. Grays are usually born dark and become lighter as they get older. This process takes place at a different rate in different breeds and individuals.

Horses can also appear a different color when sporting their thick, winter coats from when they have their sleek, summer coats. And if the horse is clipped to let it carry out its work more comfortably (more usual in the winter, but sometimes carried out in the summer), the clipped part of its coat may be a different shade.

Breed and Color

Breed and color are sometimes linked—for example, Fell ponies are commonly black, dark brown, or bay, although they can be gray. Many breed societies do not put colored horses in their studbooks.

Color and Superstition

There are many superstitions and prejudices about horse colors. Traditionally, chestnut mares have been seen as flighty and unreliable, although many owners of such horses will tell you this is not true. In some circles, colored horses were seen as common or somehow undesirable for many years, but colored horses are increasingly performing at the top level in many disciplines.

ROAN

BLAZE

STAR

Markings

Many horses have some white on their head and legs. These markings are very useful for identification and will be drawn onto the horse's passport or other documentation, such as a vaccination certification.

Head

A blaze is a wide white mark, usually starting above the eyes and running between them down the front of the horse's face, with the white being broad enough to cover the nose bones. If the white covers the eyes, forehead, and much of the muzzle, this is known as a "white face." A "stripe" is a narrower white mark down the face. A "star" is white on the forehead or between the eyes, and a "snip" is white on the nose, extending into the nostrils.

A horse can show these markings in combination, so it might have a star, then a gap in the middle of the face with no white markings before a snip. Or it may have a star which extends into a stripe.

WHITE

STRIPE

SNIP

STOCKINGS (WHITE LEGS)

LEFT

In the United States, horses with white leg markings, such as these stockings, are described as "chromey," meaning "flashy." "Stockings" only become "socks" when they finish below the fetlocks.

Legs

A horse can have white markings on any, all, or none of its legs. A stocking is when the white extends from the foot to between the fetlock and the knee or hock, while

STOCKINGS

on a sock the white finishes at the fetlock or below. If a horse has patches of color in the white, most commonly on the coronet band, these are called "ermine marks."

Acquired Markings

As well as markings the animal is born with, horses can have acquired markings. These can be the result of accidental damage. A horse may grow white hair after a cut, for example, and many horses have some white hairs on their withers where they have been rubbed by a saddle or rug.

Acquired markings also include those deliberately put on the horse for identification. Some horses are branded with a hot iron, resulting in a pattern in the coat, which identifies their breed or breeder. These brands are usually on the shoulder, hindquarters, or saddle area.

Freezemarking is a popular way of marking horses as a deterrent to thieves and to make the horse easier to identify if it is stolen. Horses are usually freezemarked under the saddle. Superchilled markers are used, which destroy the pigment so the hair grows back white. Each horse is marked with a unique four-digit number. Gray and light-colored horses are given a bald freezemark, so the markers are held on longer and the hair follicle is destroyed. This is usually done on the shoulder to prevent the saddle from rubbing on a bald mark.

Other methods of identification include microchipping (where the horse has a tiny, permanent, unique chip inserted under the skin of its neck, which can be read with a special scanner) and stamping the horse's hooves with the owner's zip code (which has to be redone regularly, as it grows out).

Whorls

Whorls are like a human's hair parting; places where the hair swirls around to grow in a different direction. They are commonly found on the forehead, at the top of the neck, and on the chest. Head and neck whorls, and those on other parts of the body on horses with few identifying features, are usually marked with a cross on the horse's passport or other identification document.

BEHAVIOR AND PSYCHOLOGY

Most horses today are kept for pleasure or competition. They are trained to carry humans and behave in a certain way. Although they live in an environment which is not natural for them, the majority of horses adapt and learn to fit into a society which is human- rather than equine-driven. Some of their natural responses may become muted, but horses do not lose their instincts, and many reactions that humans see as annoyances or faults are simply natural behavior coming through.

Herd Instinct

In the wild, horses are herd animals, living in groups for company and protection. The herd leader is usually a mature female, with the group made up of females, foals, and immature youngsters. As colts reach maturity, they will leave and form bachelor groups. A mature stallion will live on the edge of the herd, claiming his harem of mares by scent-marking piles of feces and urination spots. The stallion's harem may incorporate a number of small bands, each under an alpha female, but his position is always vulnerable to be challenged by a younger stallion.

Horses are therefore highly sociable animals, and many are unhappy if they have to live alone. They can also become distressed if they are left on their own in the short term. For example, if a horse is left in the field when its companions come in, it may gallop around or jump the fence to join them.

Some horses are naturally leaders in the herd, while others are happy to follow. When a new group of horses are turned out together, there is likely to be some galloping around and squealing as the horses sort out who is the boss.

BELOW
Horses in the wild live in small groups (herds) that include several mares and youngsters, as seen, and are watched over by a stallion.

BELOW
This piebald is warning the palomino to keep its distance by flattening its ears and kicking out with its hind leg.

BOTTOM
Grooming, primarily along the neck, withers, back, and flanks, is an important part of bonding and socialization within the "herd."

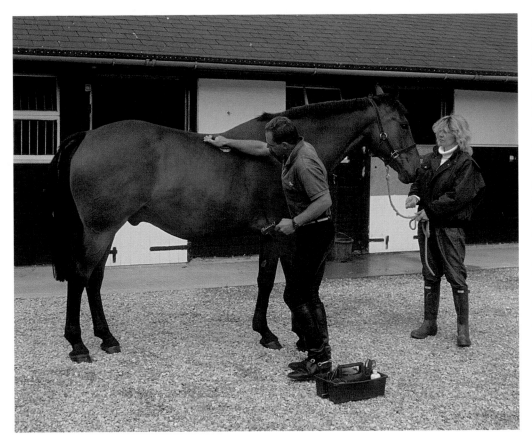

have a routine in their daily lives and work. They are intelligent animals, with long memories of good or frightening experiences. They learn by repetition, and many are willing and even anxious to please. This means that they can be highly trained—for example, to take on narrow jumps on cross-country courses or perform difficult dressage movements.

Different Temperaments

Horses vary widely in their temperament. This is partly linked to their breed, so a Thoroughbred is likely to be more flighty and "sharp" than a heavier type. But individuals are also different in their natures, and much is governed by the horse's treatment.

Communication

Much of equine communication is through physical signals and body language. Some of these signals are easily recognizable by humans, such as laying back the ears as a sign of displeasure or aggression. Horses also use smell, releasing pheromones, which other horses can sense, from the skin glands, and touch, such as mutual grooming. Horses also communicate vocally, such as through squeals and whinnying.

Flight Instinct

Horses are naturally prey animals, herbivores that evolved to eat grass and run away from predators. Although horses will fight if forced to do so, their first instinct when confronted with danger is flight.

In the domesticated situation, this instinct means horses spook or shy away from unusual sights and sounds.

Horses can often hear or see potential danger earlier than humans and will jump away quickly. As horses are so big and strong, it is easy for humans to be hurt accidentally if they are not alert to this potential unpredictability.

Learning

Horses are creatures of habit and will be happiest if they

A horse's behavior will be altered partly by its short-term management—for example, many horses are more relaxed if they spend longer in the field and less time cooped up in a stable. Much of the horse's later behavior is dictated by how it is treated and trained during its first interaction with humans when it is a youngster.

Care, Management & Riding

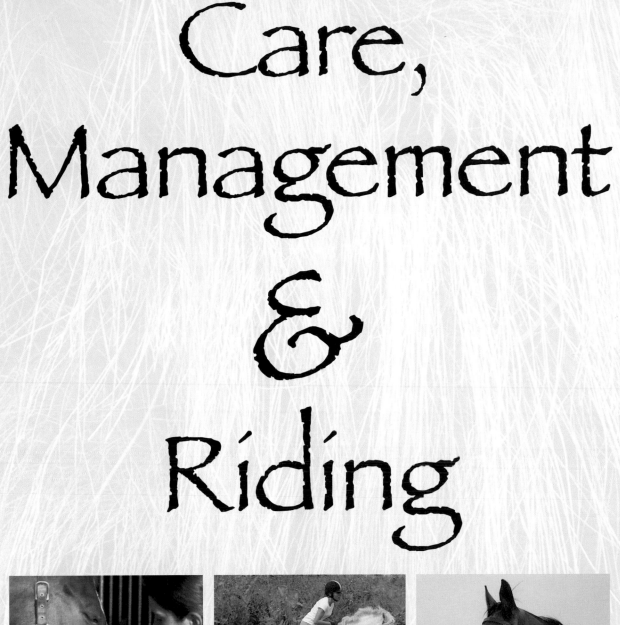

CHOOSING AND BUYING A HORSE

Choosing to become a horse owner is a major decision, one which should be carefully thought out, especially if this is your first venture into owning horses. It is both exciting and easy to rush into buying the first horse you see. Take your time, and consult an expert. Make sure that you see a range of horses so that you develop an idea of what you want, and most importantly, what is best for you. Be prepared to keep looking until you find the right one.

It is worth taking the time to find the right horse when looking to buy. Once purchased the horse becomes a major part of your life , with a strong bond forming between horse and owner.

Points to Consider

First, all prospective horse owners should ask themselves whether they should own a horse. Are you prepared to devote the necessary amount of time to taking care of it? Do you have somewhere sufficient to keep it? Perhaps most importantly, can you afford to buy one and sustain the accompanying costs?

Horses are a big responsibility. They require care all year round, in all weather conditions, despite whether you are sick or busy. Do you have someone you can turn to for advice and support and who could look after the horse in case of an emergency?

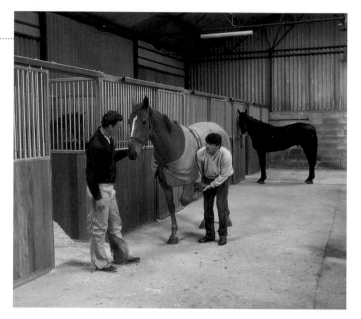

Are You Experienced Enough?

No one should buy a horse without having the knowledge and experience to take care of it. Of course, you will learn a great deal as you go along, but a basic level of riding ability and a rudimentary understanding of a horse's needs are essential. Although it is wonderful to have your horse at home, it is often more sensible to keep your first horse at a livery stable. This should mean you have help caring for it and can ask the stable owner for advice. Many people learn to ride in riding schools, and despite having reached a sophisticated standard of equitation, are surprised how different it is and how much hard work is involved in owning your own horse.

> **LEFT**
> *It can be beneficial to keep your horse at a good livery stable, such as this pictured, where there are professionals on hand to help.*

How Much Do You Want to Spend?

Horses can cost anything from a few hundred to many millions of dollars. It is a good idea to work out your budget and then stick to it. Be realistic; you are not going to find your dream event horse for nothing, but be wary of spending tens of thousands on a first horse. You may decide horse owning is not for you, and it is best to stick a toe in the water before diving in. Remember that the initial amount to purchase the horse is only the start. Make a careful list of what you will need to buy for tack, rugs, and a grooming kit. Work out how much it will cost to keep it at a stable, or if the horse will live at home with you, what the extra costs will be in terms of electricity and water, as well as hay, hard feed, bedding, stable, and fencing maintenance, grass upkeep, and tools. Factor in vet's fees, as well as routine expenses such as vaccinations, worming, and farriery.

What Type of Horse?

There are so many different types of horses that it can be difficult to decide which one

> RIGHT
> *Cob types such as this are often sensible in nature and quiet to handle. They are also good weight carriers and are equipped for the larger rider.*

is best for you. Don't be too ambitious; it is often better to be underhorsed than overhorsed. Ask your teacher, who should have a good idea of what will be best for you. Consider in what circumstances you will be keeping it: if the horse is to live out in a field all the time, it may be better to get a hardy, native breed than a thin-skinned Thoroughbred. What do you want to do with it? If your ambitions lie in the show ring, you will need to carefully choose a horse that is true to type with good conformation and good appearance. If you are nervous, make sure you are looking for a sane, sensible horse; an ex-racehorse may be tempting and cheap, but would a sturdy half-bred or cob be better for you?

Fascinating Facts

The most expensive horse ever sold was a 2-year-old, Florida-born colt, reportedly going for $16,000,000 on February 28, 2006. However, as of September 2007, Green Monkey was still to run his first race . . .

> LEFT
> *Different breeds have different characteristics, and it is worth considering these before purchasing one. Thoroughbreds, such as the one pictured, can be sharp in temperament, which is not always beneficial for a novice owner.*

check carefully that the horse you see is the one advertised.

Horse Dealers

The advantage of going to a dealer's stable is that they will often have a selection of horses to show you, instead of just one. As long as you check that the dealer has an excellent reputation within the horse world, this can be a good way to buy a first horse, as they are more likely than a private seller to take an unsuitable horse back. Their reputation relies on client satisfaction, and good dealers are experienced at finding the right horse for the right person.

Where to Look

There are many places to look for a horse to buy. The main ones are:

Trade Papers and Magazines

The equestrian press is often the best place to look for horses. Remember that all horses sound great in an advertisement; do not take all the seller says at face value. Local papers often have an equine section, and sometimes better value can be found here than in the classified sections of magazines.

The Internet

There has been a vast increase in the amount of horses advertised for sale on the Internet in recent years. A quick search will reveal many sites, with horses ranging from top competition animals to small ponies. Many horse dealers now have their own websites, which can be a useful tool, but check how often the ads are posted and updated. It is easy to fall in love with a horse that was sold months ago. Never buy a horse without going to see it, however, and

Auctions

Some great bargains can be found at auctions, but it is a big risk to take and best left to those with plenty of experience.

What to Ask

Don't be afraid to ask the seller as many questions as you like, and take a friend along, ideally one with lots of horse experience.

• Before you arrive, ask for the horse to be left out in a field so that you can see it being caught and brought in.
• Look carefully at the horse and its conformation. Does it have any lumps, bumps, or scars, and what is the explanation for them?
• Has it ever suffered from any serious veterinary problems?
• How old is the horse, and how big is it? What sex is it?
• How is it bred?

• What has it done? Does it have a competition record? Has it been hunting?
• Why is it being sold?
• Does it bite, kick, buck, rear, or suffer from a stable vice such as crib-biting, wind-sucking, or box-walking?
• Does the horse suffer from any seasonal problems, such as sweet itch in the summer or mud fever in the winter?

• Is it vaccinated, and does it have a passport? (In the United States, horses take the same nationality as their owner when applying for a passport.)
• Watch it being tacked up.

Fascinating Facts

A common nickname for horse racing is The Sport of Kings.

How does it react to the bit being put in its mouth or the girth tightened? Does it stand still when it is being mounted?
• Ask to see it ridden, on the flat and over fences. In its home environment, expect it to go as well as it can.
• Ride it, first in an enclosed environment, and then ask if you can take it for a short hack. This should give you a chance to see how it reacts to traffic.

Most importantly, ask yourself whether you like the horse, whether you feel confident around it, is it the type you are looking for, and is it worth the money the seller is asking.

FEEDING

When you have bought your horse, check what its previous owner has been feeding it. This is important not only as a guide but also because abrupt changes in a horse's diet are not advisable. You will also need to know about the principal rules of feeding, how much you should feed your horse, and the different types of feeds available. It is also important that you understand how different feeds break down into the three main types and ensure that you feed your horse in the correct combination and proportions.

ABOVE

Horses are "trickle feeders"— their digestive system is designed to cope with small amounts of food fairly continuously. Horses in the wild will graze for up to 18 hours a day.

intestine have time to adapt accordingly.

• Feed something succulent every day.

• Horses are creatures of habit and thrive on routine. Feed at approximately the same time every day.

• Don't feed immediately before or after exercise.

• Make sure that all feed and water buckets are cleaned regularly.

How Much Should You Feed Your Horse?

It is not easy to work out how much your new horse needs to be fed, and it can be a case of trial and error. The following calculation should provide a rough guide that you can adapt to your own horse:

Take the horse's weight in kilograms (either weigh it on a weighbridge or use a weight tape), and multiply it by 2.5. Divide the total by 100. The resulting figure is how much total food the horse requires per day. So a 16-hh horse might weigh 600kg (600 x 2.5 / 100 = 15). This means that the horse should receive 15kg (35 lbs) of food.

Horses are grazing animals, and most of their diet should be grass or hay. For a horse in medium work, a good rule of thumb is that 70 percent of its diet should be roughage, and 30 percent should be made up of concentrates, such as oats, barley, sugar, beets, etc.

This is obviously dependent on the horse's age, temperament, and size. A Welsh pony will very rarely need concentrates in its diet and will survive well on relatively poor grazing, while a fit Thoroughbred may need large amounts of concentrates to supply it with the energy it needs.

Principal Rules of Feeding

• Feed small amounts of food regularly.

• Feed the best-quality food that you can afford. Cheap food is a waste of money, as its nutritional values are low.

• Feed according to the type of horse, its temperament, the amount of work it is doing, and the condition it is in.

• Make sure that clean, fresh water is always available.

• Introduce changes to a feeding routine gradually, so that the bacteria in the horse's

Feed Types

Feed is split into three main groups: roughage, concentrates, and vitamins and minerals.

From top clockwise: rolled oats, horse and pony nuts (also called cubes or pellets), and flaked barley.

Roughage
For most horses and ponies, roughage means grass, which should almost always provide the main part of a horse's diet. Mature horses in little or no work are unlikely to need anything else, as is the case with small, native ponies. Hay is dried, baled grass, and is fed in the winter when grass is poor and not plentiful. Other forms of fiber include haylage, which is richer than hay and may not be good for native ponies and horses who suffer from obesity. Chaff is chopped hay or straw and can be fed to bulk out small feeds and to prevent a horse bolting from its food too quickly.

Concentrates
These are divided into mixes and nuts, and "straights." "Straights" are oats, barley, sugar beets, and linseed. Mixes and nuts are these core components mixed together in varying quantities to form a range of pre-balanced feeds for all types of horses.

Barley should be cooked for at least two hours before feeding or bought in a pre-cooked formula, as it swells up in a horse's stomach. It is a carbohydrate-rich food that is good at putting on condition and giving slow-releasing energy.

Oats should be fed crushed, rolled, or cooked. They are easily digestible and palatable but are high in energy and not appropriate feed for many types of horses and ponies.

Sugar beet is a byproduct of the sugar industry and therefore high in energy and very palatable. It is useful for putting on weight and for tempting shy feeders to eat. It comes in cubes, which must be soaked in cold water for 24 hours before feeding, or shreds, which should be soaked for 12 hours. Linseed is poisonous to horses unless it is cooked until the shiny seeds split and become jellylike. Fed in small quantities, it is excellent for putting on condition.

Vitamins and Minerals
Many horse owners like to give their animals extra vitamins and minerals, often unnecessarily. Sometimes there is a need to supplement the horse's usual diet, but it is wise to consult an expert first. A salt or mineral lick is often popular. Other supplements such as garlic, for respiration, and various additives to improve hoof quality or aid joint suppleness can be useful. But it is easy to spend a fortune on trendy products that your horse really does not need.

The small bowl of pellets shows sugar beets before they has been soaked. Underneath is a large bowl of soaked sugar beets that are now ready for feeding.

ENVIRONMENT

There are two main ways to keep a horse: principally outside (in a field) and principally inside (in a stable). Not all horses are adaptable to either. It is perfectly possible to keep a horse outside, rugged or unrugged, but it is useful to have a stable to bring it in to if necessary, such as for veterinary treatment. Hardy, native types cope best with this type of management. More highly-bred horses may also cope, but many prefer to be stabled at night during the winter.

Grass-kept Horses

The bare minimum amount of land on which a horse can be kept is 0.4 ha (one acre), but it is much easier on a plot of 0.8–1.2 ha (two to three acres). This allows the land to be divided up and rested as necessary.

Fencing
Make sure that your field is well fenced. The best fencing is solid post-and-rails, with either tall bushes or trees for shelter. But taut, plain wire (*not* barbed wire) or a thick bush can be used, although bushes must be checked regularly for gaps. The gate should be made of treated wood or metal and be high enough to stop horses from jumping out.

For your convenience, make sure that it is properly hung and has a secure lock. If the gate opens onto a road, a chain and padlock are advisable. Check all fencing frequently for damage and weakness.

It is nice for horses to have a field shelter where they can escape the worst of the winter weather and avoid the flies in the summer. If you keep more than one horse together, check that the shelter has a

wide-enough entrance to prevent one horse from trapping another in there, and some sort of bedding should be provided so that horses are not standing either in deep mud or on hard concrete. Always leave the cobwebs in the corners to catch the flies.

Water
Your field must have a clean, fresh supply of water. A tank linked to the water supply with a means for replenishing it is ideal. A running stream is fine, as long as it does not have a sandy bottom which the horse could suck up while drinking. If buckets are used, they will need to be filled up a couple of times a day and more often in the summertime.

LEFT

Horses must be provided with an adequate shelter to protect them from the elements (hot and cold), and the shelter must be large enough to accommodate the number of horses using it.

Ponds without a stream running through them should not be used—the water becomes stagnant—and old bathtubs with sharp edges are also hazardous. Remember that in the winter, water may freeze over and will need to have the ice broken up in it.

Grass

It can be tricky to provide your horse with enough grass without it being too little or too much. Grass grows especially lushly in the spring and fall and may need to be restricted at these times. Small areas can be partitioned off with electric fencing. In the winter, the growth and quality may be insufficient, and the horse's diet will need to be supplemented with good-quality hay.

Grass management is important. Investigate whether it needs fertilizing, removing all horses while this is done. Especially long grass may need to be cut and the clippings should be removed. Buttercups are a sign that the grass is poor and that it may need to be reseeded with a carefully selected assortment of grasses.

Check your field regularly for poisonous plants. These include ragwort, which has distinctive yellow flowers and if eaten is likely to prove lethal. Others include: yew; deadly nightshade; bracken; foxgloves; acorns; laburnum; privet; black and white bryony; ivy; locoweed; Johnson grass; field horsetail; tall fescue; perennial ryegrass; hemlock; common pokeweed; common cocklebur; hemp

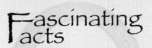

Fascinating Facts

Horses have only four natural gaits: the walk, the trot, the canter, and the gallop.

BELOW

Some horses (especially native pony breeds) are able to spend the winter out without being rugged, but others will need a weatherproof rug such as seen in this picture.

dogbane; white snakeroot; yellow and white sweet clover; common milkweed; and some mustards.

Management

All horses kept in grass need to be checked twice daily. They should be groomed less than stable-kept horses in order to preserve the coat's natural oils, which help keep it warm and waterproof. Rugs should be removed and replaced every day and feet checked for stones.

If you are feeding several horses in the field, space out the feeds or piles of hay to avoid fights and to ensure each horse gets enough.

RIGHT

This is not an ideal way to feed hay as much is wasted, and there is a chance of bullying. It is better to leave a number of small piles of hay that allows each horse its own. Only as much hay should be put out as is eaten—it is preferable to feed smaller amounts of hay more frequently than to provide one large pile as pictured.

stable to get stuffy. Also, all light switches and appliances should be covered and out of the reach of the horse.

Bedding

There are many types of bedding, and you should consider which works best for you and your horse. Do not be tempted to skimp on bedding; horses like to lie down and should be able to do so in comfort and without damaging their knees and hocks.

Straw is warm, can be banked high at the sides, and drains well. It is also the cheapest form of bedding, coming either in small bales or big round ones. But some horses suffer from dust allergies, which can cause respiratory problems. These animals will need a dust-free form of bedding, such

All stable appliances need to be safe and out of reach of the horse. Light switches should have a plastic covering, as shown here.

as good-quality shavings, wood chippings, or paper. Hemp is a new, dust-free form of bedding but can be expensive.

Shavings are easy to muck out and warm but can get very wet and heavy because they do not drain well.

Well-fitted rubber matting on top of the stable floor stops horses from having to stand on cold concrete and provides support for their feet and joints. Mats must be pulled up and scrubbed from time to time.

Stable-kept Horses

The Stable

A pony stable should be a minimum of 12 ft. x 10 ft. (3.6 m x 3 m); a horse should not be kept in a stable less than 12 ft. x 12 ft. (3.6 m x 3.6 m),

ideally made of stone, which has the advantage of being cool in the summer and warm in the winter. But there are many modern stable companies who will build you durable, well-designed, wooden stables at a reasonable cost.

It is useful to have hard ground outside the stable so that you can tie your horse up outside to be groomed and to be mucked out. Inside, the floor should slope slightly toward a drain at the front of the stable, so that urine does not collect. The stable door should be at least 3 ft., 7 in. (1.1 m) high and fastened by bolts at both the top and the bottom.

The stable must be well ventilated. It is better for horses to be well rugged in cold weather than for the

Wood chips and shavings are a good form of bedding. They are very absorbent and easy to work with. They should be stored somewhere dry, for example a barn, such as that pictured.

Mucking out

You can either muck your horse out completely every day, removing all droppings and wet patches, or "deep-litter" the bed. This means picking up the droppings, and then putting more bedding on top to absorb the moisture. A thick, warm bed can be built up like this, but it will need to be removed about once a month, and it is more difficult to keep horses and rugs clean with this system. Muck heaps should be placed away from the stable, away from any water supply, and downwind of the stable to prevent dirty straw from being blown back.

Water

Water can be provided either in buckets, which need to be filled up and cleaned out, or by way of an automatic system which self-fills as the horse drinks. This is obviously less labor-intensive, but some horses do not like to drink from these, and with this system it is impossible to check how much a horse is drinking daily.

Hay and Feed

Hay should be fed in a net, which must be tied up high enough to prevent a horse from getting its hoof caught in it, but slightly lower than eye level so that seeds do not fall into the horse's eyes; on a rack; or in piles on the floor. This last method is more wasteful but is also more natural, as the horse feeds with its head down, as it does in the wild. Feed can be placed in a manger, which will need to be regularly cleaned out; in buckets, which may be in danger of being kicked over; or in a trough, which can be clipped straight on to a horse's door.

Tack and Feed Rooms

Tack rooms must be properly secured, with substantial locks and an alarm system. All tack should be marked, as should rugs.

Feed rooms should also be kept locked. Feed bags should be placed in barrels or at least on pallets to prevent the bags from becoming soggy. A tap with hot running water will make life easier.

LEFT

Stable-kept horses must be turned out for a period of time daily or exercised. They cannot be kept in for days at a time; it is detrimental to their physical and mental health—the exception being in the case of illness or injury.

Exercise

Horses cannot just be left in their stables all day. If they are not turned out for a few hours, which is the best and most natural way of managing them, they must be properly exercised, either ridden or on the lunge, every day.

Rugs

If a horse is kept in a stable during the winter, it can actually become colder than its grass-kept counterpart because it is not moving around and keeping warm. It will therefore need rugging, especially if it has been clipped. Modern stable rugs, made of nylon with padded fillings, come in many weights from light to heavy. It is good practice to use a thin, cotton sheet as the bottom layer, which should be washed once a week. This saves the rest of your rugs from getting dirty and keeps the horse cleaner. All rugs should be washed, and if they are outdoor rugs, rewaterproofed a couple of times a year.

Outdoor rugs are called "New Zealand rugs" and are both warm and waterproof. If a horse comes in from the field wet, it may be better to leave the rug to dry on the horse if you do not have a system of drying the rug quickly, as it is unpleasant for a horse to have a cold, damp rug put back on in the morning.

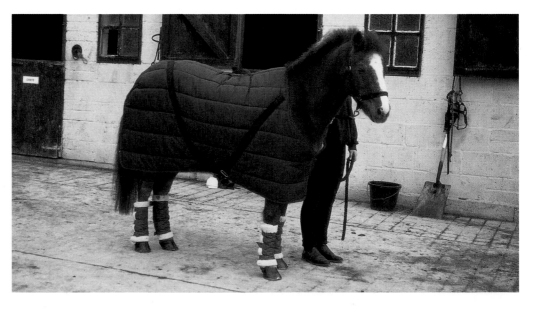

Traveling with a Horse

Everything possible should be done to ensure that a horse has a good traveling experience. Bad travelers have been made that way, usually by bad driving, and it may be difficult to reestablish their confidence.

Clothing

When traveling, horses should wear adequate leg protection, either traveling boots or bandages. Boots are much easier to put on, especially for inexperienced owners, but bandages may be more appropriate on very long journeys, because if applied correctly, they provide a degree of leg support.

A tail bandage and tail guard will keep the tail from being rubbed and protect it. Do not, however, put the tail bandage on excessively tightly. A poll guard, made from foam or a bandage wrapped around the headpiece, is advisable on long journeys and for bad travelers.

Rugs will depend on the weather. In the summer, a sweatsheet or cotton sheet may be enough; in the winter, a sweatsheet and thick, wool, traveling rug with a surcingle (a type of girth or band used to keep a blanket, saddle, or pack secure around the middle) to keep them in place might be needed.

Transportation

Horses travel either in a special truck or a horse trailer pulled by a four-wheel-drive vehicle. Each should have

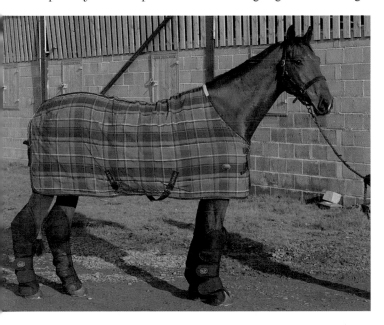

rubber matting and a small amount of bedding on the floor and must be well maintained and frequently checked for safety.

Horses often like to spread their legs for balance when traveling, and for this reason it is safer to have partitions that are not solid attached to the floor. Always drive slowly and carefully, and remember to anticipate braking and turning much sooner than you would in a car.

Journeys

Plan long journeys carefully, and arrange to have stops every three hours. This rests horses and is an opportunity to give them a drink and replenish their haynets. You might also walk them around to stretch their legs, but never unload on the side of the road, and make sure you will be able to get them to load again, otherwise it might be safer to leave them in the trailer until you reach your destination.

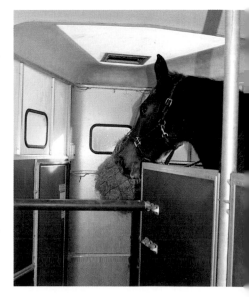

GROOMING AND MAINTAINING

Regular grooming should be part of your daily routine with your horse. It keeps your horse's skin and coat healthy and clean. Horses that are stable-kept should be groomed more thoroughly than those that are kept on grass, as they have less need of the coat's natural oils and have a tendency to become scurfy underneath their rugs. It is also an opportunity to spend time with your horse and to bond with it outside of a riding situation.

Grooming Kit

The term "grooming kit" is given to the collection of brushes and tools that we use to clean our horses. Here are some of the most useful:

Dandy Brush

This stiff brush is used to remove mud and is used on the legs and body. Avoid using on sensitive clipped areas or on the mane or tail.

Body Brush

A body brush is a soft-bristled brush used to deep-clean scurf from the coat. It is used on the whole body together with a metal curry comb. Also use a body brush to brush out the tail and on delicate areas such as the head.

Curry Comb

A plastic or rubber-toothed curry comb can be used in small circular motions on the coat to loosen and remove mud, excess hair (when the

horse is shedding its coat), and scurf. It can be useful on sensitive horses that object to hard brushing with a dandy brush. Metal curry combs should be used only to

clean dirt and scurf out of a body brush and not on the horse itself.

Hoof Pick

This is a blunt metal or tough plastic hook which is used to remove dirt and stones from horses' hooves. Be careful with the sensitive parts of the hoof, and always pick downward away from the heel to avoid damaging the frog.

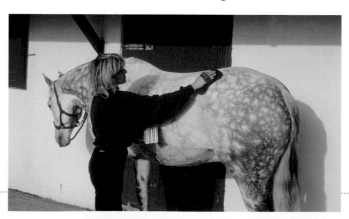

horses love a bath on a hot day to cool down; if you have to wash them on cold days, use warm water and dry them thoroughly.

Sweat Scraper

This is a tool with a handle and a curved rubber strip with which you scrape off excess water after washing your horse.

Hoof Oil

Hoof oil, applied with a small brush, is like nail polish for horses and is a cosmetic touch used to make them look attractive on competition and hunting days. It has a drying effect on the hoof, and should be used on special occasions, such as competitions and vacations.

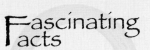

Fascinating Facts

All kinds of extra horse products are available—from conditioners to "make up!"

BELOW

Hoof oil really enhances the look of the feet and should be used when showing and competing.

Mane Comb

A wide-toothed comb of metal or plastic is used to comb out the mane and can be used gently on the tail.

Water Brush

A soft brush with tightly-set bristles, this brush is used with water to remove stains from the horse's coat and sweat marks. It can be used for cleaning hooves and for brushing out manes and tails.

Sponge

Sponges are used for washing horses or for cleaning areas such as the eyes, nose, and dock.

Shampoo

Horses who live outside most of the time shouldn't be washed often because of the loss of the coat's natural oils. When you do wash your horse, such as after strenuous exercise or before a competition, use special horse shampoos which are gentler than the ones we use. Some

Stable Rubber

This is a finishing cloth used to provide gloss to a coat and remove final traces of scurf. It is often used in the show ring to make the horse look its best just before the judge examines it.

Scissors

Round-ended, blunt scissors can be used to trim unwanted hair around the horse's chin and muzzle and remove feather from their fetlock joints. They are also used to shorten the tail but should never be used on the mane.

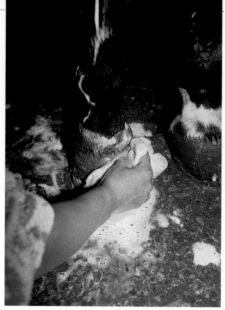

Grooming Tips

How to Wash a Tail

Soak the tail in a bucket of lukewarm water to loosen the dirt. If you cannot fit the whole tail in a bucket, wet the top part of the dock with a water brush. Shampoo with a special equine shampoo, and rub vigorously. Rinse thoroughly, changing the water as it becomes soapy. Squeeze out the water with your hands, and swing the tail to help get rid of any remaining water. Comb through the ends gently to prevent tangles. To help the tail remain untangled, spray lightly with a show-sheen product and brush through with a body brush a few strands at a time.

Turning a Horse out for a Show

Wash the mane a few days before (*see* Helpful Hints). On the morning of the show, thoroughly wash the horse's whole body and tail to remove dirt and stains. Scrub hooves and socks. Make sure you dry the horse thoroughly, especially if the weather is at all cold. First use a sweat scraper to get rid of surface water, and then rub down with a towel. Braid the horse's mane and tail (see section on how to braid), and rug and bandage the horse up until you are almost ready to enter the ring. Next carefully apply hoof oil, and use a chalk block to make the horse's socks white. A drop of baby oil can be used to emphasize its eyes and muzzle, which should have been sponged clean first. Run a stable rubber over the coat to remove all final traces of dust, and check that the horse's braids are still neatly in place.

Helpful Hints

Don't wash your horse's mane the day before a show. It will be slippery and more difficult to braid. Instead, wash it a couple of days earlier so that some of the natural oils return.

RIGHT

Always wash the mane thoroughly a few days before the show, making sure to remove all scurf, dust, and dirt. Be careful not to get soap into the horse's eyes.

Grooming Horses That Live Outside

If a horse is grass-kept and without rugs, the skin should be in a healthy condition, and it is unnecessary to groom it unless it is being ridden. Grooming should be limited to:

• picking out the feet every day and checking the shoes.
• brushing down with the dandy brush to remove mud and sweat marks. (After exercise, do not wash down, but allow the sweat to dry and then brush it off.)
• sponging out the eyes, nose, muzzle, and dock.

If the horse is rugged, the skin will become scurfy in the same way as that of a stable-kept horse, and more regular and thorough grooming will be required.

Strapping

Strapping is a traditional way of improving muscle tone and development by rhythmically "thumping" the horse's shoulders, quarters, and neck with a leather massage pad, followed by "sliding" the pad over them. It is rarely used these days except by old-fashioned horsemen and women, but done correctly it can be tremendously useful and beneficial. It should be attempted only by people who know what they are doing or else a lot of damage could be done. Get someone experienced to show you how to do it.

Helpful Hints

Sick horses or those on enforced box rest should be groomed regularly. It provides stimulation for their coat and most importantly their muscles, which are not being used at the time, and makes them feel as though they are getting some attention.

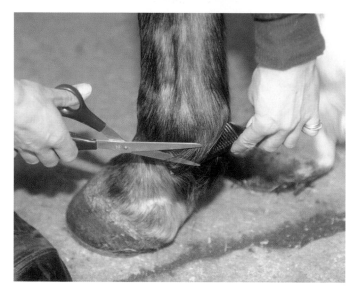

them. Always clip against the direction of the hair growth, and use long, sweeping strokes. Pull the skin tight over any difficult spots, such as the elbows and stifle joints. Work quickly, and if the clippers become very hot, allow them to cool off before starting to clip again. Make sure that the blades are sharp and well oiled, and send the blades away to an expert to be resharpened and maintained when they become dull.

Trimming

Trimming the excess hair away from areas such as the head and legs can improve the horse's appearance. Use a pair of dull scissors to remove unwanted hair from the coronet band at the top of the hoof and the back of the heels and fetlock joint (known as "feather").

Helpful Hints

Never clip the inside of the ears. The horse needs this hair for protection and warmth. In order to clean up aroundyour horse's ears, just trim the most wispy pieces of hair carefully with a pair of dull scissors.

BELOW

Be careful when clipping the horse's head. Some horses do not like the noise and sensation of it and will react, although the horse pictured is very relaxed.

Trimming and Braiding

Clipping

Clipping involves removing part of the horse's winter coat with electronic clippers. It is done so that horses become less sweaty during winter work, makes grooming easier, allows horses to dry faster, and means that cuts, grazes, and lumps can be spotted more easily.

How to clip Introduce horses that have not been clipped before to clippers gradually. Let them become accustomed to the noise of the clippers first, and use a helper to stand at their head to reassure

Helpful Hints

The hair will stick to your clothes when clipping, so make sure that you wear overalls, from which it can easily be brushed off, or a plastic coat or jacket.

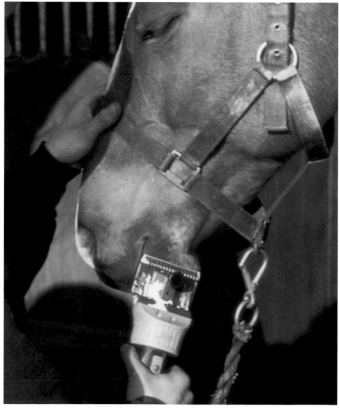

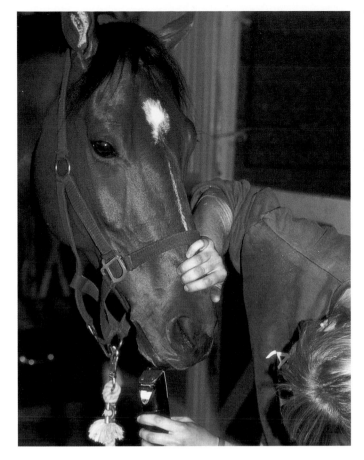

Mane and tail pulling Always use a comb to "pull" tails and manes, not a pair of scissors. This achieves a more natural look. Take a small section of mane, backcomb it, and tug the remainder out sharply. Do a little at a time, and it is easiest for the horse to do this after exercise, when the body is warm and the hair comes out more easily.

Braiding

Braiding manes and tails is done to improve a horse's appearance and make it attractive at competitions, showing, and hunting.

Braiding a mane Brush the mane and wet it so that it lies flat. Divide the short, well-pulled mane into small, equal sections with rubber bands. Starting at the top, braid each section tightly, and secure the bottom either with a rubber band or using a needle and thread, depending on which you find easier. Roll up the braid to form a "knot," and either stitch with the thread or secure with another rubber band.

Tradition used to have it that you made either seven or nine braids along the neck and one at the forelock, but these days you can choose how many looks best on your horse—or how many it takes you to reach the end of the neck.

Improving the appearance of the neck Thick, chunky braids will make the neck look shorter and bulkier; smaller braids will lengthen the neck and slim it down. Dressage horses often have many small braids fastened with white tape, while show horses usually have bigger, more spaced-out braids sewn in, in order to look cleaner.

To trim the horse's "beard" underneath its chin, either use scissors or a quiet pair of clippers. Trim close to the jawbone, and gently stretch the loose skin to achieve a clean appearance. Some people remove the horse's chin whiskers with a pair of scissors, but others believe horses need these whiskers as a part of their sensory equipment.

Trim the end of a horse's tail to around 5 in. (12 cm) below its hocks. This will not prevent the tail from being used to swat flies, but will keep it out of the wintry mud.

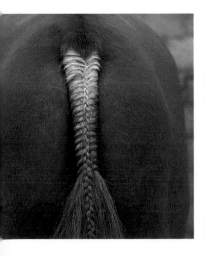

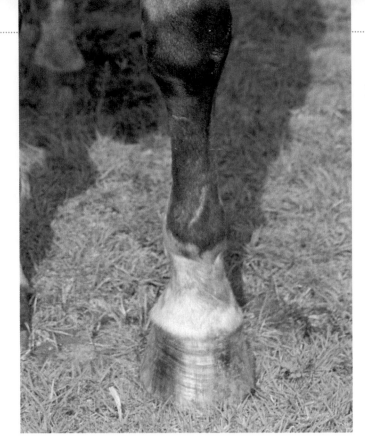

Shoeing a Horse

There is a growing trend to leave horses unshod, and for certain horses, with careful hoof trimming this may be satisfactory. But for the majority of the horse population, the application of metal shoes allows them to do the work expected of them. The art of shoeing horses is called "farriery," and the person who shoes your horse is a "farrier." Each horse's hooves are different, and it is important to find a farrier who will take time to understand what your horse needs.

The Structure of the Hoof

The exterior is made up of three parts: the wall, the sole, and the frog (*see also* page 34). All three are non-sensitive and contain neither nerves nor blood, which is why nails can be driven through the wall and why the frog and wall can be trimmed back without causing pain or bleeding.

The wall This is the part of the hoof visible when the foot is on the ground. It grows down from the coronet, like a fingernail.

The sole This thin structure protects the hoof from injury from underneath and is slightly concave, in order to provide grip.

The frog This wedge-shaped structure grows down from the heel on the bottom of the horse's hoof. It is the horse's anti-slipping and anti-concussion pad and should remain flexible and cushionlike.

How Often Should My Horse Be Shod?

Most horses will need to be shod every four to six weeks, depending on how quickly their hooves grow and how much work they are doing. Even when the shoes are not badly worn, the hoof will have grown and need to be trimmed.

Signs That a Horse Needs To Be Shod

- The foot is long and out of shape.
- The shoe has worn thin.
- The shoe is loose or has come off.
- The "clenches" (the nail heads that protrude from the hoof wall) have risen up and stand out.

The Farrier's Visit

Before your farrier arrives, make sure that your horse's legs and feet are clean and dry and that it is standing in an appropriately sheltered place, preferably with a flat, clean surface.

To remove a shoe, the farrier cuts all the clenches, using a buffer and driving hammer. He then pries the shoe off with pincers. The overgrowth of hoof wall is removed with a knife, and ragged parts of the sole and frog are trimmed away. A rasp is then used to give the foot a level bearing surface.

The new, hot shoe is then taken to the hoof on a pritchel and seared to the hoof to check that the shoe fits the shape of the foot. After any

adjustments, the shoe is cooled in water and nailed on. The first nail is usually hammered into the toe and out from there. The end of the nail, where it penetrates from the wall, is turned over and twisted off, leaving a small "clench." The clenches are cleaned up with the rasp, and the toe-clip is tapped lightly back into position.

The Newly Shod

Foot Check that:
• the shoe has been made to fit the hoof, not the hoof made to fit the shoe.
• the type and weight of the shoe is suitable for the horse.
• the frog has been correctly

trimmed: it should make contact with the ground on soft surfaces, as its serves as a concussion pad.

• no daylight shows between the shoe and the hoof, especially at the heel region.
• the heels of the shoe are not too long nor too short.

Helpful Hints

Metal studs can be attached to the heel of a shoe to decrease the risk of slipping. It is better to use one on the inside and one on the outside of each shoe to maintain the balance of the hoof. Studs come in various shapes and sizes; as a general rule, small, pointed studs are used when the ground is hard and bigger, squarer ones when the ground is soft and wet.

HEALTH

K eeping a horse healthy means constant vigilance. The horse cannot tell you if something is wrong, so your perception and assessment of its condition are vital to its well-being. You will also need to take certain active steps to maintain your horse's health, such as worming. Learn what is and isn't normal for your horse, and maintain an eye for any signs of deterioration or change. Any deviations from the signs of good health listed below should be noted and appropriate action taken as quickly as possible.

Signs of Good Health

• The horse should be standing and behaving normally.
• It should be alert and confident.
• There should be no signs of sweating while at rest, except in very hot weather.
• Its eyes should be bright and wide open.
• The membranes under the eyelids and the linings of the nostrils should be salmon pink in color.
• It should be eating well and chewing normally.
• Its coat should be sleek and lying flat, not dull and "stary."
• Its limbs should be free of heat and swellings.

• It should be standing evenly on all four feet. Resting a hindleg is normal; resting a front leg is a cause for concern.
• Its urine and feces should be normal in color and passed at the normal rate. Horses fed on hay will pass light-colored, yellowy-brown feces, while those at pasture will pass dark green feces.
• The skin should move easily over the horse's ribs, which should neither be too visible nor obscured by excess fat.

ABOVE
The horse in this picture is an example of a horse in good health. The coat is shiny, ears pricked up, and eyes alert.

• While at rest, the horse's temperature should be within the range of 99.5°–101.3° F.
• At rest, the horse's respiration (breathing) rate should be 10 to 20 inhalations per minute.
• At rest, the horse's pulse should be 36 to 42 heartbeats per minute.

Routine Healthcare

Vaccination

All horses must be vaccinated against tetanus, a serious disease picked up from bacteria in soil that can result in death. If you do not know the vaccination history of your horse, it must have an initial set of injections and a booster shot every year.

Flu vaccinations are optional but recommended and are mandatory if you wish to compete at an affiliated level in any discipline. The set consists of an initial injection, a second one between 21 and 90 days later, a third one between 115 and 210 days after the second, and annual boosters after that. These need to be six-monthly if

you are competing under International Equestrian Federation (FEI) rules.

Always ensure that your horse's vaccinations are up to date. If they fall behind, you will have to start over again.

ABOVE

This horse is wearing a speculum, or mouth gag, which keeps the mouth open, allowing the equine dentist to work on the teeth more efficiently.

Worming

All horses and ponies can suffer from worms, caused by ingesting immature larvae while grazing. It is important to control these worms through pasture management and a worming program.

Droppings should be picked up from the pasture, or if the field is too big for this to be practical, have the field

harrowed so that the droppings are broken up and spread. Do not graze horses with donkeys, as the latter pass on lungworms.

Wormers usually come in the form of a paste, which can be

"injected" into the mouth so that the horse eats it. Take advice from your vet about a sufficient worming program; there are different types of wormers to combat different worms. On average, horses should be wormed every six to eight weeks.

Teeth

It is good practice to have your horse's teeth checked at least once a year, either by your vet or a qualified horse dentist. Some horses will never need anything done to their teeth, while others may need regular treatment and rasping on sharp edges and uneven wear.

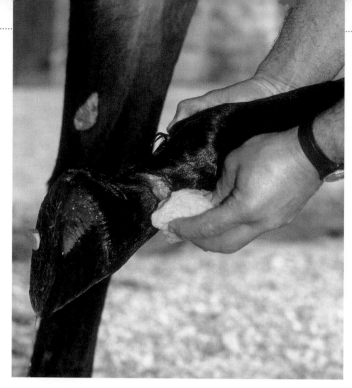

First Aid and Wounds

There are several different types of wounds. Some you will be able to manage yourself, but others will need veterinary attention. If in any doubt, call the vet—it is better to be safe than sorry. Keep the vet's phone number close by to minimize delays.

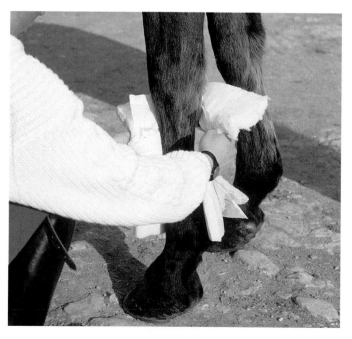

Minor Wounds
Superficial grazes, scrapes, and small cuts can be managed by clipping away the surrounding hair and cleaning thoroughly. To wash the wound, use a mild antiseptic solution in warm, clean water from a clean bucket. If you do not have antiseptic handy, kitchen salt will work. Soak cotton pads in the water and gently rub the wound, changing the cotton pads frequently.

Do not apply an ointment or powder because these make dirt stick and attract infection. If possible, apply a non-stick pad and then a bandage. Keep the horse in a stable, if possible, because it is easier to keep the wound clean. Also, check that the horse's tetanus vaccinations are up to date.

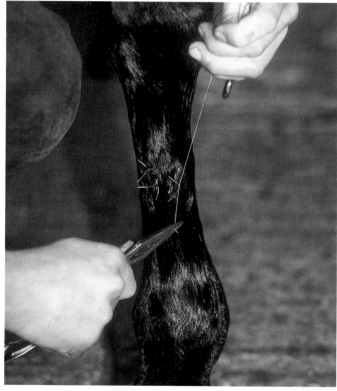

When to Call the Vet
Always call a qualified veterinarian in the following situations:

• if blood is spurting from the wound
• if the wound is on the foot, over a joint, or near a tendon, or at the eye. Infection in the foot is difficult to treat once established. Wounds near joints are dangerous because of the risk of joint oil (synovial fluid) leaking out of the joint capsule and serious infection resulting. If a horse falls over on the road and damages its knees, seek veterinary advice, however superficial the injury may look
• if the cut is big enough to need stitching, whether it is jagged-edged or clean-edged
• if the horse has picked up a puncture wound. This is a small, deep wound, perhaps from a nail or sharp-pointed object. The danger is that they are easy to miss, and because of their depth, may have damaged the internal structures of the horse or contain foreign bodies and dirt that you cannot see. They are difficult to clean out and may need to be poulticed

If you have called the vet in an emergency, there are a few things you can do to help the situation. If blood is spurting out, push a clean cotton pad into the wound and either hold or bandage it into place.

With all major wounds, try to prevent the horse from panicking or moving too much so that further damage is minimized. Make sure that you have warm water and some clean towels ready.

Deep wounds, where the blood is not spurting out, can be liberally hosed with cold water until the vet arrives. This will constrict the blood vessels and help stop the bleeding.

Girth Galls and Saddle Sores

If a horse's tack does not fit properly, it will rub and cause a sore patch. Wash the area with a weak antiseptic solution, and when the skin has healed, harden it up with an antiseptic solution. Most importantly, find out what is rubbing and take steps to prevent it. A fleece girth-guard should be used until the problem is solved. For saddle sores, do not ride the horse until they are completely healed, and seek the advice of a saddle maker.

RIGHT

Girth galls such as this pictured can quickly become open sores if they are not noticed. They must be allowed to completely heal before the horse is saddled again, and the girth should be changed.

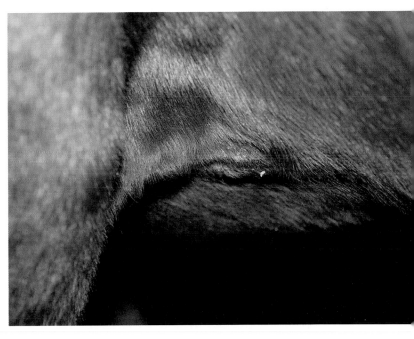

LEFT

Cold hosing is an excellent therapy for any type of bruised injury on the legs or feet and helps reduce inflammation.

Mouth Injuries

Badly fitting bits or those with sharp or worn edges can damage the mouth, especially if combined with rough riding. Cracks to the corners of the mouth are most common, which can become very sore. Check the bit for damage or pinching, and change it accordingly. Applying calendula cream, or hemorrhoid cream formulated for humans, will help heal the sores. In bad cases, you may have to refrain from using a bit for a few days.

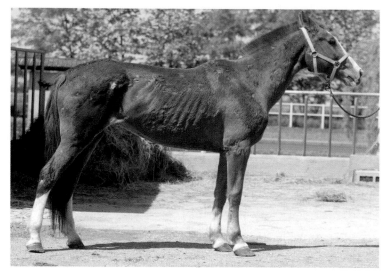

Signs of Bad Health

Common signs of sickness include:

- dullness and depression
- failure to eat and sudden weight loss
- a dull and "stary" coat
- patchy sweating at rest
- box-walking and general unease
- getting up and lying down repeatedly
- ears laid back
- runny, weeping eyes
- a runny nose
- abnormal pulse and respiration rates
- a higher temperature
- swelling or heat in a leg
- resting a foreleg or shifting constantly from one leg to the other
- lameness
- drinking more than normal and urinating more than normal
- discolored feces and urine, or feces of an unusual consistency
- patchy hair loss
- coughing
- skin lumps

- aggression toward other horses or humans
- disinclination to socialize with other horses in the field
- poor performance and poor exercise tolerance

It is important to know what is "normal" for your horse, especially its respiration and pulse rates and temperature.

Taking Your Horse's Temperature

Lubricate the bulb of a thermometer, preferably a digital one, and gently insert it into the horse's rectum. Do not stand directly behind the horse in case it kicks, and hold the tail out of the way. Hold on to the thermometer firmly (plenty of these have been lost inside horses, which necessitates a visit to the vet), and leave for two minutes or until it beeps if it is digital. Withdraw the thermometer, and read the temperature. Make sure that you wash the thermometer thoroughly.

Taking the Pulse Rate

The easiest places to feel the pulse are where the facial artery crosses the jawbone and just below the horse's elbow. Make sure that you take the pulse rate with your fingers, not your thumb, which has a pulse of its own. Count the number of pulses in 15 seconds, and multiply by four to get a reading.

Taking the Respiration Rate

Watch the horse's flanks move in and out, and count for a minute. Breathing should be regular and quiet.

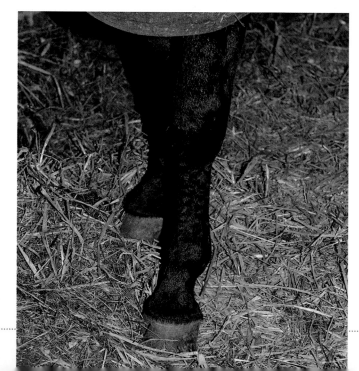

LEFT
Whenever a horse rests or "points" a front leg, as seen here, it indicates pain in the limb and should be investigated immediately.

ABOVE
When checking the horse's pulse rate, always use your fingers and not the thumb—this is because the thumb has its own pulse, which confuses the reading.

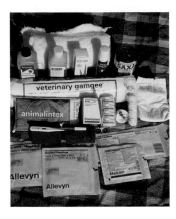

Common Ailments and Treatment

All horse owners should possess a basic first-aid box containing the following:

- cotton pads
- dull-ended scissors
- a thermometer
- antiseptic solution for cleaning wounds
- a variety of different-sized dressings
- surgical tape
- gamgee pads
- a selection of bandages
- self-adhesive bandage,

such as Vetwrap
- Animalintex or similar impregnated multi-layered poultice
- Epsom salts
- a clean bowl or small bucket
- Vaseline
- your vet's and farrier's phone numbers

Lameness

Many horse owners will have to cope with some degree of lameness in their horse at some point. It can range from mild to severe and be sudden in onset or gradual. If both forelegs or both hindlegs, or all four legs, are affected, it can be difficult to detect because there may not be an obvious limp; the stride

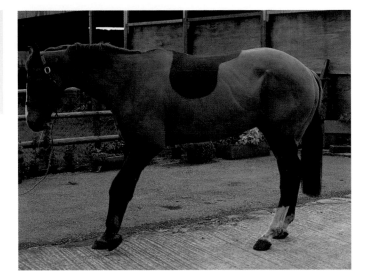

length may just be shorter or the horse may be unwilling to go forward freely.

Almost all lameness is a result of foot pain (the most common reason) or damage to the leg's soft structures, such as tendons and ligaments.

Laminitis

Laminitis is a painful condition of the feet caused by inflammation of the laminae, which are sensitive membranes on the inside of the hoof wall. It can affect any horse at any time of the year, but it is especially prevalent in small ponies, especially natives, in the

spring. It has many causes, but the most common is carbohydrate overload from too much rich food, especially grass. Others include insulin resistance, too much work on hard ground, infection, lameness resulting in hoof imbalance, a hormonal disease called Cushing's, or reactions to certain drugs such as corticosteroids.

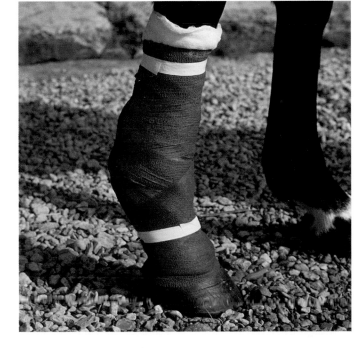

The hoof wall is hot to the touch, with an increased digital pulse. The horse will stand with its weight tipped back on to its heels and will be unwilling to move. Horses with a severe case of laminitis may lie down and refuse to get up.

Treatment Call the vet. In the meantime, make the horse as comfortable as possible. Do not remove all access to food and water, and do not hose the horse's feet in an effort to reduce the heat.

Other Sources of Foot Pain

Other forms of lameness in the foot may be the result of abscesses, where infection has built up and can cause the horse to be severely lame. Veterinary treatment will be needed to drain the abscess. Corns or bruises at the heel between the frog and the hoof wall are fairly common and are often the result of poor shoe size. Stones can become trapped in the foot and will

make a horse instantly lame. Thrush is a smelly, fungal infection on the bottom of the foot, with a black discharge oozing from the frog. Bad stable management or poor foot care is the usual cause of this ailment.

Tendon and Ligament Damage

The flexor tendons and check and suspensory ligaments at the back of the horse's lower leg are vulnerable and liable to damage because of the amount of strain they take when a horse moves. Some injuries to these do not initially cause lameness, only some heat and swelling. If you suspect damage, rest the

horse immediately, and call the vet. It is very difficult for the amateur to tell how severe these injuries are without expert advice. Early identification and treatment can make all the difference to recovery.

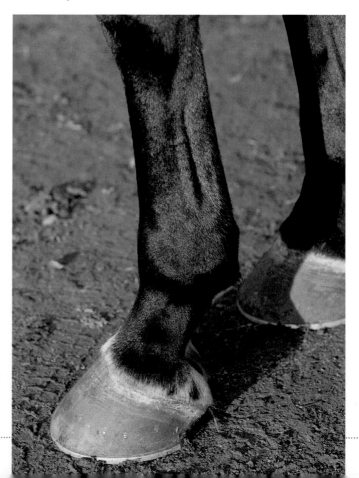

Skin Diseases

Most skin diseases are not serious and are relatively easy to treat. But they can be infectious and spread to other horses and even people, so prompt and efficient management is vital.

Ringworm This is not caused by a worm at all but is a fungal infection that affects the roots of the hair. It is identified by small, round, bare patches and is highly infectious to other horses and humans. The horse should be isolated, and all tack, rugs, and grooming kit must be thoroughly cleaned and kept separate from that belonging to other horses. Wash your hands and exposed skin after attending to the affected horse to minimize the risk of cross-infection.

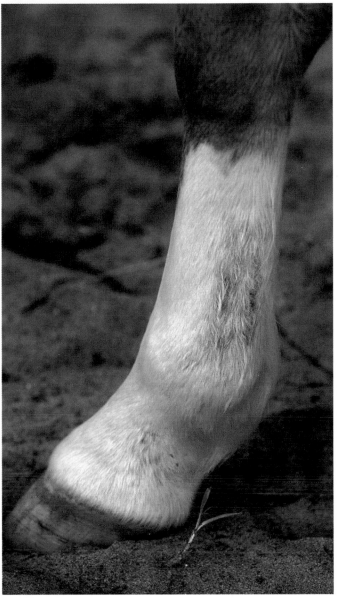

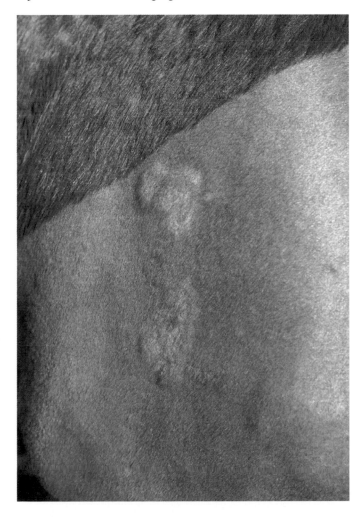

LEFT
Ringworm develops as small, round, bare patches, as seen here, although sometimes the lesions will exude a thick serum. It is a highly contagious condition and can be caught by humans as well as other horses.

Sweet itch This is an unpleasant condition caused by an allergy to mosquito bites and causes severe itchiness around the mane and tail. It affects ponies more frequently than horses and drives them to rub themselves raw. It is incurable but can be kept under control through careful management. It is helpful to keep the animal in the stable at dawn and dusk, when the mosquitoes are at their worst, and repellent should be used liberally. There are also some specifically designed rugs that have proven highly effective, made out of light cloth that tightly covers the horse from nose to tail.

Mud fever Many horses suffer from mud fever at one time or another. When the skin surrounding the heels and the lower leg is softened by moisture, bacteria enter the skin, and infection develops. The skin becomes lumpy and cracked and may puss out yellowy fluid. The horse's legs may swell up, and it can become very painful. Horses get it from standing in wet conditions and mud, and it can be prevented by keeping their legs clean and dry or covering the legs with ointment or baby oil before turning them out. Wash mud off when they are brought in after turn-out or exercise, and then dry thoroughly.

To treat, trim the hair back to help keep the legs clean and dry. Your vet will advise you on antibacterial creams to heal the infection.

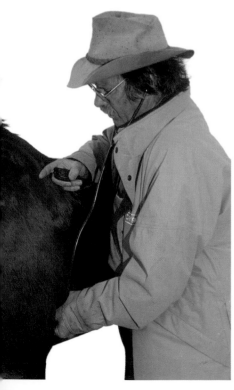

Colic

Colic means abdominal pain and has an almost infinite number of causes and levels of severity, from mild to life-threatening. Always call the vet if you suspect your horse has colic, as early treatment is essential, and surgery may be required.

Symptoms of colic The horse will look uncomfortable and uneasy and kick at its belly. There may be patchy sweating, and its heart, temperature, and respiration rates may be increased. Other signs are a failure to finish food, not passing feces as normal, and getting up and down.

Action While you are waiting for the vet, try to keep the horse as calm as possible. It may be severely distressed and potentially dangerous; if this is the case, do not interfere. But if it is calm, remove any feed or hay from the stable, and note if any feces have been passed. If the horse wants to lie down, allow it to, but prevent it from rolling if you can. The vet will assess the severity of the problem, identify the type of colic, and treat it accordingly.

LEFT AND BELOW
Do not diagnose yourself. Wait for the vet to check your horse.

Some causes of colic
- Bolting food
- Ingesting sand from a stream or sandy ground
- Working hard too close to a meal time
- Worms
- Sudden changes in diet
- Poor tooth care
- Moldy hay or hard food
- Drinking too much cold water immediately after exercise

Fitness Regimes and Training

How in shape your horse needs to be will depend on what you want to do with it, but the more in shape it is, the easier it will find it to work and the less risk there is of causing damage to its joints, muscles, tendons, and ligaments.

Allow 12 to 14 weeks to get your horse in shape enough for hard work, such as horse trials, hunting, or any form of exercise that requires considerable exertion.

Before you start
• Check that the horse's worming and vaccination programs are up to date.
• Check that its teeth are in

First stage
• Stay in walk, including road work, for at least three weeks. Start with 30 minutes a day, building up to an hour and a half.
• If the horse is returning from an injury, extend the walking period to six weeks.
• Make sure that the horse walks out in an active manner and in balance; slopping along with the reins swinging will not help get the animal in shape and muscled up.

Basic Fitness Program
This plan assumes that you are starting with an out-of-shape horse but one that is in good condition. Horses in poor condition will take longer to get in shape and will find it much harder. It would be better to spend some time improving the horse's condition before attempting to work it.

good condition and don't need rasping, and arrange for the farrier to visit and shoe the horse if necessary.
• Trim and clean up the horse's mane, tail, and heels.

RIGHT
The walk phase of the fitness regime is the most important and provides the building block for the work to come.

Second stage

• Combine walking with slow trotting for another three weeks, building the exercise up to two hours six days a week if possible. Use hillwork to build up muscle.

• Some steady trotting on good roads helps harden the legs, but do not overdo it, as it can make them jar.

• You can also introduce some schooling on flat ground, some slow cantering

for short periods, and towards the end of the six weeks, some simple jumping.

Third stage

• By this time, the horse should be ready to improve its respiratory fitness as well as its muscular fitness. Find some open ground with a good level, and start with a quarter of a mile of cantering interspersed with trotting. Build up the distance gradually until the horse is cantering for a mile at a

good, controlled pace once or twice a week.

• Slow work up a hill is beneficial; hillwork enables you to do shorter, sharper pieces of work with your horse without putting unnecessary strain on its legs by working for long periods of time.

• Hacking, schooling, and gymnastic jumping should be done on the other days of the week.

Interval Training

Interval training is a useful refinement of your basic fitness regime and can be included in the final two weeks of the program. It is designed to strengthen the horse's muscles and respiratory system by a gradual increase in "stress" and consists of repeated spells of canter interspersed with periods of walk in which the horse is allowed almost, but not completely, to recover its prework pulse rate before going on to the next interval of fast work. Not allowing the pulse to drop completely strengthens

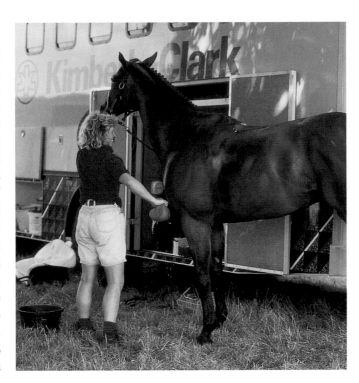

the heart, lungs, and muscles and helps them adapt to the stress placed on them. It also develops the capacity of the horse's respiratory and circulatory systems.

As an example, a horse getting in shape for a novice-level, one-day event would canter for three minutes, walk for three minutes, and canter again for three minutes, increasing the canter periods depending on how in shape you want the horse to become.

> # Fascinating Facts
>
> There are centers devoted to Equine Assisted Psychotherapy and Equine Assisted Learning, where people with problems and troubles can be helped by both two-legged and four-legged therapists.

You must be practical: tailor your horse's fitness program to match the time you have available and your facilities. Not everyone has a hill to work up or good hacking. Cantering the horse in balance around and around the school on each rein can, if done properly, be just as good if it is your only option.

Rider Fitness

Riders are increasingly aware of the need to be in shape to ride. Fitness is important because a lack of fitness for a specific activity results in early fatigue, which leads to a failure of skill and an increase in the risk of injury. If you "hit the wall" and get very tired halfway around a cross-

---
RIGHT

It is important for the rider to be in shape as well as the horse. If the rider is out of shape, it adds to the horse's burden, especially when jumping.

ABOVE

Always wash the horse down after work to remove traces of sweat from the coat and to cool it down.

---

country course, you effectively become a passenger and cannot help the horse when it needs it. We all want to ride our horses to the best of our abilities, and being out of shape makes you a less effective, less balanced

rider. It also increases your risk of injury and your risk of falling off. Even if you don't want to compete, getting in shape can help you stay safe and injury-free.

Fitness can be divided into stamina, strength, and suppleness. Stamina strengthens your heart and lungs, strength tones your muscles to allow you to do physical work without injury, and suppleness enhances mobility. For general fitness and non-competitive riding, a balance of all three is best. Depending on your riding discipline and how well schooled your horse is, suppleness and stamina are probably the most important, followed by strength. Stamina becomes more important the longer the duration of your discipline; endurance riding requires higher levels of stamina than dressage. Jockeys riding in races and event riders have to have a far higher amount of strength than endurance riders or dressage competitors.

GROWTH AND BREEDING

Deciding to breed a foal is a big decision, one that should be thought through from all angles. Is the mare you are breeding from exceptional in terms of conformation, temperament, and performance? Can you afford the stud fee of a good stallion and the associated costs with bringing a foal to life? If not, strongly consider buying a foal with proven parentage instead; it will be cheaper in the long run and less of a risk. But breeding a foal is also exciting, and if everything works out, very rewarding.

The Lifecycle of a Horse

Young Horses

A horse's life starts after an 11-month gestation period. Foals, whether they are colts (male) or fillies (female), go by these names until their first birthdays, when they become yearlings.

• Foals have small bodies with what seem like excessively long limbs and big joints and a short, fluffy mane and tail.

• Yearlings still look very young and are awkward and unfurnished. The limbs still look out of proportion to the body, and the mane and tail are still fluffy. In the Northern Hemisphere, all horses have their "official" birthdays and turn a year older on January first; the official horse birthday in the Southern Hemisphere is August first. Between January first (or August first in the Southern Hemisphere) and the actual date of their birthdays, horses are referred to as "rising" to that age; i.e. "rising five" means that the horse will be five years old.

• When a horse becomes a two-year-old, it begins to look more like an adult horse. The head is defined as much as it will be as an adult, and the limbs are more in proportion. The mane and tail begin to look normal. The body, however, lacks maturity and has very limited muscles. This is not as true with Thoroughbreds, which have been bred for early maturity for centuries and race in their two-year-old year. Remember, though, that they are carrying very light weights and racing in straight lines, not being asked to balance a large human while turning circles or jumping.

formal education and work. The years from six to 12 are probably the prime of the horse's life and their best competitive years, although many horses, especially those who mature late, may achieve their best results in their teenage years.

Older Horses

A horse is generally considered to be a "veteran" at the age of 16; however, with modern advances in veterinary care, the science of feeding, and understanding of welfare issues concerning the geriatric horse, many people

ABOVE

These young Lusitano stallions are starting to look like mature horses but still have a lot of growing and maturing to do.

• Three-year-olds are distinguishable from fully adult horses only by a lack of muscle and general immaturity, and at four the horse is considered to be an adult. They are still referred to as "fillies" and "colts" until they are four, or five in the racing industry, when they become "mares" and either "geldings" or "horses," "entires" or "stallions," depending on whether or not they have been castrated.

Adult Horses

Although different breeds of horses take different amounts of time to mature, they are considered to be adult at four years of age. This is the age when they can be exhibited in anything apart from youngstock classes and when most horses apart from Thoroughbreds in the racing industry begin to receive

do not consider their horse to be "old" until it is in its twenties. Horses can live into their thirties if cared for throughout their lives.

Old horses show signs of age: the bone structure on the head looks more pronounced, the neck tends to lose muscle, the back often hollows out, and the withers stand out, and the limbs and joints may show signs of wear. The amount of work they do may need to be reduced, and the time spent warming up and cooling down should be extended.

• Does she have good breeding? Horses with good bloodlines are easier to sell.

• Has she been a good performer? Again, the offspring will be more popular if its dam has a proven competition record.

• Does the mare have a good temperament?

• Is she sound? Many people decide to breed a foal from their much-loved mare because she is no longer sound enough to be ridden. This is not good practice; the foal may inherit the same weaknesses as its mother.

Choosing a Stallion and Mare

When choosing to breed a foal, you should first think about the mare. Remember that traits are inherited from both parents; it is good to choose an outstanding stallion, but if the mare is a poor specimen it is unlikely that you will breed a champion, or even a good, useful all-rounder.

• Does she have any serious conformation faults that she might pass on to the foal?

If you can honestly answer yes to all these questions, you then need to think about the stallion you would like to use. There is a huge range of stallions available at a variety of prices. It is worth going for the best you can afford; the foal is likely to be a nicer animal and easier to sell should you decide to. Even if you plan to breed a horse for your own use, it is sensible to

• Is the stallion of a breed likely to cross well with your mare? For obvious physical reasons, it is not a good idea to cross a Shire horse with a Welsh pony, and non-traditional outcrosses, such as a part-heavy horse/part-Arab are unlikely to inherit the strengths of both and none of the weaknesses and will be harder to sell.

BELOW AND RIGHT

The conformation of the stallion should be carefully assessed, as should his temperament, competition record, and fertility.

society? This will ensure that he is true to type and a good example of the breed.
• Is he a well-made horse with good movement, and would his conformation complement that of your mare? Two horses with weak hindlegs are very unlikely to produce one with a good hindleg.
• Is he sound?
• Does he have a good fertility rate?
• Is his stud fee within your price range? Some studs offer reductions to mares with proven competition records, so it is worth investigating this.

• When is the fee due? Often if the mare is not in foal by a certain date, or even does not give birth to a live foal, you may get a free return to the stallion.
• How far away is he? How practical will it be to travel your mare a great distance to be covered?
• Does the stud have a good reputation for getting mares in foal and for looking after your mare well while she is in residence.
• What job do you want the foal to do? Try not to breed indiscriminately out of sentiment. Pick a stallion that is a dressage sire if you want a dressage horse or an eventing stallion if you want to produce an eventer.

ABOVE

Morgan horses, such as this fine stallion, are especially popular in America and are often crossed with Arab or Thoroughbred to produce small show horses.

think about the future. Your circumstances may change, and a healthy and strong foal will have a much better chance of a decent life.

• Does the stallion have an established breeding record, i.e. has he sired suitable foals before? It is safer to choose a well-recognized sire than one that is just starting out on a career at stud, especially if you are a first-time breeder.
• What is his performance record? If he has not competed, why is this?
• Is he graded with a breed

The Breeding Process

AI or not?

Breeders must decide whether they want to use artificial insemination (AI) or have their mare covered by the stallion. If they choose AI, the semen can either be frozen or chilled. Fertility rates with frozen semen are often lower than with chilled, and it has a short life span once unfrozen.

Advantages of AI

• You don't have to transport your mare to stud.
• You have a wider range of stallions to choose from, especially from abroad.
• There is much less risk of sexually transmitted diseases.
• There is less of the risk of

injury to the stallion or mare that can occur during traditional breeding.
• There is better quality control on semen.

Disadvantages of AI

• It is more expensive than a stallion covering a mare.
• You need good infrastructure to transport the semen and a vet that specializes in AI to administer it.
• Some semen will not survive the thawing / cooling process.

Mares should have a thorough pre-breeding assessment before undergoing AI, which should take into account any previous breeding history and the age of the mare: fertility declines after the age of 10,

although many mares conceive at much higher ages. Accurate prediction of ovulation is important because the best time for AI with chilled semen is in the 24 hours leading up to ovulation. Pregnancy rates will generally fall if

insemination is outside of this range. This time interval is shorter than if fresh semen or natural mating is used, and the window of opportunity is even shorter with frozen semen.

stallion; if she doesn't, she will be examined by a vet a few days later. This will be done by manual palpation and with an ultrasound scanner. The usual pattern for scanning is 15 to 18 days after covering, again at 21 to 28 days, and once again at 35 to 40 days.

- Keep stress to a minimum.
- Reduce the risk of infection, which could cause abortion or fetal damage, by keeping her away from young stock, horses-in-training, and competition horses.
- Make sure that she has regular veterinary examinations, and check that her vaccinations are up to date.

In-Hand Breeding

The most commonly used method on studs is in-hand breeding, where the mare and stallion are brought together just for mating and are held by handlers. This should

interrupted and so that several foals can be born at the same time, rather than just one, as in theory there is no limit to the amount of eggs that can be fertilized and transferred to recipient mares.

Care of the Mare

To give a mare the best chance of producing a strong, healthy foal and of recovering quickly from the birth, good care during her pregnancy is important.

- Make sure that she has adequate nutrition. She will not need extra food in the early months, but consult a nutritionist later on to ensure that she is getting the right vitamins and minerals,
- Light exercise is a good idea; she will tell you when she no longer wants to be ridden.

always be carried out by professionals, and all precautions must be taken to minimize damage to the mare or stallion.

Embryo Transfer

This is a relatively new method of producing a foal, where the mare whose egg is fertilized does not carry the foal to term, as this is done by a surrogate mare. It is increasingly used on top competition mares so that their careers are not

However, it is very expensive and requires highly specialized veterinary expertise.

Pregnancy

It is important to establish whether a mare is pregnant as soon as possible and that she is carrying just one fetus. Twin fetuses are rarely successful and are often aborted or die shortly after birth. If a mare remains at stud, she will be "teased" about 12 days after mating to see if she responds to the

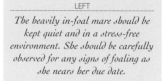

LEFT
The heavily in-foal mare should be kept quiet and in a stress-free environment. She should be carefully observed for any signs of foaling as she nears her due date.

and one hour, and the feet can appear out of the vulva after about 15 to 20 minutes. They should be followed by the nose, then the head, shoulders, and chest.

It is usually at this stage that the amniotic sac is broken, and the foal can breathe. The rest of the foal's body should then appear, with the hind feet last. The mare will then lick and nuzzle the foal and encourage it to its feet. The placenta will probably be expelled some time after this. If the process described above does not happen fairly quickly, the vet should be called immediately.

Foaling and the Young Foal

Mares are either foaled at their owner's home or at stud. For first-time breeders, it is advisable to have your mare foaled at stud by experts, just in case something goes wrong. Make sure that you are there, too, so that you can learn what to do next time. Very occasionally, a disaster happens and either the mare or foal is lost during foaling. There are special organizations and charities that can help by finding a foster mare for a motherless foal or a motherless foal for a mare who has lost hers, which can make the whole experience less painful for both the horse and the humans involved.

Foaling

Some mares foal outside in the field, but many are brought inside to a special foaling box. This must be large enough, with a thick bed and high banks of bedding against the walls. Most mares give birth at night or in the early morning, and most prefer to do so alone if possible. Mares "wax up," where the teats secrete a waxy solution, before giving birth, but this can be misleading and happen a while before the foal is ready to be born.

When she is ready, the mare will become restless and pace around, holding her tail to one side. After the allantoic sac is broken and fluid gushes out, the mare will usually lie down. A normal labor will last between only 30 minutes

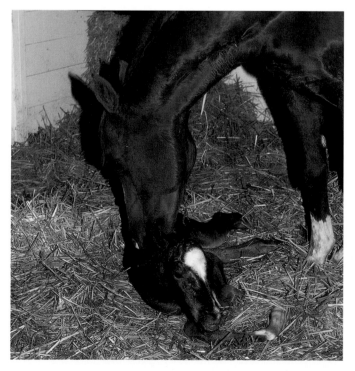

After foaling it is imperative that the foal suckle as quickly as possible to ingest the infinitely important colostrum that is only present for a limited time in the mare's milk.

The Young Foal

A normal foal should be attempting to stand within 20 minutes of birth and should be up within one hour, and it should suckle within an hour or two. Once on its feet and sucking, it should become increasingly well coordinated; after all, in the wild a foal must be able to travel with the herd within a few hours. Any delay in these timings means the vet should be consulted, as a delay in dealing with a weak foal could be serious. A foal's legs are 90 percent of the length that they will be as an adult.

Like a human infant, the foal receives nourishment and antibodies from the colostrum in milk that is produced within the first few hours or days following birth. The mare needs additional water to help her produce milk for the foal and may benefit from supplementary nutrition.

The mare and foal are usually kept apart from others for a few weeks and then turned out in a group with other mares and foals. At about four weeks, the foal will begin to eat grass and grain alongside its mother, and at 12 weeks the foal needs more nutrition than the mare can supply from milk alone. Foals grow quickly, and can gain 3 lbs (1 kg) a day.

Foals are typically weaned at about six months, but some are left on the mare longer. Most foals accept weaning easily, but some will become upset by it, and it is better if they have company around the same age and do not have to live alone at this stage.

Helpful Hints

It is a good idea if a foal receives some basic training, such as being taught to lead, having a headcollar put on, and being groomed, as well as having their feet picked up, inspected, and trimmed by the farrier.

Foals benefit from being turned out with others so they can socialize and play—the herd environment is their natural one.

TACK AND EQUIPMENT

I t is easy to accumulate large amounts of tack and equipment, such as boots and rugs, for your horse, most of which you will use only once and which can cost you a fortune. Invest in smaller amounts of the best-quality saddlery you can afford, and clean and maintain it carefully to ensure that it lasts. Also, make sure that it is not left lying around where it could easily be stolen: there is a demand for second-hand tack originating from stolen goods.

Saddles, Girths, and Stirrups

Saddles

A good saddle is essential and should be treated as an investment. It should be

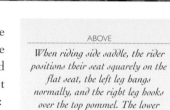

comfortable for both horse and rider, and expert advice from a saddle maker should be sought. The three most popular types of saddles are:

• **general-purpose saddle** This is designed for all types of riding and general activities. It is sensible to buy this as a first saddle, as it can be used for both dressage and jumping. It will be fairly forward-cut without being as extreme as a jumping saddle, with a knee roll.

• **jumping saddle** This usually has a flatter seat than

a dressage saddle and is designed for riding with short stirrups, so it has a forward-cut saddle flap and knee and thigh rolls to help keep the rider's leg in place.

• **dressage saddle** This is generally the most deep-seated saddle and often has a high cantle. The stirrup bars are farther back than on a saddle predominantly used for jumping. The girth straps are longer than usual, and it is used with a short girth to prevent the girth buckle from lying under the rider's thigh.

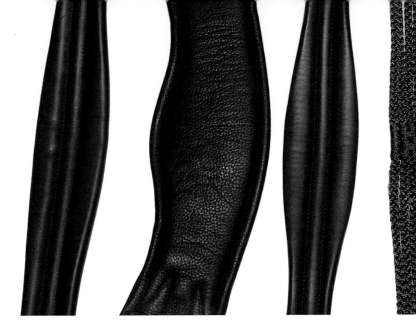

Girths

Girths secure the saddle on a horse's back, and it is really important that they fit well and are in good condition. Check the stitching regularly. Girth sizes are determined by how long they are from end to end, including the buckle, and are measured in inches. There are three main types of leather girth: the three-fold, where a single piece of leather is cut straight and folded over to form three layers; the Balding, which starts straight with two buckles but divides into three strips that cross over and are stitched together to reduce the width of the girth behind the horse's elbow where it could rub; and the Atherstone, which is also shaped to provide comfort for the horse but is one solid strip of leather.

Girths can also be made out of webbing, soft nylon, or synthetic fabrics, which are easy to wash but do not last as long as leather girths, string, or a variety of synthetic leathers.

Stirrups

Stirrup leathers and stirrup irons should be good quality and well maintained; it is not fun if your stirrup leather breaks halfway around a crosscountry course or during a long-distance ride. Irons should be made out of stainless steel, not nickel, which has a tendency to wear thin and break. They should be large enough to allow about 0.5 in. (1 cm) at each side of the rider's foot; getting your foot stuck in the iron is very dangerous if you fall off. But don't use stirrup irons that are too big and allow the whole foot to slip through. Rubber treads attached to the irons are a good idea, as they prevent the foot from slipping.

Stirrup leathers are made of ordinary leather (cowhide), rawhide, or buffalo hide. The leathers tend to stretch when new, so check that the holes are still level with one another. It is also a good idea to switch the leathers over from time to time, as the one on the left stretches more because of the additional pressure of the rider mounting and dismounting.

Fascinating Facts

The fastest horse ever recorded was Secretariat, who holds the world record for finishing a mile and a half in two minutes and twenty-four seconds at the 1973 Belmont Stakes.

at the other to the bit rings.

• **bit** This is the main device for communicating with the horse and comes in an almost infinite variety of shapes, sizes, and materials. The cheekpieces and reins are attached to the bit by buckles, hooked billets, or stitching.

• **reins** These are the long strips of leather between the bit and the rider's hands, down which communication signals are passed. Make sure that they are the correct width for the rider's hands and the right length.

• **noseband** This aid to control fits around the horse's nose and is a separate piece of leather that attaches only to itself but fits through the browband loops and over the head under the headpiece. It comes in a variety of forms, such as the cavesson, which is the standard simple noseband; the drop, which fits below the bit and is stronger; and the "flash," a combination of the two.

The Double Bridle

This has two bits, called the "bridoon" (snaffle) and the "curb" and an extra headpiece and cheekpiece,

called a "slip-head," is used to secure the bridoon. They are buckled on the right side, where all other bridle straps are attached on the left. The curb bit must have a curb chain attached to it, and a lip strap should be threaded through the "fly" (extra) link in the center of the curb chain to hold it in place. As there are two bits, there are also two sets of reins, and it is a good idea to make these slightly different from each other so that it is easy to tell which set controls which bit.

In Roman mythology, the god Neptune, though credited with being god of the sea, was held in higher esteem by the Romans for also being Neptune Equester, the god and patron of horses and horse racing.

Bridles and Bits

There are three main types of bridles: snaffles (any bridle used with one bit), double bridles (with two bits), and bitless bridles.

The Snaffle Bridle

The snaffle bridle is made up of the following parts:

• **headpiece and throatlash** Made from the same piece of leather, the headpiece goes over the top of the horse's

head, and in conjunction with the cheekpieces, keeps the bit in the horse's mouth. The throatlash extends down from the headpiece and fastens around the horse's throat to keep the bridle in place.

• **browband** This attaches to the headpiece and goes around the brow at the front of the head to prevent the headpiece from slipping back.

• **cheekpieces** These keep the bit in place by attaching at one end to the headpiece and

ABOVE

The long metal shanks that form part of this bitless bridle act as levers, so when contact is made, pressure is exerted on the front of the nose, at the poll, and behind the jaw by the curb chain.

The Bitless Bridle

These are usually used to keep a horse with a sore mouth in work while the damage heals but can be useful if a horse is especially fussy or difficult in his mouth. They rely on nose pressure and leverage to control the horse. The most common form is the hackamore.

Bits

The snaffle is the basic schooling bit and the most commonly used bit. It comes in a range of forms with different mouthpieces and rings or cheeks, each of which have a different action in the horse's mouth. Some popular ones include the eggbutt snaffle, the loose-ring snaffle, the French link, the straight-bar snaffle, the Dr. Bristol, or

ABOVE

Pelham bits should preferably be ridden with two reins, though they can be ridden with one through the use of a leather coupling, as seen.

the hanging-cheek snaffle. Gags are a type of snaffle but more severe than most, and as well as acting on various parts of the horse's mouth, also apply poll pressure.

Pelhams are a combination of the curb and the bridoon from a double bridle in one bit. Critics say that this blunts the effectiveness of the bits and is a less sensitive aid, but many horses go well in them. They should be worn with a curb chain. Some riders have "roundings," which enable just one rein to be used. Some pelhams, such as the Kimblewick, are designed to be used with a single rein, but most, such as the Rugby, globe, half-moon, or broken, are used with two reins.

LEFT

Gags should always be used with two reins, as seen here. They are a severe bit and exert pressure on the poll, while also applying upward pressure to the corner of the mouth that acts to raise the head.

Martingales and Reins

There are three types of martingales: standing, running, and Irish.

Standing Martingale

This is used to stop the horse from raising its head too high. It consists of a piece of leather, which loops around the girth and passes between the horse's front legs, through a supporting loop on the neck strap, to the cavesson noseband. It should not be fitted too tightly and should not be used to hold the horse's head down.

Running Martingale

This is a more moderate way of encouraging the horse not to carry its head too high and takes effect only when the horse raises

its head beyond the angle of control. It attaches to the girth between the forelegs; after it passes through the rubber ring on the neck strap that holds it in place, it divides into two. Each of these two ends comes with a metal ring, through which the reins are passed. Make sure that it is not too tight, or more commonly, too loose. As a rough guide, when the martingale is attached to the girth and both rings are taken to one side, it should be long enough to reach the horse's withers.

RIGHT

Running martingales should always be used in conjunction with rubber martingale stops. These are positioned on the rein between the bit ring and the martingale ring.

Helpful Hints

Always use martingale "stops," which are pieces of leather or rubber that fit onto the reins and stop the martingale rings from getting caught on the bit or the rein fastenings.

LEFT

Standing martingales attach to the back of a cavesson noseband and prevent the horse from raising its head above a certain level.

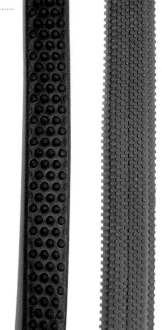

Irish Martingale

This is simply two metal rings connected by a leather strap approximately 4 in. (10 cm) long. The reins are threaded

through it under the horse's neck. It is most commonly seen in racing and is used to keep the horse's reins in place and stop them from flying over its head.

Reins

Reins are available in several materials:

• **leather** Plain leather is attractive, gives the best feel, and is most correct in the show ring but can become slippery in the rain or on a sweaty horse. Braided leather

is less slippery but is expensive and can be difficult to clean.

• **rubber** Rubber-covered leather, either on one side of the rein or both, gives the best grip. When a pair of these reins becomes ratty, do not throw them away immediately; often they can be recovered with rubber by a saddler, as long as the leather underneath is strong.

• **webbing** These give good grip, and if they have leather "bars" on them, do not slip.

• **string** These are often good for children because they are especially pliable and should not slip, but they may not be attractive enough for competing adults.

Lunging reins Lunging reins are long webbing reins that fix on to a lunging cavesson (a special type of padded, leather headcollar used for lunging) and allow the horse

to move in a circle around the lunger. They should be at least 23 ft. (7 m) long and have a rotating clip joint.

Side reins Side reins are used when lunging a horse and run from the bit to the saddle or surcingle to encourage correct carriage and flexion. They are made from webbing or leather, sometimes with added elastic inserts for flexibility. They should be carefully attached and adjusted by an experienced person and must be the same length on each side. It is advisable to warm

the horse up on the lunge without them and then clip on the side reins when the horse is ready to work.

Lead reins Lead reins, made out of webbing and leather, attach via two clips to each bit ring. They are used to lead animals in hand, such as stallions, and in in-hand and leading-rein classes in the show ring.

Brushing Boots

These are worn while the horse is being ridden and protect the cannon bones and the sensitive structures in that area, such as tendons and ligaments, from damage. They are shaped to fit the contours of the leg and come in different sizes. The fastenings should be on the

are shaped, and attach with straps.

Knee Boots and Hock Boots

These protect the horse while traveling and are made out of thick felt or synthetic material. They are also sometimes worn for exercising on the road and for hunting in countryside where there are walls to be jumped. The top straps must be fastened tightly and the bottom strap loosely, so that there is no restriction of leg movement.

Boots

There are many types of boots designed to stop the horse from injuring itself or being injured. The main ones are traveling boots, brushing boots, overreach boots, knee boots, and hock boots.

Traveling Boots

Worn while traveling, these boots are made out of synthetic fiber, either padded or lined with fleece and fastened with Velcro straps. They cover the whole lower leg from above or below the knee or hock to the coronet band. They must fit correctly and not slip down. Modern boots are so good that it is hardly ever necessary to travel horses in bandages now, except on long journeys.

outside of the leg with the strap ends pointing back. They are made out of leather, Neoprene, and synthetic fibers.

Overreach Boots

These fit around the lower pastern and hoof, protecting the coronet band and bulb of the heel. Simple overreach boots are made out of a single piece of ridged rubber and are pulled on; sophisticated designs are made from padded, synthetic materials,

Helpful Hints

Clean your boots thoroughly after use, as mud and sweat will rub the horse and give it sores. Straps should be kept soft and pliable and should be checked regularly for weaknesses.

underneath the stable rug to help keep both the rug and the horse clean. In really cold conditions, a cheap blanket or comforter can be used between layers of rugs and held in place with a surcingle.

Sweat Rugs

These are made out of cotton mesh, synthetic "breathable" fabrics or towels, and are used on a sweating horse while it cools down to prevent chills, while traveling, or to help dry a horse after it has been washed.

Summer Sheets

These are made out of cotton and are used as an underrug, for traveling in the summer, or to protect a clean, groomed horse from dust and flies.

Rugs

Not all horses need to wear rugs, but horses that have been clipped or those with fine coats will need extra protection from the cold and bad weather.

Turnout Rugs

Called "New Zealand rugs," these are designed for outdoor use. They should be both warm and waterproof. Old-fashioned canvas lined with wool is satisfactory but heavy, and there are many modern rugs that are light, easy to handle, rugged, warm, and weather-resistant. They are fastened with cross-surcingles under the horse's stomach and often have leg straps or fillet strings under the tail. It is

important that they fit well, allow for movement, and do not rub.

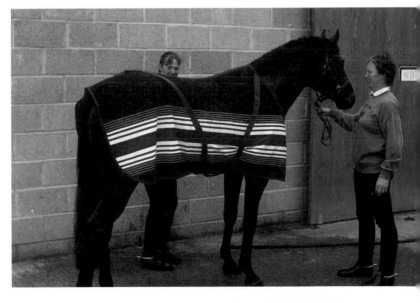

Stable Rugs

A variety of rugs for indoor use is available. They come in all fabrics and are padded to different weights. The less bulky ones are machine-washable, and it is a good idea to use a cotton sheet

Equipment Care

Tack

Saddles, stirrups, bridles, and martingales should all be cleaned regularly. Using a cloth and warm water, remove all the mud, grease, and scurf from tack, then rub in glycerine saddle soap with a sponge. The bottoms of saddles and bits should be washed after each ride, and numnahs (saddle pads) and saddle cloths should be washed as soon as they become dirty: this may be after each ride and certainly if the horse has sweat a lot. From time to time, take the bridle apart and clean each part separately before putting it back together. Girths should be washed to remove sweat and mud and to prevent girth galls.

Give your tack a good inspection every six months, and check for signs or wear and tear. Never compromise on safety, and take anything with loose stitching to the saddle maker. Check your saddle tree by holding the pommel and cantle and squeezing together gently. If the leather on the seat wrinkles, it may have a broken tree. Check that bits have not developed sharp edges and are not wearing thin.

Rugs

Stable rugs and sweat rugs, if made out of modern, synthetic materials, can be washed and dried. Older, heavier rugs, such as those made from jute, will not wash easily, and these should be combined with a washable sheet as an underrug and can also be brushed. Some outdoor rugs can be washed but will need to be rewaterproofed after. Scrubbing the worst of the mud and stains off is often enough, although there are specialist cleaners who will wash and repair your rugs for you. Check all bindings and straps regularly; horses are good at breaking them.

Boots and Bandages

These should be washed, either in a machine, or if leather, by hand and soaped after each wearing. Fastenings should be repaired and replaced as necessary.

RIDING AND TRAINING

Riding is the reason most of us own a horse. Achieving harmony and understanding between horse and rider may be a long, slow process, but it is the aim of all who ride and worth working hard to reach. Good instruction from a qualified teacher who you find easy to understand and who truly wishes to help you improve is extremely valuable. Don't be afraid to "try out" a few instructors in an effort to find the one with whom you click best, and be clear about what you want to achieve.

Riding Gear

The most essential part of your riding gear is a hard hat that complies with the most recent safety standards. It is better to sacrifice elegance for comfort and safety than to compromise your head, and hats should come with a chin strap. Appropriate boots should be worn; these should have a heel to prevent the foot from slipping through the stirrup. Short boots are more comfortable if worn with half-chaps to protect the lower leg. Tennis shoes are *not* appropriate nor safe. It is a good idea to wear gloves when riding, even in the summer, to help prevent blisters and rubs. Jodhpurs or breeches are the best clothing for your legs, but many people ride happily in jeans or sweatsuits if just hacking. Hacking jackets are best when saved for competitions and hunting. Make sure that your clothing is light and comfortable and tight enough to avoid restricting movement or becoming entwined in tack.

The Paces

The horse has four basic paces: walk, trot, canter, and gallop. At all paces, the rider should be in balance and harmony with the horse, and the horse should be going in a balanced, rhythmical manner.

Walk

This is a four-time gait, and should be purposeful and regular. The sequence of footfalls is: left hind, left fore, right hind, right fore. The horse always has two feet on the ground at the same time.

Trot

The trot is a diagonal, two-time pace, with two beats to a stride. The sequence of footfalls is: left hind and right fore together, then right hind and left fore together, with a moment of suspension when all four feet are above the ground, in between.

Fascinating Facts

Advanced dressage horses can be trained in variations of the "trot," including the "Piaffe," which is essentially where the horse trots on the spot with hardly any forward motion.

BELOW
The walk is a four-beat gait. A good walk should be purposeful and positive, and the horse should be encouraged to step forward and cover the ground, rather than ambling along.

Canter

The canter is a three-time pace with three beats to the stride. When the left foreleg is leading, the sequence of footfalls is: right hind, then left hind and right fore together, then left fore. The leading leg is always last. When the right foreleg is leading, the sequence of footfalls is: left hind, then right hind and left fore together, then lastly right fore. There is a moment of suspension after the leading leg touches the ground.

Gallop

This is the fastest pace of the horse, and a proper gallop (instead of a speedy canter) is a four-time movement. The sequence of legs with the left fore leading is: right hind, left hind, right fore, and lastly the leading leg, the left fore, followed by a moment of suspension when all four legs are off the ground. The

sequence of footfalls with the right fore leading is: left hind, right hind, left fore, and lastly the right fore, followed by a moment of suspension.

When a horse is going in the correct way in all four basic paces, it is time to move on to more advanced work. This can include changes within the individual paces:

collection and extension. In collected paces (walk, trot, and canter), the rhythm and tempo remain the same but greater activity is shown. Each step is higher and shorter, covering less ground, and the speed is thus decreased. Extension (extended walk, trot, and canter) is the opposite; again, the rhythm and tempo remain consistent, but the horse covers more ground with each stride without hurrying and losing the regularity. Both require more impulsion (controlled energy) than the basic paces.

The Basics

Mounting and Dismounting
Before you can ride your horse, you have to get on it. Check the girth is tight enough to ensure that the saddle will not slip around. Pull the stirrup irons down, and check the stirrup length is approximately right. To do this, pull the stirrup leathers down, put your hand at the top near the buckle, and lift up the stirrup iron. It should approximately reach your armpit.

We generally mount from the "nearside" (the left), but it is important to be able to do so equally well from both sides. Stand with your left shoulder to the horse's left shoulder, and take the reins into the left hand, which should then be placed in front of the withers. Put your left foot into the stirrup iron, and pivot to face the horse. Place your right hand at the back of the saddle, and spring lightly up,

being careful to lower yourself into the saddle and not to land heavily on the horse's back. Put your right foot into the stirrup, and quietly gather up the reins in both hands. Although everybody should be able to mount from the ground, it is in fact often better for the horse's back to use a mounting block.

It is equally important to be able to dismount from both sides, and the horse should be used to you doing this. But usually we dismount from the nearside. Remove both feet from the stirrups, and gather the reins in the left hand. Put your left hand on the horse's neck, and lean forward. Swing your right leg back over the horse's hindquarters, allowing both feet to slip to the ground. Bend your knees and land lightly, clear of the horse.

Do not swing your leg over the front of the saddle and jump off facing out. This is dangerous—if the horse moves while you are getting off, you can fall and land on your back with your head near the horse's front feet.

BELOW
When mounting, place your left foot in the nearside stirrup and your right hand to the back of the saddle, jump, and land lightly and fluidly in the saddle.

Adjusting the girth and stirrups while mounted It is important to be able to change the length of your stirrups and to tighten or

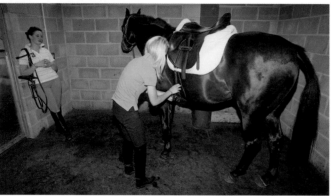

loosen your girth without getting off. To alter the right stirrup, do not take your feet out of the stirrups but draw up your leg, hold the reins in the left hand, and use the other hand to adjust the stirrup leather. To adjust the girth on the left-hand side, hold the reins in your right hand and put your leg forward over the knee rolls of the saddle. Lift up the saddle flap, and adjust each girth strap as necessary, being careful not to pinch the horse and that the buckle guards are lying flat over the girth buckles. Ideally, the girth buckles should be at the same height on the girth straps on both sides of the saddle.

The Rider's Position

The rider should sit squarely in the saddle at the lowest part. You should feel your seatbones are carrying equal amounts of weight on each side, and your back should be straight. Don't be tempted to sit rigidly upright; your whole body should be supple and without tension, with the seat, thighs, and knees lying relaxed and straight. The ball of the foot should rest on the bar of the stirrup iron, with the natural drop of the rider's weight keeping it in place. The rider's ear, shoulder, hip, and heel should form a straight line, and another straight line should pass from the rider's elbow through to the hand and along the rein to the horse's mouth.

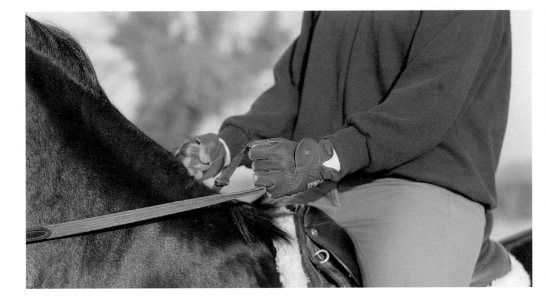

Fascinating Facts

Anna Sewell's first and only novel, *Black Beauty: The Autobiography of a Horse*, was first published in 1877 and was an instant bestseller, with an aim to abolish the mistreatment of horses, which won some success by helping end the use of the checkrein, a strap used to keep horses' heads held high that was damaging to the horses' necks.

ABOVE LEFT

This rider is holding the reins correctly and is beginning to establish contact.

Holding the reins

To carry the reins correctly, they come from the horse's mouth through the rider's third finger and little finger across the palm and over the index finger, with the thumb on top. It is important that the third finger holds the edges of the rein in the joints nearest the palm and that the fingers are closed securely but without tension.

When holding two reins—for example, if you are using a double bridle—hold as for the single rein, except that the little finger of each hand should divide the reins. The bridoon rein is usually held on the outside.

Contact

This refers to the relationship between a rider's hands and the horse's mouth down the reins. It is important to be able to move your hands independently of the rest of your body and to keep them still and soft, despite other parts of your body being in motion. When you take up the reins, you should feel some weight in your hands. This consistent weight, which should be flexible and soft but always present, should stay the same at all times and at all paces. The horse should accept this consistent contact happily but will do so only if the rider is in harmony with the horse, responsive, and can "go with" the movements of the horse's head and neck without tightening or dropping the contact.

The hands should be held with the thumbs on top and the backs of the hands facing out. Wrists should not be floppy nor too stiff.

and keep the stirrups on the ball of your foot. Try to maintain a steady and even contact on the reins. Learning to trot is probably the hardest part of learning to ride; walk and canter are much easier, but practice makes perfect.

At Canter

At canter, the rider's weight usually stays in the saddle. Supple hips are important to absorb the movement of the three-time beat of the canter, and the upper body should move in rhythm with the horse. If the rider tenses his back, he will bump in the saddle, and the experience will be uncomfortable for both the horse and rider.

At Gallop

At gallop, the rider should carry her weight out of the saddle and onto the knees and stirrups. The reins and stirrup leathers will need to be shortened to allow this. The upper body should be inclined forward but with the weight posed over the center of gravity. Balance is essential.

Movement

Riders must learn to position themselves correctly at all paces and to stay balanced and in harmony with the horse at all times. The more supple and flexible a rider is, the better that person will learn to ride.

At Walk

The only difference between the rider's position at halt and at walk is that the body moves slightly at the hips and waist in rhythm with the horse's

natural movements, and the elbow and shoulder joints move to allow the rider's hand to follow the movements of the horse's head and neck.

At Trot

In rising trot, the rider rises from the saddle for one beat and sits in the saddle for the alternate beat (also called "posting"). The rider's shoulders should lead the movement in order to stay in balance without tipping forward and allowing the weight to come forward on to the horse's shoulders. The back should remain straight; do not allow your body to collapse at the waist. Keep an even weight in the stirrups,

The Aids

The aids are how the rider communicates with the horse and are divided into "natural" aids and "artificial" aids.

Natural Aids

The legs These are used to encourage the horse and to ask the horse to change pace and direction. The inside leg asks for impulsion (energy) from the horse and

The voice This is a useful aid, especially in training the young horse and when used in conjunction with the other aids. It is also used to reward the horse, praise it, soothe it, or if necessary, discipline it.

Artificial Aids

The whip is used to teach respect for the rider's leg aid or to correct the horse. But be careful to never to use it in anger. It is almost always because the horse does not understand that it disobeys; this is your fault, not the horse's. It can be useful to reinforce the leg aid if the horse does not respond and to

ABOVE

This horse is wearing a running martingale, and the rider is carrying a long schooling whip, which should only be used lightly, but it is a useful aid for encouraging the horse to move forward.

to keep its mind on the job, by way of a quick tap behind the leg. Never hit a horse on the head or any other sensitive part of his body.

Spurs are made out of metal and fit around the rider's heel. The short shank at the point of the heel can be used to give a more refined leg aid and should be used only by experienced riders.

to encourage it to bend correctly. The outside leg controls the hindquarters.

The hands These should keep an even contact with the horse's mouth at all times. They are the principal methods of communication and should be used carefully. The inside hand is used for direction, while the outside hand controls and regulates the speed and pace and controls bend. Used in conjunction with the legs, they are also your "brakes." All movements of the hands should be subtle and clear: remember that you are asking a question through a very sensitive part of the body, i.e. the mouth.

RIGHT
The central horse is being asked to trot across the diagonal, that is, from one corner of the school to the opposite one, in order to change the rein (direction) in which it is traveling.

Basic Maneuvers

Changing Pace

To change pace up, or increase speed, make sure that the quality of the pace you are in is as good as possible. Sit softly in the saddle and give a firm nudge with the legs, while avoiding restricting forward movement with the hands. To ask for canter, balance the horse in trot, sit for a few strides, bring the outside leg back behind the girth while keeping the inside leg on the girth, and give the horse a firm nudge with the outside leg. Keep the contact constant and avoid leaning forward.

To change down a pace, or decrease speed, maintain good contact, keep the leg on to ensure impulsion is not lost, and ask the horse to slow down with a light "pull" on the reins.

The Halt

The halt should be "square," i.e. the horse is standing still and straight with its weight balanced equally over all four legs. To ask for halt, repeat the instructions to decrease pace but make the aid a little firmer, and remember to use the leg as well as the hand. Never tug sharply at the horse's mouth or fail to prepare the horse for the transition.

Turns and Circles

When circling or turning, the rider wants the horse's body to bend equally from poll to tail. Make sure that you resist the temptation to twist your own body; keep the hips and shoulders parallel to those of the horse, and turn your head only to indicate the direction you want to take. Your inside hand controls the direction, so ask the horse to turn with a firm but sympathetic aid. Keep the outside hand back to control the pace, and stop the horse's neck from bending too much without its body following. The outside leg stays on the girth, while the inside leg may nudge the horse to encourage the horse to change direction and bend.

BELOW
This horse is demonstrating a "square" halt. Its front legs and back legs are parallel, as seen, and it is standing balanced and ready for another command.

BELOW
The rider is guiding this horse around a circle. The horse and rider should remain in balance while moving around a circle.

Jumping

Rider Position

To jump successfully, riders need to shorten their stirrup leathers by a couple of holes. This closes the angles at the knees and ankles,

which should help give you a balanced and secure position over the jump and allows you to balance over the center of gravity without putting pressure on the horse's back. Practice the "jumping position" in walk,

trot, and canter before attempting to jump. Hold your weight out of the saddle (as for galloping), keeping the head up and hands forward. To practice

the position required over the fence itself, halt the horse and fold forward from your hip joints with a flat back and chin up. Make sure that your lower legs stay in the correct position, neither too far back nor too far forward. Push your hands forward slightly along the horse's neck without dropping the contact and without using the neck to balance yourself. Practice again until you can do it smoothly and without overbalancing.

Phases of the Jump

A horse's jump is divided into five phases:

• **Approach** The horse must be going forward in balance, with plenty of impulsion and in a good rhythm. This is the most important phase of the jump and the one that usually determines how good the jump itself will be.

• **Take-off** The horse lowers its head and stretches its neck before take-off to assess the fence, and as it

ABOVE

The horse should make a nice, rounded, and athletic shape over an obstacle when jumping, as seen here over this upright fence.

takes off it shortens its neck, raises its head, and lifts off the ground, folding its forelegs beneath it. The horse's hocks come underneath it, and as its hind feet touch the ground, the horse stretches its head and neck and uses its hindquarters to spring forward and upward.

• **Moment of suspension** The horse is stretched to its fullest in the air, with a rounded back.

• **Landing** The horse straightens its front legs, raises its head to balance itself, and touches down with first its front and then its back legs.
• **The getaway** The final phase should see the horse's hocks coming underneath it to rebalance and reestablish a good rhythm.

BELOW
As the horse lands, his head and neck come up to balance himself. This is seen here as this horse lands after jumping an oxer fence.

RIGHT
This horse is jumping through a double, which is a combination of two jumps with a carefully measured distance in between.

Starting to Jump

Start with trotting poles to get you and the horse used to the idea of negotiating obstacles. These are heavy poles placed approximately 4 ft., 3 in.–5 ft. (1.3–1.5 m) apart for a horse; for a pony, place them roughly 3 ft., 3 in.–4 ft., 6 in. (1–1.35 m) apart. They teach balance, rhythm, and engage-

ment, and help the rider judge distances and "get their eye in." Use at least three poles to stop the horse from jumping them in one try, and trot over them on each rein and from each direction. Do not canter over them unless you have increased the distances between them to account for the increase in stride length.

Add small jumps (cross-poles or uprights) into the grid, starting with two trotting poles and one jump at the end, until you and the horse are jumping a variety of obstacles in a straight line. Next, begin to build small courses, remembering to repeat each exercise on each rein to prevent the horse from becoming one-sided.

Fascinating Facts

Jumping Distances
Aproached in canter, a one-stride double for a pony will be approximately 20–24 ft. (6.1–7.3 m) in distance. A two-stride double is about 31–34 ft. (9.4–10.4 m). For a horse, the distances will be about 23–25½ ft. (7–7.8 m) for a one-stride distance and 34–36 ft. (10.4–11 m) for a two-stride distance. A bounce (no stride in between; the horse takes off as soon as it lands) will be about 10–12 ft. (3–3.6 m) for a pony and 11–14 ft. (3.3–4.3 m) for a horse.

Training a Young Horse

It is important that a horse's early education is done correctly. It is best left to those who know what they are doing; however, if you decide to train your young horse yourself, be sure to progress slowly, and take plenty of advice and help from experts.

Here are four golden rules to follow:

• Always be consistent and patient. Do not rush: horses like routine and need to have their confidence developed.

• Remember that young horses learn all the time. Make use of every opportunity to teach them something new, and make sure that you never cut corners with their education.

• Try to imagine life as your horse sees it. It will help you to understand when and why it is frightened and will help you anticipate how your horse will behave in certain situations.

• Remember that all horses need discipline: they will learn to take advantage if they can, and it is essential that they respect, but do not fear, you.

All horses are different and will take different amounts of time to adjust to new situations and learn new things. You must be prepared to adapt your training regime to your horse, and do not panic if things take longer than you predicted.

Lunging and Long-reining
Lunging can be used throughout a horse's active life as a method of training or just for exercise. It teaches the horse to listen, to understand voice commands, and to trust and obey the trainer. Done correctly, it will also increase concentration, strength, and rhythm. It is a good way for a young horse to learn without the added problem of having to balance a rider on its back. Be careful to lunge in big circles that do not put unnecessary pressure on its young joints, and do it for short periods of time. Voice commands must be simple and clear, and take time to make sure that your horse understands what you are asking.

Long-reining is when a person walks behind the horse, controlling it by the use of two reins attached to the bit, then taken through rings on the side of a roller. It is not easy to do well but once mastered is an excellent way of getting the young horse to move forward confidently and of developing the horse's outline, balance, and understanding before it begins to be ridden. The horse can be schooled through all movements at all paces in the school and asked to go out along lanes and tracks. Take care to make all commands clear, and remember that you are directly attached to the young horse's very sensitive mouth.

Starting to Ride

It is a good idea to work with an assistant in the beginning. Start by riding in the school or a small area to allow you and your horse to get used to each other and to the idea of riding. Gently teach the horse, using a light, firm aid to start, stop, steer, and turn. Do not ride tight circles or ask anything too ambitious too quickly.

As soon as it is safe to do, start to hack out to maintain your horse's interest and forward thoughts. Try to get the horse used to hacking with a companion or on its own. And don't just slop along down the road: hacking is a great way to school the young horse. Introduce hillwork to help balance your horse and improve its fitness.

ABOVE
Long reining is a useful method of training for a young horse and helps the horse gain confidence and athleticism.

Negotiate hazards whenever possible: open and close gates, walk down to the river, inspect that tractor on the side of the road, walk past those cows . . .

RIGHT
Hacking out gives the horse a break from school work and helps keep his interest. Hacking out with another horse will give a young horse confidence.

have to cost the earth, and the greater variety the young horses sees the better. Make sure that you give it a chance to jump ditches, water, and small combinations before you take it to a small competition. Hunting is an excellent way of introducing young horses to a variety of terrain and types of obstacles in a herd atmosphere.

Use every opportunity to put your horse in social situations and to introduce it to new things and occasions. Not only will it be fun for both of you, but also it will have the added benefit that when you take your horse to its first event, it will take it all in stride. It is important to stay calm and confident; never lose your temper or take it out on the horse. Remember that you are in charge, and be firm but sympathetic. Horses do not think like humans, and it is unfair to expect them to do what we want if we do not give them the correct signals.

Practice "schooling" (i.e. straight lines, bends, and transitions) on tracks and in fields; your horse will learn that schooling is not something that only takes place in the confines of a school or arena.

Starting to Jump
The best way to teach a young horse to jump is to find small, natural obstacles while out hacking. This takes away from the enormity of the occasion and lets the horse know that jumping is a perfectly usual thing to do and no big deal is to be made about it. Keep fences, whether outdoors or in a school environment, small and straightforward,

and praise the horse when its completes the task successfully. Be careful to give the horse all the help that you can; present

it correctly and do not overchallenge it.

Use your imagination when building fences; they do not

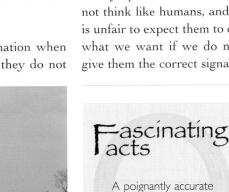

Fascinating Facts

A poignantly accurate inscription found at the Horse Park in Kentucky reads: "History was written on the back of a horse."

LEFT
Many horses really enjoy jumping. Keep them interested by jumping different types of fences, including show jumps and cross-country fences.

COMPETING

Although winning should never be the be-all-and-end-all of why you ride, competing is, for many people, an enjoyable way of socializing with other people and horses and a good way of checking that their riding and training are progressing in the right way. It is a good idea to try a variety of disciplines before you settle on one or two to do; consider what is best for you and your horse, what you prefer, and what is practical.

Show Jumping

Show jumping, or stadium jumping, is a jumping class in which horses and riders negotiate a course of brightly colored fences that are easily knocked down. Heights range from "clear round" classes over fences 1 ft. (0.3 m) high to the towering fences seen in international Grand Prix classes.

BELOW

The jumps in a show jumping course will all be different—some are brightly colored, and others are creative. Most courses will include at least one combination of either two or three jumps in a line and on a measured distance.

Equipment

Riders wear breeches, boots, either a shirt and tie or stock shirt and stock, a tweed, black, or blue jacket, and a crash helmet that conforms to current safety standards. It is a good idea to wear gloves. Long hair should be neatly tied up or secured in a hairnet.

Horses should be presented looking their best and usually wear forward-cut saddles specifically designed for show jumping. Most horses wear protective leg boots, often open-fronted tendon boots.

Rules

The course will include verticals, spreads, double, and triple combinations, with turns and changes of direction appropriate to the level of competition. The purpose is to jump cleanly over a set course within an allotted time. Time faults are given for exceeding the time allowance. Jumping faults are incurred for knocking fences down and for refusals. Horses are allowed a limited number of refusals; either one or two, depending on the rules under which the class is judged, before being eliminated. A refusal can also lead to a rider going over the time allowed. Placings are based on the lowest number of faults accumulated. Those who jump clear in the first round of the competition usually have a jump-off over a raised and shortened course, and the course is timed; the fastest clear round over the jump-off course wins.

Competitors should walk the course carefully beforehand. This is a chance for the rider to walk the lines he or she will actually ride, finding the fastest and best possible paths.

Types of Jumps

- **Vertical** An upright fence made out of poles or planks with no spread.
- **Filler** Not a type of fence but a solid part below the poles, such as a gate, flower boxes, or a roll-top.
- **Oxer** A spread fence, wider than a vertical. In essence, a vertical with a back pole added on a separate set of wings.
- **Square oxer** Both top poles are of an equal height.
- **Ascending oxer** The farthest pole is higher than the first.
- **Swedish oxer** The poles slant in opposite directions, so that they appear to form an X shape when seen head on.
- **Triple bar** A spread fence using three elements of graduating heights.
- **Wall** This type of jump is usually made to look like a brick wall, but the "bricks" are constructed out of a lightweight material and fall easily when knocked, so as not to damage the horse.
- **Hogsback** A type of jump where the tallest pole is in the center.
- **Combination** Usually two or three jumps in a row, with no more than two strides between each. Two jumps in a row are called a "double," and three jumps in a row are called a "triple." If a horse refuses the second or third element in one of these combinations, they must jump the whole combination again, not just the part they refused.
- **Fan** The rails on one side of the fence are spread out by degree, making the fence take the shape of a fan.
- **Open water** A wide ditch of water which a horse must jump over cleanly.
- **Liverpool** A ditch or large tray of water under a vertical or oxer.

Principal Events

The principal international show-jumping events, held under the rules of the Fédération Equestre Internationale (FEI), are the Olympic Games, held every four years; the World Championships, also held every four years on the "even-numbered" years between Olympics; the annual World Cup; and continental championships, run every two years. Nations Cup competitions take place throughout the world several times a year. Each show-jumping nation also has a national championship.

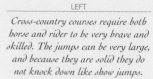

Challenging to both horse and rider, this is a test of boldness and bravery and should be approached with energy and confidence.

• **Stone walls** Solid fences such as these are easy to jump but require bold riding and bravery on the part of the horse.

• **Roll-tops** These are wooden fences with a rounded profile which are forgiving and easy to jump.

• **Drops** The horse will not know that it is to land lower than its take-off spot, but the rider will, so it is up to

Cross-Country

Cross-country is when riders and horses tackle a course of solid obstacles laid out in open country. A cross-country fence can be designed into almost any shape, and the higher up the levels a rider progresses, the more imaginative the designs become. Cross-country is the middle and most influential, element of eventing, which is discussed later on.

Cross-Country Fences
These can include:

• **Arrowheads** These are narrow fences shaped like triangles, with the point toward the ground, designed to test accuracy and straightness.

• **Coffins** These are combination fences, consisting of an upright set of rails, with one or two strides to a ditch, then a farther one or two strides to another set of rails.

The horse must approach the fence in a short, bouncy canter, in balance, and in a good rhythm, and the rider must keep his or her riding strong and determined.

• **Corners** These are a V-shaped fence that can have an angle of up to 90 degrees, meant to be jumped on a line perpendicular to an imaginary bisecting line of the angle, as close to the narrowest point as possible. It is a great test of accuracy and requires precise riding, as there is no room for error.

• **Trakehners** The trakehner is a rail hanging over a ditch.

the rider to make sure that the horse is well balanced, with its weight on its hocks. The rider should lean back and slip the reins but be ready to gather the horse up again on landing.

• **Steps and banks** These are tests of a horse's power and agility and should be approached from a short, bouncy canter.

• **Open ditches** These are more intimidating to the rider

than the horse, and the rider should therefore ride strongly and confidently, maintaining balance and rhythm, and remember to keep his or her head up and not to look down into the bottom of the ditch.

Hunter Trials

These are solely cross-country competitions, usually organized by riding clubs, Pony Clubs, or hunts and most often held in the spring or fall. They take place in open fields, and competitors jump a course of wooden jumps usually of fairly basic design. The aim is to jump a clear round, and the winners

are decided by several methods from those who jump clear, such as using a "timed section;" this is part of the course, including jumps and perhaps a gate that must be opened and shut again,

where riders have to go as fast as possible within the limits of safety. Some hunter trials are judged on style, or in the case of pairs classes, on how well each pair stays together over the fences.

Equipment

Riders must wear an approved crash helmet and a body protector. Generally cross-country colors (a colored rugby shirt and hat

cover) are worn, but a plain sweatshirt and your standard hat cover are perfectly acceptable. It is a good idea to wear long sleeves to protect your arms, and never jump in anything but the correct footwear. Always remove all jewelry. Most people put protective overreach and brushing boots on their horses' legs, and the saddle may be secured with an overgirth.

RIGHT

When riding over a cross-country course, it is customary to put protective boots on the horse's legs and overreach boots on its front feet. The rider will also wear a body protector, as seen.

Dressage

Dressage is simply the correct training of horses. Any horse, from a Welsh Pony to a Thoroughbred, can do well, and dressage training will be of benefit to any horse undertaking any job. Competitive dressage, run internationally under the rules of the FEI but in individual countries by national governing bodies, is a way of testing that you and your horse are training along the right lines. Affiliated dressage starts at preliminary

level and continues through to Grand Prix. Dressage also forms the first part of the three-day event.

The Arena

There are two sizes of arenas: 66 ft. x 132 ft. (20m x 40 m)

and 66 ft. x 198 ft. (20m x 60 m). The smaller arena is used for the lower levels of both pure and eventing dressage, while the "long" arena is used at the more advanced competitions.

The letters along the sides of the arena indicate where movements should take place. In the short arena, the letters, starting clockwise at A, run A-F-B-M-C-H-E-K, with D, X, and G on the center line. The letters in the long arena are A-F-P-B-R-M-C-H-S-E-V-K, with D-L-X-I-G on the center line. X always marks

the center of the arena. At the start of the test, the horse enters at A and progresses down the center line. The judge sits at C; as a rider progresses up the levels, there will also be judges at up to four other letters: B, E, M, and H.

Scales of Training

The training scale is used as a guide for the correct training of the dressage horse. It is not meant to be a rigid format, but a series of "building blocks" with which to progress. Each element is interconnected. First defined in Germany, their German meanings are

more encompassing and comprehensive than the words in English. The six scales are:

• relaxation (*Losgelassenheit*)
• rhythm and regularity (*Takt*)
• contact (*Anlehnung*)
• impulsion (*Schwung*)
• straightness (*Geraderichtung*)
• collection (*Versammlung*)

buy an expensive dressage saddle that they may not use again. Horses have braided manes, but their tails are usually left unbraided. Turnout is very important.

count for the final team score. From 2008, the Olympic teams will consist of only three riders, so all three scores will count. The scoreboard is then wiped

Fascinating Facts

The great tradition of horse racing was brought to America when the British colonized the country—leading to the first formal racetrack being founded in Long Island, New York, in 1665.

This elegant combination of horse and rider are competing in a top-level competition. The rider is wearing the top hat and tails required for this level of competition.

Horses are not permitted to wear boots or bandages or training aids such as martingales. Novice horses wear snaffle bridles, and advanced horses compete in double bridles. Dressage saddles, designed to help the rider to adopt the correct position and with straight flaps to avoid hindering the horse's movement, are used—although beginners would be advised to start in a general-purpose saddle rather than

Principal Events
The Olympics, World Championships, and cont-inental championships run in a four-year cycle. At these, team medals are contested first, and all four team members ride the Grand Prix test, which is divided into two parts on consecutive days. The three best scores from each nation are added up to

clean, and the top 25 riders from the team competition go on to perform the Grand Prix Special, battling for gold, silver, and bronze individual medals. The top 15 from this then go on to a further competition for another set of medals for the Grand Prix Freestyle (*Kür*), which is performed to music of the riders' choice.

Equipment
At lower levels, riders wear tweed, black, or blue coats with a shirt and tie or stock and stock shirt, and either a crash helmet or hunting cap, although the former is recommended for safety. At advanced competitions, a tailcoat with a yellow vest and top hat is correct.

important to leave yourself enough time to walk the show jumping and cross-country courses thoroughly and to work out your approach to each fence.

Between phases, cool your horse down, untack the horse if appropriate, and make sure that it is comfortable. It is unwise to leave your horse tied to the back of the truck

levels. Many Pony Clubs and riding clubs also run unaffiliated one-day events at novice and open standard, and horse and rider combin-

Eventing

Eventing is possibly the ultimate test of horse and rider. The competitor is expected to complete a dressage test, cross-country round, and show-jumping round, so must be proficient in all three phases and

prove boldness, accuracy, suppleness, trainability, and stamina.

One-Day Events
At affiliated level, each country's national body runs one-day events, where all three elements take place on the same day at a variety of

ations should be proficient at these before attempting affiliated competition.

You will be given set times by the organizers at which you must do each phase; there will usually be an hour or more between each one. The dressage is always performed first, and then the show jumping and finally the cross-country, although the last two phases are sometimes switched. It is

or trailer if you are not in available, in case it breaks free. Leave yourself enough time to warm up correctly for each phase; it is no fun to be in a hurry, and you will not perform to your best. After the cross-country, dismount after crossing the finishing line, loosen the girth, and walk the horse back to the truck. Wash the horse down thoroughly to cool it off and remove sweat, and walk it until its heart rate has returned to normal. Check the horse carefully for any lumps, bumps, and cuts that it might have picked up across country, and let it drink—but do not let it drink too much too quickly because it might develop colic.

All riders must walk both the cross-country course, as seen here, and the show-jumping course before riding it. This enables them to determine the angle at which the fences should be jumped and also measure the distances between jumps.

Fascinating Facts

The Horse is featured in the Chinese zodiac, and according to folklore, those born in a certain animal's year are said to have specific personality traits shared with their animal zodiac. Those born in the year of the Horse are known to be intelligent, independent, and free-spirited.

RIGHT

Both horse and rider must be immaculately prepared when being presented for the veterinary inspections at events.

Three-Day Events

These are run under the auspices of the FEI, which is the governing body of all horse sports internationally. They start at CCI* level, and the top level is CCI****. There are six CCI**** events in the world each year: Badminton and Burghley in Great Britain, Kentucky in the U.S., Luhmuhlen in Germany, Pau in France, and Adelaide in Australia.

Although they are called three-day events, the competitions actually take five days from start to finish. The first veterinary inspection, where the horses are trotted up in front of the ground jury (panel of judges) for soundness, takes place on Wednesday. There are then two days of dressage on Thursday and Friday. The cross-country phase is completed on Saturday, and the show jumping, preceded by a final veterinary inspection and trot-up, finishes the event on Sunday.

completed a short section of "roads and tracks," to be completed in trot in a certain time, then galloped around a steeplechase course, then underwent a short section of roads and tracks, which led them to the 10-minute box. Here horses were washed and cooled down and inspected by the vet during a 10-minute interval, then they set out on a tough cross-country track of several miles. Almost all events have now adopted the shortened version of a three-day event, however, which does not include roads and tracks or steeplechase. Riders must be sure, therefore, that they have warmed their horses up

A three-day event is very demanding for horse and rider, and both must be in peak physical condition. Until recently, Saturday's cross-country phase was termed the speed and endurance section. Riders and horses first sufficiently to undergo such a demanding test without these elements, which were in effect preparation for cross-country, and be sure that their horses are prepared to complete the course without distress.

ABOVE
By having a panel of several judges, as seen at this jumping competition, there is no room for error. They are perfectly situated in the ring to evaluate each individual competitor.

Showing, Gymkhanas, and Other Events

There are a multitude of activities that you can do with your horse, either competitively (such as showing, endurance riding, team-chasing, or driving) or non-competitively (such as fun rides and hunting). The only important thing is to find something that both you and your horse enjoy and are capable of, and the best way to do this is to try a range of different options.

Competing is a good way of measuring the progress you are making as a rider and as a trainer of your horse, and it is a good incentive to improve,

*ABOVE
It is important for the horse and rider to practice at home and be prepared physically and mentally for competitions.*

but it should not become all-important, and you must be realistic in your expectations.

The key to all success is preparation. Practice at home what must be done in the show ring, and make sure that your tack, horse, and clothing are clean and ready the night before. Get there in plenty of time, and check whether things are running in order before you get your horse out of the truck or trailer. Leave enough time to dress, warm up, and give the horse a final polish before your class; if entering more than one class, ensure that they do not clash.

Showing

"Showing" is a very broad term but basically covers classes judged on conformation, way of going, turnout, and paces. At the top end, your horse will have to be a beautifully

behaved runway model with exceptional presence, but there are many local shows with classes for all types. Some are for specific breeds or types, such as native ponies or colored horses; others are judged on suitability, jumping, turnout, or simply the pony the judge would most like to take home. Working hunter classes will require you to jump a round over rustic fences, and then those who complete this successfully will be asked to come back into the ring and perform a show.

There are also many in-hand classes, where the horses are not ridden but shown by someone on the ground. These may be a good starting point if you are nervous about riding in front of other people. All young stock and breeding stock are shown in-hand, and there are classes for almost all types of horses in-hand at many shows.

Helpful Hints

Keep your individual show short and sweet, and design it to show your horse off to its best advantage. Use the ring cleverly, and plan your show in your mind long before starting.

The judge may have many horses to watch that day and will appreciate a concise show.

RIGHT (TOP & BOTTOM)
There are many different types of gymkhana games, but for all of them the pony and rider have to be very athletic and quick.

Usually, all competitors walk, trot, and canter around as a group in ridden classes and then are asked to give short, individual shows. The judge may then ask to see the horses or ponies without their saddles and trotted up in front of them and will then pick a winner. Remember that showing is subjective; what one judge likes another will not, and it is best to shrug your shoulders and plan for another day if things do not go as planned.

Turnout is very important, and horses should be as clean and neat as you can manage. Your appearance is important, too; find out the correct attire for the class you are entering, and make sure that you are spotless and prepared. Most classes will require horses and ponies to be braided; however, classes for native ponies and Arabs do not.

Gymkhana

Gymkhana games are often offered at local shows and Pony Club events and consist of a series of races while carrying out different activities. Some popular ones include:

• bending race
• egg-and-spoon race
• walk, trot, and canter
• ride and run
• apple bobbing
• sack race

Fast, nippy ponies are best adapted to these, but there is no reason why the average horse should not try them out, provided the rider continues to ride well and not get carried away in the heat of the moment by wrenching the mount's head around, walloping the horse, or just riding poorly in general.

Endurance

Endurance riding is long-distance riding over various types of terrains. This can be a very rewarding sport for those who do not wish to show or jump their horses and is known for its friendliness and approachability at the lower levels. Arab horses are especially well adapted to it because of their great stamina, but any type of horse can do well. Rides start at just a few miles in distance but progress up the grades to

ABOVE RIGHT
Arabian horses such as these are especially well adapted to endurance riding, since they naturally have great stamina and are very tough.

international competitions, which can be as much as 100 miles (160 km) in a single day and many more over several days. Fitness of both horse and rider is crucial, and there are well-regulated veterinary inspections.

Hunting

Hunting has always been an excellent training ground for horse and rider and great fun for both of them as well. It teaches horses to cross different terrains and jump a variety of obstacles in company and is a good way of getting young, inexperienced horses socialized and going forward. It is never mandatory to jump, and there are many hunts who jump little or not at all. Contact your local pack for more details and

to ask whether you may join. Horses should wear clean, well-fitting tack, and riders should be neat and tidy. Remember that you will be in the saddle for a long time, and it is important to be warm and comfortable.

BELOW
Horses that hunt are generally very brave and tackle the biggest of fences and hedges, as seen. Irish horses are famous for their qualities as good hunt horses.

Fun Rides

These are organized by local hunts, Pony Clubs, or riding clubs and consist of riding in groups or alone around a preset course, which will often include optional jumps. They are an enjoyable, relaxed way of getting used to riding in public and a way to educate your horse about how to behave with other horses without the pressure of competition.

Competition Checklist

If you go to a competition or other outing with your horse, you will need some of the following items, depending on the type of event in which you are taking part. It is better to take too much than too little, and you will soon know what is necessary and what is not.

Horse
• Saddle and numnah (saddle pad)

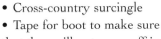
RIGHT
Western show classes require slightly different clothing than English ones. Here the handler and horse are beautifully presented for a "halter" class in western showing.

• Stirrups and stirrup leathers
• Girth
• Martingale/breastplate if worn
• Basic first-aid kit, including your vet's telephone number
• Braiding rubber bands / needle and thread
• Grooming kit: dandy brush, body brush, curry comb, hoof pick, stable rubber, hoof oil, and brush / mane comb
• Two buckets: one for washing and one for your horse to drink from
• Sponges and sweat scraper
• Sweat rug and surcingle
• Traveling boots
• Tail bandage
• Headcollar and rope
• Water carrier and plenty of water

For jumping
• Brushing boots, overreach boots, bandages, and gamgee tissue
• Studs and tools to put them in and take them out

• Cross-country surcingle
• Tape for boot to make sure that they will not come off in the middle of a round

Rider
• Approved standard hat
• Jacket
• Shirt and tie, or stock shirt, stock, and stock pins
• Light-colored breeches or jodhpurs
• Boots, or jodhpur boots and half-chaps
• Hairnet
• Basic human first-aid kit
• Whip / spurs as required
• Gloves
• Body protector
• Cross-country shirt and helmet cover
• Waterproof clothing for wet conditions and sunscreen for hot days

The Breeds

EVOLUTION AND PRIMITIVE BREEDS

In accordance with Charles Darwin's (1809–82) theory of evolution, horses have evolved just like other animals over the millennia into the types and breeds that we see today. Through studying fossils, scientists can trace the original horse, the *Eohippus*, or dawn horse, back around 60 million years. They can also learn about the horses that followed —*Mesohippus, Miohippus, Merychippus,* and *Pliohippus*—through to the modern horse, *Equus caballus*. The past helps up understand the story of the horse today.

Eohippus, the Dawn Horse

The origins of horses seen today can be found in the animal known by scientists as the *Eohippus*, or dawn horse, which existed up to 60 million years ago until around 40 million years ago. Scientists know that the *Eohippus*'s ancestors were part of the Condylarth group, which had five toes on each of their four feet and from which all creatures with hooves evolved. The *Eohippus* had just four toes on its front two feet and only three toes on the back feet. It also had pads on its feet similar to those of dogs. As distinct from today's horses, it was also only about 14 in. (35 cm) tall, although some dawn horses were as small as 10 in. (25 cm) and others a little bigger than 18 in. (45 cm).

The remains of these animals have been found in and around Wyoming, as well as in Europe. In 1867 the most complete remains of a dawn horse were found embedded in rock of the Eocene period in Wyoming State.

Dawn horses are thought to have roamed in areas around the world, including Europe, America, and Asia. Scientists suggest that these dawn horses lived in jungle habitats, as they were designed to eat the leaves of shrubs. They also suggest that the horse's coats were dark with lighter spots, which would act as camouflage in wooded areas.

BELOW
The Konik retains many characteristics of a primitive horse, especially seen in its dun or grullo coat coloring with a dark, dorsal stripe.

BELOW
Eohippus, or Dawn Horse, was a tiny animal with four toes on its front feet and three on its back feet.

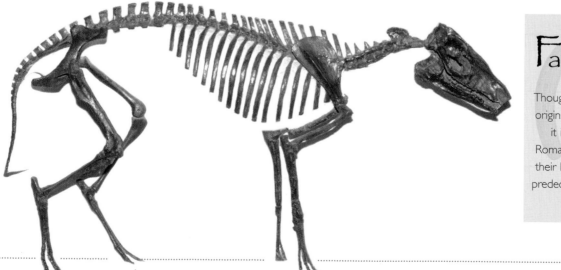

Fascinating Facts

Though it is hard to trace the origins of the first horseshoe, it is suggested that the Romans appeared to protect their horses' hooves with the predecessor of the horseshoe, the hipposandal.

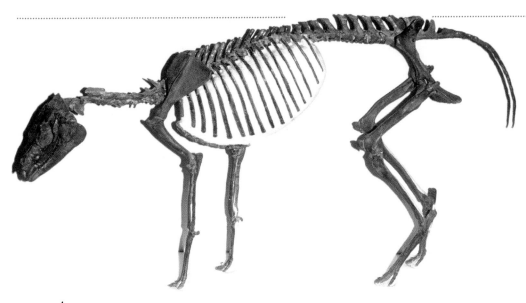

same time, their muscles developed to allow greater movement, and ligaments supported the foot.

Pliohippus

The first single-hoofed horse was *Pliohippus*, which evolved around six million years ago. *Pliohippus* was the archetype for today's modern horse, *Equus caballus*, which was established one million years ago. *Pliohippus* was just over 4 ft. (120 cm) in height and had a stiff, upright mane. This species' head was also bigger and its neck longer than its predecessors. The ligaments in the legs developed even more to allow for greater speed and agility.

Mesohippus and Miohippus

After *Eohippus* came the *Mesohippus* and *Miohippus*. The *Mesohippus* existed in the Oligocene period around 35 to 40 million years ago. It had only three toes, with the central toe larger and longer than the other two. They were on average 4 in. (10 cm) bigger than the *Eohippus*. It is thought that the horse's territory must have changed to firmer footing, and as a result more toes were no longer required. The increase in the horse's size and number of teeth also suggests they may have begun foraging for a variety of taller foliage.

Scientists believe that at this time the horse's coat also changed to a more solid color and that their eyes were positioned to allow for more lateral vision. This, and the animals' increased size, made them more adept at fleeing predators; despite this *Mesohippus* was extinct by the mid-Oligocene period.

The *Miohippus* was a larger version of the *Mesohippus*, standing at 24 in. (60 cm), and it had an increased number of incisor teeth, again pointing to a change in diet.

The *Miohippus* developed around 30 million years ago and marked the gradual change of horses from browsers to grazing animals.

Merychippus

The *Merychippus* developed next, during the Miocene period. These animals were around 36 in. (90 cm) high and had less rounded backs than their predecessors, being more reminiscent of today's horses. They balanced even more weight on their central toes, although they still had three toes on each foot. With their bigger frames and longer necks, the *Merychippus* could reach high branches, and their teeth were stronger so as to be able to grind grasses. By now, the eyes and head were shaped to allow a greater degree of vision from all around the animal. At the

Equus caballus

The species *Equus caballus* was established around one million years ago. This species moved continents over the land bridges that existed until around 9,000 B.C. from America to Europe, Asia, and Africa. The animals became extinct in America around 8,000 years ago and were replaced by the Spanish conquistadores only in the 1500s.

Primitive Horses

Scientists generally agreed that there were three principal types of primitive horses that formed the basis for today's breeds. These are the Asiatic Wild Horse, the lighter Tarpan previously found in Eastern Europe and the Ukranian steppes, and the Forest Horse.

The primitive Tundra Horse no longer exists, but it is thought to be an ancestor of the Yakut, a tough, small

horse standing around 12.2 hands (hh), that can cope with the freezing conditions of the Arctic Circle. Although a primitive breed, it is not one that is believed to have had an effect on modern breeds.

The Forest Horse
The Forest Horse was thought to stand up to 15 hh and be of stocky frame. They were believed to have inhabited Europe around one million years ago but no longer exist. They had big, wide hooves and a coarse coat, being a hardy type predecessor of today's heavy horses.

Przewalski's Horse
The Asiatic Wild Horse came from the central Asian steppes and is the only true wild horse still in existence today. It is also known as Przewalski's Horse after the

Russian explorer Nikolai Mikhailovitch Przhevalsky (1839–88), who described the horse in 1881 after one of his expeditions.

Tarpan
The Tarpan inhabited Russia, Eastern Europe, and the Ukranian steppes. The last, true, wild Tarpan died in 1880, but a semi-wild herd now roams in Poland. The breed is thought to have influenced lighter stock today. The breed has a dark stripe running along its back and generally has a short, wide neck. They stand about 13hh.

The Konik
Those Tarpans that exist today in Poland have been redeveloped using the Konik horse, which bears a strong resemblance to the breed, and Przewalski stallions. The Konik is a Polish breed genetically similar to the extinct Tarpan. It exists in

reserves in areas including the Netherlands, Latvia, and the United Kingdom.

Sorraia
The Sorraia horse is an ancient breed discovered about 1920 that has outlived the Tarpan and other types of wild horses. Some argue that the Sorraia is an original wild horse, but others doubt whether selective breeding has influenced the type.

Icelandic Horses
Icelandic horses are said to bear a closer resemblance to primitive breeds because they have not been influenced by selective breeding since the Vikings introduced them to Iceland from Scandinavia and Britain.

ABOVE
The Sorraia is an important and ancient breed that has influenced the development of the Spanish Horse breeds.

BELOW
The Forest Horse gave rise to horses such as this, heavy in stature with large, rounded hooves and a thick, insulating coat.

Bosnian

The Bosnian pony is an ancient breed originating from the former Yugoslavia. The type resembles the Konik and Huçul breeds. The Bosnian pony is thought to be the product of Tarpan and Przewalski breeding. The breed is used

today for farm work, as well as a pack and riding animal. These ponies are notoriously sure-footed over difficult terrain. They have large heads, short, thick necks, and straight backs in keeping with the primitive breeds.

Fjord

The Norwegian Fjord horse is though to be one of the oldest breeds in the world. Believed to have migrated to Norway around 4,000 years ago, it has been selectively bred for about half that time. The origins of the breed are debated, but it is thought to have come from Przewalski lines. The Fjord is primitive in color as

well as type, and has a thick coat allowing it to endure tough winters.

Gotland

The Gotland pony has lived on the wooded moors in Sweden for thousands of years. It is believed that the breed descends from the wild Tarpan.

Friesian

The Friesian horse is an ancient breed thought to have descended from the primitive Forest Horse. Native to the

Netherlands, the breed has influenced some modern British native types, including the Fell pony.

WILD AND FERAL HORSES

Wild horses are those whose ancestors were not domesticated, whereas feral animals have domesticated ancestors who were at some point released into the wild. There are several types of feral horses in many different countries, from Mustangs in the United States to Brumbies in Australia. Canada has Sable Island horses and Namibia the Namib Desert horses.

Przewalski's Horses

Przewalski's are believed to be the only remaining true, wild, primitive breed in existence. Only a few hundred of the breed are thought to exist today. They roam parts of Central Asia in small herds of five to twenty. A few can also be seen in captivity. The breed was though to be

extinct until rediscovered by Russian explorer Przhevalsky (Przewalski is the Polish spelling of his name) in 1881. They have large heads, long ears, no forelock, and lighter colored muzzles. They are light in color with a dark, dorsal stripe and stripes on their legs, and they stand about 12 to 13 hands (hh).

Mustang

Mustangs are said to be descendants of Iberian horses with Andalusian or Barb blood that were brought to Mexico and spread throughout North America.

During the 1800s Mustangs escaped and were released into the wild and formed herds. Later, some of these stallions were replaced with different types, such as Thoroughbreds, in attempts to improve the breed.

Since the 1900s the number of feral Mustangs in the United States has decreased dramatically as the horses were sold for meat or military uses. The animals came under protective law from

the 1970s, but there are still thought to be fewer than 25,000 in existence, in areas such as Nevada and Montana.

Exmoor

Exmoor, in the southwest of England, has high moorlands that are home to herds of feral Exmoor ponies. These are the oldest ponies in Great Britain. As well as the original stock,

breeders continually try to improve the breed. The animals roam free until the fall, when mares and foals are rounded up to be inspected and branded by the breed's society.

There are fewer than 1,000 in the world, but the Exmoor National Park Authority has founded two herds that are protected in their natural environment.

The ponies are about 12.3 hh and are generally brown, bay, or dun. Their most distinctive marking is their mealy muzzle. They have broad foreheads, thick necks, wide backs, and short legs, all characteristics that link them more closely with primitive breeds.

Fascinating Facts

The first evidence of a nailed-on horseshoe appears around A.D. 500–600 and is credited to the Celts of Gaul.

The Australian Brumby lives a feral existence, although they are routinely rounded up and sold and can make riding horses.

For centuries the Exmoor pony existed on the moor with little human interference. In the past 200

These horses are especially tough and brave and are favored by the French cowboy for herding the dangerous Camargue bulls.

years, however, changes such as enclosure of parts of the moor and crossbreeding of native ponies has affected them.

Brumby

The Brumby ponies are free-roaming in Australia. The feral breed is found across the country including south-eastern areas, the Northern Territory, and Queensland. The breed is thought to have been established from the escaped horses of European settlers. Many horses also arrived in Australia from South Africa, the U.K., and Indonesia. There is thought to be a fair amount of Thoroughbred influence.

Over the years some of the feral horses have been rounded up and sold.

Camargue

The free-roaming Camargue horses are found in south-eastern France on the watery plains and salt marshes. The ancient breed is believed to

These diminutive and rare ponies are not always correct in their conformation, but they are extremely hardy.

have been crossbred with other breeds, including Arabian blood. They stand from around 13.2 hh to 14 hh.

Misaki

The Misaki is a pony native to Japan and dates back around 2,000 years. There are only about 100 of the breed still in existence, and it is considered an endangered species. The feral horses live in national parks and stand around 12.2 hh to 13.2 hh, with most being black or bay in color.

THE EQUUS FAMILY

Pliohippus, the first single-toed animal related to today's horse, developed during the Pliocene period around six million years ago and stood more than 4 ft. (120 cm) in height. Today's horse emerged from the *Pliohippus* in the later part of the Ice Age, being known as *Equus caballus*. Zebras, asses, and hemionids also evolved from the *Pliohippus* and are part of the genus *Equus*.

At the end of the Ice Age, horses existed in Europe and Asia, but zebras were prevalent in South Africa, asses in north Africa, and hemionids in the Middle East. While horses were being domesticated in Eurasia, on the other side of the world their *Equus* family counterparts were also being put to use.

Zebras

There are only three main species of zebras still in existence—the plains, Grevy's, and mountain zebras. The quagga, another variety of zebra, became extinct in the 1800s.

Plains Zebra

The plains, or common, zebra is also known as *Equus quagga* or Burchell's zebra, and can be found in parts of eastern and South Africa, as well as in captivity. They are on average 13.3 hh, with males weighing more than females. Like all zebras, they have distinctive black-and-white markings that are vertical on the body and horizontal on the legs. Some coats have an area of brown hair between the black and white hair. For all zebras, these lines serve as camouflage.

In the wild, zebras live in dry habitats and have to migrate to find water and food. They graze on a variety of grasses, as well as plants, leaves, and other forage. These animals are hunted in the wild by, for example, lions and crocodiles. They inhabit open plains, when possible, to give them the best chance of spotting predators from a distance and therefore being able to flee. They live in herds with one stallion to each few mares and their young.

There are generally agreed to be four types of plains zebras, all with differences in their markings—the Grant's zebra, Chapman's zebra, Selous' zebra, and Burchell's zebra (confusingly, a subspecies as well as the alternative overall name).

Grevy's Zebra

Grevy's zebras live in dry, savanna habitats in parts of Kenya, Ethiopia, and Somalia. These zebras cope with dry, hot habitats and even survive for periods of time without water. They have large, wide ears and especially distinctive and narrow stripe patterns. Their bellies, however, are usually completely white. They are the largest of the zebras, standing at around 15.3 hh. They, too, live on grasses and foliage. Again these animals live in small family or bachelor herds.

When born after a gestation period of 13 months, Grevy's zebras are light brown with darker brown stripes, again for camouflage. They were until recently poached widely

for their distinctive skins, causing numbers to diminish and the species to become endangered. Such hunting is now banned in Kenya.

Mountain Zebra

There are two subspecies of mountain zebras that live in southern parts of Africa—Hartmann's zebra and the Cape Mountain zebra, which is an endangered species and is therefore given protection in Kenyan national parks.

They largely inhabit the desert-type areas of southwest Africa.

Donkeys

The common domestic donkey or ass stands around just over 3 ft. (1 m) high. There are also miniature breeds, however, that can be almost half this height, and other breeds that can reach up to 15 hh. Donkeys originate from North Africa and are built to endure hot climates and desert landscapes.

Despite being from the same species, donkeys differ from horses in that their bray is not like a horse's neigh, they have long ears, they do not have forelocks, and their manes tend to be short and stiff. They have shorter tails than horses and are often flatter at the withers and across their backs. They can be a variety of colors, including black, brown, and gray, and have a dorsal stripe that forms a cross at the withers.

Mules

Mules are a cross between a horse or pony and a donkey. The offspring of a male donkey and female horse is correctly referred to as a "mule," whereas a female donkey and a male horse would produce a "hinny."

Hinnies and mules differ in stature and temperament, and mules are more common, being generally preferred. Broadly speaking, mules are said to have a horse's body with a donkey's limbs, which are straighter than those of a horse. They have longer ears than horses and similarly short manes to donkeys. Again, like donkeys, they have low withers and flat backs.

The hinny, in contrast, tends to have the body of a donkey, but the ears are shorter than those of a mule and the mane and tail longer and fuller. Their legs are stronger and the hooves less upright, the body rounder and deeper, and the head shorter and narrower.

It is possible for a mule to be bigger than both its parents, and mules tend to live longer than either other species, too. Mules are generally stronger and hardier and have more stamina than hinnies. Mules are popularly used to carry tourists on riding vacations in areas of difficult terrain, as they are sure-footed and reliable, despite their stubborn reputations.

predominantly brown coat. They are recognizable for their especially long legs. Some onagers are endangered species. They have been used to pull carts but also have a bad reputation for being difficult to tame.

The Mongolian kulan is a type of hemionid found in desert habitats of Central Asia and standing between 12 hh and 13 hh. Their numbers are declining due in part to poaching. They are

grassland areas. They are one of the biggest types of wild asses, standing around 14 hh. Kiangs have large heads and short, upright manes like donkeys. Their coats, like other onagers, change color with the seasons and are more chestnut in the summer and darker in the winter. Their

---
BELOW

The Tibetan Wild Ass, or Kiang, is similar to the Mongolian Kulan but is better adapted to its mountainous environment.

Hemionids

Hemionids are half-asses, possessing some attributes of horses and donkeys. Also known as Asian wild asses, or onagers, hemionids live in desert habitats in areas such as India, Israel, and Syria.

ABOVE

The Hemionid, or Asiatic Wild Ass, is distinctive through the length of its leg bones and is notoriously difficult to train.

They tend to be slightly bigger than donkeys and have a black, dorsal stripe and

said to run even faster than a Thoroughbred, reaching speeds of up to 40 mph (75km/h). They have especially large nostrils, allowing them to take in large amounts of air per breath and therefore compensate for the thin air of their habitat.

The kiang is another subspecies of hemionids. The kiang is native to Tibet, where they live in wooded and

---
LEFT

The Mongolian Kulan, which is now a rare breed, is especially notable for the speed at which it can run.

---

bellies are all-white, a characteristic of several types of zebras, asses, and hemionids. They have a dark, dorsal stripe running from their manes to tails. Wolves are a threat to these animals, as are human poachers.

Fascinating Facts

According to superstition, the luckiest horseshoe comes from the hind leg of a gray mare, but if you hang any horseshoe upside down the luck runs out.

EXPLAINING BREEDS

So what is a breed? A breed is a subspecies of an animal—in this case, a horse or pony. Horses and ponies of the same breed will, to a greater or lesser extent, resemble each other physically in size, shape, and sometimes color. They may also have similar traits in terms of their physical capabilities, such as speed, and their temperament. A true "breed" is one with a true-breeding population, which reliably passes on the same characteristics to offspring again and again. But many "breeds" of horses exist that are too recent to be totally true-breeding, as this is a process that takes multiple generations to establish.

ABOVE

The Arab horse has been influential in the majority of all "modern" horse breeds and almost always improves the stock it is crossed with.

Arabs and Thoroughbreds

The Arab is the oldest breed of horse and the only one which is truly pure. With the Barb, from North Africa, and the Spanish horse the Andalusian, it is one of the three breeds that have had the greatest influence on light horses all over the world.

The Thoroughbred developed chiefly from Arab blood, but it is a larger, faster specimen. Nowadays, the Thoroughbred is the most influential breed in the world. It is also an example of a breed with a "closed studbook." Only animals whose parents are registered in the studbook (or another registry recognized by the studbook) can be admitted into such a studbook.

The studbook for the Thoroughbred horse in the United States is the *American Stud Book*. In the United Kingdom, it is the *General Stud Book*. This has been published every four years since 1793 by Weatherbys, which administers racing in the U.K. All Thoroughbreds can be traced back to the first edition of the *General Stud Book*.

ABOVE

The Thoroughbred is one of the best known, classiest, and important breeds of horse in the world.

Old and New

Some breeds of horses are old and well-recognized, while others are more recent and are still developing. Examples of old breeds include the United Kingdom's native ponies, which developed over hundreds of years of natural selection to survive in wild regions such as the Welsh mountains and Exmoor.

The Cleveland Bay is another ancient breed in the U.K. but one which has been influenced by humans. A bay packhorse was bred in an area of Yorkshire including Cleveland in the Middle Ages. It was known as the Chapman Horse because it transported the goods of chapmen (traveling traders). Andalusian and Barb blood was introduced into the Chapman Horse to create the Cleveland Bay in the latter part of the 1600s.

LEFT

Sadly the numbers of this magnificent breed, the Cleveland Bay, have greatly diminished and efforts are underway to restore it.

Mazury, with Arab and Thoroughbred influences, too. The Pony of the Americas is another recent breed, which is now very popular in the

the world, some with more stringent requirements for inclusion than others. There are also organizations, such as International Sporthorse Registry & Oldenburg Registry

ponies and then introducing some Arab and small Thoroughbred blood.

An example of a very new breed is the Wielkopolski, which originated in Poland in the 1960s. It is a cross between two now-extinct Polish breeds, the Poznan and the

United States. This breed originated in 1954 when an Appaloosa mare was crossed with a Shetland stallion. Welsh ponies and other breeds including Arabs and Quarter Horses have also contributed to the Pony of the Americas.

ABOVE

The distinctive and elegant Pony of the Americas is an athletic and popular breed that has proved its merit in the competitive forum.

Essentially, breeds are created by people taking individuals of different breeds with certain characteristics and trying to fix those characteristics through selective crossbreeding and inbreeding. The breed can come to bear little resemblance to its original, foundation stock. For example, the American Shetland is an artificial breed with little in common with its Scottish ancestors. This breed was developed by crossing finer Shetlands with Hackney

BELOW

The Wielkopolski is a Polish success story. The young breed has proved to be exceptionally talented for producing sports horses.

Studbooks

There are many studbooks for different breeds all over

North America, which accept horses of different breeds but have rules for inclusion based on breeding, performance, and progeny, and which hold gradings (tests to determine suitability for breeding) for stallions and mares.

Fascinating Facts

The phrase "That's a horse of a different color" originated in Shakespeare's *Twelfth Night* in 1601.

TYPES

"Types" of horses are not breeds but usually a group of breeds that share similar characteristics or are used for a specific activity, such as polo or hunting. They do not have a breed registry and may either be one of a certain number of different registered breeds or horses of mixed and indifferent breeding that are alike in appearance, behavior, or use. Polo ponies, cobs, hacks, hunters, draft horses, gaited horses—all are examples of "types" of horses.

Polo Pony

All horses used to play the sport of polo are referred to as "ponies," although most of them will be significantly bigger than the official maximum height of a pony (14.2 hh, or 57 in. / 147 cm). Most polo ponies measure between 15 hh and 16 hh and are usually Thoroughbreds. Many ex-racehorses find a second career in polo, but there are also studs that

purpose-breed polo ponies, especially in Argentina. There the ponies may be a combination of Thoroughbred blood and the native Criollo breed. Polo ponies need to be fast, agile, and quick-thinking—and, due to the rough nature of the sport, brave. They are competed with hogged (shaven) manes.

Riding Pony

The term "riding pony" is usually used to refer to show ponies, originally developed in the United Kingdom but now found worldwide. Ranging in

height from around 12 hh to 14.2 hh, they are fine, elegant creatures that more resemble small horses than traditional ponies. They are usually a mix of either Thoroughbred or Arab blood with Welsh and developed after the Second World War when small Thoroughbreds and Arabs were turned out on the Welsh

hills to improve the stock. There are three main types: the show pony, which looks like a miniature show hack or Thoroughbred; the show hunter pony, which is just as elegant but stockier and able to carry a little more weight; and the working hunter pony, which has more substance and is more "workmanlike" than the other two types.

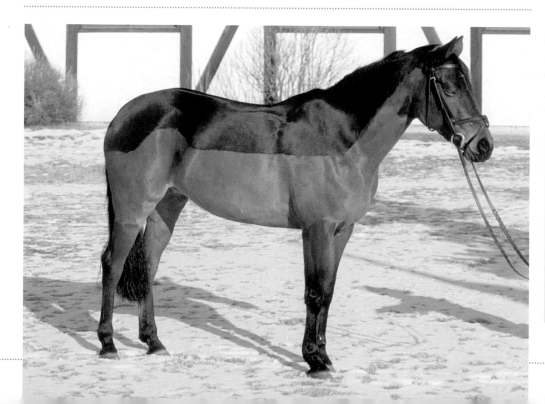

Fascinating Facts

The first female jockey, Diane Crump, broke onto the scene in 1969 and became the first woman to ride in a pari-mutuel race in North America.

Hunter

"Hunters" can either be show hunters or "working" hunters, i.e. those whose job it is to go hunting, termed in the United States a "field hunter." Show hunters in the United States are usually judged on how well they perform over a course of fences; show hunters in the United Kingdom are usually exhibited on the flat. Turnout, attitude, movement, and conformation are important. In the United Kingdom, show hunter classes are divided into lightweight, middleweight, and heavyweight sections and are won by quality animals that demonstrate substance, manners, and elegance.

Field hunters must have the stamina, manners, jumping ability, boldness, and speed to carry their riders over a variety of terrain for several hours at a time. They come in an infinite variety of shapes and sizes but are united by possessing the characteristics listed above.

Hack

Hacks are the most elegant members of the showing community and should have superb movement, manners, and conformation. They are primarily Thoroughbreds, and classes are divided into small hacks (up to 15 hh) and large hacks (up to 15.3 hh). Disobedience and misbehavior are severely punished in hack classes—they are supposed to perform an advanced show smoothly, calmly, and obediently. The type originally developed from the classy riding horses that ladies and gentlemen used to parade around in Hyde Park in London, England, in the 1800s in order "to be seen."

Cob

"Cobs" are small, stocky horses with compact bodies, short legs, and steady dispositions. They are usually of unknown or mixed breeding; perhaps an Irish Draft horse crossed with a hunter mare with a little Thoroughbred blood. They are different from Welsh Cobs, a separate breed. It is said that the classic show cob has "the head of a lady and the backside of a cook." Show cobs in the U.K. are divided into three classes: lightweight cobs, exceeding 58 in. (148 cm) and not exceeding 61 in. (155 cm), able to carry up to 196 lbs (90kg); heavyweight cobs, exceeding 58 in. (148 cm) and not exceeding 61 in. (155 cm), able to carry more than 196 lbs (90kg); and maxi-cobs, exceeding 61 in. (155 cm). They are shown hogged (manes clipped off).

Warmblood

"Warmblood" is a generic term used to describe a group of sport horses, originally developed in Europe, that resulted from a cross between coldbloods (draft horses) and hotbloods (Arabs and Thoroughbreds). Especially used in show jumping and dressage due to their good movement and trainable temperaments, there are a number of different types— such as Swedish Warmblood, Dutch Warmblood, Trakehner, Danish Warmblood, Selle Français, Hanoverian, and Holsteiner. Each has slight

variations, but they are similar types. They have become increasingly popular in the eventing world since more emphasis was placed on the dressage phase, but many event riders still prefer the Thoroughbred's bravery. The warmbloods' studbooks are carefully regulated, and stock are performance-tested, with the emphasis placed on rideability and temperament.

Draft Horse

These are large, heavy horses originally used for pulling agricultural machinery and for farmwork, such as Shires, Clydesdales, Percherons, and Suffolk Punches. Although rarely used for their traditional occupations in the modern day, the breeds are still preserved through the show ring and for exhibitions.

Often they are crossed with lighter breeds, such as the Thoroughbred, to produce sporting horses and riding animals. They have been developed for strength,

docility, patience, and stamina, with muscular builds. Their conformation tends to be more upright through the shoulders than most riding horses in order to equip them better for pulling carts and machinery.

Palomino Horses

Palomino is a color, not strictly a type, but is often seen as one, and there are separate showing classes for them. Any breed or type can be registered as palomino providing it has a golden-colored coat and white mane or tail. Some breeds that have palomino representatives are the American Saddlebred, Tennessee Walking Horse, Morgan, and Quarter Horse. The color is fairly rare in the Thoroughbred but does occur, and it is recognized by the Jockey Club (the breed registry for thoroughbred horses in the U.S., Canada, and Puerto Rico).

Mountain and Moorland

The term "mountain and moorland" is used to describe the breeds of ponies native to the British Isles. Shetlands, Exmoors, Dartmoors, and Welsh Sections A and B ponies are called the small breeds, whereas Highlands, Connemaras, Dales, Fells, New Forests, and Welsh Sections C and D ponies are the large breeds. They are shown in their native state—untrimmed with unpulled and unbraided manes. They are hardy and designed to survive in relatively poor grazing

ABOVE

Gaited breeds have an inherent ability to perform their different gaits, though some horses will have a greater aptitude for them than others.

areas and often become fat and "overtopped" unless their nutritional intake is carefully controlled.

LEFT

This Shetland pony is classified as a mountain and moorland pony.

Gaited Horses

This is the collective term for horses that perform the smooth, four-beat, intermediate gaits known as "ambling." Ambling is usually faster than a walk but slower than a canter. There are two basic types: lateral, where the front and hind feet on the same side move in sequence; and diagonal, where the front and hind feet on opposite sides move in sequence. Examples of gaited horses include the American Saddlebred, the Paso Fino, the Tennessee Walking Horse, the Racking, some Saddlebreds, and the Icelandic horse. The latter's four-beat gait is known as the "tolt" and is a surprisingly comfortable way to cover long distances over rocky terrain.

BELOW

In the show ring, mountain and moorland ponies should be presented with their mane and tail in their naturally long state.

Ponies

It is hard to believe that the world's vast array of pony breeds—from the Shetland of Scotland to the feral herds of Assateague and Chincoteague to Indonesia's dancing Sumbawa—derived from two "prototypes."

Pony Type 1 is thought to have lived in northwest Europe and is similar to the Exmoor and the Icelandic. It was usually brown or bay and stood a little over 12 hh. It probably had the Exmoor's distinctive "toad eye" and "snow chute" to protect its tail, as well as the double-layered coat that made it extremely resistant to wet and cold.

Pony Type 2 was considerably larger than Type 1, standing around 14–14.2 hh. It probably looked very similar to the Przewalski, with a convex profile and the dun color, with dark points and dark dorsal stripe. Like Type 1, it was resistant to cold and inhabited northern Eurasia. Its modern counterpart might be considered the Highland Pony.

A Plethora of Ponies

From these two types, we now have myriad breeds of ponies. In England, Scotland, and Wales alone, there are the Exmoor and Dartmoor from southwest England, the New Forest from the south, the Fell and Dales from the north, the Shetland, Eriskay, and Highland from Scotland, and the four Welsh Pony and Cob breeds. Even Ireland has her own breed, the beautiful and hardy Connemara.

All over the world, there is virtually no country that does not have its own pony breed. The United States has her own American Shetland, which bears little resemblance now to its Scottish cousin, and the grandly named Pony of the Americas, as well as the American Walking Pony, with its delightfully named "Merry Walk." Norway has her Fjord; Africa, the Basuto and Nigerian; China, her Guoxia; and Indonesia, the Java and Sandalwood. And in Spain and Portugal, there is the Sorraia—the unassuming forerunner to the majestic Andalusian and Lusitano.

AMERICAN SHETLAND

Shetland

TEMPERAMENT: calm, gentle, intelligent

ORIGINS: United States

SIMILAR BREEDS: Shetland, Hackney Pony

HEIGHT: maximum 46 in. (117 cm)

COLOR: all colors

PERSONALITY TYPE: warm-blooded

USE: child's pony, harness

Unlike its Scottish ancestors, the American Shetland Pony is a fine-limbed, athletic, little animal, elegant as well as sturdy. The ponies were first introduced to the United States in the 1800s, where their strength, stamina, and durability were to prove invaluable in pulling the ore carts for America's mining industry. Mechanization ended the Shetland's career in the mines, but the introduction of Welsh Pony, Hackney, and other blood refined the breed, and it became a highly sought-after child's pony.

Hackney Blood

After just over 100 years, the American Shetland Pony bears little resemblance to its shaggier Scottish cousin. An altogether more elegant creature, it stands higher than the 42 in. (107 cm) upper height limit in the Scottish Shetland Pony Stud Book, with animals being registered up to 46 in. (117 cm).

The infusion of Hackney blood has given it a smaller, more delicate head, almost Arabian in profile, as well as the distinctive high-stepping action. The diamond-shaped head is slightly dished, with large eyes and a small muzzle set on a long, slender neck. Its body is compact and muscular and comparatively narrow through the shoulders and girth, making it a perfect choice as a child's first pony. It has a good, level topline, long hip, and high-set tail, with straight legs.

In Harness

While its calm nature and gentle disposition make it a perfect child's pony, the American Shetland is also a superior driving animal.

Intelligent and strong, hardy and trainable, this pony retains the native characteristics of its island heritage. The American Shetland Pony Society recognizes two types: the Classic, as described here, and the Modern Shetland, a far showier animal with a higher proportion of Hackney blood. Both types are extremely popular in the United States and can sell for high prices.

CHINCOTEAGUE/ASSATEAGUE

HEIGHT: 12–13 hh

COLOR: all colors

PERSONALITY TYPE: warm-blooded

TYPICAL USE: children's riding pony

TEMPERAMENT: intelligent, willing

ORIGINS: United States

SIMILAR BREEDS: Mustang, Welsh, Arab

Marguerite Henry made these ponies famous in her renowned book, *Misty of Chincoteague* (1947). But fact is often stranger than fiction, and it has been suggested that the wild herds of Assateague and Chincoteague islands, off the coast of Maryland and Virginia, swam to the islands from a shipwrecked galleon. It is more likely, though, that the ponies have descended from horses that were brought to Assateague Island in the 1600s by mainland owners.

Charming for Children

Although they are often called wild, the equines on Assateague are actually feral—they are descendants of domestic animals that have reverted to a wild state. The ponies can be tamed and make charming children's mounts, being sturdy, intelligent, and willing.

The ponies vary in appearance. Some resemble Welsh or Arabian; others are more like Mustangs. They are usually between 12 and 13 hh, although some are bigger. All common colors are seen, including pinto or paint. They

LEFT

These ponies live a mostly feral existence, although those that are captured and tamed make excellent children's ponies.

have expressive heads, with a broad forehead, slightly dished profile, and tapered muzzle with large nostrils. Their eyes are large, and they have small, wide-set, tipped-in ears.

Saltwater Cowboys

Grazing on the islands is poor, and some of the herd are removed from Assateague as foals and fed a high-protein diet to increase their size. Almost 80 percent of the ponies' diet is saltmarsh grass, and because of the high percentage of salt in their diet, the ponies drink twice as much water as normal equines, giving them a bloated appearance.

To keep the herds to a reasonable level, the Chincoteague Volunteer Fire Company, which manages the herd on the Virginia end of Assateague Island, holds an annual pony penning each July. The ponies are rounded up by "saltwater cowboys," and at low tide, they are swum across from Assateague to Chincoteague, where they are auctioned off. The remainder are swum back to the island.

PONY OF THE AMERICAS

TEMPERAMENT: gentle, obedient, intelligent

ORIGIN: Iowa

SIMILAR BREEDS: American Shetland, Shetland, Appaloosa

HEIGHT: 11.2–14 hh

COLOR: spotted

PERSONALITY TYPE: warm-blooded

TYPICAL USE: child's riding pony, show

America's eponymous pony breed owes its existence to one animal—a black-and-white spotted colt called Black Hand. In 1954 an Iowan Shetland breeder named Les Boomhower was offered an Arab-Appaloosa mare who was in foal to a Shetland stallion. When the foal was born it was white with black patches, one of which, on its flank, looked like a handprint—and from there it got its name. Boomhower, a lawyer, set up a new breed registry with his friends, and the Pony of the Americas was born.

Strict Criteria

The first registered Ponies of the Americas were subject to strict criteria before they could be entered into the new registry. The pony's head had to be small and neat and slightly dished like that of the Arab, with neat, fine ears and expressive eyes; the body had to be compact and muscular and the coloring Appaloosa. It had to have clean, straight legs and good feet.

The spots on the pony's coat had to be visible from a distance of 40 ft. (12 m), but a variety of coat patterns—blanket spot, leopard spot, and roan—were permitted. The ponies were intended for children, so they had to be gentle, obedient, and easy to train.

Delightful Character

Its gentle disposition and small size were to make the Pony of the Americas the perfect mount for a nervous child. The permitted size of the breed increased over the years, and infusions of Welsh, Mustang, Arab, and Appaloosa blood were used to refine it. By the 2000s the Pony of the Americas was more like a little horse—a little horse with an attractive appearance and delightful character that make it an enduring success.

Fascinating Facts

Black Hand was to found an extremely popular new breed—15 years after his birth, there were 12,000 registered Ponies of the Americas; by 1996 there were 40,000.

ABOVE

These fine-limbed and well-conformed ponies reflect the Arab and Appaloosa blood of their heritage, as well as the Shetland pony. Roans like this are rare for the breed.

AMERICAN WALKING PONY

HEIGHT: up to 14 hh

COLOR: any solid color

PERSONALITY TYPE: warm-blooded

TYPICAL USE: leisure, riding, show, harness

TEMPERAMENT: intelligent, kind, obedient

ORIGIN: Georgia

SIMILAR BREEDS: Tennessee Walking Horse, Welsh Pony

How do you like the sound of a Merry Walk? The American Walking Pony, first registered as a breed in 1968, is said to be seven-gaited, and as well as the charmingly named Merry Walk, can perform the Pleasure Walk, Western Walk, jog-trot, trot, lope, and canter. The breed was founded using the Tennessee Walking Horse and Welsh Pony to produce an exceptional animal with smooth gaits and an elegant appearance.

Jumping Ability

It is a tall pony, standing up to 14 hh, with exceptionally comfortable gaits and the

arched neck and delicately dished face of the Welsh Pony, from which it also inherited its jumping ability. Intelligent and gentle, it is a versatile breed with presence and quality, making it highly successful in the show ring. The Welsh blood also means that it makes a good, light, hunter pony.

The American Walking Pony has the typically small, refined head of the Welsh Pony set on a well-muscled neck and sloping shoulders to allow for freedom of movement. Its chest is broad and deep, the back compact, and the hindquarters muscular. It can be any solid color, but bright palominos and liver chestnuts with flaxen manes and tails are in high demand.

Unique Gaits

The Pleasure Walk and the Merry Walk are unique to the breed, both being faster than an ordinary walk, with the Merry Walk the quicker of the two with less head movement. Both gaits are exceptionally light and smooth and therefore comfortable for the rider. To ensure the American Walking Pony retains these characteristics, only horses that have been registered with both the Walking Horse and the Welsh Pony societies are available for stud. It continues to be popular, as its reputation gains momentum.

Fascinating Facts

The American Walking Pony is sometimes called a "dream walking," a nickname it picked up because of its smooth gaits, including the unusual Merry Walk.

LEFT

These elegant ponies combine the best characteristics of their ancestors — the Welsh pony and the Tennessee Walking Horse.

WELARA

TEMPERAMENT: gentle, calm but lively

ORIGIN: California

SIMILAR BREEDS: Arab, Welsh

HEIGHT: 11.2–14.2 hh

COLOR: all solid colors

PERSONALITY TYPE: warm-blooded

TYPICAL USE: child's pony, show

An attractive and gentle creature, the Welara was developed as recently as 1981, ultimately the result of a breeding experiment by Lady Wentworth, a British peeress whose influence on Arabian horse breeding has had a deep and lasting effect and who in the 1920s used the Arabian stallion Skowronek on Welsh Pony mares imported from the Coed Coch Stud in Wales. The Welara exhibits both Arabian and Welsh characteristics, being intelligent and eager, as well as a beautiful animal. It inherits the dished face of both the Arab and the Welsh and the presence of both breeds.

Great Beauty

The Welara is a large pony of tremendous quality and exceptional good looks. The mixture of Welsh and Arabian blood can vary—purebred Arabs that are too small to be registered as Arabians can actually be accepted into the Welara register—and all colors are accepted, except spotted, which is not permissible in either foundation breed.

RIGHT

This is a very recent breed developed through crossing Welsh stock with Arabs to produce a quality, intelligent, small pony.

CHOCTAW

TEMPERAMENT: intelligent, lively

ORIGIN: Mississippi

SIMILAR BREEDS: Mustang

HEIGHT: 13.2–14.2 hh

COLOR: all colors

PERSONALITY TYPE: warm-blooded

TYPICAL USE: riding, trekking, pack

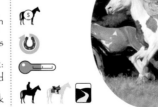

For the Native Americans, the arrival of the horse in the 1500s with the Spanish transformed their lives. Its speed and endurance were a tremendous boon to the buffalo-hunting peoples, but the Choctaw, a tribe whose homeland centered in Mississippi and who were agriculturalists rather than hunters, also put the horse to good use. They used a small strain of Spanish horse—standing between 13.2 and 14.2 hh—that became known as the Choctaw Pony.

Cow Sense

The Choctaw was a hardy, spirited, intelligent, little horse with good "cow sense" (they were also used for herding cattle), considerable stamina and endurance, and noted agility. To the Choctaw, these ponies signified wealth, prestige, glory, and honor. They were also used to barter for other goods.

When the tribes were forced to leave their homelands, the Choctaws took their tough, little horses with them to Oklahoma. Threatened with extinction due to outcrossing, the Choctaw Pony is currently being preserved.

CAYUSE INDIAN

HEIGHT: 14 hh

COLOR: all colors

PERSONALITY TYPE: warm-blooded

TYPICAL USE: riding, pack

TEMPERAMENT: spirited, intelligent

ORIGIN: Canada/United States

SIMILAR BREEDS: Mustang, Barb

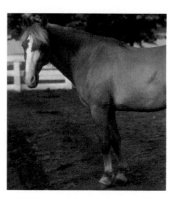

Although the term "cayuse" was applied in general to the little horses ridden by the Native Americans, the Cayuse Indian Pony is recognized as a specific breed. It originated in the northwest and is believed to have descended from French-Norman horses imported to Canada in the 1600s, which had a lot of Percheron blood. This influence would have given the breed **bone and substance and the ability to trot for long periods of time.**

Colorful Influence

The French Canadians later brought their horses into what is now the United States, where they bartered them for goods with the Pawnee Native Americans, who took them farther west. They later crossed these sturdy horses with the lighter Spanish Barb to produce an equine with speed and endurance.

The Cayuse Indian Pony became a recognized breed in the 1800s, and its colorful traits—the French influence

> **RIGHT**
> *The Cayuse pony does not always exhibit the best conformation, but it is renowned for its stamina and trotting ability.*

bred spots and color splashes —can still be seen in American Appaloosa and Pinto horses.

SABLE ISLAND

HEIGHT: 14–15 hh

COLOR: bay, brown, black

PERSONALITY TYPE: warm-blooded

TYPICAL USE: feral, trekking

TEMPERAMENT: tough, hardy

ORIGIN: Nova Scotia, Canada

SIMILAR BREEDS: Iberian

For more than 500 years, herds of feral ponies have lived on Sable Island off the coast of Nova Scotia. Little is known about their ancestry, but they do display some characteristics of the Spanish breeds, suggesting that they may trace back to the Spanish who came to the New World in the 1500s.

Harsh Environment

Sable Island Ponies today rarely stand higher than 14 hh, perhaps as a result of the

harsh conditions of their barren, island home. Tough, hardy, and enduring, they are sure-footed and "good doers," thriving on meager rations.

The feral herds show a wide range of characteristics but are mostly dark colored (with the occasional palomino), with straight or slightly convex profiles. They have short, straight necks, thick manes, a straight back, and short, clean legs. They also grow thick, wooly coats.

Sable Island's feral ponies can be tamed and broken to ride if caught young. They make good trekking ponies, although their small stature make them better for children than adults.

GALICEÑO

TEMPERAMENT: brave, hardy, tractable

ORIGIN: Mexico

SIMILAR BREEDS: Iberian

HEIGHT: 14 hh

COLOR: all solid colors

PERSONALITY TYPE: warm-blooded

TYPICAL USE: riding, herding, pack

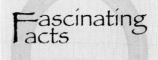

Despite its short stature, Mexico's native equine is regarded as a horse rather than a pony. Standing little more than 14 hh, it has few pony characteristics, with a nicely proportioned head, alert ears, short, muscular neck, and narrow chest and body. But although it is finely built, the Galiceño has a tough constitution and great stamina. It can travel at a fast running walk, which is smooth and comfortable but also covers plenty of ground. The Galiceño is still used by Mexican cowboys for herding.

Considerable Beauty

It is a breed of considerable beauty and substance, with a refined head, large, lively eyes, and a small muzzle. Its short neck is set on prominent withers and sloping shoulders; its body is smoothly muscled, with a short, straight back, sloped croup, and high-set tail. It has clean legs with strong, well-shaped joints and usually excellent feet. All solid colors are seen, but albino and pinto are not permitted.

LEFT

Although small in stature, the Galiceño is horselike in its conformation and is especially elegant. It is prized by the Mexican cowboy.

Spanish Influence

Like so many horse breeds of the Americas, the Galiceño probably owes its existence to the Spanish conquistadores who arrived in Mexico in 1519. It has much in common with the Sorraia and Garrano ponies of Portugal and Spain and gets its name from Galicia in northern Spain. These animals were taken to South America in the 1500s and retain much of their Iberian characteristics. The fast, smooth, running walk that the Galiceño still performs was a much-prized gait in Spanish horses.

The Galiceño is quick and agile, alert, and quick to learn. While its small size and gentle nature make it an ideal child's pony, it is strong enough to carry an adult.

Fascinating Facts

A horse can produce nine tons of manure every year.

It has considerable stamina and endurance and is gaining increasing popularity in the United States, where the registry was set up in 1959.

DARTMOOR

HEIGHT: 12.2 hh

COLOR: brown, bay, black, chestnut, occasionally gray or roan

PERSONALITY TYPE: warm-blooded

TYPICAL USE: riding, trekking, harness

TEMPERAMENT: gentle, willing, kind

ORIGIN: England

SIMILAR BREEDS: Exmoor

There are references to England's Dartmoor Pony dating back to 1012, and it is known that during the reign of Henry I (1100–35), when Dartmoor was a royal forest, a stallion was taken from the moor to be bred to royal mares. The Dartmoor Pony today is a good-looking, sturdy, native breed with a gentle temperament and rugged hardiness that make it a popular child's pony, although it is strong enough to carry an adult.

Wild and Free

Dartmoor itself, in southwest England, is an upland area of moorland and granite tors. Rising in places to more than 2,000 ft. (600 m) above sea level, it receives the full force of the Atlantic gales. Its indigenous breed had to be tough to survive and developed a thick, shaggy coat and hardy constitution. They were used in the tin mines and on farms and later to escort work groups to and from the prison in Princetown—this practice continued into the 1960s. The breed's docility and obedience made it popular with the whole family—

LEFT

The Dartmoor is a rugged and sturdy pony with a calm and equable temperament, making them excellent for children.

Dartmoor Ponies would be used to transport the farmer's wife and children to church in a cart. Once broken to harness, it makes a superb driving pony.

Rare Breed

There are only around 5,000 Dartmoor ponies left in existence today, and it is listed by the Rare Breeds Survival Trust as "vulnerable." Since 1988, positive steps have been taken to restore the more pure-type Dartmoor Pony to its natural habitat. Mares belonging to Moor farmers have been run with a pedigree registered stallion on an enclosed part of the moor for the summer. These mares are then returned to the open moor until they foal. It is hoped that this will encourage the farmers to return to breeding the purebred Dartmoor and give visitors the chance to see the true Dartmoor Pony flourishing in its native environment.

Fascinating **F**acts

Bookmakers at racecourses use a sign language called "tic-tac" to secretly communicate changes in the betting odds of a horse to each other.

EXMOOR

TEMPERAMENT: kind, biddable, hardy

ORIGIN: England

SIMILAR BREEDS: Dartmoor

HEIGHT: 13.2 hh

COLOR: dun, bay, brown

PERSONALITY TYPE: warm-blooded

TYPICAL USE: riding, trekking, harness

Evidence suggests that the Exmoor is England's oldest breed of pony. Archaeological material dating back some 60,000 years bears an uncanny resemblance to today's breed, and it is thought that they are direct descendants of the first horses to walk to Britain before it became an island. They roam the bleak, open moorland of southwest England and have developed into a tough, resilient, little equine able to withstand the harshest conditions.

Unique Features

Battered by wind and rain, Exmoor is cold and wet, and its equines had to survive on meager rations and with little shelter without human intervention. The breed evolved, and possesses two features that are unique to it: the "toad eye" and "ice chute." The toad eye has a fleshy "hood" to keep out wind and rain, while the ice chute (or snow chute) is a fan of short, coarse hairs at the top of the tail that funnels off rainwater. The Exmoor also has a double-layered winter coat, a short, fine layer that acts as "thermal underwear," and a coarser, greasy top layer as a "raincoat."

The only permitted colors are dun—usually with a black dorsal stripe—bay or brown, and it is instantly recognizable through its "mealy" muzzle, a lighter color around its mouth and nostrils.

Endangered Breed

Almost wiped out during the Second World War, when troops training on the moor used its native wildlife as target practice, the Exmoor is still rare, listed by the Rare Breeds Survival Trust as "endangered." And what a tragedy it would be if the breed were lost; these attractive little ponies, with their distinctive, mealy muzzles, make excellent child's ponies with their sweet nature and tough constitution. They are also among the purest equine breeds, with no outcrossing of other blood to "improve" the stock.

ABOVE

The Exmoor is Britain's oldest native pony breed and also its purest. Sadly the breed is listed as being endangered due to rapidly decreasing numbers.

LUNDY

HEIGHT: 13.2 hh

COLOR: all solid colors

PERSONALITY TYPE: warm-blooded

TYPICAL USE: riding, competition

TEMPERAMENT: gentle, hardy

ORIGIN: England

SIMILAR BREEDS: Welsh, New Forest

Contrary to popular belief, the ponies of the island of Lundy, situated off the southwest coast of England, are not closely related to the area's Dartmoor and Exmoor ponies. A comparatively new equine breed, the Lundy Pony was developed in 1928 using New Forest and Welsh Section B bloodlines. The island's then owner, Martin Coles Harman, imported 34 New Forest mares and let them run with a Welsh stallion. The stallion died after only one year, having produced just a single offspring.

Height and Substance

Coles Harman's vision was a pony of style and height, a good-looking equine with quality and substance. The one colt the deceased stallion left behind proved his breeder's vision; he was a creamy dun with black points named Pepper and was to be the foundation of the herd. Allowed to breed unchecked, the herd on the island grew, until in the 1930s around 50 were rounded up and sent to the mainland to be

sold. During the Second World War, when the shipping lanes were closed, the herd increased to around 100 ponies.

The herd was moved to the mainland in 1980, but the breed society formed in 1984 returned some of the ponies to the island later in the same decade. Connemara and Welsh Mountain Pony blood have been introduced, but otherwise the breed has had no outside influence.

Good Doer

Still a rare breed, the Lundy Pony is attractive and hardy, with a wide, deep chest, sloping shoulders, and hard, sound legs. It has a neat head and short, muscular neck. Common colors are

---
LEFT

The Lundy, of which there are sadly only a small number, is a well-conformed pony with a natural aptitude for jumping and a quiet temperament.

---

dun, roan, palomino, bay, and liver chestnut. It is a good doer and strong but is gentle enough to be a suitable child's mount. It has natural jumping ability and would make a good hunting or competition pony.

HACKNEY PONY

TEMPERAMENT: intelligent, spirited

ORIGIN: England

SIMILAR BREEDS:
Fell, Hackney Horse, Thoroughbred

HEIGHT: 12–14 hh

COLOR: bay, black, brown, chestnut

PERSONALITY TYPE:
warm-blooded

TYPICAL USE: driving, show

High-stepping, elegant, and spirited, the Hackney Pony is a breed in its own right and not a scaled-down version of the Hackney Horse. It owes its existence to one man, Christopher Wilson, who bred the Hackney Horse St. George to a Fell mare in 1866 and then interbred the resulting offspring to make a fixed type—for some years they were known as Wilson Ponies. Left out on the inhospitable Fells with little food or care, the breed became hardy and resilient.

Exaggerated Action

By 1880 the Hackney Pony was an established breed and in high demand for its stamina and good looks. The pony has a fine head with tapering muzzle and large eyes, small, neat ears, elegantly arched neck on powerful shoulders, and low withers. Its back is compact, and it has fine legs with good joints. The feet are small and hard and often allowed to grow long in the toe to accentuate the action. Ponies are usually bay, black, or brown, with the occasional chestnut, with some white markings.

Fascinating Facts

The Hackney Horse gets its name from the French *haquenée*, a language commonly spoken in the country in Medieval times, meaning a riding horse with an especially comfortable gait.

ABOVE LEFT

The Hackney is one of the most elegant and refined pony breeds. It has a naturally extravagant, high-stepping movement and is athletically built.

The high-stepping gait is exaggerated in the Hackney Pony—it lifts its knees almost to its chest and brings its hocks right under its body. This action is not just for show; it can move at good speed with minimum bounce on a cart or carriage.

Fluid and Energetic

Its showy good looks make the Hackney Pony popular, and its fluid and energetic gait is spectacular. While the breed has a tendency to pugnaciousness, its spirit and intelligence make it a joy to watch. It is the king of the show ring, exploding across the arena with pistonlike speed—head and tail carried high and proud—appearing suspended in the air for a moment at the highest point.

FELL

HEIGHT: 12–14 hh

COLOR: Black, bay, brown, gray

PERSONALITY TYPE: warm-blooded

TYPICAL USE: driving, riding, trekking

TEMPERAMENT: docile, brave

ORIGIN: England

SIMILAR BREEDS: Friesian, Dales, Hackney Pony

There were probably small, dark ponies native to England's northern hills—the word "fell" derives from the Norse word for "hill"—when the Romans invaded in 55 B.C. The Romans brought with them their handsome black Friesian horses, and when they left, they left these horses behind to breed with indigenous stock. The result was the Fell Pony, which retains a striking resemblance to the Friesian Horse. The modern Fell Pony combines strength, agility, and style.

Sixth Sense

Before mechanization, the Fell Pony was in great demand as a family all-rounder—it would work on the farm, was used for shepherding, and pulled the family carriage. Fell Ponies were used to carry wool from the Lake District along ancient packways to wool merchants and to carry lead from the mines in England's northwest to the smelting works on the northeast coast. Strong but docile, placid, and sure-footed, the Fell was the perfect dual-purpose pony. It seemed to have a "sixth sense," knowing the safest track through marshy ground or the safest descent on a rocky hillside.

Royal Endorsement

The Fell Pony suffered, as did many breeds, with the arrival of mechanization; however, as riding became a more popular leisure activity, the Fell enjoyed a resurgence. When more and more people started carriage driving, the Fell's strength and uniformity of type made it an obvious choice.

It has the good looks of the Friesian horses in its ancestry, with a small, chiseled head, bright eyes, and neat, small ears. Its neck is of medium length, its shoulders sloping, and its back long and well muscled. Its legs and feet—which have characteristic blue horn—are good, and it has fine feather at its heels. Its mane and tail are long and fine. It is a pony fit for a king—or at the very least a duke.

Fascinating Facts

The Duke of Edinburgh, who shaped the sport of carriage driving in the United Kingdom, drove a team of perfectly matched Fell Ponies until he retired from the sport in 2006. He has represented Britain at several European and World championships.

LEFT

The magnificent Fell pony is a strong-limbed and muscular animal that has a majestic bearing and even temperament.

NEW FOREST

TEMPERAMENT: intelligent, friendly, willing to please

ORIGIN: England

SIMILAR BREEDS: Lundy Pony

HEIGHT: 14 hh

COLOR: all solid colors, except blue-eyed cream

PERSONALITY TYPE: warm-blooded

TYPICAL USE: riding

Commoners who lived in the royal hunting ground of the New Forest in southern England, created by William the Conqueror in c. 1079, had been occupying the area since long before then. After a series of struggles, including being thrown off the land and harsh punishments for breaking forest law imposed by the sovereign, the commoners were finally granted grazing rights, and since then the people of the New Forest have been allowed to graze their ponies in the region. The New Forest Pony—a mixture of Arab, Thoroughbred, Welsh, and Hackney—is an attractive, intelligent animal with little fear of humans and an innate willingness to please.

The modern New Forest is agile, strong, and hardy, able to carry an adult with ease but narrow across the girth, making it an excellent child's mount. It rarely exceeds 14 hh, and there is no lower height limit, although smaller animals tend to be more "ponyish." Skewbalds, piebalds, and blue-eyed creams are not permitted.

LEFT
The New Forest pony is a sound and tough animal that is well adapted to its semi-feral existence in the New Forest area of Southern England.

Quality and charm

While the ponies freely graze the Forest, every fall they are rounded up in the annual "drift" and either kept on as breeding stock or auctioned off. Although the best stock was not always retained—the Commoners naturally wanting the highest prices for those ponies sold—the breed society endeavors to keep this native equine's quality and charm. It makes the perfect all-rounder for a horsey family.

Roaming Free

Ponies have roamed free in the New Forest for centuries, and it was not until the end of the 1800s that concerted efforts to maintain and improve the stock were made. A polo pony named Field Marshall had considerable influence on the New Forest breed during 1918, and other blood, including Dartmoor, Exmoor and Highland, has also been used. Since 1930 no further outcrosses have been introduced, making the breed more uniform.

DALES

HEIGHT: 14.2 hh

COLOR: black, brown, bay

PERSONALITY TYPE: warm-blooded

TYPICAL USE: driving, riding, trekking

TEMPERAMENT: calm, intelligent

ORIGIN: England

SIMILAR BREEDS: Friesian, Fell

Like its close cousin the Fell, the Dales Pony has its roots in the northeast of England and was used primarily as a pack pony. Both breeds had links to the now defunct Galloway Pony, but the Dales takes its name from the Yorkshire area of the U.K. Certainly the Fell—or Wilson Pony, as it was once known—had influence on the breed, as did the Norfolk Trotter and later the Clydesdale, which was used to increase the height of the Dales Pony.

Military Favorite

Due to its hardiness and strength, the Dales was a superlative packhorse and was, for a time, bred specifically to serve the thriving lead-mining industry —they were renowned for their ability to transport heavy loads over rough terrain at speed, sometimes traveling up to 200 miles (320 km) in one week. For the same reasons they were a valuable asset to the hillside farmer; their speed and endurance made them popular for trotting races, and their agility was prized in the hunting field. Later they were used widely in the military, their sure-footedness, strength, and stamina carving them a niche in both world wars.

Flashy Gait

The Dales was less affected by mechanization than many native breeds because of its versatility. The pony could work on the farm all day, six days a week, and still be able enough to transport the farmer and his family to church and go for a day's

ABOVE

These ponies are incredibly versatile and have been used for riding, driving, and packing. They have exceptional paces and a calm, willing temperament.

hunting. The Yorkshire farmers also enjoyed trotting races but could not afford to keep a horse separately just for racing. So the Dales was increasingly bred to Galloways and Norfolk Trotters, resulting in the fast, flashy gait it shows today. These old bloodlines are reflected in the breed's coloring—although grays and the occasional roan are sometimes seen, most Dales Ponies are black, brown, or bay.

SHETLAND

TEMPERAMENT: intelligent, willful

ORIGIN: Scotland

SIMILAR BREEDS: Highland, Fell, Dales

HEIGHT: 42 in. (107 cm)

COLOR: all colors

PERSONALITY TYPE: warm-blooded

TYPICAL USE: riding, harness

An ancient law of the Shetland islands states that any man who "cut any other man's horsetail" would do so "under the pain of ten pounds." This exorbitant fine (for the times) was an indication of how valuable, and how valued, these tiny equines were on the islands off the northern coast of Scotland.

Ninth-Century Evidence

A stone carving from the 800s found on the Shetland island of Bressay depicts a priest mounted on a very small, well-proportioned pony. Certainly it is believed that the Shetland is Britain's oldest native breed.

On these bleak islands off the northern coast of Scotland, fishing was the main source of income, and the Shetland

ABOVE

These charismatic little ponies are incredibly hardy and intelligent, as well as being extremely strong for their small stature.

Pony provided raw materials for necessary equipment; their coarse tail hair made excellent fishing nets and lines. Life on the islands was hard for all the inhabitants. The ponies had to cope with a hostile environment, poor grass, hard, wet ground, and continual driving winds. To conserve body heat, the ponies had short limbs, a short back, a thick neck, and small ears. Only the hardiest and most intelligent animals survived.

Island Mystery

How equines arrived on the islands in the first place remains a mystery. The first settlers may have brought them there, and Viking stock mixed with British to create a distinct type. These early hybrids probably combined predecessors to the Fell, Dales, and Highlands and a Scandinavian type with Oriental bloodlines. Or one story has it that animals

from the Spanish Armada flagship, *Gran Grifton*, which foundered off the coast of Fair Isle, were somehow stranded in Shetland—though of course this is many centuries later than the evidence on the stone carving.

Whatever its history, the hardy little Shetland has proved its resilience a thousand times over.

Fascinating Facts

It may be the smallest of the United Kingdom's breeds, but the Shetland is, pound for pound, believed to be the strongest known equine.

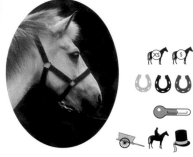

ERISKAY

HEIGHT: 12–13.2 hh

COLOR: gray, black, bay

PERSONALITY TYPE: warm-blooded

TYPICAL USE: riding, harness, competition

TEMPERAMENT: honest, amenable, intelligent

ORIGINS: Scotland

SIMILAR BREEDS: Highland

And while other breeds in the region were being "improved" with the introduction of other equine blood, such as Norwegian Fjord, Arabian, and Clydesdale, because of the remoteness of the islands the Eriskay was left to breed pure. But this also led to the decline of the breed, with only about 20 ponies left by the 1970s. Thanks to a dedicated group of people, the Eriskay Pony was saved from extinction, and it is believed that there are now around 300 of them.

Family Pony

The Eriskay makes an excellent family pony, and despite its diminutive size, is well adapted to almost any equestrian sport, including driving. It is tough and hardy, able to live out in the harshest of conditions, and is attractive, too. It has a neat head, with a wide forehead, tapered muzzle, and large, bold eyes. Its shoulders are sloping and its back strong, with a sloping croup. It has clean, strong limbs and good feet.

Most Eriskays are born brown or black, turning gray as they age, although some retain their dark color into adulthood.

Perhaps the most pure of the Scottish breeds, the Eriskay is thought to be a direct descendant of the Celtic Pony and is the only surviving native pony of the Hebrides Islands off western Scotland. They are similar to those ponies depicted on ancient Pictish stones found in the north and west of the country. A distinct and separate breed to the Highland and the Shetland, the Eriskay Pony is almost extinct.

People-Friendly

Able to survive on meager rations and tough enough to withstand the harsh conditions of the far northwest of Scotland, the Eriskay also developed as a people-friendly, amenable creature— the animals lived closely with their human owners, and bad temperaments were not tolerated.

HIGHLAND

TEMPERAMENT: intelligent, calm, willing

ORIGIN: Scotland

SIMILAR BREEDS: Shetland, Fell, Dales

HEIGHT: 13–14.2 hh

COLOR: dun, bay, black, gray

PERSONALITY TYPE: warm-blooded

TYPICAL USE: riding, competition, harness, pack, stalking

Native to Scotland's mountain areas, it is thought the Highland spread into the country after the retreat of the glaciers 10,000 years ago. Certainly there have been horses in

> **BELOW**
> *The robust Highland pony is extremely versatile, making an excellent riding pony as well as being used for driving, trekking, packing, and stalking.*

the Highland region and the Western Isles for millennia, and it is sometimes said of the breed that "it is too old to know how old it is." The modern pony still has "primitive" markings of the earliest equines and is the only British native breed still to do this without any conscious selection.

Versatile and Willing

The Highland was originally a crofter's pony—a vital asset to the crofters, or small-holding farmers, who eked out an existence in this harsh environment. Versatile and strong, the pony could work the land and was strong enough to carry heavy loads for long journeys. It was a farm horse, a packhorse and a carthorse all rolled into one. The Highland is hard-working and willing and has an inbred sure-footedness ideal for the treacherous terrain. It is still used on Scottish estates today, and Highland Ponies tend to dislike being stabled, so it is economical to keep.

Ancient Markings

An attractive equine, the Highland can be all ranges of dun—mouse, brown, blue, yellow—and has the ancient markings: the eel stripe, shoulder stripes, zebra markings on the legs, and dark mane and tail. Grays and the occasional liver chestnut with silver mane and tail are sometimes seen. Its head is alert and well carried, with a broad muzzle and deep jowl. It has a good length of neck and a deep chest, with plenty of heart room. It has powerful quarters with good, strong legs and clean, flat hocks. Its limbs are sturdy with plenty of bone.

Today's Highland is, perhaps more than any other breed, versatile enough to compete in and excel at every equestrian discipline.

WELSH MOUNTAIN (Section A)

HEIGHT: 12 hh

COLOR: all solid colors

PERSONALITY TYPE: warm-blooded

TYPICAL USE: riding, harness

TEMPERAMENT: gentle, spirited, intelligent

ORIGIN: Wales

SIMILAR BREEDS: Welsh Sections B, C, D

The Welsh Mountain Pony's Arabian heritage is clear in its dished face, but it is far from being just a "pretty toy." The Welsh Mountain Pony—or Section A in the Welsh Pony and Cob Society Studbook—is the foundation of all the Welsh breeds and has roamed the hills and valleys of Wales for centuries. It was certainly there before the Romans, and its Arabian inheritance is possibly due to their abandoning their horses when they withdrew in 410 A.D.

Semi-Feral

Led by proud stallions, bands of Welsh Mountain Ponies

survived and thrived in the harsh environment they inhabited. Galloping across mountains and leaping ravines, they made the most of their inherent sure-footedness and endurance. Nature's rule of "survival of the fittest" could have been written about the Welsh Mountain Pony—it is a tough, sound, and hardy little creature, with a strong streak of native intelligence.

These attributes mean that it has always been in high demand, whether as a strong, sound, working pony for riding or for driving. There is evidence it pulled the chariots in ancient sport arenas; it has also worked in the mines. Yet its gentle nature means that it makes an excellent child's mount.

Most Beautiful

The Welsh Mountain Pony is also, perhaps, the most beautiful of Britain's mountain and moorland breeds. Its small head has neat, pointed ears, big, bold eyes, and a wide forehead. Its

Fascinating Facts

Even an edict of Henry VIII (1509–47), that all horses standing under 15 hh should be destroyed, failed to eliminate the Welsh Mountain Pony. Hidden in desolate areas where its would-be slayers were reluctant or unable to go, it continued to live, reproduce, and thrive.

LEFT

The Welsh pony breed is highly attractive and has had a positive influence on many other breeds. The Section A is the smallest of the Welsh ponies.

jaw is clean-cut and tapers to a small muzzle. The silhouette of its face should be concave —or dished—but never convex nor too straight. Its neck is of good length and its shoulders sloped to well-defined withers. The limbs must be set square, with good, flat bone and round, dense hooves. It carries its tail high and proud.

The Welsh Mountain breeds true, passing on its best qualities and its undeniable beauty to its offspring.

WELSH PONY (Section B)

TEMPERAMENT: gentle, kind, intelligent

ORIGIN: Wales

SIMILAR BREEDS: Welsh Sections A, C, D

HEIGHT: up to 13.2 hh

COLOR: all solid colors

PERSONALITY TYPE: warm-blooded

TYPICAL USE: riding, show

As riding became more and more popular, there was a growing demand for a child's pony, an attractive and safe mount standing under 13.2 hh. The idea was to keep the enduring qualities of the Welsh Mountain Pony but to refine them and breed a taller animal, without losing its charm and essential pony character. The result, which is Section B of the Welsh Pony and Cob Society Studbook, is an elegant creature, with the beauty of the Welsh Mountain Pony but standing a full hand and a half higher and appearing finer—a true riding pony.

Darley Descendant

To produce the taller, riding type of pony, a stallion named Merlin—a direct descendant of the Darley Arabian that founded the Thoroughbred—was used on Welsh Mountain mares. The resulting ponies were sometimes referred to as "Merlin's." It is possible that other breeds, perhaps New Forest and Hackney as well as the larger Welsh Section Cs, were introduced.

Hardy, balanced, and fast, these ponies were for generations the primary form of transport for Wales' hill farmers, herding sheep and wild ponies over rough, mountainous country. They had to be tough and strong and so only the very best were bred from to retain these qualities in future generations.

Show-Ring Success

The Section B keeps all the desired characteristics of its smaller counterpart but has more quality; an extremely good-looking pony, its fine head, well-balanced body, and low, smooth action make it a natural for the show ring. It has an innate jumping ability, so it makes a good all-rounder for the young rider while retaining the Welsh Mountain's sweetness and gentle nature, making it ideal for a nervous youngster.

LEFT

The Welsh is perhaps the most striking of the British pony breeds and is renowned for its excellent and extravagant movement.

The Welsh Section B can hold its own among top-class riding ponies and can turn in a top-level performance in almost any competition arena.

WELSH PONY (Section C)

HEIGHT: 13.2 hh

COLOR: all solid colors

PERSONALITY TYPE: warm-blooded

TYPICAL USE: riding, harness, competition

TEMPERAMENT: kind, equable, intelligent

ORIGIN: Wales

SIMILAR BREEDS: Welsh Sections A, B, D

Desire for a bigger animal than the Welsh Mountain and the Section B but one still possessing the essential pony characteristics led to the use of Andalusian, the now-extinct Pembroke Carthorse and Norfolk Trotter, and more recently, Hackney bloodlines to create a handsome, versatile all-rounder that was hardy and strong yet kind and willing. That animal is the Welsh Pony of Cob Type, or Section C of the Studbook.

True All-Rounder

Spanish blood provides the breed's substance and good looks, and it was further refined using Arabian and Thoroughbred blood. Its head is fine and intelligent, with neat, small ears and a bold eye. It has a good length of neck, strong, sloping shoulders, a muscular body, and clean legs with hard, dense hooves. Some silky feather is permitted, and all solid colors are seen (grays are rare). The Section C has good jumping ability. It makes an ideal harness pony or an excellent child's hunting pony, and it would not be out of place in the dressage arena.

WELSH COB

HEIGHT: no upper height limit

COLOR: all solid colors

PERSONALITY TYPE: warm-blooded

TYPICAL USE: riding, driving, all-rounder

TEMPERAMENT: even-tempered, willing, clever

ORIGIN: Wales

SIMILAR BREEDS: Welsh Sections A, B, C

In silhouette, the Welsh Cob (Section D) should look like a scaled-up model of the Welsh Mountain Pony. An ancient breed, it has been a chariot horse, a knight's charger, a warhorse, and an all-round form of transportation. Julius Caesar, arriving in Britain in A.D. 55, admired the British chariot horses. The Welsh Cob, also known as a "rouncy," was used to lead the legendary fighting horses known as "destriers" in battle. To this day the Cob's powerful and ground-covering trot is its defining feature.

Arabian Influence

It is known that animals native to Wales date back to 1600 B.C., and after the Crusades (1100–1500) Arabian horses left behind were taken into Wales and used on local stock. In the 1700s and 1800s, Norfolk Trotter and Yorkshire Coach Horses were used to add height and substance. The Welsh Cob crosses especially well with the Thoroughbred to produce an excellent hunter or competition horse, but the purebred Cob competes with success in almost every equestrian discipline; its spectacular action is proving to be popular in the dressage arena.

CONNEMARA

TEMPERAMENT: kind, intelligent, equable

ORIGIN: Ireland

SIMILAR BREEDS: Irish Hobby (extinct)

HEIGHT: 12.2–14.2 hh

COLOR: predominantly gray, though all solid colors are permitted

PERSONALITY TYPE: warm-blooded

TYPICAL USE: riding, driving, all-rounder

Wild and beautiful, Connemara, on Ireland's west coast, has been home to the ponies that bear its name for centuries. It is sometimes thought that the Spanish horses of the conquistadores, perhaps shipwrecked off Ireland's treacherous coastline, were the basis for this sturdy and rugged mountain and moorland breed. It is likely, though, that small equines inhabited this craggy, lunarlike landscape millennia before to evolve into Ireland's only native breed.

True Survivors

Most probably, Celtic warriors brought their dun-colored ponies to the country and used them to draw war chariots and carts along the beaches and plains of their new home. It is known that the tribes of western Ireland were mounted, and it may in fact be that when some of the Spanish Armada was shipwrecked off the Connemara coast in the 1500s, horses swam to the shore and bred with the native stock.

Whatever their origins, Connemara ponies are true survivors, able to thrive in the harsh environment and hazardous, rocky coastal terrain, where one wrong step could send them crashing to their deaths.

Farmer's Friend

Connemara farmers caught and tamed these wild ponies, and they proved themselves to be invaluable. Hardy and thrifty to keep, the ponies could easily carry heavy loads, whether clearing rocks from the land or carrying seaweed for fertilizer or turf cut from the bogs that served as fuel for cooking and heating. The pony would pull the cart to carry the farmer and his family to church on Sundays. The farmers would usually choose to own a mare, so they could breed a foal to supplement their sparse income.

Arabian and Thoroughbred blood has latterly been used to refine the breed, but the Connemara remains hardy, versatile, and equable, with quality and jumping ability— a great family pony.

BELOW

The rugged and beautiful Connemara is Ireland's only native pony breed and is noted for its surefooted movement and athleticism.

LANDAIS

HEIGHT: 11.3–13.1 hh

COLOR: bay, brown, chestnut, black

PERSONALITY TYPE: warm-blooded

TYPICAL USE: riding

TEMPERAMENT: intelligent, lively, gentle

ORIGIN: France

SIMILAR BREEDS: Welsh Section B

Landais

Said to resemble a miniature Arab, the Landais—one of just three pony breeds native to France—is a good-looking, gentle creature with origins tracing back to the early 700s, when it lived wild in the forests of the region. Since then it has been heavily influenced by foreign blood, most notably Arabian, first introduced around the time of the Battle of Tours (also known as the Battle of Poitiers) in A.D. 732, and again in the early 1900s.

Mostly Amenable

The Landais is sometimes referred to as the Barthais, which was once a separate breed, although slightly bigger and heavier. It is not known when the two breeds merged, and little is known about the Landais itself. What is certain is that it

LEFT
The attractive and small Landais pony reflects the Arab influence in its ancestry through its quality appearance and good action.

originated in the Landes region of southwest France and is an amenable riding pony with athletic paces and innate jumping ability. It is friendly and easily trained, although it can be a little willful.

Ponies are usually dark colors —bay, brown, chestnut, and black—with a neat, ponyish head, thickset neck, prominent withers, straight back, strong,

muscled legs, thick mane, and high-set tail.

Endangered Breed

In the early 1900s there were around 2,000 Landais ponies, but by the Second World War numbers were in serious decline, with only around 150 remaining. To avoid too much inbreeding, some Welsh Section B blood was introduced to keep the Landais' pony qualities. There is also evidence of some Spanish influence, but since 1981 the breed's studbook has been closed to less than pure animals to prevent further outcrossing. The breed is officially recognized as being endangered, with fewer than 100 purebreds still remaining.

The modern Landais clearly shows its Arabian heritage and makes an excellent child's pony—it would be a tragedy if it were allowed to die out altogether.

POTTOK (Basque)

TEMPERAMENT: quiet, calm, willing

ORIGIN: France

SIMILAR BREEDS: Welsh Section B, Landais

HEIGHT: 11.2–14 hh

COLOR: all colors, except gray

PERSONALITY TYPE: warm-blooded

TYPICAL USE: riding, harness, competition, pack

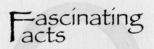

Prehistoric engravings found in caves in the Pyrenees Mountains of the Basque region of France show the existence of a pony, or small horse, more than 10,000 years ago. Whether the Pottoks are ponies or small horses—their name, pronounced "pot-ee-ok," comes from the Basque word *pottoka*, which means "small horse"—is open to debate, but they are thought to descend from the Magdalenian Horses of 14,000–7,000 B.C. This, in turn, is thought to be related to the ancient Tarpan.

ABOVE
The elegance of these ponies' appearance belies their toughness and stamina. They are popular riding ponies and are also used for packing.

Rounded up

Although only around 150 Pottoks remain in the region, they were once integral to Basque life. They were used primarily as pack animals—it is said partly to smuggle goods between France and Spain, their dark color acting as perfect camouflage for night journeys—or in the mines from France to Italy.

Sturdy and sure-footed, the Pottok was uncomplaining and enduring, able to work for long hours and cover great distances.

Now all the ponies in the Basque region are in ownership and no longer wild, although they still run free in the mountains. They are traditionally rounded up on the last Wednesday in January, branded for identification, and either sold or returned to the mountains as breeding stock.

French Champion

The Pottok is a tough, little creature of considerable endurance. It is sturdy and robust, with a comparatively large head for its size, small ears, short neck, long back, and shaggy mane. It has small but sturdy hooves for mountain walking, which is what made it such a good pack pony. Since the late 1970s, however, there has been increasing demand for the Pottok as a riding animal, especially as a child's mount because of its calm disposition. Today it is also finding growing acceptance as a dressage mount.

Fascinating **F**acts

In 1983 a purebred Pottok named Kuzko was French national champion in a discipline combining dressage and show jumping.

ARIÈGEOIS

HEIGHT: 13.1–14.3 hh

COLOR: black

PERSONALITY TYPE: warm-blooded

TYPICAL USE: pack, harness, riding

TEMPERAMENT: calm, quiet, equable

ORIGIN: France

SIMILAR BREEDS: Dales, Fell

Fascinating Facts

An Ariègeois pony was presented to the British Prime Minister Tony Blair in 1997.

RIGHT
The Ariègeois is an especially striking breed, often used for driving, that is renowned for its calm, even, and forgiving temperament.

Stocky, sturdy, and hardy, the Ariègeois, named after the Ariège River between Roussillon and Catalonia, bears a strong resemblance to the Fell and Dales pony breeds of Britain and to the cave drawings found in its native home. Some of the carvings and wall pictures in Niaux in the Ariège, made by Cro-Magnon man, are recognizably the Camargue horse; others, just as certainly, show the Ariègeois in its winter coat with its characteristic "beard."

Ancient Breed

The Ariègeois is sometimes referred to as the Merens Pony and almost certainly has Eastern blood, perhaps crossed with the heavy pack mares of the Roman legions to add substance and bone. It is certainly an ancient breed—Julius Caesar describes it accurately in his commentaries on the Gallic Wars of 58–51 B.C.

Perhaps because of the remoteness of its mountain home, the Ariègeois was almost unknown until the 1900s, when its reputation as a superlative pack pony began to spread. Because of its dark color, it was valued by the smugglers who worked along the Spanish border and was crucial to hill farmers from the region, for whom the tract or was virtually useless because of the terrain, and in the mines.

Mental Balance

In Ariège, most of the breeders raise the ponies out in the open air all year round. The foals are born in the spring snow, and there are rarely any problems. In June the herd is led up to the summer pastures to spend several months in total freedom in the high mountains. This life with the herd gives the Ariègeois the mental balance for which it is known.

The Ariègeois is always solid black in color, its coat taking on a rusty sheen in the winter—white markings are rare. Its mane and tail are thick and long, and vital to a mountain breed, it has good, hard feet.

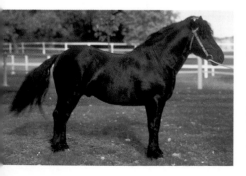

ASTURCÓN (Asturian)

TEMPERAMENT: hardy, placid

ORIGIN: Spain

SIMILAR BREEDS: Galician, Galiceño, Sorraia

HEIGHT: 12.2 hh

COLOR: black

PERSONALITY TYPE: warm-blooded

TYPICAL USE: riding, pack

Also known as the Asturian, this breed originated in northern Spain and is known to be at least 3,000 years old. While its ancestry is not well documented, it is thought to be a hybrid of Garrano, Sorraia, and Celtic Pony. The Romans referred to these equines as Asturcóns and apparently thought well of them; Pliny the Elder (A.D. 23–79) described them as a small horse that did not trot but moved its legs on each side together. They were also popular in France in the Middle Ages.

Ladies' Mount

The Asturcón's unusual gait, a kind of amble, was unique to the breed and made for an extremely comfortable ride, so the ponies were popular as ladies' mounts. Known as "palfreys" in England, they were called *haubini* in France, the word becoming "hobbye" and from there "hobby horse." Some Asturcón blood was introduced into Ireland, where the Irish Hobby was greatly admired. The amble is an inherited rather than learned gait, and there have been ambling horses in China, Turkey, Mongolia, and Siberia. Neither the Garrano nor the Sorraia, thought to be the Asturcóns close relatives, have this gait.

In Decline

The Asturcón is also closely related to, and sometimes referred to, as the Galician after the region of northwest Spain, and both have had some influence on the Galiceño Pony of Mexico. It has a small though rather heavy head with a straight

ABOVE

This ancient breed has a natural gait, best described as an amble, which is especially smooth, even, and comfortable to ride.

profile, small ears, and large eyes. Its neck is long and thin with a flowing mane, and it has high-set withers, a long, straight back and a low-set tail. Although not especially good-looking, it is well shaped and very hardy.

As recently as the 1970s there were thought to be some 20,000 of these ponies living semi-feral in the hills of northwest Spain, but their numbers have since been in decline.

SORRAIA

HEIGHT: 14 hh

COLOR: dun

PERSONALITY TYPE:
warm-blooded

TYPICAL USE: stockhorse, riding

TEMPERAMENT: gentle

ORIGIN: Portugal and Spain

SIMILAR BREEDS: Garrano, Asturcón, Mustang

The Sorraia's distinctive gray-dun coloring (also known as "grullo") with black mane and tail betray its genetic links with the extinct ancient Tarpan, and this breed is an ancient one, sometimes also having the primitive dorsal stripe. It originates in the area between the Sor and Raia rivers—from which it gets its name—that run through Portugal and Spain. It is also sometimes known as the *marismeño*, or the "horse of the swamp."

Sorraia was used to herd the fighting bulls of the region and other livestock.

The breed was discovered in Portugal in the 1920s by Portuguese scientist Ruy d'Andrade, who coined its name and who, by selecting

LEFT

Surprisingly, the slightly unprepossessing looking Sorraia horse is an ancient breed that gave rise to the magnificent Iberian horses—the Andalusian, Lusitano, and Alter Real.

Foundation of Glory

The tough little Sorraia is thought to form the basis of the mighty Iberian horses, the Andalusian and the Lusitano, as well as the less influential Alter-Real. It is hard to believe that such an unassuming creature could have been the foundation of such glory. DNA from the breed has also been discovered in the Mustangs of North America, and it is thought that the indigenous Iberian breed was taken to the New World with the conquistadores, where it bred with other equines. The grullo coloring still occurs in the Mustang.

The modern Sorraia is always grullo or dun with no white markings, and sometimes it has stripes across its neck, shoulders, and back. Foals are born with the zebra-striped markings all over, which acts as excellent camouflage in the wild.

Saved from Extinction

While the Sorraia is nothing much to look at, it is renowned for its ability to withstand extremes of climate, especially dry, hot conditions, and to survive on short rations. Its

hardiness and agility made the Sorraia highly valuable to local stockmen. Once captured and tamed, the

30 of the little equines to run as a protected herd, saved it from almost certain extinction.

GARRANO

TEMPERAMENT: quiet, willing

ORIGIN: Portugal

SIMILAR BREEDS: Sorraia

HEIGHT: 12–13 hh

COLOR: bay, chestnut, brown

PERSONALITY TYPE: warm-blooded

Use: pack, harness, riding

The Garrano, or Minho, is closely related to the Sorraia. Some ponies have distinct, Arabian, dished faces, the result of infusions of Arab blood implemented by the Portuguese Ministry of Agriculture. The modern Garrano is a slightly more refined pony than its ancient ancestors (which played a role in the development of the influential Iberian breeds), although some still bear a resemblance to the extinct Tarpan. It has a pretty head, small ears, and large, lively eyes. Good-looking, with both speed and stamina, it resembles a scaled-down version of the mighty Andalusian and Lusitano.

Influential Breed

It has a comparatively long neck, straight shoulders, a deep, wide chest, and a short, compact back, with sloping quarters, a low-set tail, short, strong legs, and very hard feet. Inherently sure-footed, the Garrano travels easily over the steep, densely wooded terrain of its homeland in the Minho and Tras os Mentos regions. A popular military pack pony, it is also competed in the region's trotting races and makes a good harness pony.

PENEIA

TEMPERAMENT: amenable, quiet

ORIGIN: Greece

SIMILAR BREEDS: Pindos

HEIGHT: 10–14 hh

COLOR: roan, chestnut, black

PERSONALITY TYPE: warm-blooded

TYPICAL USE: agriculture, harness, pack, riding

The Peneia, or Pinia, is found in the Ilia and Achaia regions of Greece's Pelopponese. This rare pony breed is probably closely related to the Pindos, with outcrosses to Anglo-Arab, Anglo-Norman, and Nonius. The breed's studbook was started only in 1995, but the Peneia is thought to be an ancient breed. As of 2002 there were only 231 breeding mares and 69 stallions.

Stamina and Endurance

The Peneia is extremely tough and hardy, with sound constitution and great stamina. Used for all forms of work, it has a very amenable temperament and is sure-footed across rough terrain. It tends to be heavily framed, with a coarse head, muscular neck, broad, strong back, and very sound legs, but it is often cow- or sickle-hocked with weak underdeveloped hindquarters. It has a stilted, uneven stride but does have an innate jumping ability. Peneia stallions are often used to breed mules.

LEFT

As with most of the Greek breeds of ponies, the Peneia is renowned for its hardiness and stamina.

SKYROS

HEIGHT: 11 hh

COLOR: bay, brown, gray, dun

PERSONALITY TYPE: warm-blooded

TYPICAL USE: harness, pack, agricultural

TEMPERAMENT: gentle, docile

ORIGIN: Greece

SIMILAR BREEDS: Exmoor

This tiny pony, which gets its name from the Greek island it inhabits, is facing extinction, and the race is on to save it from dying out completely. As of 2001 there were just 93 breeding mares and 52 studs. There are now believed to be fewer than 150 ponies on the island, and not all of these may be purebred. They resemble a smaller version of England's Exmoor Pony and are thought to be at least as ancient as their more northerly cousin.

Parthenon Connection

It is thought that the ponies were introduced to Skyros by Athenian colonists in the 400s to 700s—some believe they are the little equines seen on the frieze at the Parthenon—and they made the most of their island habitat. They are fairly unprepossessing, with a small head (which often has the same mealy muzzle and prominent eye of the Exmoor), straight shoulders, narrow body, and short legs with small feet.

Skyros is an island of contrasting halves, the north side being lush and fertile, while the southern side is less hospitable and more mountainous. During the winter months when food and water are plentiful, the ponies live in the southern mountainous part of the island commonly referred to as the *vouno*. At the onset of summer they migrate north in search of water and food.

Semi-Feral

The ponies continue to live a semi-feral existence on Skyros. Farmers on the island round them up at harvest time for threshing grain, although increasing mechanization has reduced this practice. They are also used to breed mules, and the existence of some of these progeny left on Skyros further threatens the breed's ability to procreate. While it is illegal to export the ponies, donkeys or mules may be exported and sold, which makes it more economic to breed them.

RIGHT
This is a small and tough breed of pony that lives a semi-feral existence on the Greek island of Skyros.

PINDOS

HEIGHT: 13 hh

COLOR: bay, brown, black, occasional roan

PERSONALITY TYPE: warm-blooded

TYPICAL USE: agriculture, riding, harness, pack

TEMPERAMENT: stubborn, willful

ORIGIN: Greece

SIMILAR BREEDS: Peneia

Sometimes known as the Thessalonian Pony, the Pindos is an ancient breed raised in the Thessaly and Epirus regions of Greece— it is thought to be a descendant of the now-extinct Thessalonian Horse, which was developed by the Greeks and renowned for its courage and beauty. Greece, however, is not an ideal place for breeding horses—it has harsh weather conditions and poor, infertile soil. These conditions, and the mountainous region the Pindos inhabits, have produced a pony noted more for its endurance than its good looks.

Climbing Ability

The Pindos, while not much to look at, is an inordinately hardy and enduring pony with functional abilities that more than make up for its lack of aesthetic beauty. It has all the qualities that accompany a mountain breed, which include remarkable climbing abilities. It is also agile and sure-footed, with hard feet and a sound constitution. It is a good doer and able to withstand baking heat and punishing winters, with temperatures still as low as 9° F in the early spring. The Pindos pony is also long-living, with animals of 40 years old or more recorded.

It is used by the local people of the region for agricultural work, plowing, harness, pack, and riding—despite its small stature, the Pindos is strong enough to carry an adult.

Willful

The Pindos has an unattractive, coarse head with a small eye, a medium-length neck and back, and a narrow frame. The hindquarters are poor, and the high-set tail indicates Eastern influence, as do their fine legs and tough hooves. They are usually dark in color with no white markings, although the occasional animal will have a light-colored mane and tail, perhaps the result of an unsuccessful attempt to introduce Haflinger blood. The pony has a reputation for being willful and stubborn.

Fascinating Facts

A subspecies of the Pindos exists as an endangered wild herd on the island of Kefalonia, off the coast of western Greece. They are known as the Ainos Horses, named after the island's Mount Ainos, the third highest mountain in Greece. It is believed there are around 20 of these ponies left.

BELOW

The Pindos is a very old breed thought to be a descendent of the Thessalonian horses of ancient Greece.

BARDIGIANO

HEIGHT: 13 hh

COLOR: bay, black, brown

PERSONALITY TYPE: warm-blooded

TYPICAL USE: riding, pack, agriculture

TEMPERAMENT: quiet, kind

ORIGIN: Italy

SIMILAR BREEDS: Avelignese, Haflinger

Although it is native to the northern Appenine region of Italy, the Bardigiano bears a striking resemblance to Britain's Exmoor Pony, as well as southern Italy's Avelignese, Austria's Haflinger, and the Spanish Asturcón (Asturian). Both the Haflinger and the Avelignese have a common ancestor in the Arab stallion El Bedavi, and the Bardigiano is noticeably Eastern in appearance, with a neat head, broad forehead, tapered muzzle, and slightly dished face, with not even the merest suggestion of coarseness.

Producing Mules

During the First and Second World Wars, Bardigiano mares were used to produce mules for the military, the effect being a sharp decline in the number of good breeding stock. The introduction of outside stallions almost proved disastrous, as the breed began to lose its distinctive sure-footed and robust. It has a quiet, kind temperament, which makes it an excellent child's pony, as well as being adaptable to farm work, light draft, and as a pack animal.

Roman Ancestors

The Bardigiano is undoubtedly related to an ancient breed of horse, named the Abellinium by the Romans, but has adapted to its rough mountain habitat and is a small, attractive creature. It retains pony characteristics, such as its pretty head, with a deep chest, strongly built body, and short, sturdy legs with hard joints and plenty of bone.

It has the thick, full mane and tail of many pony breeds, and the mealy muzzle so distinctive in the Exmoor sometimes occurs, suggesting again the closeness of the ancestry of both breeds. Like the Exmoor, it is not very affected by cold and damp.

characteristics. In 1972 a committee was formed to reestablish and protect the breed.

Today's Bardigiano is a useful and attractive equine, tough and enduring as most mountain breeds, as well as

Fascinating Facts

A foal usually inherits its father's (sire's) looks and its mother's (dam's) constitution and personality.

AVELIGNESE

TEMPERAMENT: placid, hardy

ORIGIN: Italy

SIMILAR BREEDS: Haflinger

HEIGHT: 13.3–14.3 hh

COLOR: chestnut with flaxen mane and tail

PERSONALITY TYPE: warm-blooded

TYPICAL USE: trekking, pack

Italy's version of the Haflinger is a strong, robust, little animal that takes its name from Avelengo, an area of the Alto Adige, which has been an Italian region since 1918, and is used mostly for pack and draft. It bears a striking resemblance to the Haflinger—both breeds contain bloodlines that can be traced back to the Arabian stallion El Bedavi— but stands slightly bigger than its Tyrolean cousin, reaching around 14.3 hh. It is widely bred in Tuscany, Emilia, and central southern Italy, although it is also found throughout the country and is believed to be the most prolific Italian breed.

Oriental Influences

Although the Avelignese is considered a coldblood and exhibits many coldblood characteristics, it almost certainly has Oriental influences. It is undeniably attractive, with a small head of considerable quality, a broad forehead tapering to a fine muzzle, and a short, crested, and muscular neck. Its powerful shoulders are ideal for carrying a harness collar, and it has a broad, deep chest and wide, compact back.

Its hindquarters are muscular and well rounded, and its shoulders are upright, so its stride is fairly short. It has generally good legs with hard, dense bone, well-formed joints, and some feathering around the fetlocks. Its feet are exceptionally hard and well formed.

ABOVE

The resemblance of the Italian Avelignese to the Austrian Haflinger is striking—both breeds share similar bloodlines that trace back to the Arab stallion El Bedavi.

Unflappable Nature

The breed is always a bright chestnut, with flaxen mane and tail—a pleasing combination—and is very versatile. The stocky Avelignese has the typically placid coldblood temperament, which makes it an ideal mount for children, novices, or nervous riders, and has sufficient stamina to be used for endurance riding. But it is also used extensively for working the land in its mountainous homeland, where motorized vehicles are impractical. It is surefooted and strong and virtually unflappable.

DÜLMEN

HEIGHT: 12.3 hh

COLOR: dun, black, brown

PERSONALITY TYPE: warm-blooded

TYPICAL USE: riding, driving

TEMPERAMENT: tough, trainable

ORIGIN: Germany

SIMILAR BREEDS: Senner (extinct)

LEFT
The Dulmen is an ancient breed and retains its primitive coloring and physique. It is Germany's only surviving native pony breed.

As a country most famous for its warmblood breeds, it is perhaps strange that Germany possesses only one native breed of pony—there used to be a breed called the Senner that existed in the Teutoburg Forest, but this is now extinct. The Dülmen is an ancient breed found near the town of the same name, in the Merfelder Bruch. Ponies have been documented as being in this area since the early 1300s. The Dülmen's exact origins are unknown, but it is thought to have developed from primitive equines.

The Last Wild Herd

The Dülmen used to live in large wild herds throughout Westphalia, but during the 1800s, when land was divided and parcelled out separately, they began to lose their natural habitat. There is only one remaining wild herd. This is owned by the Duke of Croÿ and roams around 860 acres of the Merfelder Bruch. This area combines a wide diversity of small habitats, ranging from woodland to heath and open moorland.

The ponies are left largely to their own devices, foraging for food and seeking shelter, with little outside assistance. The ones that survive are invariably the strongest, and as a breed they are exceptionally tough and resistant to disease.

Tameable and Trainable

The Dülmen is easily tamed and trained and makes an excellent child's pony. It is also used as a driving pony and for working the land. Although not especially attractive—they tend to be coarse and their hindquarters are poor—they are highly valued for their hardiness and adaptability. Many still retain the primitive dun coloring—the browns, chestnuts, and blacks seen suggest infusions of foreign blood at some point in the breed's past.

Fascinating Facts

Each year on the last Saturday in May, the Dülmen are rounded up in the traditional Wildpferdefang, and the colts are separated. The colts are sold at public auctions and the mares returned to the Merfelder Bruch with one or two stallions.

HAFLINGER

TEMPERAMENT: happy, willing

ORIGIN: Austria

SIMILAR BREEDS: Avelignese

HEIGHT: 13.2–15 hh

COLOR: all shades of chestnut, with flaxen mane and tail

PERSONALITY TYPE: warm-blooded

TYPICAL USE: light draft, harness, pack, riding, competition

All modern Haflingers must be able to trace back to the breed's foundation stallion, 249 Folie, a descendant of the influential stallion El Bedavi. Folie was bred to a Tyrolean mare, and the breed's name comes from the village of Hafling, high in the southern Tyrolean Mountains in what are now Austria and Italy. The Austrian Haflinger bears the famous Edelweiss brand mark—a flower with an 'H' in the center—and the breed is sometimes referred to as the "Edelweiss Pony."

Golden Pony

The Haflinger is instantly recognizable by its glorious color—its coat ranges from pale, shimmering gold to rich, glowing chestnut and every shade in between—and flaxen mane and tail. Most Haflingers stand around 13 hh, although bigger animals are sometimes seen. In the Second World War, the military demanded stockier, sturdier equines, and the Haflinger breeders obliged, but from then on the emphasis was again placed on elegance and height.

ABOVE

The Haflinger is a popular and versatile pony breed, whose elegant appearance reflects the influence of Arab blood early in the breed history.

And the Haflinger is an elegant creature. It has a lean, refined head with a large, lively eye, a medium-length neck with well-defined withers, and good, sloping shoulders. Its deep, broad chest and muscular back make it a powerful equine, and it has excellent legs and hard feet. Haflingers often live beyond 40 years old.

Happy Nature

Tyrolean artwork from the early 1800s shows a small but noble equine carrying packs and riders across the steep alpine trails, and the modern Haflinger retains this sure-footedness. Many of the mountain villages are accessible only by these narrow, rocky paths, and the agile Haflinger was invaluable to the villagers. But its happy nature makes it an ideal family horse, too, and there is not much to which it is unable to turn a hoof—it can be used for light draft, harness, or pack work, and competes successfully in a wide range of equestrian disciplines.

KONIK

HEIGHT: 12–13 hh

COLOR: dun with black dorsal stripe

PERSONALITY TYPE:
warm-blooded

TYPICAL USE: agriculture, harness

TEMPERAMENT: gentle, hard-working, eager to please

ORIGIN: Poland

SIMILAR BREEDS: Tarpan (extinct), Hucul

Konik translates as "little horse"—it is a Polish diminutive that actually means "horsie"—and Poland's native breed is perhaps more of a horse than pony, although it stands barely 13 hh. It bears a strong resemblance to the Tarpan, a now-extinct European breed, and it is thought that farmers captured the remaining wild Tarpans and bred them to their domestic horses. The Konik certainly has many features of the Tarpan, including the primitive coloring of dun with dark, dorsal stripe and dark points.

Valuable Commodity

The modern Konik has the gentle nature and eagerness to help that made it so popular with Polish farmers —this is a horse that works

hard to please and is a valuable commodity. It is also used under harness and for light draft work, for which it is well adapted, being hardy, robust, and self-reliant.

It has a quiet temperament and is easily managed. It is a stocky equine, with a large head, short, strong neck set on low withers, upright shoulders, broad body, deep girth, and strong, sound legs.

ABOVE
The ancient Konik breed is close in appearance to the Tarpan and retains primitive physical characteristics in its coloring and conformation.

Some Arab blood has been introduced for refinement, so occasionally other colors than its distinctive dun do occur. Today the Konik is mostly bred at the Polish state stud of Jezewice and at Popielno, where careful selection ensures the breed continues.

Breeding Program

In the 1900s several attempts were made to breed back a Tarpan-like horse using Koniks, Przewalski's Horse,

Icelandic horses, and Gotlands. Semi-wild herds of Koniks now exist in nature reserves in the Netherlands, Latvia, and the United Kingdom, where it can be seen in Kent and Cambridgeshire. While the attempts to recreate the Tarpan may not have been entirely successful, it can do no harm to try and preserve the reliable and sturdy "little horse" of Poland.

Fascinating Facts

7.1 million Americans are involved in the industry as horse owners, service providers, employees, and volunteers.

HUCUL

TEMPERAMENT: hardy, placid

ORIGIN: Poland

SIMILAR BREEDS: Tarpan (extinct), Konik

HEIGHT: 12.1–13.1 hh

COLOR: bay, black, chestnut, dun

PERSONALITY TYPE: warm-blooded

TYPICAL USE: riding, pack, light draft

Hroby, Ousor, Pietrousu, and Prislop—and the horses were carefully bred to preserve the purity of these bloodlines. In 1922, 33 ponies were sent to the then Czechoslovakia to establish a herd there that would become known as the Gurgul line. The studbook for the breed was opened in 1982.

LEFT

The Hucul, with its sturdy build, is very strong and this, combined with its tractable temperament, makes it popular in its home country for riding, packing, and light draft work.

The Hucul, one of the oldest breeds of native pony in Europe, resembles the extinct Tarpan perhaps more than any other. It dates back to the 1200s and is believed to be the result of crossing Mongolian Horses with the wild Tarpan. It originated in the Carpathian Mountains in Eastern Europe—it is sometimes called the Carpathian Pony or the Mountain Tarpan. Borders have changed many times throughout history along this mountain range, and both Romania and Poland could lay claim to being the Hucul's country of origin.

influence, a distinct breed evolved into a robust and enduring little equine. It is compact and muscular, with a deep, broad chest and exceptionally strong neck and back. It has an attractive head with large, expressive eyes and small, mobile ears. Its legs are strong and sound, and it has excellent feet—the Hucul rarely needs to be shod.

As the Hucul was used and bred by a variety of people in a variety of places, slightly different types emerged—the Hucul of Romania was different to the Czech and Polish versions. Today Huculs are bred mainly in the Bucovina region of Romania, as well as Hungary, regions of the Czech and Slovak republics, Poland, and the Ukraine.

Foundation Stallions

The Hucul's isolated mountain home is in the Eastern Carpathians, a region called Huzulland, which has a harsh, unforgiving climate. With no other equine

Different Versions

The first stud farm was established in Roaduti, Romania, using five foundation stallions—Goral,

KLEPPER (Torijski)

HEIGHT: 14.3–15 hh

COLOR: chestnut, bay, dun, gray

PERSONALITY TYPE: warm-blooded

TYPICAL USE: agriculture, riding, pack, tourism

TEMPERAMENT: willing, obedient

ORIGIN: Estonia

SIMILAR BREEDS: Vyatka

Estonia's native breed is one of the few that has been little influenced by outside blood. In its turn it played an important role in the development of the now-extinct Obva breed and the Vyatka. It has also been used with, variously, Hackney and Ardennais blood to create the Toric (*see* page 337). The original Klepper first arrived in Russia via Novgorod as early as the 1300s, when it was in demand for its willing temperament, good working qualities, and adaptability.

Foundation Mares

As agriculture developed and demand for good working horses increased, the Klepper was crossed with larger breeds to give it more size and strength. The Tori Stud was established in 1856 with 47 mares and seven young stallions. As well as breeding pure Kleppers, the stud also crossed them with light harness and saddle breeds; the best mares resulting from the cross were used to develop the Toric. The purebred stallion Vansikasa, a horse of great strength and endurance, won many championships, and its daughters were foundation mares of the Toric.

As with so many equines, mechanization was to have a devastating effect on the Klepper, and it is no longer bred on mainland Estonia, surviving only on the islands of Saaremaa, Hiiumaa, and Muhu. It is thought there are only around 1,000 purebreds left.

Long-lived

The Klepper today is also known as the Torijski. It is an attractive and amenable equine. Standing up to 15 hh, it has a well-proportioned head with a wide forehead, although there is a tendency to coarseness; the neck can be on the short side, and the withers are set low. The chest is very wide and deep, and the Klepper has short, clean legs

ABOVE

There are very few purebred Kleppers left, their numbers having dropped dramatically with the arrival of mechanization.

and extremely solid hooves. The breed is long-lived, with some horses reaching 40 years old.

ZEMAITUKA

TEMPERAMENT: quiet, biddable

ORIGIN: Lithuania

SIMILAR BREEDS: Konik

HEIGHT: 13.2–14.2 hh

COLOR: dun, black, brown, bay, palomino

PERSONALITY TYPE: warm-blooded

TYPICAL USE: riding, light draft, agriculture

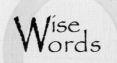

Also called the Zhumd, this is an ancient breed originally from Lithuania on the Baltic Sea, and closely related to the Konik and therefore the ancient Tarpan. Little is known about the breed, except that very few are left in existence. Its natural habitat is harsh and unforgiving, with poor forage and freezing temperatures. The Zemaituka has developed into a tough little equine, able to survive on meager rations.

ABOVE

The Zemaituka is closely related to, and bears a resemblance to, the Konik, pictured, with both breeds displaying primitive coat colors and characteristics.

Sporting Horses

Over the years other breeds have had influence on the Zemaituka, including native Russian blood and light horse breeds from Poland. More recently Arabian blood has been introduced, which can be seen in the animal's surprisingly fine head. There were, at one point, two distinct types of Zemaituka:

a finer quality riding type and a heavier light draft type. This distinction has been blurred as, after the Second World War, conscious effort has

Wise Words

"If you want a kitten, start out by asking for a horse."—Anon

been made to increase the breed's size and bulk, making it adaptable to both riding and light draft.

Today's Zemaituka is an attractive, sturdy creature with a gentle, biddable nature and an endearing eagerness to please. Despite its rather solid and massive frame, it is generally agile and athletic. When crossed with a lighter breed, such as a Thoroughbred, it produces excellent sporting horses.

A Good Doer

The Zemaituka is a good doer, with considerable stamina and endurance, and is seemingly unaffected by fatigue. It has an attractive head with large, kind eyes and small, mobile ears. It has a well-muscled neck, broad, deep chest, straight shoulders, a compact, straight back, and a sloping croup with low-set tail. Its legs are short and muscular (although the breed has a tendency toward poor hocks), and its feet are well formed and hard. The most common color is dun or mouse dun, with a dark dorsal stripe and black points —indication of its ancient origins. Blacks, browns, bays, and palominos occur.

BELOW

The Polish Wielpolski, pictured, and Arab blood was used to refine the Zemaituka, lending it greater elegance and making it adaptable to riding and light draft work.

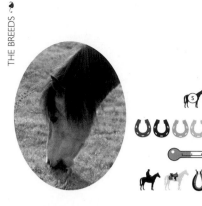

BOSNIAN

HEIGHT: 13–14.2 hh

COLOR: bay, black, brown, gray, palomino

PERSONALITY TYPE: warm-blooded

TYPICAL USE: riding, pack, agriculture, light draft

TEMPERAMENT: quiet, docile

ORIGIN: Bosnia

SIMILAR BREEDS: Hucul, Konik

The Bosnian is the third of the three Balkan breeds, together with the Hucul and the Konik. They are all ancient breeds, and the Bosnian is thought to be the result of a cross between the Tarpan and Przewalski's Horse, also known as the Asiatic Wild Horse. Since the 1900s it has been selectively bred to ensure the endurance of the breed, which suffered serious decline following infusions of Oriental blood.

LEFT

The Bosnian pony is a small and tough breed, which has much in common with the ancient Hucul and Konik breeds.

During the 1940s three stallions—Agan, Barat, and Misco—had an important influence on the breed, generally improving it. Agan and Barat were probably pure or almost pure Przewalski, while Misco was of a lighter, finer type.

Useful and Functional

The modern Bosnian retains the primitive appearance but also possesses quality and refinement. It has a heavy head with a straight profile, full forelock, and small ears. A short, muscular neck joins long, sloping shoulders, a deep, wide chest, and a straight back with sloping hindquarters. The primitive dorsal stripe and black points are sometimes seen, although most solid colors occur.

It is an extremely useful and functional little animal, adapted to riding, light farmwork, or draft and pack, as it is sure-footed enough to cross rough terrain inaccessible to motorized vehicles. Hardy and tough, its docile temperament makes it easy to handle and safe to ride.

State Control

Oriental blood was introduced by the Turks during the Ottoman Empire, and the resulting deterioration of the breed was rectified by infusions of more Tarpan blood. Selective breeding in the 1900s has saved the breed, which is highly prized, and for many years, when Bosnia was part of the former Yugoslavia, the principal center for breeding the Bosnian was the Borike Stud in Bosnia. Stallions were strictly controlled by the state, but the mares were under private ownership.

RIGHT

The Hucul, pictured, Konik, and Bosnian are the three Balkan breeds and share many similarities, especially in their stocky conformation.

KAZAKH

TEMPERAMENT: placid, docile

ORIGIN: Kazakhstan

SIMILAR BREEDS: Mongolian Pony

HEIGHT: 14 hh

COLOR: grullo, bay, brown, chestnut, palomino

PERSONALITY TYPE: warm-blooded

TYPICAL USE: riding, pack, meat

Originating in Kazakhstan and primitive in origin, the Kazakh is one of the breeds with its roots in Przewalski's Horse. A true working breed, it is sturdy, hardy, and strong, with great stamina and a thick, waterproof coat. Its short, choppy stride can make it uncomfortable for riding, but it is a good pack animal.

Subtypes

Over the years the Kazakh has been subject to infusions of outside blood, not all of them successful. There are two known subtypes—the Dzhabe and the Adaev—with the latter being of lighter frame and generally more lively. The Dzhabe has a plain, coarse head and short, muscular neck leading to straight

shoulders and back, and is commonly bay or liver chestnut. The Adaev type has a much more refined head, slightly longer neck, pronounced withers, and compact body. It is usually bay, gray, palomino, or chestnut. Both types have strong legs and good, hard feet. The Adaev is more adapted to riding, with a smoother stride.

VYATKA

TEMPERAMENT: willing, docile, hardy

ORIGIN: Russia

SIMILAR BREEDS: Konik, Klepper

HEIGHT: 14.2 hh

COLOR: roan, dun, bay, brown, chestnut

PERSONALITY TYPE: warm-blooded

TYPICAL USE: pack, harness, light draft

The rare Vyatka, or Vyatskata, originated in the region around Russia's Vyatka and Obva rivers. The pony probably descended from the Tarpan, with Konik and Estonian / Klepper influences. It was affected by edicts from state breeders during the reign of Peter the Great (1672–1725); and Estonian horses imported to the Urals for use in the mining industry in the 1700s were likely crossed with the native Vyatka breed.

Sharply Declining Numbers

The result was a sturdy equine of speed and extraordinary endurance, able to thrive on meager rations. It made an excellent light draft horse. With increasing mechanization and more intensified agriculture, however, numbers fell sharply.

The Vyatka's ancient roots are clearly seen in its most common chestnut or bay roan coloring, with a black, dorsal stripe along its back and zebra stripes on its forelegs. Some also have a wing-shaped marking over the shoulders. Brown, bay, and chestnut are also seen, as well as the much less common

black. It has a small, clean-cut head, a strong, thick neck, a deep girth, and powerful shoulders and hindquarters.

PONEY MOUSSEYE

HEIGHT: 12 hh

COLOR: gray, chestnut

PERSONALITY TYPE:
warm-blooded

TYPICAL USE: riding, pack,
light draft

TEMPERAMENT: quiet, easygoing

ORIGIN: Cameroon

SIMILAR BREEDS: Nigerian

Poney

Little is known about the Poney Mousseye, which comes from Cameroon, a country on the west central coast of Africa. The tiny equine—it stands barely 12 hh—probably has common roots with the Nigerian, which in turn probably dates back to the Barb, which, taken to Nigeria by the nomads, mated with the local ponies. Although this is the received wisdom, it is entirely possible it was the other way around, with the Nigerian descending from the Poney Mousseye.

Disease-resistant

A rare breed, the Poney Mousseye is found mainly in areas around the Logone River. This particular region is notorious for the tsetse fly, the bite of which carries sleeping sickness, also known as African trypanosomiasis,

which can cause brain damage, and if untreated, death. The Poney Mousseye, however, appears resistant to the disease, while other equine breeds are not.

Easygoing

The Poney Mousseye has remained largely uninfluenced by other breeds because of its geographic isolation, and whatever its origins, the modern Mousseye certainly shows little of its supposed Barb roots. It has a

plain head with straight profile, which tends to be on the heavy side; a short, thick neck; and a long back. It has a sloping croup—perhaps betraying its Barb origins—a compact body, and short but strong legs. The only defect is occasionally underdeveloped hindquarters. Versatile and easygoing, the Poney Mousseye makes a good,

LEFT
The purity of the Poney Mousseye breed has remained relatively intact due to their geographic isolation.

ABOVE
The precise origin of the Poney Mousseye is unclear, but they often show a striking similarity to the Barb, pictured.

willing, child's riding pony and is strong and hardy enough for light pack work because of its great stamina and endurance.

The Nigerian, while similar in appearance to the Poney Mousseye, is larger, standing up to 14.2 hh. It has the same sweet nature and stamina and is just as resistant to heat.

BASUTO

TEMPERAMENT: brave, affectionate

ORIGIN: Lesotho, Southern Africa

SIMILAR BREEDS: Cape Horse

HEIGHT: 14.2 hh

COLOR: chestnut, bay, brown, gray, white markings

PERSONALITY TYPE: warm-blooded

TYPICAL USE: riding, trekking, polo

This tough, brave pony was developed in Lesotho (formerly Basutoland), a country landlocked by South Africa, in the 1700s and 1800s from the region's Cape Horse. Both breeds descended from the first horses introduced to South Africa by the Dutch East India Trading Company, which brought four equines to the Cape area in 1653. These horses were probably Arabian and Persian and founded the Cape Horse, a large, quality creature that served as a popular warhorse.

Stamina and Bravery

The Basuto was smaller and stockier but tough and sure-footed, traits it almost certainly developed to cope with the rocky and hilly terrain over which it was ridden, sometimes at considerable speed. Possessing incredible

Fascinating Facts

It is possible today to appreciate horses in South Africa by going on a safari horse trail in the Western Cape area.

BELOW LEFT
The Basuto pony is renowned for its stamina and speed over the most treacherous terrain. They are spirited and affable in temperament.

stamina and bravery, the Basuto grew in popularity, and this was almost its downfall—in high demand, hundreds of thousands of them were exported, and many of the best were killed in action during the Boer War at the end of the 1800s. With so many spread out in different areas, and some of the best breeding stock cut down in its prime, the Basuto was almost wiped out.

Polo Pony

An attractive little equine, the Basuto has a large but neat head set on a long neck, with straight shoulders and long, straight back, ending with a muscular, sloping croup. It has good, tough legs and sound, hard feet. Although technically a pony—the Basuto rarely stands taller than 14.2 hh—it does have horselike qualities, including an exceptionally long stride.

Today the Basuto is often used for racing—making good use of that long stride—or polo, where its speed and agility are great assets. Its friendly, amenable nature makes it a good mount for a child, and its stamina means that it is an excellent pack pony. There is currently a concerted effort to save the Basuto breed.

BURMESE

HEIGHT: 13 hh

COLOR: brown, bay, black, chestnut, gray

PERSONALITY TYPE: warm-blooded

TYPICAL USE: pack, trekking

TEMPERAMENT: quiet, willing

ORIGIN: Burma

SIMILAR BREEDS: Manipuri, Bhutia, Spiti

The Burmese, bred by the hill tribes of Burma's Shan, is sometimes called the Shan Pony. Superbly adapted to its mountain environment, this ancient breed is resistant to the harsh climate and sure-footed enough to traverse the steep, rocky terrain at speed. Its short, choppy stride is well adapted to the rugged topography.

Function Not Beauty

The Burmese probably developed from the Mongolian, with Oriental influences. It is neither especially speedy nor athletic and is rather unprepossessing to look at, with emphasis on function rather than beauty. It does have a fine head, with a straight profile and a pleasingly wide forehead. Its long, muscular neck is in proportion to its body, but its back tends to be too long. The withers are not pronounced, and its shoulders are straight. It has a deep, wide chest, fine but strong legs, and small, hard hooves. Quiet and willing, it is an ideal mount for children or beginners.

RIGHT

These small, tough ponies are ideal for packing and trekking over mountainous terrain and are especially surefooted.

Fascinating Facts

The Burmese's stamina is renowned. In 1887 an equestrian explorer named George Younghusband traveled 1,800 miles (2,900 km) on a Burmese called Joe, which the adventurer described as a "lovable scamp."

MANIPURI

HEIGHT: 13 hh

COLOR: most solid colors, pinto

PERSONALITY TYPE: warm-blooded

TYPICAL USE: polo, racing, military

TEMPERAMENT: intelligent, alert

ORIGIN: Burma / India

SIMILAR BREEDS: Bhutia, Spiti, Burmese

The Manipur Cavalry was respected and feared throughout upper Burma during the 1600s. Part of the credit for this must go to the agile, tough, and athletic Manipuri. A cross between the ancient Mongolian Wild Horse and the Arabian, it was later used in the Second World War and as a transportation animal. Before it was a warhorse, however, the Manipuri was the original polo pony.

Polo by Torchlight

The King of Manipur introduced polo in the 600s. Later, Akbar the Great (1542–1605), a polo aficionado, played the game at night by torchlight and had his own huge stables, which can still be seen today in Agra.

The intelligent Manipuri, with its speed and stamina, was a natural for the game, but its small stature counted against it. As polo's popularity spread, over the years the upper height limit for polo ponies was increased and then abolished altogether. Still the Manipuri remains popular. Undeniably attractive, it has a muscular neck, broad chest, well-sprung ribs, and compact body, with sloping shoulders, muscular hindquarters, a sloping croup, strong legs, and good feet.

BHUTIA AND SPITI

TEMPERAMENT: willing and quiet,
though can be bad-tempered

ORIGIN: India

SIMILAR BREEDS: Tibetan, Manipuri, Burmese

HEIGHT: 12–13.2 hh

COLOR: gray, chestnut, roan, bay

PERSONALITY TYPE:
warm-blooded

TYPICAL USE: pack

High in the Himalayan region were three distinct types of pony—the Bhutia, Spiti, and Tibetan. Probably descended from ancient Mongolian strains, over centuries they have interbred to the extent that many of their individual characteristics have long been lost. They are now categorized as the "Indian Country Bred," although the Tibetan Pony retains some of its purity. The Bhutia is found today in Nepal, Bhutan, and the Sikkim and Darjeeling regions of India, while the Spiti is found in the Kangra Valley in northeastern Punjab.

Self-sufficient

Bhutia and Spiti are frugal feeders and thus economical to keep. They are incredibly tough and self-sufficient. Both are plain and thickset, with a comparatively large head with a pronounced jaw, short neck, low withers, sloping quarters, and deep chest. The shoulders are a little upright and straight. The legs tend to be short but very strong, with exceptionally hard feet.

Excellent pack ponies, they can make good riding ponies, as they have stamina and endurance.

BELOW
Bhutia and Spiti, like these rugged ponies seen here in the wetlands of Mongolia, are very self sufficient.

MONGOLIAN

TEMPERAMENT: quiet, biddable

ORIGIN: Mongolia

SIMILAR BREEDS: Przewalski's Horse

HEIGHT: 12.1 hh

COLOR: dun, bay, brown, black

PERSONALITY TYPE:
warm-blooded

TYPICAL USE: riding, racing

Purported to be largely unchanged since the time of Genghis Khan (1206–27), the Mongolian is an ancient breed that resembles Przewalski's Horse, of which it is believed to be a direct descendant. There are thought to be around three million Mongolian Ponies. Able to survive on minimal rations, it is used for riding and racing, which play a big part in the Mongol lifestyle.

Prized Attributes

Even today, the ponies live out on a plateau 6,000 ft. (1,820 m) above sea level, in punishing winds and a winter temperature that goes down to –40° F. Breeders believe that when stall-fed, the pony loses its great speed and exceptional hardiness, both highly prized.

The ponies retain many of the primitive characteristics, though not all have dun coloring and black points. Small and stocky, they have a large head, short legs, and very long manes and tails—and considerable stamina. Racing ponies with a child in the saddle will run at full gallop over a distance of 22 miles (35 km) and keep running even if the rider falls.

CHINESE GUOXIA

HEIGHT: 11 hh

COLOR: bay, roan, gray

PERSONALITY TYPE: warm-blooded

TYPICAL USE: riding, harness

TEMPERAMENT: calm, willing

ORIGIN: southwest China

SIMILAR BREEDS: Mongolian

A bronze statue of a pony recovered in southwest China is thought to be of a Guoxia and is dated at 2,000 years old. The word Guoxia translates as "under fruit tree horse," so it may have been that the pony, which is small in stature, worked in orchards collecting the fruit. Little is known about the Guoxia, and it was thought to be extinct before it was rediscovered in 1981.

Marauding Tribes

Not especially horse-orientated, the Chinese were forced to deploy mounted warriors and even breed their own horses in defense against the marauding nomadic tribes who continually attacked the nation's borders. The tough, hardy Guoxia is probably a descendant of the Mongolian, and through it, Przewalski's Horse.

It has a comparatively large head, with small, alert ears, a short neck, straight shoulders, a short, straight back, strong legs, and very hard feet. Its generally gentle, friendly nature makes it an excellent child's first pony. Very strong with considerable stamina, it is also used in harness, despite its small size.

RIGHT
The gentle Chinese Guoxia makes a good child's pony.

TIBETAN

HEIGHT: 12.2 hh

COLOR: usually bay or gray

PERSONALITY TYPE: warm-blooded

TYPICAL USE: riding, trekking, pack, light draft, racing

TEMPERAMENT: energetic, willing

ORIGIN: Tibet

SIMILAR BREEDS: Mongolian

Although Tibet's native pony breed is undoubtedly descended from the Mongolian, it has remained largely pure for many years and is revered for its incredible strength and endurance. The Dalai Lama historically keeps Tibetan Ponies, and a Tibetan Pony was often sent as a gift to the Chinese emperor, especially during the Tang and Ming dynasties.

A Versatile Friend

An excellent worker, resilient, and energetic, the Tibetan is used for light draft, riding, and packing. Extremely sure-footed, in some parts of Tibet it is the only form of transportation. It is also used for trekking, which is becoming more popular. Despite its small size, the Tibetan is ridden in racing, with its swift turn of foot.

It has a straight head, pronounced jawline, and small ears and eyes. Its short, muscular neck is set on flat withers and straight shoulders. It has a straight back, broad, powerful hindquarters, strong, straight legs with solid joints, and hard feet. It is usually bay or gray, but most solid colors are seen.

TOKARA

TEMPERAMENT: gentle, placid

ORIGIN: Japan

SIMILAR BREEDS: Misaki, Hokkaido, Kiso

HEIGHT: 12 hh

COLOR: bay, brown, chestnut, roan

PERSONALITY TYPE: warm-blooded

TYPICAL USE: riding, light draft

Once numerous, these little ponies are now rare, although a preservation project is underway. They were discovered in 1950, when a Dr. Shigeyuki Hayashida found a group of small equines living in the south side of the Tokara Islands and gave them their name. They were thought to be the descendants of horses taken to the island in the 1800s, and the people used them for farming, transportation, and for processing the sugarcane grown in the area.

National Treasure

The Tokara suffered a severe decline after the Second World War. In an attempt to preserve the breed in a near original form, a number of animals were taken to Nakanoshima on Tokara Island, where

they range freely during the year and are rounded up for pest extermination, inoculation, and veterinary treatment every 12 months. The breed has been designated a Japanese national treasure.

MISAKI

TEMPERAMENT: wild

ORIGIN: Japan

SIMILAR BREEDS: Tokara, Hokkaido, Kiso

HEIGHT: 13.2 hh

COLOR: bay, black, chestnut, cremello

PERSONALITY TYPE: warm-blooded

TYPICAL USE: tourism

The wildest of all Japanese breeds, the Misaki originates in the Miyazaki Prefecture on the island of Kyushu and lives in the meadows of the Cape Toi, or Toimisake—the word *misaki* means "cape." It has been rarely handled by humans, and like the Tokara, has been declared a national treasure in Japan.

The first known record of the Misaki is in 1697, when the Akizuki family of the Takanabe Clan took the wild horses under its protection and created a stud farm.

Tourist Attraction

The ponies were still left to run wild, but they were

rounded up once a year to select animals for taming and domesticating and probably to castrate any males deemed unsuitable for breeding. The same system is used today—the ponies are rounded up, inoculated and treated for parasites, and checked over for their general health. A rare breed, there are thought to be around 100 left. The region is popular with tourists, and the wild ponies are a great attraction.

HOKKAIDO

HEIGHT: 13 hh

COLOR: most solid colors

PERSONALITY TYPE: warm-blooded

TYPICAL USE: riding, draft

TEMPERAMENT: placid, willing

ORIGIN: Japan

SIMILAR BREEDS: Mongolian, Kiso

Also known as the Dosanko or the Hokkaido Washu, the Hokkaido lives on Hokkaido's Pacific coast. Originally taken to the island by Japanese herring fisherman, they were left there when the fishermen returned home in the fall. Those that survived the cold and bears were rounded up when the fishermen returned.

Nanbu Descendants

The Hokkaido is considered a descendant of the Nanbu, which was used primarily as a military animal. Those taken to Hokkaido were probably inferior specimens. Left to forage in the harsh, mountainous terrain, only the hardiest survived, developing the enduring strength for which the breed is known. Even-tempered, docile, and a strong, willing worker, it is bigger than most of the Japanese breeds. Its slightly primitive appearance suggests a relationship with the Mongolian. It has a large, plain head, a short neck, thickset body, slender legs, and exceptionally hard feet. It rarely has any white markings, and dun coloring with a dorsal stripe is common. Many Hokkaidos are natural pacers.

KISO

HEIGHT: 13 hh

COLOR: most solid colors

PERSONALITY TYPE: warm-blooded

TYPICAL USE: riding, harness, light draft

TEMPERAMENT: gentle, tractable

ORIGIN: Japan

SIMILAR BREEDS: Mongolian, Hokkaido

Were it not for the Japanese custom of keeping a sacred white horse at certain shrines, the Kiso would have died out completely, as the breed's diminutive size meant that breeding pure was discouraged. Then during the Second World War, a government edict demanded that all Kiso stallions be castrated, but one was discovered at a Shinto shrine that had been deemed a holy horse and was therefore not gelded.

Last Purebred

This horse, called Shinmei, was put to a mare called Kayama, and in 1951 bred a colt called Dai-san Haruyama —the last of the purebred Kiso. The breed has been saved from extinction by back-breeding, but there are thought to be only around 100 left. Records exist of horses being bred in the Kiso region as early as the 500s. According to legend, during the 1200s some 10,000 were produced as cavalry mounts for the famous warrior Kiso Yoshinaka's army. The Kiso undoubtedly owes much to the Mongolian, and dun coloring with black points and dorsal stripe is common.

NORDLAND

TEMPERAMENT: energetic, even-tempered, willing

ORIGIN: Norway

SIMILAR BREEDS: Icelandic

HEIGHT: 12–13 hh

COLOR: chestnut, bay, brown, gray

PERSONALITY TYPE: warm-blooded

TYPICAL USE: riding, harness, pack

The Nordland's resemblance to Przewalski's Horse and the Tarpan suggests that Norway's native pony is an ancient breed—well-preserved finds from Viking graves indicate an equine presence in the country that dates back centuries. It is thought to have arrived in Norway from the east, which supports this theory, and perhaps in search for food then concentrated —and developed—in the northern part of the country. It is called, variously, Nordland, Northlands, Lyngen, and Lyngshest, and at one time there were two very distinct types of this pony.

Almost Extinct

The two variations were the Lyngen type from the district in northern Troms of the same name, and the smaller Norland type which was essentially based on examples from the Lofoten district. The Lyngen version was bigger and heavier and almost always chestnut in color, while the Norland type was much finer, resembling closely the now-extinct Lofoten Pony. The two types have, however, interbred, and the modern Nordland is basically of one type— although there are still some individuals that are clearly one or the other—with all solid colors occurring except the primitive dun.

> ### ABOVE
> *The Nordland breed faced extinction after the Second World War, when their numbers were dangerously low, but recent breeding programs have helped to improve the situation.*

The breed was at the brink of extinction after the Second World War, due to a poor economy, sparse food, and a general shortage of animals, but a breeding program fortunately saved it for future generations.

Fascinating Facts

Horses have been put through their paces in Norway every October since 1991 at the Oslo Horse Show, part of the Western European League in show jumping.

Equable Temper

The modern Nordland has a plain head with thick mane, medium-length back, sloping croup, and sturdy legs and is generally sound and free from health problems. It is long-lived, surviving into its thirties, and also retains its fertility to advanced age. Easily trainable and willing to work, it has an equable temperament and makes a good child's mount. It is also used for pack and harness.

FJORD

HEIGHT: 13.2–14.1 hh

COLOR: all shades of dun

PERSONALITY TYPE: warm-blooded

TYPICAL USE: riding, harness, pack

TEMPERAMENT: calm, gentle

ORIGIN: Norway

SIMILAR BREEDS: Przewalski's Horse, Icelandic, Exmoor

Ice Age cave paintings of ponies of 30,000 years ago bear a strong resemblance to today's Fjord Pony, a Norwegian breed that gets its name from the country's famous waterways. It is thought to have migrated to Norway around 4,000 years ago, perhaps part of the vast herds that came to the Scandinavian peninsula. It has the distinctive primitive coloring of dun with black points, black dorsal stripe, and zebra striping on its legs and shares several similarities with Przewalski's Horse.

Approximately 90 percent of Fjord Ponies are brown dun, the other 10 percent being red dun, gray dun (grullo), gold, or yellow dun, although this last is very rare. The occasional bay or brown Fjord is also seen. It is an attractive equine, with a pretty head that is less heavy than that of Przewalski's Horse and is sometimes dished. It has large eyes, small, mobile ears, a short, crested neck, a powerful body with a deep girth, and excellent legs and feet.

Unique Trait

A unique characteristic of the Fjord is its striking mane—the center hair of the mane is black, while the outer hair is white. The mane is traditionally cut short so that it stands erect, trimmed into a crescent shape to enhance the graceful curve of the neck. The white, outer hair is then trimmed slightly shorter to display the dark line down the center. In all the Fjord is a pleasing picture of equine excellence.

> **LEFT**
> *The heavyset and thick-framed Fjord pony reflects the primitive characteristics of its ancient history.*

The Vikings used the Fjord as a warhorse and then a farm animal—the Vikings were thought to be the first Western Europeans to use horses for agricultural purposes— for which the Fjord's sure-footedness, strength, soundness, and exceptional stamina have made it invaluable. It has an extremely equable temperament and is easily trained.

GOTLAND

TEMPERAMENT: intelligent, lively, gentle

ORIGIN: Sweden

SIMILAR BREEDS: Przewalski's Horse

HEIGHT: 11.2–13 hh

COLOR: dun, bay

PERSONALITY TYPE: warm-blooded

TYPICAL USE: riding, harness

It has been called a "living relic of the past," and it is known that the Gotland pony of Sweden is an ancient breed. There have been wild ponies on the Lojsta Moor, on the Swedish island of Gotland, since the Stone Age. It is known in Sweden as the Russ, a word derived from the Norse word for "horse," and in Gotland itself as the Skosbagga, which means "forest ram." The ponies have inhabited the island for about 5,000 years, although it is not known how they first got there, nor whether those early equines were the same as today's Gotland.

Roaming Free

Discoveries made at an Iron Age village called Vallhagar (220 B.C.—A.D. 500), a few miles from Lojsta Moor, show that horses became increasingly common as domestic animals during that period, but the Gotland lived in semi-wild freedom in the forests. Farmers kept the ponies to work the land and often had a herd of them roaming free to be captured when they needed new stock. The free ponies would forage for themselves, only returning to the farms if there were food shortages.

It was these farmers who were to save the breed from extinction. By the early 1900s there were only around 150 Gotlands left, as agricultural policies had changed and the "forest rams" were damaging crops. Food shortages and meat rationing during the First World War meant that the Gotland was also hunted for meat.

BELOW

The attractive and versatile Gotland pony is used for riding and light draft purposes and has an especially equable temperament.

Saved from Extinction

The Gotland farmers fenced off an area of around 200 acres and introduced to it eight Gotlands, and this tiny herd formed the beginning of a breeding program to save the equine. It was successful —today there are around 9,000 Gotlands in Sweden and more elsewhere, the breed proving popular for its equable nature and attractive appearance.

Fascinating Facts

Gotlands are still watched over on the Lojsta Moor. Each season is marked by an annual Gotland activity: releasing the stallion to the herd each June, judging in July, and weaning the foals from the mares in November.

JAVA/TIMOR

HEIGHT: 12.2 hh

COLOR: all colors

PERSONALITY TYPE: warm-blooded

TYPICAL USE: tourism, harness

TEMPERAMENT: willing, quiet

ORIGIN: Indonesia

SIMILAR BREEDS: Sumba / Sambawa, Sandalwood

Indonesia's little pony may lack the beauty of the Arabian, but the breed is certainly unique in its heritage. It is thought to be related to the Chinese horses and date back to the fifth century B.C. When the Dutch settled in Indonesia and her islands in the late 1500s, the Arabs they traded with brought over Arabian and Barb horses to influence the islands' native stock. The Java and the Timor take the name of the islands on which they originate.

Great Stamina

The desert breeds' influence is apparent in the Java's hardiness; it is extremely tough and very strong—despite its small stature, it can carry an adult. It can survive on little feed and has great stamina, although it is also known for its occasionally uncertain temper.

On the island of Java, the ponies are used to pull *sados*, two-wheeled carts that are used to transport whole families and their combined possessions, which they do with ease. They are popular with tourists, who marvel at the sight of the tiny equines pulling such huge loads.

Australian Pony

The Timor, found on the island of the same name off the southern end of the Malay Peninsula, is equally important to the islanders—it is used for everything from riding and driving to light farmwork and working with cows. A frugal feeder, like the Java, it is also quick and

---

LEFT

The Java pony is not known for its good conformation, but looks can be deceiving, and it is one of the toughest and strongest breeds for its diminutive size.

---

agile. It tends to be smaller than the Java, standing between 10 and 12 hh, but is

equally unprepossessing, with a large head carried almost horizontally on a short neck, prominent withers, short back, and sloping croup, with good legs and hard feet. Large numbers of the Timor were exported to Australia, where they have played a part in the development of the local pony breeds.

SUMBA/SUMBAWA

TEMPERAMENT: willing, cooperative

ORIGIN: Indonesia

SIMILAR BREEDS: Java, Timor, Sandalwood

HEIGHT: 12 hh

COLOR: predominantly dun

PERSONALITY TYPE: warm-blooded

TYPICAL USE: riding, pack, tourism

Named for the two islands they inhabit, the Sumba and Sumbawa are essentially the same, developed from Chinese and Mongolian

breeds. Possessing all the admirable traits of Indonesia's native breeds, they are famed for an unusual reason—they dance.

Bells are attached to the pony's knees, and it dances with surprising elegance and grace to the beat of tom-tom drums. The breed may not be especially beautiful, but to see it dance is a joy to behold.

Primitive Roots

The Sumba/Sumbawa is primitive in looks, being predominantly dun with dorsal stripe, black points,

and zebra stripes on its legs. It is found in the Nusa Tenggara province, the west of which is formed of two main islands, Lombok and Sumbawa; the east of over 500, the biggest ones being Flores, Sumba, and Timor.

These islands have poor grazing, yet the ponies thrive. Agile and fast, like the Java and Timor, they are able to carry or pull weights far out of proportion to their tiny stature.

BATAK

TEMPERAMENT: willing, easy to manage

ORIGIN: Indonesia

SIMILAR BREEDS: Java, Timor, Sumba/Sumbawa, Sandalwood

HEIGHT: 13 hh

COLOR: all colors

PERSONALITY TYPE: warm-blooded

TYPICAL USE: riding, pack, harness, light draft

Once used primarily as a sacrifice to the gods, today the Batak of Indonesia fulfills a less gruesome role. It still plays a central part in the lives of the people of Sumatra, where it is found and is highly regarded. Like other Indonesian equines, it is probably Mongolian in origin but has been improved by Arabian blood

and selectively bred. It is probably the next best-quality Indonesian breed to the Sandalwood and is used to improve the ponies of the other islands.

Easy Keeper

Arabian blood is apparent in the Batak's good looks—it

has the fine, chiseled head and high-set tail also seen in the Sandalwood. It is an easy keeper, obliging and gentle, and economic to

keep. It is lightly built, with a slender frame and narrow chest. Its legs are sometimes poor, but it has good, hard feet.

Another Indonesian breed, the Gayoe, also found in central Sumatra, is thought to be a substrain of the Batak, but it is a stockier, more sturdy creature.

SANDALWOOD

HEIGHT: 13 hh

COLOR: all colors

PERSONALITY TYPE: warm-blooded

TYPICAL USE: riding, harness, agriculture, light draft, racing

TEMPERAMENT: quiet, biddable

ORIGIN: Indonesia

SIMILAR BREEDS: Java, Timor, Sumba/Sumbawa

Named after the sweet-smelling wood that is one of the islands' main exports, the Sandalwood is the best of Indonesia's pony breeds, having considerably more quality than the others. This is largely due to greater infusion of Arabian blood. It is known that the Dutch settlers imported Arabian stallions to Sumatra, the biggest of the islands that make up Indonesia, and used them on selected mares to produce a quality equine, which in turn was exported to the other islands to improve their stock.

Beauty and Grace

The Sandalwood breed still retains a high percentage of Arabian blood and has inherited that breed's beauty and grace. It is a very versatile pony, with great stamina and endurance, as well as speed and agility. But it also has a quiet, biddable nature, which makes it an excellent child's pony.

ABOVE

These ponies are elegant and refined, as seen, and have a high percentage of Arabian blood in them.

The Sandalwood has a nicely proportioned head— sometimes with the slightly dished face of its Arab ancestors—small, alert ears and intelligent eyes. It has a short, muscular neck (on which it carries its head slightly higher than the other Indonesian breeds), a deep chest, long, straight back, and sloping croup. It carries its tail high and has slender legs, with the good, hard feet that typify the islands' ponies.

Three-Mile Races

The breed has also been used to improve Australia's ponies, but it has another role in its homeland. Racing is hugely popular in Indonesia, and the swift little Sandalwood, with speed a part of its Arabian heritage, is raced over distances of two and a half to three miles. In Malaysia, where it is frequently exported, the Sandalwood is crossed with Thoroughbreds to produce bigger, faster racehorses.

It has also inherited the Arabian's immunity to heat— the Sandalwood rarely breaks a sweat.

BALI

TEMPERAMENT: quiet, biddable

ORIGIN: Indonesia

SIMILAR BREEDS: Java, Timor, Sumba/Sumbawa, Sandalwood, Batak

HEIGHT: 12–13 hh

COLOR: predominantly dun

PERSONALITY TYPE: warm-blooded

TYPICAL USE: riding, pack, harness, light draft

Indonesia's island jewel has its own breed of pony, the eponymous Bali. The pony's ancient origins are apparent in its rather primitive appearance—it is often dun with black dorsal stripes and black points—although there is evidence of Oriental influence. It is probably Mongolian in origin, with infusions of Eastern blood from horses imported by the Dutch in the 1700s.

Minimal Rations

The Bali is not selectively or consistently bred, so it does have conformation faults, but it is noted for its strength (in comparison to its size) and for its hardiness. It is used to transport stones and coral from the beaches for building, as well as for riding, trekking, and sightseeing by tourists. The breed can exist on minimal rations and needs little in the terms of care, and as with all of Indonesia's ponies breeds, it has exceptionally good, hard feet.

AUSTRALIAN

TEMPERAMENT: intelligent, lively

ORIGIN: Australia

SIMILAR BREEDS: Indonesian breeds

HEIGHT: 12–14 hh

COLOR: all solid colors

PERSONALITY TYPE: warm-blooded

TYPICAL USE: riding, show

With its fine head, arched neck, and sloping shoulder, the Australian Pony oozes quality. Its good looks and presence are perhaps surprising, considering Indonesia's rather unprepossessing little Timor formed the foundation of the breed, but later infusions of outside blood refined Australia's pony to make it the equine supermodel it is today. The Timor was taken to Australia in 1803 —the country had no indigenous horses or ponies, so horses did not appear until the British First Fleet arrived in 1788, bringing with it equines.

Founding Sire

Later, several stallions exported to Australia were to have a profound effect: two Exmoors—Sir Thomas and Dennington Court— imported in the mid-1800s; a Hungarian stallion called

Bonnie Charlie; and Dyoll Graylight, a Welsh Mountain which arrived in 1911. This last is considered a founding sire.

The influence of the Welsh Mountain Pony and earlier infusions of Arabian blood are clear in the Australian Pony's concave profile and high-set, gaily carried tail.

Light Horses

The term "light horse" is used to describe any equine over 15 hh that is not one of the heavy draft breeds. A light horse should be well proportioned, with a narrow body and sloping shoulders and a greater distance from wither to ground than the length of the body. Like a golden thread running through a bolt of silk, the blood of the Arabian runs through the world's horse breeds. The Arabian's prototype was Horse Type 4, a refined creature standing around 14 hh with a concave profile and high-set tail. It came from Western Asia and was resistant to heat, especially the dry heat of the desert. Today's Caspian Horse is its nearest modern equivalent.

Horse Type 3 stood about 14.3 hh and was long and narrow in the body, goose-rumped with a long neck and long ears. It inhabited Central Asia and was, like Type 4, able to tolerate heat. Its nearest equivalent today is the Akhal-Teke.

A Pervasive Influence

The influence of the Arabian on the world's horse breeds cannot be underestimated. Without the Arabian, we would not have the Thoroughbred, with all its fire and might. The Arabian influence also extends to the Welsh Mountain Pony, which has its charming dished face and plays a part in the world's mighty warmbloods, the success story of the 1900s.

Perhaps the only modern horses largely uninfluenced by the Arabian are the Iberian kings, the Andalucian, and the Lusitano. But the Barb, an ancient breed similar to the Arabian that also played a part in the development of the Thoroughbred, was probably the ancestor of the Spanish horses. It, in turn, gave us the Lipizzaner, Vienna's dancing white horse.

Arabian blood has been used in the development of so many breeds, such as Russia's splendid Orlov Trotter and India's distinctive Kathiawari and Marwari. And as horses evolved, they changed the lives of humans across the entire planet. This is summed up beautifully by an anonymous poet:

Look back at our struggle for freedom,
Trace our present day's strength to its source,
And you'll find that man's pathway to glory
Is strewn with the bones of a horse.

BANKER (Shackleford)

TEMPERAMENT: calm, friendly

ORIGIN: North Carolina

SIMILAR BREEDS: Mustang

HEIGHT: 13–14.3 hh

COLOR: bay, brown, chestnut, dun

PERSONALITY TYPE: warm-blooded

TYPICAL USE: feral

These feral horses eke out an existence on the wild and barren islands off North Carolina's Outer Banks, of which one is called Shackleford—the breed is also sometimes known as the Shackleford Horse. It is most probably Spanish in origin. Although the British colonized these islands, Bankers display many characteristics of the Mustang. The isolated environment, however, **means that they have developed into a distinctive breed and remained pure.**

Heat and Hurricanes

The Banker has adapted to be able to survive on meager rations of marsh grass and scratching through sand to get to water supplies. It is exceptionally tough and hardy, with a good turn of speed, and unlike many feral breeds, is calm and friendly. They regularly experience—and survive—extreme heat, hurricanes, swarms of insects, and winter storms, but the breed is increasingly rare and there are very few left.

RIGHT

These feral horses are very hardy and have adapted to their environment exceptionally well, tolerating the extreme heat and cold of the climate.

FLORIDA CRACKER

TEMPERAMENT: willing, intelligent, spirited

ORIGIN: Florida

SIMILAR BREEDS: Mustang

HEIGHT: up to 15.2 hh

COLOR: all solid colors

PERSONALITY TYPE: warm-blooded

TYPICAL USE: ranching, Western riding

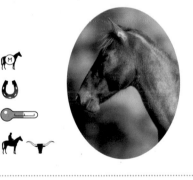

Florida's cowboys were nicknamed "crackers" because of the noise their whips made when they flicked them in the air, and the name was extended to the region's small, tough cattle and the agile little horses the cowboys used to work them. They trace back to the Spanish horses brought to the Americas in the 1500s; **however, because of the isolation of this part of the country, they developed into a distinct and separate breed.**

Lost Demand

The breed suffered a downturn in the 1930s. Cattle were moved from the Dust Bowl of the drought-stricken Great Plains into Florida during the Great Depression, and they brought with them a parasite called screwworm. Instead of herding and driving the cattle, the cowboys now had to rope them and treat them for the worm. Demand for the Cracker was lost as the cowboys instead turned to the bigger, stronger Quarter Horses. This breed was saved by a handful of ranchers who continued to breed and preserve the Florida Cracker for future generations.

MUSTANG

HEIGHT: 13–16 hh

COLOR: all colors

PERSONALITY TYPE:
warm-blooded

TYPICAL USE: ranching,
rodeo, Western

TEMPERAMENT: brave, spirited, independent

ORIGIN: United States

SIMILAR BREEDS: Florida Cracker

North America's wild horse gets its name from the Spanish word *mesteño*, or *monstenco*, meaning "wild" or "stray," and today's Mustang still roams free across the western United States in huge numbers. The Mustang is Spanish in heritage— descending from the horses brought to the New World in the 1500s by the conquistadores. Over the past 500 years, many other bloodlines have been introduced, including Arabian, French, and the German East Friesian, but the Spanish blood is still evident.

The East Friesian was introduced in the late 1800s, when the United States government bought the heavy horse from the Germans to pull artillery wagons. It is almost certain that some of these horses escaped and mated with the wild Mustang.

Captives to Freedom

The arrival of the horse changed the lives of the Native Americans, and as European settlers pushed farther and farther west, they brought more horses with them. These horses either escaped or were freed in Natve American raids, and the tribes themselves bartered with or captured horses, adding to the mix. Wild stallions would also tear down fencing to reach mares. The Native Americans learned to ride and passed on this skill.

In 1680 the Native Americans rebelled against Spanish rule, and the Europeans left behind thousands of their horses as they beat a quick retreat. Rather than round the horses up, the Native Americans left them to roam free.

Poor Conformation

Although the occasional dun with dorsal stripe gives away the Mustang's Spanish origins—tracing back to the little Sorraia, which in turn was to found the mighty Iberian horses—most of today's Mustangs have little or no Spanish blood. The lack of a monitored and selective breeding program means that the horse comes in a wide variety of colors, including all solid colors, as well as pintos and paints. Appaloosa markings, palominos, buckskins and blacks have largely been bred out, although some do still occur. Sorrel and bay are the most common colors.

RIGHT

The American Mustangs live in large feral herds and are descended from the original Spanish horses introduced by the conquistadores in the 1500s.

Some Mustangs may stand only 13 hh; others up to 16 hh. One of a staggering 18 hh has been recorded. Most are around 14.2 hh. They often have poor conformation, with a plain head, short neck, upright shoulder, and poor legs. They are, however, very tough and hardy, with innate intelligence and plenty of courage.

Living Symbol

By the year 1900 there were an estimated two million Mustangs in the United States. Previously, large numbers of feral horses had posed no problems. As the Western states became increasingly settled, however, the herds of Mustang were encroaching on grazing land for cattle, and the ranchers began to regard them as a pest.

A haphazard and indiscriminate form of culling began, and by 1926 the Mustang population had been halved—by 1970 only around 17,000 remained. To protect the horse, Congress labeled the Mustang a "living symbol of the historic and pioneer spirit of the West," and passed the Wild Free-Roaming Horse and Burro Act in 1971, putting it under federal protection. There are now an estimated 40,000 wild Mustangs, the welfare of which is overseen by the Bureau of Land Management.

The Kiger Herd

In 1977 a small herd of Mustangs was discovered in the remote area of Beatty's Butte, Oregon, which were strikingly similar in color and conformation and which bore the primitive markings. Testing by the Kentucky University found Spanish markers in their blood, suggesting that they carry the original Spanish genes. They are almost all dun, or one of its variations, and have markedly better conformation than the more common Mustangs. They are called Kiger Mustangs and have their own breed registry.

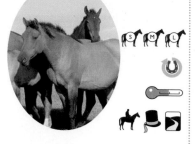

AMERICAN BASHKIR CURLY

HEIGHT: 13.3–16 hh

COLOR: all colors

PERSONALITY TYPE: warm-blooded

TYPICAL USE: riding, competition, Western, trail

TEMPERAMENT: calm, gentle, friendly

ORIGIN: United States

SIMILAR BREEDS: Morgan

The United States' popular "horse with a permanent wave," the Bashkir Curly is something of an enigma. It was first discovered in 1898, when a young man named Peter Damele and his father were riding in a mountain range near the town of Austin, in the remote high country of central Nevada, when they came across three horses with coats formed of tight ringlets all over their bodies. From that day on there have always been curly-coated horses on the Damele range, and many Bashkir Curly Horses in the United States can be traced back to the Damele herd.

Russian Mystery

But how did the horses get there in the first place? For some time it was thought that the Curlies traced back to the Russian breed called the Bashkir, which was perhaps taken to North America by Russian settlers in the 1700s and 1800s. But horses were not widely used by the Russians, and they were likely to be the more hardy Yakut, rather than Bashkir or its close relative, the Lokai, from Taijikistan, which also had a curly coat.

RIGHT

The origins of the American Bashkir Curly are unclear. The smaller Russian Bashkir Curly developed in the harsh Ural Mountains of Russia and is an ancient breed.

Horses with curly coats are nothing new—similar equines were depicted in art and statuary in early China as far back as A.D. 161. The origins of those in the United States may never be fully explained, but they have been embraced with great enthusiasm.

"Marcel" Wave

The American Bashkir Curly is intelligent, gentle, curious, calm, and affectionate. Its curly coats can be of three distinctive types: ringlets of several inches in length; the deep marcel wave; or crushed velvet, a soft, dense pile of curls. The preferred mane is kinky and can also be split, hanging on both sides of the neck. The tail may be ringlets or wavy. The breed sheds its coat in the summer, although it sometimes retains curls in its short, broad ears and has curly eyelashes. It is naturally gaited, moving at a smooth, running walk.

Fascinating Facts

American Bashkir Curly foals are born with thick, crinkly coats that are reminiscent of astrakhan and are very friendly and affectionate, characteristics the breed retains into full adulthood. People who are allergic to horses are often unaffected by the Bashkir Curly.

NOKOTA

TEMPERAMENT: intelligent, calm, reliable

ORIGIN: United States

SIMILAR BREEDS: Mustang

HEIGHT: 14.2–17 hh

COLOR: roan, gray, black, overo

PERSONALITY TYPE: warm-blooded

TYPICAL USE: competition, riding

Although it is received wisdom that all horses in the United States are Spanish in origin, having arrived with the conquistadores, the Sioux and Lakota Native Americans claimed to have horses before the Europeans arrived. Certainly the horses of the Northern Plains, which includes the vast grasslands of North Dakota, were Native American horses, and it is known that the tribes bred selectively, choosing only the best horses to continue the line—tribal chiefs were proud of their equines.

Evaded Capture

When Chief Sitting Bull surrendered to the U.S. Army in 1881 in Fort Buford, North Dakota, his horses were confiscated and sold on.

Some of them were sold to the Marquis de Mores, founder of the town of Medora, gateway to what is now the Theodore Roosevelt National Park in North Dakota. The Marquis allowed his horses to roam free, and although on his death in 1896 they were rounded up and sold, some of them evaded capture. When the national park boundaries

were fenced in during the late 1940s, small bands of wild horses were inadvertently enclosed within.

These came to be called the Nokota—a distinctive, separate breed with an exceptional bone structure, gentle disposition, and considerable athletic ability.

"All-Terrain Vehicle"

The Nokota is generally blue roan (a rare color but dominant in this breed), red roan, gray, or black, often with a bald (white) face and blue eyes. It has a straight or slightly concave profile, broad forehead, large, kind

ABOVE

The Nokota horse is a finely built, elegant animal of exceptional athletic ability, which with its tractable nature makes it a popular riding horse.

eye, and long, thick mane and tail. It stands between 14.2 and 17 hh and is large-boned and rangy.

The modern Nokota is sometimes referred to as the "equine all-terrain vehicle," reflecting its stamina, durability, and athleticism. Exceptionally sound, with good legs and solid feet, it is low-maintenance and requires minimum care. Nokota owners rarely go back to any other breed.

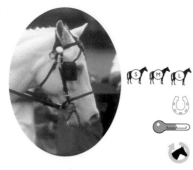

AMERICAN CREME AND AMERICAN WHITE

HEIGHT: 14–16.2 hh

COLOR: white or cream

PERSONALITY TYPE: warm-blooded

TYPICAL USE: all uses

TEMPERAMENT: generally good

ORIGIN: United States

SIMILAR BREEDS: varying breeds are used; color most important

Fascinating Facts

China not only has the most people in the world but also has the most horses—with 10,000,000.

LEFT

The American White must have pink skin pigment, and they generally have pale blue or amber eyes.

A horse called Old King, foaled in 1908, was to found a new breed, now known as the American Creme or American White. Old King was true white with pink skin; he had dark brown eyes, which he passed on to 90 percent of his progeny. He also passed on his color—when bred to a colored mare, he achieved 50 percent white and 50 percent colored, and up to 80 percent of his descendants throw white stock.

Breeding Legacy

Caleb and Hudson Thompson purchased Old King to found

a new breed then named the American Albino. Caleb and his wife, Ruth, promoted the horse through the White Horse Troupe, which performed such spectacular feats as a six-horse tandem ride, team jumping with the rider standing rather than sitting, high and broad jumping over cars or human "hurdles," and movements of the High School.

In 1937 the American Albino Horse Club was formed to record the descendants of Old King, who died of swamp fever in 1924. The

first horse registered was Old King's grandson, Snow Chief 2nd, who left a breeding legacy in his son, White Wings, who sired 108 foals, all but three being white.

Amber Eyes

Old King and his descendants are not albino, and the American White and American Creme have none of the "weaknesses" associated with albinos such as deafness or blindness, although they are sensitive to sunlight. The American White may have no slight pigmentation of hair and must have pink skin; all eye colors, including amber and very pale blue, are acceptable.

The Creme must have pink skin, which may take on a deeper tan color known as "pumpkin." Its coat may vary

from a very pale ivory to a deeper rich cream. Its mane and tail can range from pure white through to shades of cream to a cinnamon; its eyes are usually pale blue or pale amber.

APPALOOSA

TEMPERAMENT: docile, quiet, energetic

ORIGIN: Northwestern United States

SIMILAR BREEDS: Quarter Horse

HEIGHT: 14–15.2 hh

COLOR: variations of spotted

PERSONALITY TYPE: warm-blooded

TYPICAL USE: riding

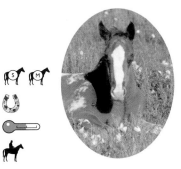

The Nez Perce tribe of the American Northwest was long famed for its superb horses and for their mastery of them. The explorer Meriwether Lewis noted in a diary entry from February 15, 1806: "Their horses appear to be of an excellent race; they are lofty, elegantly formed, active and durable . . . some of these horses are pied with large spots of white irregularly scattered and intermixed with black, brown, bay, or some other dark color." The Nez Perce were the only tribe to breed selectively, and the Appaloosa was the result.

ABOVE

The distinctive spotted coat patterning of the Appaloosa make them especially attractive. There are a number of different spot configurations in the breed.

Spotted Coat

Known as a "Palousie horse" —a reference to the Palouse River that flows through the region of north-central Idaho and eastern Washington from where the breed originated— the name was soon shortened to Appalousey, then Appaloosa, which was officially adopted in 1938. The Appaloosa is noted for its speed, stamina, and endurance—and for its striking coat patterns. There are 13 recognized coat base colors and six acceptable patterns—snowflake, leopard, spotted blanket, white blanket, marble , and frost – although the horses can exhibit a myriad combinations of base colors and patterns.

Good-looking

Spots aside, the Appaloosa is a good-looking creature. It has a small, neat head with a straight profile set on a long muscular neck, and deep chest with good, sloping shoulders. It has a short, compact back with rounded, muscular quarters. It has good, strong legs and hard feet. Its mane and tail are thin and sparse.

Its gentle temperament and kind nature makes it an excellent riding horse, and it has considerable speed and stamina. The Appaloosa also makes a genuine all-round family horse and is a suitable mount for the most nervous of novice riders. The breed's delightful disposition wins hearts as easily as its striking coat turns heads.

MORGAN

HEIGHT: 14.1–15.2 hh

COLOR: all solid colors

PERSONALITY TYPE: warm-blooded

TYPICAL USE: all uses

TEMPERAMENT: gentle, kind, intelligent, spirited

ORIGIN: United States

SIMILAR BREEDS: Standardbred, Quarter Horse, Tennessee Walking Horse

A Vermont schoolteacher and businessman named Justin Morgan acquired a colt foaled in 1789 and named him Figure. The colt's breeding is not clear—and is the subject of much speculation—but it was thought to be by a stallion called True Briton, a much-admired sire of the times. Figure was a handsome bay, with spectacular paces and a gentle disposition. He was also athletic, fast, and smart, with so much stamina, endurance, and ability that tales soon spread of the great "Justin Morgan horse."

and his abilities to his offspring. He lived to be 32 and served numerous mares during his long lifetime—and founded the United States' first light horse breed.

Gold Rush

Figure's legacy was carried by three of his sons, Sherman, Bulrush, and Woodbury, back to which all modern Morgans can be traced. And the breed grew with the emerging American nation. Morgans worked alongside

their owners clearing fields and forests; they provided transportation to the market and to church on Sundays. Figure's descendants pulled stagecoaches throughout New England. Young men from Vermont answered the call of the Gold Rush on the Morgan's back; the First Vermont Cavalry fought the Civil War mounted on Morgans; and Union General Sheridan rode a Morgan into battle. The cavalryman was only ever as good as his horse, and the Morgan was in high demand as a cavalry mount and artillery horse.

By the 1840s breeders in Vermont and New Hampshire were making a concerted effort to concentrate Morgan lines,

President's Mount

The Morgan Horse, as Figure was increasingly known, could outwalk, outrun, out-

trot, and outpull any other equine. Although he was not especially big, standing just over 14 hh, his beauty, presence, and good manners were deemed worthy for the President of the United States —in 1817 he carried President James Monroe on a muster-day parade ground in Montpelier, Vermont.

Figure was also prepotent, passing on his good looks

and by locating second-, third-, and fourth-generation descendants of little Figure, they established the foundations of the new breed. By the mid 1850s Morgans were selling for high prices and were gaining a fine reputation across the United States for their beauty, speed, agility, and temperament.

Foundation Breed

Morgans are exceptionally good-looking, with a refined, neat head with a slightly concave profile, broad forehead

tapering to a fine muzzle, large, kind eye, and small ears. Their neck is elegantly arched and set on well-angled shoulders, with a broad chest, short back, sloping croup, and deep, compact body. They have strong legs with flat, dense bone and round, hard hooves. Their proud bearing gives them presence as well as beauty.

But the Morgan was never merely a case of "Handsome is . . ."—the breed is athletic and enduring, with both speed and stamina, making it one of the world's most versatile equines. It can be used for almost any equestrian discipline, in either a Western or an English saddle, and is highly successful in driving, show jumping, and dressage.

It has also contributed to the formation of other American breeds, including the Quarter Horse and the Tennessee Walking Horse, to which it has passed on some of its spirit, its abilities, and its good looks.

Family Member

The Morgan remains popular today, with around 150,000 listed on the registry (first established in 1894) in all 50 U.S. states and around the world. A calm and sensible ride, it makes a superb all-rounder, and its charming nature and gentle disposition mean that its popularity is unlikely to wane. Those who have bought a Morgan say that they have not only purchased a horse, but they have also welcomed a new family member.

MORAB

HEIGHT: 14.3–16.1 hh

COLOR: all solid colors

PERSONALITY TYPE: warm-blooded

TYPICAL USE: competition, riding, show

TEMPERAMENT: intelligent, kind, spirited

ORIGIN: United States

SIMILAR BREEDS: Morgan, Arabian

As its name suggests, the Morab is a mixture of two of the most beautiful horse breeds: the ancient Arabian and the more recent Morgan. The coining of the name "Morab" is accredited to the newspaper tycoon William Randolph Hearst (1863–1951), who crossed his Morgan mares with the Arabian stallions Tsar and Ghazi specifically to create versatile horses for his California ranch. With the mix of the "desert" type horse, the Arabian, and the athletic ability of the Morgan, these horses were perfectly adapted to the rough terrain.

Unequaled Beauty

The Morab proved both incredibly versatile and hardy. The early remount horses used by the United States military were generally thought to be Morgans crossed with either Thoroughbreds—a breed which, of course, was founded by Arab stallions—or Arabians, and were renowned for their extreme endurance.

Considered to be one of the founding sires of the Morab breed is a registered Morgan stallion named Golddust, a palomino foaled in 1885 renowned for his golden color, his outstanding trotting record, and his unequaled beauty. He was by a registered Morgan stallion named Vermont Morgan and out of a daughter of an imported Arabian stallion Zilcaddie. Golddust sired 302 foals.

Bona Fide Breed

When William Randolph Hearst died in 1951, much of his breeding program—and almost the Morab—was lost. But American breeders were still producing Morab horses, and their cause was taken up by a woman named Martha Doyle Fuller, who produced Morabs for the show circuit, on which they excelled. Her daughter, Irene Miller, dubbed "Mrs. Morab," started the first breed register in 1973.

While some consider Morabs to be "half-Arabs" or "half-Morgans," they are a bona fide breed, as they pass on their distinguishing characteristics to their progeny. The accepted breed standard for today's Morab is 25/75, although the most common is 50/50—one Morgan parent and one Arabian, with the endurance, ability, and abiding beauty of both.

ABOVE

The Morab was developed through crossing Morgan horses with Arabs, the result generally displaying the best of both, as pictured.

PINTO

TEMPERAMENT: varied

ORIGIN: United States

SIMILAR BREEDS: Mustang

HEIGHT: all heights

COLOR: dual-colored

PERSONALITY TYPE: warm-blooded

TYPICAL USE: all uses

Fascinating Facts

A colored horse descended from two solid-colored parents of a usually solid-colored pure breed is called a "crop out," and is usually overo.

LEFT

Part-colored horses, called Pintos (or Paints), are further described by the configuration of their markings. This horse is a "tobiano."

Pictures of horses with broken coats—skewbald or piebald or tricolored—have appeared in art for centuries, suggesting that the "colored" horse is nothing new. There is evidence of colored coats in the wild horses of the Russian Steppes, which suggests the introduction of "pintos" or paints in Europe possibly as early as during the Roman Empire. The Europeans brought horses to North America, some of which escaped or were set free to form the wild herds, among them those with broken coats.

Magical Powers

These horses were in turn domesticated by the Native Americans, whose tribal chiefs prized the flashy skewbald or piebald above all others, believing them to have magical powers that would protect the chief in battle. The settlers, too, realized the value of the horse, and they were to use them in festivals and parades. Other breeds were later used to improve the stock and to produce larger animals, but the broken coat continued to appear. An 'American Paint' horse is a specific breed of pinto colouring that can trace its pedigree back to registered American Quarter Horse or Thoroughbred bloodlines.

Color Patterns

There are two recognized Pinto color patterns: tobiano (the most common) and overo. A tobiano appears to be white with large spots or splashes of color, originating from the head, chest, flank, and rump, often including the tail. Legs are generally white, and the white crosses the center of the back or topline, although the colored areas are larger than the white areas. Overo is a colored horse with jagged patches of white markings, usually around the side or belly and spreading toward the neck, tail, legs, and back. Its face is often white—the term "bald" was applied to a horse with a white face.

STANDARDBRED

HEIGHT: 15–16 hh

COLOR: bay, brown, black

PERSONALITY TYPE: warm-blooded

TYPICAL USE: racing, riding, show

TEMPERAMENT: docile, willing

ORIGIN: United States

SIMILAR BREEDS: Morgan

A new breed of only about 200 years old, all Standardbreds can be traced back to a horse named Hambletonian 10, foaled in 1849, and were required to be able to trot one mile in 2 minutes 30 seconds—giving them the name. One mile is still the standard distance of harness races. The first races were contested along roads, with men betting with each other about who had the quicker horse. The streets were cleared specifically to hold these races—many U.S. cities still have a Race Street.

BELOW

Many Standardbreds "pace" when they trot; this is when they move their legs on the same side of their body together, rather than in conventional diagonal pairs.

Amazing Turn of Foot

Hambletonian's great-grandsire was an English Thoroughbred called Messenger, foaled in 1780 and exported to the newly formed United States just after the American Revolution. The Standardbred still has much in common with the Thoroughbred, not simply its amazing turn of foot. It is not a big horse, standing around 15.2 hh, but has a longer body than the average Thoroughbred. But perhaps its biggest claim to fame is that it toppled the mighty Morgan as the American's favorite horse.

Trotting races—pacing was to come later—were a major sport in the United States in the 1800s, and the Morgan was the undisputed

ABOVE

The Standardbred is a trotting horse used primarily for harness racing and is one of the world's fastest trotting animals.

king of the racetrack. But it was to be a Standardbred that still holds the record—trotting the mile in 1 minute 55 seconds.

Two-Minute Mile

Although neither Messenger nor Hambletonian ever raced, they left behind a legacy of swift, agile horses that race-hungry Americans took to their hearts. Hambletonian left some 1,355 offspring, and his son, Dexter, set a new record for the time of 2 minutes 17 seconds.

Standardbred champions became household names— Flora Temple, the "bobtail nag" of Stephen Foster's much-loved song "Camptown Races" (1850); Goldsmith Maid, who won 350 heats in her career; world champions Maud S. and Nancy Hanks.

Pacers—horses that move laterally rather than diagonally, as in the trot— began to gain acceptance, and the sport's first two-minute mile was recorded in 1897 by the pacer Star Pointer. One of the most popular Standardbreds ever was a pacer called Dan Patch, which was also one of the

fastest, recording the first sub-two-minute mile on September 8, 1906.

Standardbreds can be either pacers or trotters—pacers are often referred to as "sidewheelers" and tend to be faster than trotters because of the smoothness of the action. A third gait, running, often manifests itself in harness racing, but the horse must return to its natural gait or face disqualification.

Competitive Nature

The Standardbred possesses the inherent good looks of the

Thoroughbred but is generally more muscular. The head is refined—the occasional suggestion of a Roman nose is sometimes seen, but infusions of Morgan and Arabian blood have made this increasingly rare—and set on a medium-length neck and sloping shoulders. The back is long; the hindquarters are muscular but sleek. The Standardbred has good, strong legs and hard feet.

It is competitive, which makes it so successful on the racetrack, but willing and calm with a kind nature. Bay, brown, and black are the most dominant colors, although solid colors occur.

Million-Dollar Prize

Although Standardbreds are used for riding (both Western and English) and show, harness racing continues to be the breed's primary occupation. There is even a race named the Hambletonian, a prestigious annual

event for three-year-old Standardbreds that is the most famous North American trotting race. The Hambletonian prize is a grand $1.2 million. Two races for pacers, the Meadowlands Pace, held in Meadowlands,

New Jersey, and the North America Cup in Woodbine, Ontario, Canada, both carry a $1 million prize. In each event the winning owner receives half the prize money, the rest is divided between the next four finishers.

Fascinating Facts

The British racehorse Humorist, who won the English Derby in the early 1920s, should never have been able to race. He died shortly after the Derby, having suffered from a tubercular lung condition that led to a massive lung hemorrhage.

RACKING HORSE

HEIGHT: 15.2 hh

COLOR: all colors, including spotted

PERSONALITY TYPE: warm-blooded

TYPICAL USE: riding, showing

TEMPERAMENT: docile, kind, friendly

ORIGIN: United States

SIMILAR BREEDS: Tennessee Walking Horse

Neither a pace nor a trot, the "rack" is an exceptionally comfortable, bilateral, four-beat gait—sometimes known as the "single-foot" because only one foot strikes the ground at any time. The Racking Horse became popular on the vast plantations in the South before the Civil War, when it was realized that the horse could be ridden comfortably for several hours because of this smooth, natural gait. The fact that the horse was also very beautiful did nothing to harm its reputation.

State Horse

The Racking Horse's unique gait is natural—that is, it is inherited rather than learned. The horse moves swiftly, appearing to jump from one foot to another while its head remains still, but its shoulders and quarters are very active. It is an easy gait to sit into for beginners, while veterans appreciate its smoothness and athleticism.

Determined to preserve and promote the Racking Horse as a distinctive breed, an Alabama businessman

named Joe Bright was instrumental in forming the Racking Horse Breeders' Association of America

ABOVE
These beautiful horses have a very fast, very smooth, natural gait called the "rack," which makes them extremely comfortable to ride.

(RHBAA), established in 1971; in 1975 the Racking Horse was declared to be Alabama's state horse.

Enchanting Breed

The breed is thought to have its roots in the Tennessee

Walking Horse, to which it bears a resemblance. It is noble and elegant, with a refined head, long, graceful neck, sloping shoulders, full flanks, and muscular quarters. It has fine legs and round, hard feet. As well as being undeniably beautiful, with a graceful and noble bearing, the Racking Horse has an enchanting nature, being kind, calm, and very people-friendly—all traits that make it the ideal mount for even the most nervous beginners.

To be accepted into the RHBAA registry, the horse must first demonstrate the unique natural gaits that give the breed its name.

PALOMINO

TEMPERAMENT: varied

ORIGIN: United States

SIMILAR BREEDS: Morgan, Quarter Horse, Saddlebred, Tennessee Walking Horse

HEIGHT: 14–17 hh

COLOR: all shades of gold, with white mane and tail

PERSONALITY TYPE: warm-blooded

TYPICAL USE: varied

The color of a newly minted gold coin, the Palomino has been prized by emperors, kings, and queens and was the subject of Greek mythology and great art alike. Queen Isabella of Spain (1451–1504) was a huge fan of the Palomino—the color is still sometimes called "Isabella"—and pale golden horses feature in Sandro Botticelli's celebrated painting *The Adoration of the Magi* (c. 1478–82). During the Crusades, the Emir Saladin presented Richard the Lionheart with a Palomino horse.

Royal Choice

The history of the palomino color will probably never be known. Horses of an iridescent gold occur in the Barb, although palomino Arabians and Thoroughbreds are not accepted by their respective registries. The gold horse with ivory-colored mane and tail appears in ancient tapestries and paintings of Europe and Asia, as well as in Japanese and Chinese art of past centuries. Isabella I kept a full 100 of these glorious creatures, and

only members of the royal family and nobles of the household were permitted to own one. It is well documented that Isabella sent a Palomino stallion and five mares to New Spain, which was to become Mexico; from there the golden horse spread into Texas and California.

Shades of Gold

The ideal color of a Palomino is that of a new 14-carat-gold coin, but shades can range from light through to medium to dark gold. The mane and tail should be pure white, ivory, or silver, although up to 15 percent dark or sorrel hair is permitted. The skin is usually

gray, black, brown, or mottled, without underlying pink skin or spots, except on the face or legs. The eyes are black, brown, or hazel.

There are three basic divisions of Palominos (which is a "color" breed, rather than a true breed). The stock type is Western horses, predominantly represented by Quarter Horses, while the Golden American Saddlebred is, of course, typically represented by Saddlebreds, and the pleasure type is exemplified by Morgan, Arabian, and Tennessee Walking Horses.

Fascinating Facts

Cowboy actor and entertainer Roy Rogers' horse Trigger was a Palomino and as famed as his owner as a star on the television and silver screen. Another well-known Hollywood Palomino was Mr. Ed, the "talking" horse of the 1960s television series with the same name.

ABOVE
Palomino horses, with their beautiful gold coloring and pale mane and tail, are highly sought after.

QUARTER HORSE

HEIGHT: 14–15.3 hh

COLOR: all solid colors

PERSONALITY TYPE: warm-blooded

TYPICAL USE: Western, riding, rodeo, ranching

TEMPERAMENT: gentle, brave, intelligent

ORIGIN: United States

SIMILAR BREEDS: Mustang

aid to be the United States' oldest horse breed, the Quarter Horse is thought to have its roots in the Chickasaw ponies acquired from the Native Americans, short, blocky little equines of Spanish descent containing Arab, Barb, and Andalusian blood. It is a common misconception that the "quarter" part of the breed's name denotes the proportion of Thoroughbred blood—although it was certainly used later to improve and refine the Quarter Horse. In fact, the name refers to the distance—a quarter of a mile—over which the horse can sprint.

Heavy Wagers

Horse racing, sprinting over a short distance, was very popular in the 1600s, and the fastest competitors became known as Celebrated American Running Horses by the British colonists. The original blocky little horse, when crossed with the English Thoroughbred, was unsurpassed. Compact but heavily muscled, the chunky little equine could sprint a short distance from a standstill, outrunning any other breed.

These first races were held in Enrico County, Virginia, with two horses racing against each other down town streets and country lanes and across flat pastures. Sizable prizes were on offer, and there was extensive heavy betting—disagreements between both owners and gamblers were common. Some of the grander Southern plantations are said to have changed hands as a result of these head-to-head matches.

Cow Sense

As more Thoroughbreds were brought to North America and the breed became more popular, the little Quarter Horse fell out of popularity. Distance racing—at which the Thoroughbred excelled—overtook the

ABOVE

Quarter Horses are one of the world's most popular breeds, in great part due to their huge versatility and intelligent, calm natures.

shorter sprint races, and oval racecourses were built specifically for the new sport. But the Quarter Horse had other talents. As a stockhorse,

it was excellent—it could gallop from a standstill, was easy to stop, and could turn on a dime. The Quarter Horse also possessed an innate "cow sense," an ability to second-guess and outmaneuver cattle. As vast cattle ranches spread across the plains in the 1800s, as settlers and pioneers moved west, the Quarter Horses went with them.

Breeding Lines Lost

Despite its widespread and increasing popularity, the Quarter Horse had no registry or breed standard until 1940, when the American Quarter Horse Association (AQHA) was established in Texas. Until then there was little or no effort made to preserve the Quarter Horse as a breed; no records were kept, and as the custom of the day was to name the horse after its owner, valuable breeding lines were lost as stallions were sold on and their names changed. A horse named Steel Dust, however, foaled in 1843, was to have a profound effect on the breed, with his progeny being called Steel Dust Horses.

Versatile Performers

Today's Quarter Horse is still the butty little creature of old, heavily muscled and compact, with a neat, attractive head set on a muscular neck and sloping shoulders, and short-coupled with powerful hindquarters and fine, strong legs. It is intelligent but kind and easy to handle and very versatile. Quarter Horses are still raced and used for ranching, but they are also good show jumpers, dressage performers, and rodeo horses.

There are 16 recognized colors of American Quarter Horse, including the most prominent color of sorrel (brownish red). The others are bay, black, brown, buckskin, chestnut, dun, red dun, gray, grullo, palomino, red roan, blue roan, bay roan, perlino (cream coat, darker mane and tail and blue eyes), and cremello.

There are now believed to be around 4.4 million Quarter Horses in the world, and the breed continues to grow in popularity.

Fascinating Facts

As they are highly trainable, Quarter Horses are also used in moviemaking—the Robert Redford movie *The Horse Whisperer* (1998) featured 17 of them.

BELOW

Quarter Horses generally have excellent conformation, being muscular through their frame with strong legs and feet. They are generally not very tall.

COLORADO RANGER

HEIGHT: 14–16 hh-plus

COLOR: spotted and solid

PERSONALITY TYPE:
warm-blooded

TYPICAL USE: ranching, riding

TEMPERAMENT: intelligent, calm

ORIGIN: United States

SIMILAR BREEDS: Mustang

During a world tour in 1878 following his presidency, General Ulysses S. Grant visited Sultan Abdul Hamid of Turkey, who presented him with two stallions on the day of his departure. One was an Arabian named Leopard; the other a Barb named Linden Tree. Both are listed in the studbooks of the Arabian Horse Club and the American Jockey Club and were to be the foundation sires of the Colorado Ranger, a breed that is far more than just a color or coat pattern.

which he proposed to call the Americo Arab. He was partly successful—using the two desert stallions, over a period of 14 years he did produce a strain of "Huntingdon horses," more than 100 in all.

Leopard and Linden Tree, although aged, had one more breeding season with another friend of General Grant's, Colonel Colby, and they left an indelible impression on his native mares—a new breed of cow horse that came to be known as the Colorado Ranger.

Although many Rangers are spotted—some 90 percent are also registered with the Appaloosa Horse Club— solid colors are acceptable.

Two Founding Sires

These two horses reached Virginia in 1879, where a friend of General Grant's, a respected horseman named Randolph Huntingdon, saw the stallions as the ideal opportunity to perfect a new breed of light harness horse,

Appaloosa Links

Today's Colorado Ranger must be able to trace back to two stallions—Patches (a direct descendant of Leopard and Linden Tree) and Max (a spotted son of the renowned Waldron Leopard). They were both acquired by a

horse breeder named Mike Ruby in the early 1930s, and he kept meticulous records of which sires he put with which mares, their offspring, and their coloring. He formed the Colorado Ranger Horse Association in 1935.

The horse has an attractive head with alert, mobile ears, a good length of neck, deep, wide chest, compact back, and powerful hindquarters. The overall impression of the breed is solid, muscular, and strong.

ROCKY MOUNTAIN

TEMPERAMENT: docile, gentle, intelligent

ORIGIN: United States

SIMILAR BREEDS: Mustang

HEIGHT: 14.2–16 hh

COLOR: all solid colors; little or no white markings

PERSONALITY TYPE: warm-blooded

TYPICAL USE: trail, pack, riding, endurance, competition

Legend has it that one day in the 1890s, a handsome horse with striking chocolate-colored coat and flaxen mane and tail stepped out of the Appalachian Mountains in eastern Kentucky. This may be myth or romanticism, but this horse, a gaited colt, came to be called the Rocky Mountain horse and was the foundation sire of a popular and enduring breed. For some years the people of the region used this colt on their own saddle mares to produce a special strain of utility horse—the region's best-kept secret.

the field, herd cattle, travel across the steep and rugged trails, and drive the carriage to church on Sundays. In short, it had to earn its keep.

The emerging breed, the Rocky Mountain, answered every call.

Fascinating Facts

Jumping is not a natural activity for horses and left to their own devices—like most creatures—they are more likely to go around obstructions.

Family Horse

For the rural inhabitants of eastern Kentucky, the horse was essential, not a luxury. Doctors, mailmen, traveling preachers, and hundreds of others relied on horses as their means of transportation, and the "Rocky Mountain" horse was ideal. Sure-footed and easygoing, the horse had an exceptionally smooth and comfortable gait, and even more importantly, stamina. For the one-horse family, the equine had to be versatile and strong; it was used to plow

Longevity

A horse breeder named Sam Tuttle is credited with preserving and continuing the Rocky Mountain Horse for the first 75 years in the 1900s. Gaited horses were becoming less popular with the introduction of good roads and better means of

RIGHT

The Rocky Mountain Horse is a relatively young breed that reflects Spanish characteristics, especially in the shape of its head, as seen in this picture.

travel, but horses were still used in the more remote areas. Even when times were hard, Sam Tuttle kept a herd of Rocky Mountain Horses and continued to produce them, most famously from a sire named Tobe. This

stallion and his offspring were in great demand.

Tobe continued to breed until the age of 34 and died at 37— he passed his longevity to his progeny, as well as his sweet nature and easy gaits.

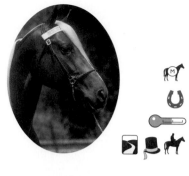

TENNESSEE WALKING HORSE

HEIGHT: 15.2 hh

COLOR: all solid colors

PERSONALITY TYPE: warm-blooded

TYPICAL USE: pleasure, trail, show

TEMPERAMENT: gentle, calm, easygoing

ORIGIN: Tennessee, United States

SIMILAR BREEDS: Morgan

That the Morgan played a huge part in the development of the Tennessee Walking Horse is beyond doubt, but several other breeds also influenced it, including the now-extinct Narragansett Pacer, Thoroughbred, Standardbred, and Saddlebred. These horses were taken to what was known as the Middle Basin of Tennessee by settlers from neighboring states such as Virginia and the Carolinas. The breed that was developed possessed an exceptional gait—the swift and smooth "running walk," for which it was to become renowned.

Fascinating Facts

If a patient with a back problem does not want to give up their riding, doctors with some horse knowledge will refer them to gaited horses—especially the Tennessee Walking Horse.

Gliding Motion

The running walk is inherited rather than learned—it cannot be taught to a horse that does not possess it naturally. It is a square, four-beat gait with a gliding motion, with the head bobbing in time. Some Walkers are known to snap their teeth in time, too, which is not considered a fault.

The horse overstrides, placing its back hoof ahead of the print of its fore hoof. It can travel at speeds of up to 12 miles (19 km) an hour and sustain them for long distances. The Tennessee Walking Horse is adapted to beginners and experienced riders alike, as this gait is supremely comfortable. The Walker also has two other notable gaits: the flat-foot walk, which is slow and

RIGHT

The magnificent Tennessee Walker is most famous for its smooth running walk, a fast, comfortable gait that is inherited rather than learned.

even, and the canter, a refined gallop with a slow, comfortable, rolling motion (sometimes known as the "rocking-chair gait"). All three are easy on the rider.

Gentle Nature

The greatest contributor to the Tennessee Walking Horse was a black stallion named Allan, with both Morgan and Standardbred lines—there was certainly some Hambletonian blood in him, from the foundation sire of the Standardbred. He passed on his considerable good looks, gentle nature, and easy gaits.

The registry was formed in 1935, and the Tennessee Walking Horse remains popular to this day because of its beauty and grace.

SADDLEBRED

TEMPERAMENT: calm, gentle, kind

ORIGIN: United States

SIMILAR BREEDS: Mustang, Morgan, Standardbred

HEIGHT: 15–17 hh

COLOR: most solid colors

PERSONALITY TYPE: warm-blooded

TYPICAL USE: riding, showing

When Paul Revere made his famous "Midnight Ride" from Boston to Lexington in 1775 at the start of the American Revolution to warn of the advance of the British Army, he is thought to have been astride a Narragansett Pacer, a horse that had great importance in the development of the Saddlebred. In those early years horses were vital to the pioneers who settled in Kentucky, and good saddle horses were highly valued. Denmark, the sire who would form the foundation of the Saddlebred, was foaled in 1839.

Warhorse

By the time of the Mexican War in 1846, the Saddlebred was well established as a breed. Prized for its beauty and utility—like the Narragansett, it was a pacer rather than a trotter— the Saddlebred also found fame in the show ring. The first "national" horse show was held in 1885 as part of the St. Louis Fair, and Saddlebreds featured prominently.

LEFT

The American Saddlebred is an especially flashy show horse that moves with an extravagant action and is one of the most exciting horses to watch.

The American Civil War saw the Saddlebred become the cavalry mount of choice for the Confederates, as the horses' extreme endurance meant that they could be marched for hours, and their bravery kept them calm under enemy fire. Generals on both sides were mounted on Saddlebreds; Stonewall Jackson rode a Saddlebred, while on the Union side, Ulysses S. Grant also had a Saddlebred as a mount. Confederate General Robert E. Lee's Traveler, perhaps the most famous horse of the war, had Saddlebred lines, his sire being the Thoroughbred Gray Eagle and his dam a mare of mixed breeding.

Worldwide Fame

Lee's Traveler possessed a smooth rack, and after the Civil War, as the soldiers disbanded, they took their Saddlebreds with them across the nation. Today the United States' superb horse breed is found in all 50 states, as well as Canada, Europe, Scandinavia, Australia, and Japan. After the Thoroughbred, it is the most popular horse breed in South Africa.

The first American Saddlebred Horse Association was established in Louisville, Kentucky, in 1891, to ensure this beautiful gaited horse continues to grow and improve.

MISSOURI FOX TROTTER

HEIGHT: 14–16 hh

COLOR: most solid colors

PERSONALITY TYPE: warm-blooded

TYPICAL USE: riding, pleasure, trail, endurance, showing

TEMPERAMENT: kind, quiet, gentle

ORIGIN: Missouri and Arkansas

SIMILAR BREEDS: Mustang, Saddlebred, Standardbred

A pleasure and utility horse, the Missouri Fox Trotter was developed in the Ozarks of Missouri and Arkansas as a breed that could carry a heavy load for long hours at a swift, ground-covering gait that was comfortable for the rider and sustainable for the horse. Neither a pacer nor a trotter, the horse uses its legs diagonally, walking with its front feet and trotting with its hind, the back foot overstepping the print of the front. This shuffling gait is sure-footed, and the rear feet slide rather than jolt, so it is extremely comfortable.

Morgan Blood

As early settlers moved into the Ozarks across the Mississippi River from Kentucky, Virginia, and Tennessee, they brought with them their own horses, a mix of Morgan, Thoroughbred, and Arabian with some other bloodlines. The horses were primarily for racing, but they became a utility breed, the broken gait being easy on both the horse and rider.

The Alsup family, who settled in the Ozarks before the Civil War, were noted

---

LEFT

The Missouri Fox Trotter is another of the gaited American breeds and produces an even, balanced gait making it comfortable when riding over distance.

---

horse breeders and had a sire named Bremmer, known not only for his good looks and racing prowess but also for his ability to pass both qualities on to his offspring. From the Kissee family came a great sire named Diamond; from the Dunns a prolific stallion named Old Skip.

Sweet Nature

These horses all played a role in developing the Missouri Fox Trotter. A line from the stallion Denmark, so influential in the Saddlebred, bred some outstanding fox-trotting horses through a sire named Chief, who left many superb progenies. The Missouri Fox Trotter gained a reputation for its ground-covering gait, its beauty, and its sweet disposition.

The Missouri Fox Trotting Horse Breeders' Association was formed in 1948, but all of its records were wiped out in a fire. Reestablished in 1955, the MFTHBA has since made great progress —by the beginning of 2005 some 83,000 horses had been registered.

CANADIAN

HEIGHT: 14–16 hh

COLOR: black, dark brown, bay, chestnut

PERSONALITY TYPE: warm-blooded

TYPICAL USE: riding, harness, competition

TEMPERAMENT: kind, sensible, sociable

ORIGIN: Canada

SIMILAR BREEDS: Arab, Saddlebred

Canada's little-known national treasure is based on French horses (such as Bretons) sent to the New World in the 1600s by France's "Sun King," Louis XIV (1638–1715). These horses were probably a mixture of Arabian, Andalusian, and Barb, the heritage of which can still be seen in today's Canadian breed. With little outside influence, the Canadian, or Cheval Canadien, evolved into a distinct breed, having to endure adverse weather, scarce food, and hard work, and became strong and tough, impervious to harsh weather, and easy keepers.

Iron Horse

These attributes earned the breed the nickname "Canada's little iron horse;" it spread into the United States, and by the mid 1800s numbered around 150,000. It was used to improve the strength and hardiness of some of the American breeds and was exported out of Canada to work in the sugar plantations in the West Indies; to the United States for the Civil War; and to South Africa for the Second Boer War (1899–1902).

Almost ironically, the number of Canada's "national treasure" dwindled rapidly in Canada. By the 1870s there were fewer than 400 Canadians left; with the advent of mechanization, the breed almost became extinct.

All-Rounder

Realizing the plight of the Canadian, enthusiasts banded together—the first studbook was produced in 1886, and the Canadian Horse Breeders Association was formed in 1895. A new studbook, with improved information, was started in 1907. In 1913 a breeding project was set up at Cap Rouge in Quebec. There are now thought to be almost 3,000 Canadian Horses.

The Canadian is a good-looking all-rounder, with chiseled head, arched neck, and the rippling mane and tail reminiscent of its Spanish ancestry. It has strong legs with plenty of bone and exceptionally good feet. It is generally long-lived, and the mares are fertile into their twenties or older. In short it is entitled to its moniker—the little iron horse.

Fascinating Facts

The Canadian Horse was adopted as a national symbol on April 30, 2002.

RIGHT AND BELOW

These horses are renowned for their excellent conformation and natural athleticism, which combined with a sensible brain, makes them good competition horses.

AZTECA

HEIGHT: 14.2–15.3 hh

COLOR: all solid colors

PERSONALITY TYPE: warm-blooded

TYPICAL USE: rodeo, bullfighting, competition

TEMPERAMENT: lively, cheerful, obedient

ORIGIN: Mexico

SIMILAR BREEDS: Quarter Horse, Andalusian

Mexico's national breed was developed only in the 1970s, but it is safe to say that it has an enduring appeal. Developed using Andalusian stallions on Quarter Horses and Criollos, the aim was to produce a breed with speed, athleticism, stamina, and power. Designed to be the ultimate all-rounder, it was also to be handsome, obedient, trainable, and brave. The ideal was reached in the Azteca—the first "full" Azteca stallion was named Casarejo, born in Texcoco in 1972.

be the foundation sire of a breed with intelligence, agility, and versatility.

To watch an Azteca at work or play is to see equine poetry in motion—its natural balance and ability to collect under itself enables it to leap sideways in the blink of an eye to avoid the horns of a bull. The Azteca excels in the bullring under the Mexican *rejonero* (a type of bullfighter) or in the *charreria* (rodeo) and naturally displays the "airs above the ground," or *haute école*, of its distant cousin, the Lipizzaner.

Natural Athlete

Casarejo was the offspring of a Spanish stallion, Ocultado, and a Quarter Horse mare named Americana. He was to

Third Generation

The Azteca has all the exceptional beauty of both the Quarter Horse and the Andalusian. Its head is lean

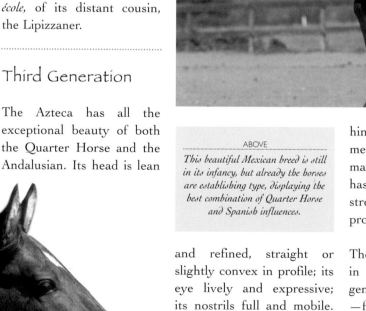

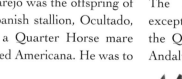

and refined, straight or slightly convex in profile; its eye lively and expressive; its nostrils full and mobile. Its neck is gracefully arched, with well-developed shoulders and deep, wide chest. It has a short, straight back with muscular

hindquarters. Its tail is medium-set, and like its mane, full and abundant. It has long, slender legs with strong joints and well-proportioned feet.

The studbook was formed in 1992, and the third generation is the pure Azteca —five-eighths Andalusian and three-eighths Quarter Horse, or vice versa. Some cutting-horse enthusiasts think that this will be a better cross—only time will tell.

MANGALARGA MARCHADOR

HEIGHT: 14.2–16 hh

COLOR: predominantly gray, bay, chestnut; other solid colors

TEMPERAMENT: intelligent

PERSONALITY TYPE: warm-blooded

ORIGIN: Brazil

TYPICAL USE: riding, competition, endurance

SIMILAR BREEDS: Peruvian Paso, Paso Fino

Its name is enchanting; the breed sublime. Brazil's national equine is founded on an Alter-Real stallion named Sublime, presented by the Emperor of Brazil, Pedro I (1798–1834), to his friend Gabriel Francisco Junqueira, an established horse breeder and owner of Campo Alegre, in 1812. By putting him to mares of Spanish and Barb descent, the Mangalarga Marchador was produced—the first part of the name comes from the stud, Hacienda Mangalarga, which subsequently bought and promoted the "Sublimes," and the second from the horse's gait, the *marcha*.

Performance Testing

Many of those first mares possessed a fast, smooth, ambling gait, which they passed on to their offspring. The Mangalarga Marchador's natural gaits are walk, *marcha*, and canter. There are two *marchas*. The Marcha Picada is a lateral four-beat gait with moments of triple-hoof support, as also found in two of the Paso Fino's gaits—the Paso Corto and Paso Largo. The Marcha Batida is a diagonal four-beat gait also showing moments of triple-hoof support.

The first registry for the Mangalarga Marchador was established in 1949 to promote and continue the breed. To be accepted, horses must pass rigorous performance testing.

World Record

The Mangalarga Marchador's Spanish origins are clear—it is a horse of considerable beauty and possesses the agility, endurance, and stamina of its ancient ancestry. There is little to which the Mangalarga Marchador cannot turn its hoof. Its agility makes it an excellent cow horse; its athleticism is adaptable to rodeo; its stamina to endurance riding and cross-country; and it possesses a natural jumping ability. It excels in the show ring, where its flying gaits, innate presence, and natural *brio* make it the horse to watch.

Fascinating Facts

The Mangalarga Marchador features in the *Guinness Book of Records* for an endurance ride of 8,694 miles (13,992 km), undertaken by two Brazilian men, which took one and a half years and was completed in 1994.

LEFT

This Spanish-influenced breed is beautiful, intelligent, athletic, and has natural flashy gaits, making it a winner in the show ring and on the ranch.

CAMPOLINA

HEIGHT: from 14 hh; no upper height limit

COLOR: all colors

PERSONALITY TYPE: warm-blooded

TYPICAL USE: riding, competition, harness

TEMPERAMENT: lively, kind, trainable

ORIGIN: Brazil

SIMILAR BREEDS: Mangalarga Marchador, Peruvian Paso

A beautiful, dark gray colt named Monarca is considered the foundation sire of the Campolina, Brazil's other equine breed (alongside the Mangalarga Marchador). It is named after its developer, Cassiano Antonio de Silva Campolina, who started the breed at his stud, Fazenda Tanque, in 1857. It was not until 1870, however, when Campolina was given a black mare named Medéia, that his eponymous breed really began. Medéia was bred to a pure Andalusian stallion, and Monarca was the result, serving 25 years in the herd of the Fazenda Tanque.

Elegant and Active

Cassiano Campolina bred Monarca to mainly Criollo mares but was determined to produce a horse with beauty, presence, and smooth, natural gaits. He used several other stallions, including an Anglo-French sire named Menelike;

a quarter-Clydesdale named Golias; Teffer, a Holsteiner; Yanke Prince, an American Saddlebred; and Rio Verde, a Mangalarga Marchador. The studbook for the Campolina Horse was closed in 1934, and no other outside breeds were permitted to be used.

Like the Mangalarga Marchador, the Campolina gaits include the *marcha picada* (lateral) and the *marcha batida* (diagonal). The breed standard for the gaits demand that they are natural, with triple support (that is, three hooves hitting the ground at the same time), comfortable, elegant, regular, and active.

Regal Bearing

But the Campolina also possesses a four-beat gait known as the *marcha verdadair* —the true march. At this powerful gait it can maintain speeds of 6–8 mph (9.6– 12.8km/h). The Campolina combines the stirring flashy gaits of the Mangalarga Marchador with the nobility and grace of the Andalusian, as well as the natural exuberance of the Peruvian Paso. It has the noble head and regal bearing of its Spanish ancestors, as well as the flash and fire of the more recent South American equine kings.

PASO FINO

TEMPERAMENT: lively, responsive

ORIGIN: Central and South America

SIMILAR BREEDS: Mangalarga Marchador, Peruvian Paso

HEIGHT: 13–15 hh

COLOR: all solid colors

PERSONALITY TYPE: warm-blooded

TYPICAL USE: riding, harness, showing

These are the horses with the "fine walk"—*los caballos de paso fino*—and never has a name been more fitting. The Paso Fino is a descendant of the horses brought to the Americas by the conquistadores; finding a continent with no horses, on their second journey to the New World, they brought with them their own, a mixture of Barb, Andalusian, and Spanish Jennet. The Jennet had a smooth, comfortable gait, which it passed on to its progeny. Today's Paso Fino has the proud carriage, grace, and elegance of its forebears.

Selective Breeding

Centuries of selective breeding by those who colonized the Caribbean and Latin America produced the Paso Fino, which flourished initially in Puerto Rico and Colombia and later in other Latin American countries. Awareness of the breed did not reach North America until after the Second World War, when servicemen stationed in Puerto Rico began exporting the horses home, where they were prized for their beauty and supremely comfortable gaits. The Paso Fino gait is performed at three forward speeds—at each the rider

should appear virtually motionless in the saddle, and there should be no perceptible up and down motion of the horse's croup.

Natural Cadence

The Classic Fino is a gait with full collection, with very slow forward speed. The footfall is extremely rapid, while the steps and extension are exceedingly short. The Paso Corto is of moderate speed, with ground-covering but unhurried steps, executed with medium extension and stride. The Paso Largo is the fastest speed, executed with a longer extension and stride but without losing any natural cadence.

With its lively but controlled spirit, natural gait, and responsive attitude, coupled with the beauty and presence of its Spanish heritage, the Paso Fino is a rare and desirable equine partner. It seems to take pleasure in the company of people and thrives not only in the show ring but also on trail and endurance rides, in dressage, rodeo, gymkhana, and as a working stockhorse.

ABOVE

These are amongst the most elegant of the gaited horses and are in high demand, due to their comfortable stride and obliging character.

Fascinating Facts

The Paso Fino is the oldest true native breed of horse in the Western Hemisphere.

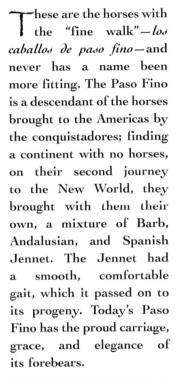

FALABELLA

HEIGHT: 30 in. (76 cm)

COLOR: all colors

PERSONALITY TYPE: warm-blooded

TYPICAL USE: show

TEMPERAMENT: gregarious, gentle, docile

ORIGIN: Argentina

SIMILAR BREEDS: Thoroughbred, Arabian

Argentina's most famous equine is extremely rare—there are only 900 registered—and its origins are open to debate. One thing is beyond doubt: the Falabella is a miniature horse, not a pony. It should look like a scaled-down model of a Thoroughbred or Arabian, with no pony characteristics at all. Although they tend to grow thick coats in the winter, in the summer they should have the sleek coat of their larger counterparts and stand no taller than 30 in. (76 cm).

Horse of the Pampas

It is thought that miniature horses, perhaps by a mutation, wandered the Argentinaian pampas for centuries. Perhaps in order to survive their harsh environment—the pampas was unprotected and whipped by fierce winds called El Pampero—and due to continual inbreeding, these horses underwent genetic changes to produce the tough little equine we know today.

The breed was developed by the Falabella family, who first saw the miniature horses in the herds run by the Mupache Native Americans around Buenos Aires in the mid-1800s. Enchanted by the little creatures, they sought to improve the breed and further refine the shape of the animal, producing an equine that stood less than 40 in. (102 cm) at the shoulder.

Harmonious Form

Thanks to Señor Falabella and his descendants, the breed that takes their name retains its unique charm. They used carefully selected infusions of Thoroughbred, Shetland, Welsh, and Criollo blood to ensure the little horses kept their harmonious form, and reduced the upper height limit to 30 in. (76 cm) from the previous 34 in. (86 cm).

Gregarious and docile, gentle and intelligent, the Falabella breeds true, passing these characteristics to its offspring. It is a good-looking equine, with clean, straight legs and good feet; an attractive, intelligent head; and fine, silky hair. It is also long-lived, often reaching 40–45 years old.

LEFT

The Falabella has the conformation of a scaled-down horse, rather than a pony, and is typically fine limbed.

CRIOLLO

TEMPERAMENT: fearless, independent, affectionate

ORIGIN: Argentina

SIMILAR BREEDS: Mustang

HEIGHT: 13.3–15 hh

COLOR: predominantly dun, chestnut, bay, gray, roan, black

PERSONALITY TYPE: warm-blooded

TYPICAL USE: riding, herding, polo

Argentina's king of the pampas, the Criollo, was originally feral, the result of Spanish horses of Andalusian and Barb descent that were left to roam free by the conquistadores for around four centuries, adapting to their new world and way of life. Life in the pampas—the grassland area around the delta of the Rio de la Plata —was tough, and only the hardiest of these feral horses survived. They in turn bred with equines brought by travelers from Brazil, Chile, and Uruguay, with Portuguese and Dutch blood later introduced via Brazil.

One-Man Horse

The Criollo, or Creole, was the natural partner to the gaucho, Argentina's cowboy. It is said that a gaucho without a horse is like a man without legs. The tough little Criollo was the perfect cow horse—agile, clever, fearless, and strong. It also had considerable stamina and was rarely tired. Said to be a "one-man horse," the Criollo is independent; however, once it gives its trust, it is affectionate and loyal.

When the British came to South America, they brought English Thorough-breds, which were mated to Criollos to refine and improve the existing stock. With the French came the Percheron, used to add bone and substance. Both almost spelled out disaster for Argentina's king of the pampas, as people began to ignore the breed's unique characteristics and natural toughness in favor of larger horses.

World's Stage

In 1910 Dr. Emilio Solanet, professor at the School of Veterinary Medicine and Agriculture in Buenos Aires, brought about 2,000 Criollos into his estancia, El Cardal. From these he selected 15 mares that would become the breeding stock of the Argentinian Criollo.

To prove the stamina and endurance of the Criollo, and reignite waning interest and faith in the breed, Dr. Solanet offered two of his horses to a Swiss schoolteacher who wanted to travel from Buenos Aires to New York. On the trip, which lasted from 1925 to 1928, Aimé-Felix Tschiffely made Mancha and Gato famous in Argentina and wrote the names of the two horses on the world's stage.

Fascinating Facts

Not only were Mancha and Gato fairly advanced in age when they made their famous trek (about 15 years), but they also each went on to live until around 40 years of age— definitive proof of the toughness of Argentina's king of the pampas.

BELOW

These are incredibly tough little horses with enormous stamina and a good brain, making them the favored mount of the gaucho, the Argentinian cowboy.

PERUVIAN PASO

HEIGHT: 14.2–15.3 hh

COLOR: all solid colors

PERSONALITY TYPE: warm-blooded

TYPICAL USE: riding, harness, showing

TEMPERAMENT: docile, willing, intelligent

ORIGIN: Peru

SIMILAR BREEDS: Paso Fino

Peru's national horse breed, the Peruvian Paso or Peruvian Stepping Horse, is the product of a judicious fusion of several Old World breeds—the Spanish Jennet gave its even temperament and smooth ambling gait, the African Barb contributed great energy, strength, and stamina, while the Andalusian imparted its excellent conformation, action, proud carriage, and beauty to the new breed. This mix of equines, introduced to Peru by the Spanish settlers, was then left in more or less isolation to evolve into a horse of great beauty and presence.

Pacers and Trotters

As the Peruvian Paso was developing, the outside world was changing. Up to the beginning of the 1600s, most horse breeds were pacers (lateral) rather than trotters (diagonal). As an ever-increasing network of roads was created, more people traveled by carriage rather than on horseback, and the trotter was better equipped to pull a carriage. At the beginning of the 1600s, it was unusual to find a horse that trotted; by the end it was rare to find one that did not.

But the Peruvian Paso, kept pure by the Peruvian people, continued to pace—of all gaited horses, it is thought to be the only one that is guaranteed to pass on its natural gaits to 100 percent of its offspring.

"Con Brío"

The Peruvian Paso has the *paso llano*, a broken, four-beat, lateral gait; the *sobreandando*, a faster gait; and the unique *termino*, a graceful, flowing movement in which the horse's forelegs roll out from the shoulders, like the arm motion of a swimmer in front crawl or freestyle. All gaits are smooth and extremely comfortable.

Although it is a different breed from the Paso Fino, there are similarities. Both horses have the presence and beauty of their Spanish ancestry, as well as the abundant flowing mane and tail. And both also have *brio*, that engaging mixture of arrogance and exuberance that makes them such a joy to watch.

Fascinating Facts

A widely perpetuated and popular myth: if a statue in the park of a person on a horse has both front legs in the air, the person died in battle; if the horse has one front leg in the air, the person died as a result of wounds received in battle; if the horse has all four legs on the ground, the person died of natural causes.

BELOW

The Peruvian Paso is one of the gaited horse breeds that always passes its gait on to its offspring.

HACKNEY HORSE

TEMPERAMENT: spirited, intelligent

ORIGIN: England

SIMILAR BREEDS: Hackney Pony, Shales

HEIGHT: 15 hh

COLOR: bay, brown, chestnut, black

PERSONALITY TYPE: warm-blooded

TYPICAL USE: harness, riding

The high stepping and extravagant Hackney horse is one of the flashiest driving horses in the world.

It is called the "Ballerina of the Show Ring," and England's Hackney Horse takes its name from the French *haquenée* (French was commonly spoken in England in medieval times), meaning a riding horse with an especially comfortable gait. Over the years it became "Hackney," a word synonymous with a general-purpose equine with legendary stamina and soundness and flashy trot that was greatly admired. These horses were highly valued by both common people and kings.

Status Symbol

In fact three monarchs, Henry VII (1457–1509), Henry VIII (1491–1547), and Elizabeth I (1533–1603) all passed Acts concerning horse breeding and the value of the Hackney; Henry VIII went so far as to penalize anyone from exporting a horse without authority.

Later, in the early 1700s, imported Arabian blood was added to the Hackney to refine the breed without detracting from its inherent qualities. As roads improved, demand grew for coach horses, and as carriages became more sophisticated, flashier, showier horses were increasingly popular. The Hackney, with its high knee action and regal bearing, fit the bill perfectly. In the flamboyant Regency period, the carriage horse became a status symbol.

Springy Step

The Hackney, when crossed with other breeds, appears to be dominant — influencing, rather than being influenced.

Hackney blood has been used in the development of other horse breeds, notably the Holstein, Gelderlander, Dutch Warmblood, Saddlebred, and Morgan. It is also used as an outcross to produce exceptional sporting horses, passing on its athleticism, speed, and stamina, as well as its good looks.

The modern Hackney has a noble outlook, with a straight or slightly convex profile, elegant head carried high on an arched neck, and sloping shoulders. It has good feet, and its legs are strong, with plenty of good, flat bone and long pasterns that give it its light, springy step.

SHALES

HEIGHT: 15 hh

COLOR: gray, chestnut

PERSONALITY TYPE: warm-blooded

TYPICAL USE: harness, riding

TEMPERAMENT: good-tempered, intelligent

ORIGIN: England

SIMILAR BREEDS: Hackney

Although it is no longer a recognized breed in the United Kingdom, the Shales, a direct descendant of and the modern equivalent to the Norfolk Trotter or Roadster, does still exist. The foundation sire of the American Standardbred was the Thoroughbred stallion Messenger, which descended from Blaze; Blaze's son, Original Shales, founded the Norfolk Roadster and is responsible for the modern Shales, as well as the high-stepping Hackney. The Roadster had similar origins to the Thoroughbred.

LEFT
The well-conformed Shales horse was instrumental in the development of the Hackney breed and remains a useful driving and riding animal.

riding horses, and these were mostly the Shales strain, which were generally gray or chestnut.

Polo Pony

The modern Shales has been bred by the Colquhoun family since 1922, when Elizabeth Colquhoun bought a two-year-old colt by Findon Gray Shales, which stood at the Duchy of Cornwall's Tor Stud. The colt, bred by the Prince of Wales, later the Duke of Windsor, was named Royal Shales.

A granddaughter of Royal Shales named Silver Shales—the female line of which traced to the renowned Thoroughbred sire The Tetrarch—was hunted as well as driven and was also used as a polo pony, proving the breed's versatility. The Shales has the good looks of the Hackney as well as its flash and fire, and it would be fortunate if the breed were to continue.

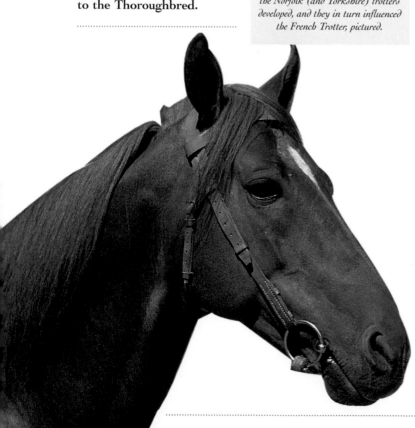

BELOW
It was from the Shales horse that the Norfolk (and Yorkshire) trotters developed, and they in turn influenced the French Trotter, pictured.

Social Change

During the 1600s and 1700s the Roadster and the Thoroughbred developed in an almost parallel way; the subsequent differences were due to social rather than evolutionary changes. The Thoroughbred was the plaything of land-owning gentry, who wanted it for hunting and racing. The Roadster or Trotter, however, was much more utilitarian—to be ridden or driven. The trot was far more adapted to that of the carriage horse.

While the carriage horse was increasingly popular—leading to the development of the Hackney—people still wanted hunters and

CLEVELAND BAY

TEMPERAMENT: sensible, intelligent, honest

ORIGIN: England

SIMILAR BREEDS: Yorkshire Coach Horse (extinct)

HEIGHT: 16–16.2 hh

COLOR: bay, few or no white markings

PERSONALITY TYPE: warm-blooded

TYPICAL USE: harness, riding, hunting, competition

Fascinating Facts

Around 1869 Fanny Drape, a Cleveland Bay-cross mare, gave a solo exhibition of jumping in hand, clearing a bar estimated to be 7 ½ ft. (2.3 m) high under which her leader ran.

LEFT

These wonderful, athletic horses were originally used primarily as coach horses, although they also make excellent riding horses.

The United Kingdom's oldest indigenous horse breed originates from Cleveland in northeast England. They were traditionally used to transport goods and materials between monasteries and abbeys in the Yorkshire Dales, and these early pack animals were called "Chapman Horses" after the name given to itinerant packmen and pedlars. When North African Barbs were imported into the area, they were used on the local Chapman mares to produce a powerful pack and harness horse.

Police Horse

The Cleveland Bay was almost wiped out with the introduction of the motor vehicle, but a few dedicated breeders kept it going, with the society being formed in 1884. As its name suggests, it is always bay colored, with few, if any, white markings. It is hardy, long-lived and possesses great stamina. Although generally sensible, it has a strong character, which if mishandled can become spoiled. It is a dominant outcross and has influenced several European warmblood breeds, including the Gelderlander, Holstein, Oldenburg, and Hanoverian. Muscular and strong, it is also good-looking, with a "hawklike" profile, well-balanced frame, good legs and joints, and sound feet. But most of all it is versatile—bred to be a packhorse or harness horse, it makes a good heavyweight hunter, and its sensible temperament means that it is also a good police horse, working well in crowds and noisy situations.

Popular Export

As the demand for carriage horses grew, the Cleveland Bay was crossed with the Thoroughbred to produce a taller, more elegant creature known as the Yorkshire Coach Horse. In the golden age of coaching, in the late 1700s, these horses were hugely popular and exported all over the world as matched pairs and teams. To this day there are still two discernible types of Cleveland Bays: the smaller Chapman type and the larger version that resembles the Yorkshire Coach Horse.

THOROUGHBRED

HEIGHT: 16 hh

COLOR: bay, chestnut, black, brown, gray

PERSONALITY TYPE: warm-blooded

TYPICAL USE: racing, competition

TEMPERAMENT: intelligent, spirited

ORIGIN: England

SIMILAR BREEDS: Arabian

If ever there were an example of equine excellence, it must be the Thoroughbred. The word is synonymous with speed, grace, beauty, and athleticism and is the given name of the most successful horse breed in the world. The English Thoroughbred —the word comes from the Arabic *keheilan*, meaning "pure blood"—is based on three foundation sires— the Darley Arabian, the Godolphin Arabian, and the Byerley Turk, each brought to England from the Middle East and named after their respective owners.

Middle Eastern Blood

As was the custom of the time, horses were known by the men that owned them— the Darley Arabian was owned by Thomas Darley, the Godolphin Arabian by Lord Godolphin, and the Byerley Turk by Captain Robert Byerley. They were brought to England from the Middle East around the turn of the seventeenth century.

The Byerley Turk is thought to be the first to be brought back, having been captured from the Turks at the siege of Buda (1686), when the Hungarian capital was part of the Ottoman Empire, and was brought to Britain in 1690. Despite the horse's

moniker, it is likely it was also an Arabian or possibly an Akhal-Teké.

Flying Childers

The Darley Arabian was purchased in Aleppo, Syria, by Thomas Darley in 1704 and was shipped to Yorkshire, where he was bred to numerous mares. The most successful matings were with a mare called Betty Leeds, resulting in two influential colts—Flying Childers and Bartlet's Childers. Through the Childers line, the Darley Arabian was the great-great-grandsire of Eclipse, of whom it was said: "Eclipse first, the rest nowhere."

The Godolphin Arabian was to be of equal importance, although he was originally

used as a "teaser" to test if mares were ready to be mated. It is said he fought another stallion for the mare Roxana, on whom he sired Cade, the father of Matchem, who was to prove especially influential on the American Thoroughbred.

American Pedigree

All this might still have been lost if it not for one James Weatherby, who published the first *General Stud Book* of the English Thoroughbred in 1791, listing the pedigrees of 387 mares, each of which could be traced back to Eclipse, Matchem, or Herod, whose great-great-grandsire was the Byerley Turk. The *General Stud Book* is still published in England by Weatherbys.

The Thoroughbred was popular in North America, too, the first export to the United States being Bulle Rock, a son of the Darley Arabian, who arrived in what was then the British colony of Virginia in 1730, at the age of 21. By the 1800s he had been followed by more than 300 others. The first volume of the *American Stud Book* was published in 1873.

Equine Powerhouse

The modern Thoroughbred retains all the beauty of its Arabian ancestry and the precocious speed of its founding sires. Its refined, chiseled head has a straight profile, rather than a dished or concave one, set on a long neck and high withers. Its

RIGHT
The Thoroughbred is noted for its elegance, beauty, and natural athleticism and is a breed that almost always improves the stock it is crossed with.

shoulders are deep, muscled, and sloping; its girth deep and its hindquarters powerful. It has strong, slender, well-muscled, clean legs and good feet.

It is an equine powerhouse that is positive proof of four centuries of careful, selective breeding. Its names—Diomed, a descendant of Herod and the first winner of the Epsom Derby;

Hyperion, Derby and St. Leger winner and hugely successful sire; Sir Archie, one of the best "American" Thoroughbreds—resonate through history.

Today 95 percent of all modern Thoroughbreds can be traced back to one of those three foundation sires—the Darley Arabian, the Godolphin Arabian, and the Byerley Turk.

ANGLO-ARAB

HEIGHT: 15.2–16.3 hh

COLOR: mostly bay, brown, chestnut

PERSONALITY TYPE: warm-blooded

TYPICAL USE: competition, riding

TEMPERAMENT: sensible, calm, intelligent

ORIGIN: Europe

SIMILAR BREEDS: Arabian Thoroughbred

This harmonious fusion between Arabian and Thoroughbred lines makes an excellennt sporting horse, the most popular cross being an Arabian stallion to a Thoroughbred mare, as this produces larger offspring than would a Thoroughbred stallion to an Arabian mare. Experiments with the two breeds began in the 1700s or 1800s and are very scientific—selective breeding used to combine the best features of two superlative equine breeds, without obviously favoring either but used to produce an excellent all-rounder.

Best of Both

The aim was to produce a horse with speed and class— the two essential attributes of the Thoroughbred—and the stamina and toughness of the Arabian, with the beauty of both. The Anglo-Arab is a natural athlete with innate jumping ability; add the Thoroughbred's speed and you get an excellent event horse.

The ideal Anglo-Arab should have no more than 75 percent Arabian blood and no less than 25 percent.

Competition Horse

The Anglo-Arab has a finely shaped head, with the slightly concave profile of the Arabian, but it should not be too dished. It has a similar outline to the Thorough-bred but generally has more substance. Its neck should be of good length and gracefully arching from the withers to the poll. Its shoulders are

LEFT

The Anglo-Arab combines the best of both Thoroughbred and Arab breeds, resulting in a horse with great speed, tenacity, stamina, and beauty.

very powerful and should slope to allow for speed and free movement. It is deep in the chest and compact through the body. It has powerful hindquarters, well-formed legs with plenty of bone and tough joints, and good, hard feet.

A naturally good mover, with a free-flowing and long-striding action, the Anglo-Arab makes an excellent saddle or competition horse. The experiment to cross two of the best equine breeds— the Thoroughbred and the Arabian—must be considered to be a resounding success.

IRISH DRAFT

TEMPERAMENT: sensible, gentle, docile

ORIGIN: Ireland

SIMILAR BREEDS: none

HEIGHT: 15.2–17 hh

COLOR: all solid colors

PERSONALITY TYPE: warm-blooded

TYPICAL USE: riding, harness, competition

Despite its name, the Irish Draft is actually a lighter, free-moving equine rather than a heavy draft breed. It did start out as an all-rounder, however, working the small Irish farms and doubling up as a hunter, as well as a harness horse to pull the trap or dogcart into town or to church. Today the breed is probably best known as an excellent outcross—mated with Thoroughbreds it produces excellent hunters and competition horses.

Strong and Handsome

It is believed that the Irish Draft has been in existence for at least 100 years, although it has come worryingly close to extinction on several occasions. To the

ABOVE

The Irish Draft is a wonderful, versatile animal with a natural affinity for jumping. It is renowned for its honest, forgiving, and amenable temperament.

small Irish farmer, his horse had to be docile, tough, and economical to keep— its traditional winter feed was young gorse put through a chaff-cutter, boiled turnips, and bran or something similar that could be spared from the cows. The breed developed into a strong, handsome equine, standing between 15.2 and 16.2 hh for mares and up to 17 hh for stallions.

Valuable Outcross

During the periods of poverty and famine in Irish history, breeders stopped registering their animals—breed enthusiasts and the Irish Horse Board endeavored to get a new studbook started. They found that hundreds of horses were going to the slaughterhouses each week, and there were very few left.

Luckily the breed was saved and has thrived, as a purebred and as a valuable outcross. In the U.K. the broodmare is acknowledged as an excellent dam of hunters when put to a Thoroughbred stallion. The Irish Draft stallion is now being used more and more to get extra bone and substance in the progeny of the lighter type mare.

The breed's excellent feet are those of a hunter rather than a draft horse and are the reason why the Irish Draft produces such wonderful competition stock.

CAMARGUE

HEIGHT: 13–14 hh

COLOR: gray

PERSONALITY TYPE: warm-blooded

TYPICAL USE: herding, riding

TEMPERAMENT: lively, good-tempered

ORIGIN: France

SIMILAR BREEDS: Solutre (extinct)

The history of the Camargue Horse is inexorably entwined with that of the tough, little bulls that live in the same region—both exist in a semi-feral state in the Camargue region of the Rhone delta. The Camargue Horse is thought to have descended from the Solutre Horse, which lived on the marshland at the edge of the Quaternary Sea during the Paleolithic period some 17,000 years ago—the musculature and skeleton of the Camargue is the same as that of the Solutre.

Fascinating Facts

Camargue horses are born dark brown or black, often with a white blaze on the forehead, but they turn gray when they reach full maturity between the ages of five and seven. Their coat lightens to white as they get older.

Horse of the Sea

Known as "the horse of the sea," the Camargue thrives in the marshy land it inhabits; it eats leafy grasses, herbs, and other ground vegetation. In the spring it grazes on samphire as well as the tender shoots of tall reeds. In the winter it survives on dried grass and on goosefoot, a tough plant that most other grazing animals cannot eat. When food is scarce, the horse may graze for 22 hours a day. When food is plentiful, it grazes only at dawn and at dusk.

It is thought that Arabian and Saracen horses may have had some influence on the

Camargue, but its natural environment has also shaped it into the rugged, little horse it is today. It has to be tough to endure the biting cold wind that roars across the delta in the winter and the fierce heat of the summer sun.

French Cowboys

The Camargue is brave, agile, and lively but is generally good-tempered and makes an excellent riding horse. Although it rarely stands much higher than 14 hh, it is considered a horse rather than a pony. It is traditionally used by the *gardians*, the French cowboys who round up the black Camargue bulls, which have a reputation for being tough and aggressive. The Camargue's delta home was designated a national park in 1928.

FRENCH TROTTER

TEMPERAMENT: quiet, biddable

ORIGIN: France

SIMILAR BREEDS: Selle Français

HEIGHT: 16.2 hh

COLOR: chestnut, bay, brown

PERSONALITY TYPE: warm-blooded

TYPICAL USE: racing, harness

Also known as the Norman Trotter, France's native breed is an intelligent but quiet equine known for its speed and stamina. It was bred as a trotting horse at the beginning of the 1800s in the Normandy region on the northern coast of France by crossing the strong Norman mares with imported English Thoroughbreds, half-breds, and Norfolk Trotters and Norfolk Roadsters. These crosses resulted in two distinct types of horses—the French Trotter and the Anglo-Norman saddle horse.

Ridden Trotting Races

The first trotting races were held in 1806 on the Champ de Mars in Paris—these were ridden races, not harness. As interest and enthusiasm for the sport grew, special racetracks were opened, the first in Cherbourg in the 1830s. The new sport received official support in 1861 with an Imperial decree, leading to the formation of its first governing body.

Five important bloodlines of the French Trotter were established: Conquérant, Normand, Lavater, Phaeton, and Fuchsia, with Fuchsia being the most influential of the early stallions. He was foaled in 1883 and sired almost 400 trotters—more than 100 of his sons produced winners.

A Great Trotting Tradition

Some Standardbred blood was introduced later to add more speed, but the Trotteur Français Stud Book closed its register to non-French-bred horses in 1937. It is only in recent years that a limited number of carefully selected French Standardbred crosses have been admitted to the studbook. In its own way the French Trotter has played an important role in the development of the Selle Français.

France has the greatest tradition of trotting racing after the United States and still holds both ridden and driven contests. The Prix d'Amérique is the premier trotting race, and the Prix de Cornulier is the ridden equivalent.

Fascinating Facts

The French Trotter is sometimes used in the sport of skijoring, where a person on skis is pulled by a horse.

LEFT

The French Trotter excels at both ridden and driven trotting races and is France's leading trotting breed.

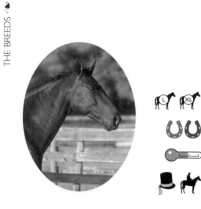

SELLE FRANÇAIS

HEIGHT: 16–17 hh

COLOR: bay, chestnut, most solid colors

PERSONALITY TYPE: warm-blooded

TYPICAL USE: riding, competition

TEMPERAMENT: willing, friendly, kind

ORIGIN: France

SIMILAR BREEDS: French Trotter, Thoroughbred, French Anglo-Arab

LEFT

The Selle Français is an athletic sporting horse that excels at competition. Unlike most warmblood breeds it has a high percentage of trotter blood in its history.

Naturally athletic, kind, willing, strong, and good-looking, the Selle Français, France's saddle horse breed, is everything anyone could want from an equine. Like all warmbloods it is a mixture of breeds, but what makes it unique is the influence of outcrosses to trotters. The Selle Français was developed in the government stud farms of Saint-Lô and Le Pin in Normandy in the 1800s by putting imported Thoroughbred stallions and Norfolk Trotters to native French stock.

French Influences

The results of these experiments were two types of horse: the French Trotter, a fast harness horse, and the Anglo-Norman, with both a saddle and heavier draft type. The saddle type of the Anglo-Norman could be considered the prototype for the modern Selle Français and is definitely the most recognized foundation stock; however, many of the local French breeds that were bred as saddle horses—such as the Vendeen, Corlais, Angevin, Angonin, and Charentais—played an important role in the breed's development. After the Second World War the emphasis was put firmly on the production of a riding horse combining speed, stamina, ability, and quality. As the Anglo-Norman began to be crossed with the regional breeds, the resulting stock became less diverse, and because of this growing similarity among the equines, in 1958 they were merged together under one name—*le cheval de Selle Français*, or the French Saddle Horse.

Sporting Horse

In less than 50 years the Selle Français has become widely recognized as one of the world's best competition horses—athletic and strong with good conformation and an intelligent and tractable disposition. The Selle Français has excelled internationally in show jumping but is also successful in eventing and in the dressage arena. It is bred to race as "AQPSA" (an acronym for *autres que pur sang association*, meaning "other than Thoroughbred"), and there seems little at which the Selle Français does not excel.

In 2002, at the World Equestrian Games in Jerez,

Spain, the French show-jumping squad took team gold, all mounted on Selle Français stallions. In 2006 Nicolas Touzaint claimed the eventing World Cup on the classy gray Galan de Sauvagère, a Selle Français; in 2007 he was European Champion.

Affinity with People

The ideal conformation of the Selle Français is that of a large-boned Thoroughbred, combining both strength and elegance. It has an attractive, expressive head set on a long

neck, sloping shoulders, strong back, and good legs with plenty of hard bone. Selle Français horses are seen in many colors, but bays and chestnuts are predominant.

A huge part of their charm is their willingness to please and their almost doglike affinity with people. They also have that extra spark that separates the superstars from the crowd, yet they remain kind and easy to handle.

While the Thoroughbred has made a huge impact on France's saddle horse, Selle Français stallions have also played a role in the development of other breeds. Notably Furioso II, Zeus, and Inschallah were important in the Oldenburg

BELOW

This is one of the most versatile of warmblood breeds and has excelled in dressage, show jumping, eventing, and even racing.

breed; Cor De La Bryère is often seen in Holstein pedigrees; Le Mexico made a contribution to the Dutch Warmblood, and Alme can be found in pedigrees of most European sport horse breeds.

The Selle Français is also becoming popular in the United States as a hunter, for which its elegance, fluid movement, and athletic jumping ability make it supremely well adapted.

FRENCH ANGLO-ARAB

HEIGHT: 16.2 hh

COLOR: all solid colors

PERSONALITY TYPE:
warm-blooded

TYPICAL USE: riding, competition

TEMPERAMENT: intelligent, willing

ORIGIN: France

SIMILAR BREEDS: Anglo-Arab,
Thoroughbred, Selle Français

Madame de Pompadour (1721–64) founded the Pompadour National Anglo-Arab Stud, which is credited with finding one of the founding sires of the French Anglo-Arab, in 1751. It was an extraordinary success story of horse breeding that was to lead to the development of the French saddle horse, the Selle Français. The stud farm, which established the first Arab breeding program in France in the late 1700s and was at the forefront of expeditions to Arabia for bloodlines, imported an Arabian stallion named Massoud from Egypt in 1820 to improve the stock.

National Studs

The other stallion was named Aslan, who came from Turkey in the early 1800s. Both stallions were bred to three Thoroughbred mares, Daer, the Cornus Mare, and the Selim Mare. They proceeded to produce the three fillies that were to be the foundation mares of the French Anglo-Arab: Delphine, Clovis , and Danae.

The stud farm's purpose was to produce exceptional, high-class, European, sport horses. Château Pompadour became a royal stud following Madame de Pompadour's death and then was reestablished by Napoleon following the

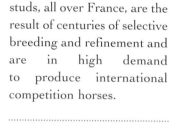

ABOVE

The French Anglo-Arab generally has excellent conformation and disposition, and it is noted for its jumping ability.

French Revolution. The Pompadour is now one of France's 23 national studs

(*haras nationaux*) that stand Anglo-Arab stallions. The stallions standing at these studs, all over France, are the result of centuries of selective breeding and refinement and are in high demand to produce international competition horses.

Correct Action

The French tradition is to breed Anglo-Arab to Anglo-Arab, rather than Arab to Thoroughbred, which produces horses of varying levels of Thoroughbred and Arab blood, usually expressed as a percentage of Arab blood. For example, a French Anglo-Arab would be registered as "41%," meaning its lineage is 41 percent Arabian and 59 percent Thoroughbred.

The French Anglo-Arab may be a little less elegant than its British counterpart, but it is tough, hard, enormously versatile, and athletic. The ones bred at Pompadour are, in general, larger and more muscular, but all the French stock are athletic types, with pronounced jumping ability and notable correctness of action.

BELGIAN WARMBLOOD

TEMPERAMENT: willing, good-natured

ORIGIN: Belgium

SIMILAR BREEDS: all warmbloods

HEIGHT: 16.2 hh

COLOR: all solid colors

PERSONALITY TYPE: warm-blooded

TYPICAL USE: riding, harness, competition

Belgium is primarily known for its heavy draft breed, the Brabant, but its own warmblood horse is a resounding success—especially as it was developed only around 50 years ago. The Belgian Warmblood was developed

mainly as a show horse, using Arabian, Thorough-bred, Anglo-Arab, and Selle Français on the country's lighter agricultural animals. These horses had already been mixed with some Gelderlander blood to add size; the Arabian and Thoroughbred lines were to add quality.

Quality and Power

Since then around 5,000 Belgian Warmblood foals have been born every year, and the demand for this elegant equine seems unlikely to wane. The horse has a head full of quality, well-placed withers, and good, sloping shoulders. Its body is compact, with a well-proportioned back and powerful quarters, and it has good legs and sound feet. Although it was bred mainly for the show ring, the Belgian Warmblood has really found its niche in the competition arena. It excels at dressage, show jumping, and three-day eventing and has become popular all over Europe and North America.

HISPANO/HISPANO-ARABE

TEMPERAMENT: lively, spirited

ORIGIN: Spain

SIMILAR BREEDS: Andalusian, Arabian

HEIGHT: 14.3–16 hh

COLOR: chestnut, black, gray, bay

PERSONALITY TYPE: warm-blooded

TYPICAL USE: riding, competition

Two of the world's most ancient and influential horse breeds have been brought together to form the Hispano, a cross between the Andalusian and the Thoroughbred, which is sometimes also known as the Spanish Anglo-Arab. When Arabian blood is added to the mix, it is known as the Hispano-Arabe, and also *tres sangres*, meaning "three bloods." The Hispano-Arabe is a cross between a purebred registered Arabian and a purebred registered Andalusian.

Arched Neck

The Hispano-Arabe usually stands between 15 and 16 hh and has the refinement of the Arabian, especially in its elegant head and the long, muscular, and well-arched neck of the Andalusian. The

shapely withers ensure good saddle placement, and its body is full and strong, with a large chest, deep and muscled with plenty of heart room. The Hispano-Arabe exhibits a solid foundation of ample, extremely dense bone and extremely strong well-shaped hooves, traits also inherited from the Andalusian.

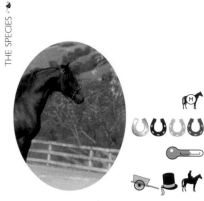

ANDALUSIAN

HEIGHT: 15.2 hh

COLOR: gray, bay, black, roan

PERSONALITY TYPE: warm-blooded

TYPICAL USE: riding, competition, harness

TEMPERAMENT: intelligent, willing, brave

ORIGIN: Spain

SIMILAR BREEDS: Lusitano, Alter-Real

Writing in the 1500s, King Henry IV's riding master Salomon de la Broue (*c.* 1530–1610) declared: "I class the true Spanish horse as the greatest, the most handsome, the most noble, the bravest, and most worthy of kings." And there are few today who would dispute that statement. The purebred Spanish horse, or *pura raza española*, is the collective term for these Iberian kings, the Andalusian (also sometimes called the Carthusian), the Lusitano, and the Alter-Real.

Pure Strain

The name "Andalusian" is taken from the sun-drenched region of southern Spain around Seville, Jerez, Cordoba, and Granada, and it is largely thanks to an order of Carthusian monks—from where it gets its alternative moniker—that it stays pure. The Monastery of Carthuja, founded in 1476 in Jerez de la Frontera, kept a small herd of Spanish horses and preserved the purest strains. The breed developed with hard, sound feet and fine body hair to counteract the rocky, dry ground and hot climate.

But the purebred Spanish horse's history begins way before the 1400s. Cave drawings dating back around 20,000 years show horses were in the region that is now made up of Spain, Portugal, and southern France during that period.

Moorish Influences

The most significant event in the Andalusian's history occurred in A.D. 710–711, when the Moors invaded Spain as the allies of Spanish lords who were at odds with their king. Within seven years they had taken possession of most of the Iberian Peninsula and named it Al-Andalus. It is known that the cavalry were mostly Berbers mounted on Barb Horses—the Arab people who also fought in

Spain were infantry, so it was the Barb and not the Arabian that was to have the most influence on the Iberian stock. But it is believed that the Andalusian had just as much influence on the Barb breed as vice versa.

Noble Appearance

The Andalusian's striking beauty and superb athleticism make it just as popular today, although it is more likely to do battle in the bullring—those same traits of speed, agility, and courage are just as essential here—or the dressage arena.

It has a noble, distinguished appearance and is most often gray, although occasionally bay, black, and roan are also seen. It is a compact horse with excellent proportions, standing around 15.2 hh. Its head is attractive, with a slightly Roman (convex) profile, a large, expressive eye, and small, neat ears. It has an abundant, slightly rippled mane and tail. Its chest is huge and its quarters lean. Its legs are clean and its feet generally good and hard; its action is energetic. The Andalusian is renowned for its ability to learn and for its excellent temperament.

Certainly, the Barb and the Andalusian have many characteristics in common. Both tend to have low-set tails and rounded croups, with short to medium-length backs. Both have well-crested, medium-length necks. The head of the Barb does show some Oriental influence but is not dished like that of the Arabian.

Weapons of Generals

Xenophon (c. 431–355 B.C.), the Greek cavalryman considered by most to be the founder of classical equitation, was hugely impressed by the horses he saw on the Iberian Peninsula and appreciated their ability to "collect"—gather their hind legs beneath the fore and fall back on their hocks. This ability, which today is valued in the dressage arena, made the Spanish warhorse swift and agile, able to turn quickly in any direction.

The Andalusian and the Lusitano, its Portuguese cousin, were the chosen weapons of generals from Hannibal to Julius Caesar; their speed, agility, and courage were unequaled and were helpful in the mastery of mounted battle.

RIGHT
This is possibly one of the most beautiful breeds of horses, as well as possessing great athleticism and a wonderful temperament.

LUSITANO

HEIGHT: 15–16 hh

COLOR: gray, black, bay

PERSONALITY TYPE: warm-blooded

TYPICAL USE: riding, bullfighting, competition

TEMPERAMENT: intelligent, willing, brave

ORIGIN: Portugal

SIMILAR BREEDS: Andalusian, Alter-Real

The Lusitano's name is derived from Lusitania, the Latin name for Portugal, and it has been recognized as a separate breed from the Andalusian only since 1966. There are considerable similarities between the two breeds, as they are both developed from Barb and Sorraia blood, but they do have some conformational differences. The Lusitano has a more pronounced Roman nose than the Andalusian and a wider forehead, and the Lusitano is considered the purer breed because it has no Arabian blood.

Majestic

The Lusitano has a more sloping croup and lower set tail than its Spanish cousin, and it is often straighter through the shoulder. Dressage expert Sylvia Loch, who founded the Lusitano Breed Society of Great Britain, wrote of the Lusitano: "To look at, it is noble rather than pretty, with aristocracy written all over its fine, slightly hawked, long face. It develops a powerful neck and shoulder, which makes it look extremely majestic in front.

"The quarters are not large, but the loins are wide and strong and the hocks long and wiry, giving it the power to bounce forcefully forward with masterful impulsion. Deep flexion is obtained from the developed second thigh and the longer than usual cannons and pasterns."

Bullring Star

In Portugal, the Lusitano is highly prized and especially valued as the mount of the *rejoneador*, or Portuguese bullfighter. Bulls are not killed in the Portuguese bullring; the aim is to demonstrate the training and schooling of the horse, its agility, and balance. It is considered a great disgrace if a *rejoneador* allows his horse to be injured during the fight.

The same characteristics that are essential in the bullring also make the Lusitano extremely efficient at other equestrian disciplines, especially dressage, or as a working and pleasure riding horse. Its excellent temperament and willingness to learn make it the perfect equine partner.

Fascinating Facts

Horses produce approximately 10 gallons of saliva a day.

BELOW

Lusitanos share many similarities with the Andalusian, although they differ notably in the shape of their head.

ALTER-REAL

TEMPERAMENT: intelligent, high-strung

ORIGIN: Portugal

SIMILAR BREEDS: Andalusian, Lusitano

HEIGHT: 15–16.1 hh

COLOR: bay, brown, gray, chestnut

PERSONALITY TYPE: warm-blooded

TYPICAL USE: riding, dressage

The Alter-Real was established by the Braganza family in Portugal in 1748, who imported 300 selected Andalusian mares from Jerez in Spain to form a national stud at Villa de Portel to produce sufficient riding and carriage horses for the Portuguese royal family. The word *real* means "royal;" the first half of the name comes from the national stud, which moved to Alter do Chão eight years later. The energetic Alter-Real was well adapted to the movements of the *haute école*, or High School.

Almost Lost

The stud was sacked by Napoleon's troops in the early 1800s, and the best of the stock was used as warhorses. Infusions of English Thoroughbred, Arabian, and Hanoverian blood were introduced to the remaining horses with dire consequences, and the breed was also lost until further Andalusian blood was added to restore the Alter-Real to its former glory.

The breed suffered another setback in the early 1900s with the dissolution of the

Portuguese monarchy—the Alter-Real stud was shut down and most of its records destroyed. It is thanks to Portugal's expert Dr. Ruy d'Andrade, who salvaged two stallions and some mares to reestablish the Alter-Real, that the breed still exists.

High-Strung

The Alter-Real is extremely adapted to the movements of the High School. It has a small, neat head with a pronounced jaw and a straight or convex profile. Its short, muscular neck is nicely arched, with pronounced withers and good sloping shoulders, and it has a compact frame, with a short back, muscular hindquarters, and a well-set tail. Its legs are strong, with slender but sturdy cannon bones and pasterns. It is generally bay but can also be chestnut, gray, or brown. It is high-strung but intelligent and is quick to learn, so it is probably best adaptable to experienced horsepeople.

BELOW

This Portugese breed had almost died out by the 1900s, although it has been restored through Andalusian influence.

SARDINIAN

HEIGHT: 15.2 hh

COLOR: bay, brown

PERSONALITY TYPE: warm-blooded

TYPICAL USE: riding, competition, police

TEMPERAMENT: trainable, sensible, calm

ORIGIN: Sardinia

SIMILAR BREEDS: Barb, Anglo-Arab, Salerno

Anglo-Arabs—with which the Sardinian was thought to have a special affinity—were imported, the most notable being Mongarry, Fanon II, and Fort Chabrol. Thirty years later more Oriental blood was introduced, which produced a military horse that was both sturdy and agile.

> RIGHT
> *These exceptionally attractive horses are appreciated for their inherent soundness and their especially amenable temperaments.*

good turn of foot and plenty of stamina, making it an excellent competition horse.

The modern Sardinian is strikingly similar to the Anglo-Arab. It is used in Sardinia and in Italy as a

Sardinia's only native equine breed is something of an enigma. Geographically, Sardinia, an island off of the west coast of Italy, is in a good location to trade with North Africa and is known to have imported North African Barb and Arabian horses for centuries, which would be crossed with the local stock. But what this local stock was, its origins, and how it came to this island in the first place are not known. The Sardinian breed was established as a fixed type in the 1400s.

When a racecourse was built in Chilivani in 1921, it sparked national interest, and Thoroughbred blood was introduced to give the Sardinian more speed.

Trainable

Four Thoroughbreds—Rigolo, Zenith, Sambor, and Abimelecco—were introduced and resulted in a good-looking, all-round athlete. The Sardinian has a neat, intelligent head with a straight profile, elegant, well-arched neck, well-proportioned body, and good sound legs and feet. It is hardy and athletic, with a

Sturdy and Agile

The Sardinian, like Italy's sporting horse, the Salerno, made an excellent military mount, being tough and trainable. In 1874 a stud was formed at Ozieri in the northwest of the island to promote and unify the breed. In 1883 several French

police horse, to which its sensible and calm temperament, as well as its inherent trainability, is well adapted.

MAREMMANA

TEMPERAMENT: steady, gentle

ORIGIN: Italy

SIMILAR BREEDS: Salerno

HEIGHT: 15–15.3 hh

COLOR: all solid colors

PERSONALITY TYPE: warm-blooded

TYPICAL USE: riding, herding, trekking

The Barb probably forms the basis for the Maremmana, bred in Tuscany but almost certainly deriving from horses from North Africa, as well as Spanish, Neapolitan, and Arabian blood. During the 1800s Thoroughbred and Norfolk Roadster blood were also introduced. The breed's name comes from the Maremma coast, a region of low marshland in the southwest corner of Tuscany. It is likely that the horse was originally bred to work the land and in harness.

Semi-Wild

The Maremmana is mainly bred in the northern region of Maremma and was established at the stud in Grosseto, although there are still herds of Maremmana running semi-wild in some local areas.

As well as being utilized as an agricultural animal, it was used by the cavalry as a troop horse and by the police force. But the Maremmana excels at working cattle, and it is frequently used by Italian ranch hands and cowboys, known as *butteri*, and demonstrates an enormous amount of "cow sense," similar to the American Quarter Horse. ("Cow sense" is probably best described as the horse's natural instinct to follow and herd cows.)

Sound Constitution

The Maremmana is not much to look at; it has a plain and coarse head (despite the Arabian, Barb, and Thoroughbred influences), short neck, weak shoulders, prominent withers, and short back. But despite its conformational short-comings, it tends to be tough and hardy, economical to keep, and generally very sound. It is also even-tempered, sensible, honest, and hard-working, so it is still in high demand as a police mount. And as Tuscany has become an increasingly popular vacation destination, the Tuscan breed has been brought into use as a trekking horse. Crossed with the Thoroughbred, the Maremmana also produces a good jumping horse, with the Italian breed's resistance to fatigue and its sound constitution.

Fascinating Facts

In the state of Arizona, it is illegal for cowboys to walk through a hotel lobby wearing their spurs.

ABOVE

This versatile breed is used for riding, trekking, and herding. It is especially good at working cattle and has an instinctive ability for this.

SAN FRATELLANO

HEIGHT: 15.2–16 hh

COLOR: black, bay, brown

PERSONALITY TYPE: warm-blooded

TYPICAL USE: riding, competition

TEMPERAMENT: robust, sensible, hardy

ORIGIN: Sicily

SIMILAR BREEDS: Sardinian, Murgese

Named after the town of San Fratello, at the foot of the Nebrodi Mountains in eastern Sicily, the San Fratellano is the closest thing the island has to a wild horse, with a number roaming free in the Nebrodi Park in what is now the province of Messina. It is thought to be very similar to the other local Italian breeds—Sicily lies off the "toe" of the boot-shaped country—such as the Sardinian, Murgese, and Sicilian, as well as the French Camargue, and more distantly the Andalusian.

Strong Warhorse

It is possible that the San Fratellano is related to the Old Sicilian Horse, which was highly regarded by the Greeks, and to the Salerno, Italy's sporting horse breed. During its long history it has been a warhorse, workhorse, and even butchered for its meat. It was popular with the Norman nobility, having been preferred by the Saracens who ruled Sicily until the 1000s. It was strong and high-spirited and could bear the weight of a knight in full armor. In the mountainous regions of Italy and Spain, strength was often an advantage over speed.

It is believed that the Norman knights who fought at the Battle of Hastings in England in 1066 were mounted on Sicilian horses.

LEFT
The San Fratellano does not always have the best conformation but is a very athletic horse, inherently sound in wind and limb.

Natural Jumping Ability

Since then English and Oriental blood have been introduced to refine the breed and improve on its heavy head, although most San Fratellanos still retain this characteristic. It is naturally athletic and sound and a "good doer" and is certainly not unattractive; it has a convex profile, balanced by a short, muscular neck, sloping shoulders, and a broad, deep chest. Its back is strong and its hindquarters are muscular and well formed. It has strong legs and good feet. It makes a good competition horse, as it has natural jumping ability.

Today there are thought to be only around 800 San Fratellanos left in Sicily.

MURGESE

TEMPERAMENT: amenable, willing

ORIGIN: Italy

SIMILAR BREEDS: Sardinian,
San Fratellano, Friesian

HEIGHT: 15–16 hh

COLOR: black, gray, chestnut

PERSONALITY TYPE:
warm-blooded

TYPICAL USE: agriculture,
riding, police

A nother rare breed, the Murgese is found in the Murge region of Apulia in southern Italy and is thought to be at least 600 years old. Its natural habitat is dry limestone hills, and like the harsh Slovenian Karst, the heartland of the old Lipizzaner, this environment invariably produces horses with good, dense bone, hard feet, and a sound constitution. The breed resembles the Friesian and is usually black in color, although chestnut and gray—a suggestion of Oriental influence—both occur.

Fascinating Facts

The left side of a horse is called the "near side" and the right side is the "off side".

RIGHT
The Murgese is a rare Italian breed that is similar in appearance to the more prolific Friesian horse.

Draft Type

During the late 1400s and early 1500s the governor of Monopoly, in the Puglia region of Italy, kept Murgese stallions and several hundred broodmares to provide remounts for the cavalry, but about 200 years ago interest in the Murgese diminished, and the breed almost died out. It

was saved, but the modern Murgese probably bears little resemblance to the older stock.

It is now a light draft horse, lacking the quality of the Irish Draft, and there is a lack of uniformity of type. The studbook was opened in 1926, and efforts have been made to improve and unify it.

Good Breeders

There are conformational faults, such as flat withers overloaded with muscle and upright shoulders, and these inhibit free movement. But

despite the limits of its structure, the Murgese is fairly active and energetic, and it is amenable, even-tempered, and economical to keep. It can be used as a light agricultural horse or as a leisure animal and is used by the Italian police. Crossed with a Thoroughbred or warmblood stallion, a Murgese mare will produce a better riding horse with more quality, good paces, and a willing nature.

Murgese mares are good breeders, being well built and roomy, and also produce the strong mules that are still used in the Murge region.

SALERNO

HEIGHT: 16–17 hh

COLOR: bay, chestnut, black, gray

PERSONALITY TYPE: warm-blooded

TYPICAL USE: riding, competition

TEMPERAMENT: kind, sensible, spirited

ORIGIN: Italy

SIMILAR BREEDS: Andalusian, San Fratellano

The result of crossing the Andalusian with Neapolitan stock, the Salerno was developed in the region bearing the same name near Naples in Italy in the 1500s as a cavalry horse —it was the official horse of the Italian army until 1947. Charles III (1716–88), Don Carlos of Naples, who would later become king of Spain, founded the first recorded stud for the breed in Persano, south of Salerno in Campania, in 1763; the breed is sometimes called the Salernitano-Persano.

Military Choice

As the Italian army encouraged competitive equestrianism, it made the cavalry mounts available to its soldiers, an act which increased the Salerno's popularity as a sporting horse. The Italian military had an equestrian jumping team, mounted mainly on Salernos, which was considered one of the best teams in the world from the end of the Second World War until the 1970s. The breed is naturally athletic, with excellent paces and natural jumping ability. It is also kind and easygoing, while being spirited and energetic as well as easy to train.

ABOVE

The Salerno is a popular Italian sporting horse breed and was used extensively by the Italian military equestrian teams for show jumping.

Best Jumper

It is thought to be Sicilian in origin, a mixture of Neapolitan, Spanish, and Oriental blood. Thorough-bred blood was introduced in the early 1900s, which greatly increased the quality of the breed. The modern Salerno is a large, upstanding horse with a handsome head with a straight profile and square forehead. Its eyes are expressive, and its neck is long and muscular. It has a well-proportioned back, good shoulders, muscular croup, and excellent, well-formed legs.

It has the reputation of being one of the best show jumpers in the world, but it is also beginning to make an impact in the dressage arena, where it may prove to be a winner because of its excellent temperament and trainability. Its kind nature makes it an amenable riding horse.

EINSIEDLER

TEMPERAMENT: sensible, calm, intelligent

ORIGIN: Switzerland

SIMILAR BREEDS: all warmbloods

HEIGHT: 16.2 hh

COLOR: all solid colors

PERSONALITY TYPE: warm-blooded

TYPICAL USE: riding, competition, harness

S witzerland's warmblood has been bred since the 900s, founded on local Schwyer stock, and gets its name from the Benedictine Abbey of Einsiedeln in the center of the country—so many of today's modern breeds have the world's monasteries to thank for their very existence. It is also known as the Swiss Warmblood, the Swiss Half-Blood, or Schweizer Halbblut. The first studbook was opened in 1655; a more comprehensive version was compiled in 1784 by a Father Isidor Moser.

three of the most important being Ivoire, Que d'Espair, and Orinate de Messil, and a Yorkshire Coach Horse named Bracken. The Swedish Warmblood Aladin also played an important role in the breed's development, as did two Holsteins—Astral and Chevalier.

In the 1960s Swedish and Irish mares were imported to Avenches, where the stud was located. Avenches continues to be discriminating in its choice of stallions, and as well as the modern Einsiedler it stands Thoroughbreds, Hanoverians, Selle Français, and Trakehners. As a result of the breeding program, the number of imports is waning.

sloping croup. Its legs are strong, with well-defined tendons and good joints.

Before an Einsiedler can be used for breeding, it has to pass rigorous tests, with stallions being tested at three and a half and again at five and mares at three. The tests include jumping, dressage, cross-country, and driving.

Fascinating Facts

New Jersey's state animal is the horse and was designated in Chapter 173 of the Laws of 1977.

BELOW

The Swiss Warmblood or Einsiedler has to pass a stringent series of tests— conformation, temperament, and ability—before being allowed to breed.

Unwise Outcrosses

The Einsiedler has had a somewhat spotted past. During the late 1600s and early 1700s some unwise outcrossing to Spanish, Italian, Friesian, and Turkish stallions proved to be a detrimental decision. Later the breed was improved by Anglo-Norman stallions,

Performance Testing

The Einsiedler is now a superlative competition horse with strength, stamina, agility, and good looks. It has a handsome head with straight or slightly convex profile; medium-length, well-proportioned neck; sloping shoulders; prominent withers; straight back, and a slightly

EAST FRIESIAN

HEIGHT: 16–17.2 hh

COLOR: bay, chestnut, brown, black

PERSONALITY TYPE: warm-blooded

TYPICAL USE: riding, competition

TEMPERAMENT: docile, placid

ORIGIN: The Netherlands

SIMILAR BREEDS: Hanoverian, Oldenburg

In its original form, the "old" East Friesian is now extinct. It was a heavy type of horse, somewhere between a draft and a warmblood, with warmblood gaits and characteristics. It was used mostly as a carriage or agricultural horse and was similar to the modern Oldenburg. Its homeland in the Federal Republic of Germany neighbored the Oldenburg region, spreading from the estuary of the Weser River to the borders of the Netherlands; it was bred on similar lines until Germany divided.

Hanoverian Influence

The East Friesian descended from a mix of Spanish, Neapolitan, Anglo-Arab, and Thoroughbred blood. Oldenburg horses were registered in the East Friesian studbook, but this was not permitted the

other way around. The East Friesian has now been absorbed into the Hanoverian —Hanoverian blood was introduced to increase the size and substance of the breed, and the East Friesian registry has joined the Hanoverian's.

WÜRTTEMBERG

HEIGHT: 16–17.2 hh

COLOR: bay, chestnut, brown, black

PERSONALITY TYPE: warm-blooded

TYPICAL USE: riding, competition

TEMPERAMENT: sensible, trainable, calm

ORIGIN: Germany

SIMILAR BREEDS: all warmbloods

Germany's oldest state stud, the Marbach Stud in Württemberg, produced this impressive warmblood, a sturdy, handsome horse standing up to around 17.2 hh, but it was not recognized as an established breed until the end of the 1800s when the breed society was founded in 1895 in Stuttgart.

The original Württemberg, which dates back to the 1500s, was probably the result of Arab stallions put to the country's heavy draft mares.

Lighter Version

The Marbach Stud was dispersed during the Thirty Years War (1618–48), and it was not until the end of the 1600s that the horse-breeding enterprise fully recovered. At that time Barb and Spanish mares were introduced to Marbach, as well as East Friesian stallions. Later, Anglo-Norman and Trakehner blood was brought in. As equestrian sports became more popular, the lighter, modern Württemberg took over from its heavier ancestors. In 1960 the Trakehner stallion Julmond arrived in Marbach, and it is considered to be the breed's foundation sire.

RHINELANDER

TEMPERAMENT: kind, sensible, trainable

ORIGIN: Germany

SIMILAR BREEDS: all warmbloods

HEIGHT: 16.2 hh

COLOR: all solid colors, but chestnut most common

PERSONALITY TYPE: warm-blooded

TYPICAL USE: competition

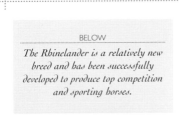

Like all warmbloods, the Rhinelander is descended from the heavy draft breeds, in this case the Rheinish, which was widely considered to be one of the best German coldbloods. As mechanization increased, the need for this heavy horse for farm work diminished, and the old draft breed is no longer recognized in its native land. The Rhinelander, although it has only been in existence for around 50 years, has already made its mark in the competition arenas of all equestrian disciplines.

New Breed

In the late 1950s and early 1960s breeders began producing a riding-type warmblood to cater for the increasing demand for leisure and competition horses. Mares by Trakehner, Hanoverian, and Thorough-bred stallions out of dams with Rheinish ancestry were crossed with stallions from Hanover/Westphalia. Stallions resulting from these crosses were then chosen to develop the Rhinelander breed. By 2003 133 stallions and 3,056 breeding mares were registered with the studbook.

BELOW

The Rhinelander is a relatively new breed and has been successfully developed to produce top competition and sporting horses.

WESTPHALIAN

TEMPERAMENT: calm, brave, intelligent

ORIGIN: Germany

SIMILAR BREEDS: all warmbloods

HEIGHT: 15.2–16.2 hh

COLOR: all solid colors

PERSONALITY TYPE: warm-blooded

TYPICAL USE: competition, harness, riding

Westphalia's coat of arms depicts a jumping horse, and like its neighbor Hanover, the state has a long tradition of horse breeding. In 1826 the state stud Landgestuet was founded in Warendorf, and in March 1904 the Westphalian Breed Registry was opened in Münster. The first Westphalians were bred based on Oldenburg blood, as well as Anglo-Norman. Since 1920 Westphalian warmblood breeding has been based on Hanoverian lines.

Dressage Star

The Westphalian first came to the attention of the competition horse world in the late 1970s, when Roman won the World Show Jumping Championship in 1978. In 1982 Fire, another Westphalian, won the jumping in the World Championships, and Ahlerich claimed the dressage equivalent. The Westphalian has a courageous, spirited temperament, but it is very willing and docile. Today the breed is used for general riding and harness work, including carriage driving. It is most talented, however, in show jumping and dressage, and some also excel in three-day eventing.

HANOVERIAN

HEIGHT: 17 hh

COLOR: all solid colors

PERSONALITY TYPE: warm-blooded

TYPICAL USE: competition

TEMPERAMENT: level-headed, kind, intelligent

ORIGIN: Germany

SIMILAR BREEDS: all warmbloods

Perhaps the best known of all the warmblood breeds—as well as the most successful—the Hanoverian originates from what was the kingdom of Hanover in the state of Lower Saxony in northern Germany. George Louis, Elector of Hanover and later King George II of Great Britain and Ireland, established the first stud in 1735 in Celle. The aim was to produce a quality horse for carriages, riding, and agriculture. It was selectively bred from local stock, Thoroughbreds, and 14 black Holstein stallions.

> RIGHT
>
> *The Hanoverian is one of the most popular warmblood breeds and was originally bred as a carriage and light agricultural animal.*

First Studbook

The Napoleonic Wars of 1803–15, especially the Sixth Coalition (1812–14), had a devastating effect on the breeding program of the Hanoverian; by 1816 there were only 30 stallions remaining—at one time there had been 100. Large numbers of Thoroughbreds were imported to Celle, until 35 percent of the stock was Thoroughbred, and this had the effect of greatly lightening the breed. The Hanoverian soon became too light to perform the agricultural tasks required, and an effort was made to increase its overall frame using more Holstein blood. The studbook, Verband Hannoverscher Warmblutzuchter, was opened in 1888.

Trakehner Influence

By 1924 the numbers of Hanoverians were rapidly increasing, and there were around 500 stallions standing in Celle. Due to the growing demand, another stud was opened in Osnabruck-Eversburg, with 100 stallions. After the Second World War there was a move toward creating a lighter type more equipped for riding—Hanoverians had been used extensively by the military—using infusions of Trakehner and Thoroughbred blood.

Today's Hanoverian is an excellent competition horse, both in dressage and jumping, and it is frequently used to improve other breeds. It probably bears very little resemblance to the original model first produced in the 1700s.

Elastic Paces

The modern Hanoverian is a noble, correctly proportioned warmblood with natural balance, impulsion, and elegant, elastic paces, characterized by a floating trot, a round rhythmic canter, and a ground-covering walk. Breeding stock is carefully inspected and selected for correct conformation, athletic ability, and inner qualities such as disposition and trainability—the Hanoverian is renowned for its level-headedness, willingness, and calm, kind temperament. It is athletic and strong and shines in all equestrian disciplines.

Substantial Equine

The Hanoverian has a straight head that is in no way coarse. Its neck is strong and well proportioned; it has pronounced withers that extend well into its back and sloping shoulders. It has a powerful body with deep girth and plenty of heart room, well-sprung ribs, and strong hindquarters with sloping croup. Its hocks are broad, clear, and well defined, its legs are strong with plenty of bone, and it has well-shaped, strong, sound feet. A substantial creature, the Hanoverian can stand up to 17 hh.

Breeding Eligibility

Breeding of this excellent warmblood is closely monitored, with only approved and graded

stallions permitted to stand at stud. All stallions must be presented for physical inspection annually to verify their eligibility for breeding. They are granted only a temporary breeding license, if they score sufficiently highly on conformation, movement, and jumping ability.

Within two years stallions must complete and pass the 100-day stallion performance test that evaluates paces, trainability, and athletic ability in dressage, show jumping, and cross-country. Mares are also tested, from the age of two and a half, when they are evaluated on type, conformation, and movement. A distinctly masculine bearing is desirable in stallions, and mares should have a marked feminine expression.

RIGHT

The modern Hanoverian is much lighter in build than its ancestors and is recognized as one of the top show-jumping breeds in the world.

TRAKEHNER

HEIGHT: 16–17 hh

COLOR: all solid colors

PERSONALITY TYPE: warm-blooded

TYPICAL USE: competition, riding

TEMPERAMENT: alert, intelligent, anxious to please

ORIGIN: Germany

SIMILAR BREEDS: all warmbloods

One of the oldest of all the warmblood breeds, this horse gets its name from the royal stud farm established in Trakehnen, East Prussia, in what is now Poland. Friedrich Wilhelm I of Prussia (1688–1740) realized that a new type of cavalry mount was needed because war tactics had changed, demanding a faster, lighter horse that also possessed power and endurance. In 1732 he moved the best of his cavalry horses to the new royal stud farm and began systematically breeding a horse that would meet these criteria.

LEFT

The Trakehner is one of the oldest and also most popular of the warmblood breeds, and it has excelled in the competitive field.

Spirit and Stability

The new cavalry mounts had to be attractive enough to be a representative horse for his officers, but additionally they had to be tough enough to survive harsh situations and come out sound. Through his efforts, the Trakehner breed (also known as the East Prussian) evolved.

The foundation stock was the small, native mares called *Schwaike*, which possessed great speed and stamina. When mated to Thoroughbred stallions, these sturdy, little mares produced a fast and willing warhorse that could also be used to work the East Prussian farms during times of peace. The object, ultimately, was to add the size, nerve, spirit, and endurance of the Thoroughbred to the bulk, stability, and nobility of the native breed. Further refinement came with the addition of Arabian blood.

refinement, perhaps more so than any other European, warmblood breed. It is a superb performance horse, with natural elegance and balance. It excels in dressage because of its elegant way of moving—the light, springy, floating trot and soft, balanced canter—and the breed also produces excellent jumpers. Perhaps the most outstanding attribute of the Trakehner, however, is its temperament—eager, alert, and intelligent, it is also sensible, accepting, and anxious to please.

Floating Trot

Today's Trakehner is characterized by great substance and bone, yet it also displays surprising

Olympic Glory

In 1787 the Trakehnen Stud was taken over by Count Lindenau, who as part of a program to improve the breed, eliminated one third of the broodmares and two thirds of the existing stallions. The first studbook was opened in 1877, and since then further Thoroughbred and Arabian blood has been introduced only when deemed strictly necessary.

The breed was soon in high demand—good-looking and athletic, Trakehners won every medal for the German Olympic Team at the 1936 Olympics in Berlin. With the Thoroughbred's speed, the Trakehner also excelled in racing, representatives of the breed winning the fearsome Pardubice Steeplechase in the former Czechoslovakia nine times in 15 years.

The Trek

Although affected by the First World War, the breed quickly recovered—it was

Fascinating Facts

The trakehner cross-country fence gets its name from the fencelines built in drainage ditches when draining the wetlands area of Trakehnen, East Prussia, in the 1600s and 1700s. These fences were also used as a test for the young Trakehner horses from the area.

RIGHT

Typically Trakehners are beautifully conformed horses and have a natural, free-flowing stride combined with great intelligence and trainability.

the Second World War that was to bring it to its knees. The defeat of Germany in 1945 led to a retreat from East Prussia, and 1,200 of the 25,000 Trakehners embarked on a three-month march, loaded down with their owners' meager possessions, to the west— this incredible journey is known simply as "the Trek." Many were mares in foal,

and a considerable number could not endure the journey. It is thought only about 100 horses survived— those that did are proof of the endurance and hardiness of the modern Trakehner.

The new studbook, the West German Trakehner Verband, was opened in 1947, as the

breed was reestablished, with remaining Trakehners being painstakingly tracked down and the bloodlines revived without being compromised.

Thoroughbred Influences

The Trakehner's Thorough-bred influences are clear. It has the refined head, long, arching neck, and regal bearing of its ancestry, with the deep, sloping shoulders and moderately long back, powerful hindquarters, and strong joints and muscles. These attributes, as well as the Trakehner's kind, honest temperament, have been used to improve other warmblood breeds.

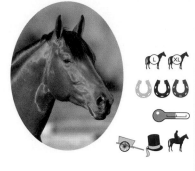

OLDENBURG

HEIGHT: 16.2–17.2 hh

COLOR: black, bay, brown, gray

PERSONALITY TYPE: warm-blooded

TYPICAL USE: competition, harness, riding

TEMPERAMENT: kind, calm, intelligent

ORIGIN: Germany

SIMILAR BREEDS: all warmbloods

First bred as a carriage horse, the Oldenburg breed has changed considerably since its development in Germany in the 1600s. The "old" Oldenburg achieved fame throughout Europe under Count Anton Günther von Oldenburg (1603–67), who was renowned as a great horseman and enthusiast of the breed. His aim was to produce a large quality carriage horse that was also able to work as an agricultural horse, and he built the royal stables and riding school in Rastede.

Eclipse Line

He began importing Spanish and Neapolitan horses and used these to cross with the East Friesian. One important stallion influential in the early development of the breed was the gray Kranich, who descended from good Spanish lines.

These early Oldenburgs would have been heavy-framed and coarse in appearance—they are documented as having a pronounced Roman nose.

In the late 1700s Barb, Thoroughbred, and Norfolk Roadster blood were introduced to add refinement. In 1897 a Thoroughbred line was introduced that is believed to trace back to the famous Eclipse.

Also around this time, Cleveland Bay stallions were used. The Cleveland Bay was a notable carriage horse of the time, as well as being extremely useful as a riding horse with a good natural jump. There were also infusions of Hanoverian and Anglo-Norman blood.

RIGHT
The Oldenburg was originally bred as a carriage horse and is still often used in competitive driving classes.

War Losses

The Oldenburg was used during the First World War by the cavalry, but the breed suffered great losses in battle. Afterwards the Oldenburg was once again mainly employed for harness and agricultural purposes, and it was not until after the Second World War that there were further efforts to lighten and improve the breed.

With the introduction of mechanization and motor vehicles, the breed again fell into decline, and it was realized by Oldenburg enthusiasts that it was necessary to focus breeding on the production of a versatile riding horse. To this effect there were further infusions of Thoroughbred blood, most notably from the stallion Lupus, and more Norman stock, especially from the stallion Condor, who had a high percentage of Thoroughbred blood.

In order to prevent the Thoroughbred characteristics, especially the "hot" temperament, from dominating, there was the continued use of Hanoverian blood, which helped maintain the excellent Oldenburg nature.

French Sires

The successes with Condor meant that Oldenburg breeders once more turned to French stallions to use on Oldenburg mares. One of the most successful was Furioso II, a highly regarded sire, and the Anglo-Arab Inschallah AA. These influences have shaped the modern Oldenburg into the supreme sporting horse it is today. The Thoroughbred blood has added speed, and the high

knee action of the original Oldenburg coach-horse type has been mostly eradicated.

The vestiges of this high action has done the Oldenburg no harm, however, in the dressage arena. The Oldenburg Bonfire was ridden to multiple World Cup dressage titles by Anky van Grunsven and individual dressage gold at the Olympic Games in Sydney in 2000.

Robust Frame

Like all warmbloods, the modern Oldenburg has the Thoroughbred's good looks, although on a more robust frame. Its head is fine and noble, sometimes with a slightly convex profile, and it has large, kind eyes. A good length of muscular neck is balanced by powerful sloping shoulders and a broad, deep chest. Deep through the girth, it has a long back, muscular quarters, and a well-set tail. The horse carries itself proudly, pushing from its hocks and powerful hindquarters for energetic, forward-going paces with active long strides.

The breed now shines in all competitive equestrian disciplines, including carriage driving, for which the Oldenburg was originally formed around 400 years ago.

HOLSTEIN

HEIGHT: 16–16.3 hh

COLOR: mostly bay

PERSONALITY TYPE: warm-blooded

TYPICAL USE: competition, harness, riding

TEMPERAMENT: honest, willing, kind

ORIGIN: Germany

SIMILAR BREEDS: all warmbloods

While it might have one of the smallest equine studbooks, there can be no doubting the Holstein warmblood breed is a resounding success. At the 1976 Olympics in Montreal, Canada, Holsteins dominated the proceedings—Granat won the individual dressage gold medal and Madrigal the silver; Albrant won the silver medal in the three-day event; and Torphy earned a silver in show jumping. The same year Emil Jung won the world four-in-hand driving championship with a team of Holsteins.

Regal bearing

The Holstein is similar to the Hanoverian and was developed in the state of Schleswig-Holstein, tracing back to a heavy warhorse from the 1300s. It was crossed with Andalusian and Arabian stock to lighten the breed, and then in the 1500s and 1600s more Spanish and some Neapolitan blood were added. These lines dominated the appearance of the Holstein, which had become an impressive large horse with a Roman nose and regal bearing.

It was well adapted to both farm and military work, but as with so many horse breeds, mechanization made it largely unneeded in the 1800s. Thoroughbred blood was then added to create a more elegant horse for riding and later on for competition.

Performance

The modern Holstein resembles its warmblood cousins, with its robust good looks, athletic versatility, and kind, honest temperament. Its noble head still has the impression of a slight Roman nose, but this in no way detracts from its beauty. It has the long neck, sloping shoulders, and powerful hindquarters that promise excellent performance.

And when the Holstein begins to move, its reputation as one of the world's finest sporting horses is displayed. With its strong haunches providing impulsion, it moves forward with elevation and suspension, creating an impression of strength, balance, and elasticity. This

Fascinating Facts

Some four million horses died in America's "Great Epizootic" of 1872. This accounted for almost one quarter of the nation's horses.

BELOW
The Holstein is another of the premium warmblood breeds and makes an excellent competition horse, being especially notable for its free-flowing action.

fluid movement, coupled with renowned intelligence, willingness to work, and a kind temperament, makes the Holstein the ideal sporting horse.

FRIESIAN

TEMPERAMENT: equable, willing, kind

ORIGIN: The Netherlands

SIMILAR BREEDS: East Friesian, Dales, Fell, warmbloods

HEIGHT: 14.3–15.3 hh

COLOR: black

PERSONALITY TYPE: warm-blooded

TYPICAL USE: riding, driving

A mere one hundred years ago the Friesian was almost extinct. It was originally a heavy draft type, like the East Friesian, probably based on the primitive Forest Horse, a huge coldblood that is now extinct, and crossed with lighter types to produce a heavy but elegant equine with a coal-black coat. It is thought to be one of the oldest domesticated breeds in Europe, native to the province of Friesland in the northern Netherlands—there are references to the Friesian throughout history.

Old Masters

Often painted by the Dutch Old Masters carrying knights into battle, the Friesian made an excellent warhorse. What it lacked in height it more than made up for in strength —it was easily capable of carrying a knight in full armor—and its extravagant knee action and proud bearing made it popular. During Spanish occupation of the Netherlands (1568–1648), infusions of Spanish blood

---
LEFT

These magnificent horses, with their noble bearing and extravagant action, were used to carry medieval knights into battle.

---

were probably added but not to its detriment. The Friesian is a horse of great beauty, with the abundant, rippling mane and tail that betray those Spanish ancestors.

Matched Black

During the First World War the Friesian was almost lost, but Oldenburg blood was used successfuly to reestablish the breed.

The Friesian added to the development of the Oldenburg and has influenced other equines, notably the American Morgan, the English Fell and Dales ponies, and the Shire.

Its Spanish heritage can also be seen in its long, fine head with its elegant, expressive face. It has a powerful neck set on excellent shoulders, a compact body, and short, strong legs with hard feet. It also has abundant feather (fine, long hair around its fetlocks) and is always black, with only a small white star permitted. It retains its high-stepping action, which makes it especially successful as a driving horse a team of Friesians, in perfectly matched black, is a magnificent spectacle.

GRONINGEN

HEIGHT: 15.2–16 hh

COLOR: bay, brown, black

PERSONALITY TYPE: warm-blooded

TYPICAL USE: riding, driving

TEMPERAMENT: kind, willing

ORIGIN: The Netherlands

SIMILAR BREEDS: Oldenburg, Gelderlander, warmbloods

The Oldenburg also played a part in the development of the Groningen, along with East Friesian and Friesian. It is somewhere between a draft horse type and a warmblood, being heavier and plainer than its more attractive cousins. What it lacks in looks it more than makes up for in stamina, endurance, and versatility. Originally bred as an all-purpose agricultural horse, it also made a good, heavyweight, riding horse and was useful in harness. It was reliable and could go all day.

BELOW

These useful and versatile horses fall between being a light draft animal and a heavyweight riding horse and excel in both capacities.

One Stallion

From about 1945 numbers of the Groningen have dwindled as the demand for powerful workhorses decreased. By the 1970s they were virtually extinct, with only one purebred stallion remaining, named Baldewijn. Since then there have been efforts by enthusiasts to preserve the breed, with recent infusions of Oldenburg blood. The Groningen now has improved conformation and is more compact, with better, more sloping shoulders, mainly due to this outcross. Later, Thoroughbred and Trakehner blood were introduced to keep the Groningen breed going without compromising it.

Sloping Shoulders

Today's Groningen is a medium-weight horse with plain features, although it does have natural presence and carriage. Its head has a tendency to be long and plain, with a straight profile and long ears. Its neck is very muscular, and its withers are reasonably prominent and long. The shoulders have

Fascinating Facts

Miniature horses are sometimes used as "guide horses" in the same way that dogs are used to help the blind.

become more sloping in recent years—probably due to the Thoroughbred influences—having originally been upright, which gave the breed a short stride. The back can be long and the croup flat. The quarters are very muscular, and the tail is set and carried high. The legs are short but strong, and it has good feet. Typically the Groningen has an excellent temperament, being willing and kind, and it is also an economical feeder.

GELDERLANDER

TEMPERAMENT: docile, cooperative, honest

ORIGIN: The Netherlands

SIMILAR BREEDS: all warmbloods

HEIGHT: 15.2–16.2 hh

COLOR: mostly chestnut, bay, gray, black

PERSONALITY TYPE: warm-blooded

TYPICAL USE: harness, riding

A far more handsome creature than the Groningen is the Gelderlander, developed originally as an agricultural horse that had enough quality to be an adaptable riding horse too. **The people of the Gelderland province of the Netherlands crossed their native mares to Andalusian, Norfolk Roadster, Neapolitan, and Norman stallions; later, infusions of Arabian, Anglo-Arab, Furioso, Holstein, and Orlov blood were added. In the 1800s English Thoroughbred, Hackney, and Oldenburg blood were introduced to the breeding.**

Fixed Type

Given the diversity of influences, it is extraordinary that a horse of such fixed type should have evolved, but the Gelderlander is widely regarded as being one of the best all-round sporting horses of modern times.

It is an extremely versatile horse, with an excellent, quiet temperament. The infusions of Thoroughbred have given the breed a certain amount of class, and it makes an eye-catching, medium-weight carriage horse. It is increasingly being used for competitive driving, to which it is well adapted, being both strong and agile with plenty of stamina.

It also makes a good middleweight riding horse and possesses a natural jumping ability—although, despite the Thoroughbred influence, it does tend to lack speed. It has great presence and elegance, with a free-flowing action and an especially stylish, high-stepping trot.

Muscular and Strong

The Gelderlander generally has good conformation, with a long, sometimes plain head and straight profile. Its neck is muscular and gently curves from broad withers to the poll; it is broad and deep

through the chest and has strong shoulders. Its back is straight and long, with muscular quarters, and its tail is set and carried high. Its legs are well-muscled and short, with good, strong joints and very hard hooves.

Numbers of the Gelderlander have decreased in recent years, although the breed is used to produce Dutch Warmbloods, which are a much higher caliber of competition horse.

DUTCH WARMBLOOD

Dutch

HEIGHT: 16–16.3 hh

COLOR: bay, gray, chestnut, black

PERSONALITY TYPE: warm-blooded

TYPICAL USE: competition, harness

TEMPERAMENT: sensible, intelligent, trainable

ORIGIN: The Netherlands

SIMILAR BREEDS: all warmbloods

A relatively new breed, the Dutch Warmblood was developed as a versatile riding horse rather than an agricultural working animal. It combines the finest elements of the Groningen and the Gelderlander with Thoroughbred, Trakehner, and Oldenburg blood. The Thoroughbred blood added quality, refinement, speed, and courage while keeping the fundamental level-headedness and calm, sensible nature of the warmblood type. The result is an extremely athletic horse, with good looks and good temper.

Sophisticated Testing

Although Dutch Warmblood stallions are owned by individuals, the breeding of the horse is monitored by the state-aided Warmbloed Paardenstamboek Nederland. Stallions may be used for breeding only if they pass the rigorous testing process. All aspects of the stallion are judged, from temperament to athletic ability and intelligence, but their conformation and movement are equally important. The stallions have their lower legs and feet X-rayed to make sure that any conformation faults are eliminated.

Mares are also tested, and the resulting offspring are closely monitored to track their success or failure as a breed standard. This process of testing is one of the most sophisticated approaches used in the world, and as a result has led to the quick growth and success of this relatively new breed.

Natural Agility

The Dutch Warmblood is an attractive, athletic horse with a free-flowing, extravagant movement that has brought it worldwide fame in the dressage arena, but its natural agility also makes it a good show jumper. Like many warmbloods, it is not the fastest horse, but further infusions of Thoroughbred blood can add speed. It has a handsome, noble head with a wide forehead, a muscular neck, sloping shoulders, deep chest, straight back, and powerful hindquarters.

The Dutch studbook is divided into three—the Rijpaardtype, or riding horse; the Tuigpaardtype, or harness horse; and the Basistype, or basic type, most similar to the traditional Gelderlander.

KNABSTRUP

Knabstrup

TEMPERAMENT: sensible, alert, intelligent

ORIGIN: Denmark

SIMILAR BREEDS: Frederiksborg

HEIGHT: 15.1–16.1 hh

COLOR: spotted

PERSONALITY TYPE: warm-blooded

TYPICAL USE: riding, harness, show

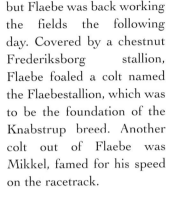

Spotted horses have existed in Denmark at least since the 1600s, when there was a popular strain of "Tiger Horses"—highly regarded, they were almost solely used by royalty and nobility; those with few spots or plain coats were used as carriage horses, as the spotted equines were hard to match up. The royal line of spotted horses died out, however, probably because of the introduction of the gray gene. The spotted horses of Denmark were resurrected through a mare named Flaebe.

Great Quality

In 1812 Villars Lunn, owner of a manor called Knabstrupgaard, bought a mare from a butcher named Flaebe—the mare was named after her owner, as was the custom of the times. It is believed she was of Spanish origin, left behind by a cavalry officer stationed in Denmark during the Napoleonic Wars. Flaebe was dark red—or *zobelfuchs*, in Danish —in color, with a white mane and tail, and her body was covered with tiny, white snowflakes. Most importantly she was a horse of great quality.

Glorious Coloring

Flaebe showed her value when she was one of two horses harnessed to take an injured man to a doctor, a journey of around 18 miles (30 km) completed in less than two hours. The first horse never fully recovered, but Flaebe was back working the fields the following day. Covered by a chestnut Frederiksborg stallion, Flaebe foaled a colt named the Flaebestallion, which was to be the foundation of the Knabstrup breed. Another colt out of Flaebe was Mikkel, famed for his speed on the racetrack.

The modern Knabstrup is just as striking, with the foundation mare's glorious coloring, the speed of her second offspring, and the robust good looks she passed on to the new breed. Sadly today it is considered to be rare.

Fascinating Facts

One reason for the tradition of mounting on the near side of a horse is that, historically, men's scabbards would be worn on the left hip and so they would get in the way if a horse was mounted from the off side.

LEFT

Sadly the numbers of this beautiful breed, with its spotted coat coloring, have become greatly reduced, although efforts are being made to preserve it. The horse pictured has a rare white coat with very subtle spotting.

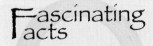

FREDERIKSBORG

HEIGHT: 15.2–16 hh

COLOR: chestnut

PERSONALITY TYPE: warm-blooded

TYPICAL USE: riding, harness

TEMPERAMENT: docile, steady

ORIGIN: Denmark

SIMILAR BREEDS: Knabstrup

Named after Frederik II (1534–88), Denmark's oldest breed is literally the horse of kings. It was first bred at the royal stud in Frederiksborg, and during the 1700s was one of the world's most famous equine breeds. It was highly prized as a reliable and elegant riding horse, well adapted to the movements of the *haute école*, a high-class carriage horse, and a superb military charger. King Frederik imported horses from Italy and Spain to lighten and refine the native stock.

Two Types

Two distinct types were bred, the riding horse and the carriage horse—for the latter, uniformity of color and markings was extremely important, as the royal carriages were pulled by six or eight perfectly matched horses. The Frederiksborg was also used to found or improve other horse breeds during the 1600s, 1700s, and 1800s.

The Frederiksborg passed on its smooth, supple action and its strength and stamina, and this was almost to prove to be the breed's downfall. So many had been exported because of its popularity that there were few left. Efforts to reestablish the Frederiksborg began in

---
LEFT

Two strains of Frederiksborg were bred, a lighter type for riding and a heavy type used as carriage horses.

---

the early 1900s, and although the breed is still fairly rare, this process could be deemed successful.

Strong and Attractive

The Frederiksborg is a strong, attractive horse, always chestnut with a flaxen mane and tail, often with white markings on the face and / or legs. Its head is well proportioned, with a

Fascinating Facts

According to superstition in Lincolnshire, England, if you see a white dog you should stay silent until you see a white horse.

straight or sometimes convex profile, pointed, mobile ears, and large, expressive eyes. Its neck is of medium length, slightly arched and muscular; its shoulders tend to be straight, and the withers are pronounced. Its back is short and straight, with a rounded croup. It has excellent legs, well muscled and strong, with broad joints, good bone, and small but tough feet.

Latterly, breeding has concentrated on breeding the riding type instead of the carriage type.

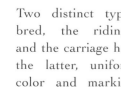

DANISH WARMBLOOD

TEMPERAMENT: amiable, tough, bold

ORIGIN: Denmark

SIMILAR BREEDS: all warmbloods

HEIGHT: 16.2 hh

COLOR: mostly bay, but any solid color

PERSONALITY TYPE: warm-blooded

TYPICAL USE: competition, riding

In 1999 a horse named Marzog, ridden by Anne Grethe Tornblad, was described by an international jury as the "best dressage horse of the century." Marzog was a Danish Warmblood. Denmark has a long history of horse breeding that dates back to the 1300s, and the monastic stud in Holstein and the royal stud of Frederiksborg both made a contribution to the Danish Warmblood. Also known as the Danish Sport Horse, it is the product of careful and selective breeding.

No Hanoverian

The Danish Warmblood studbook was opened in the 1960s, and the new breed was based on several different bloodlines. The Frederiksborg, when crossed with the Thoroughbred, produced a quality middle- to heavyweight riding horse; when Trakehner, Selle Français, and Wielkopolski blood, plus a little more Thoroughbred, were added, it improved the animal considerably and a distinct type emerged—the Danish Warmblood. Unlike many of today's warmbloods, the Danish version contains no Hanoverian.

Stringent Examination

Danish Warmblood stallions have to undergo rigorous 100-day testing, but even this stringent examination does not necessarily guarantee approval. This helps to maintain the extraordinarily high standards of the breed. The Danish Warmblood is a horse of great quality with a Thoroughbred look but with more weight and substance. It has excellent stamina, speed, and jumping ability, as well as superb natural elevation through the paces. It has a refined, attractive head set on a muscular neck, with good length of rein and a deep, broad chest. Its shoulders should be sloping and its back compact and strong. Its legs are muscular and clean, with especially well-made hock joints and perfectly formed feet. Like all warmbloods, the Danish has an exceptionally amiable temperament and is both tough and bold, with a beautiful, free-flowing movement.

Marzog is, as will no doubt be seen, one of many successful Danish Warmbloods.

BELOW

The excellent, athletic conformation and intelligence of this breed has seen it rapidly grow in popularity to become one of the leading sporting horse breeds.

SWEDISH WARMBLOOD

HEIGHT: 15.2–16.3 hh

COLOR: all solid colors

PERSONALITY TYPE: warm-blooded

TYPICAL USE: competition

TEMPERAMENT: calm, even-tempered

ORIGIN: Sweden

SIMILAR BREEDS: all warmbloods

Archaeological evidence has been found for the existence of horses in what is now Sweden dating back to 4,000 B.C., and the history of the Swedish horse closely follows that of humans in the region. The original Scandinavian horse was probably small, standing no more than 14 hh, high-spirited, and with good endurance. In the 1500s a program was started to improve the quality of these native horses. Friesians were imported from the Netherlands to increase the size of the native stock.

Divided Breeding

Following the peace treaty with Denmark in Roskilde, Sweden, in 1658, the Swedish king Carl X Gustav (1622–60) ordered a royal stud to be established in Flyinge. The horses from Flyinge and the national stud farms, which included those at Kungsör and Strömsholm, were often used in the royal stables. Other importations of various saddle breeds were made, but the larger draft breeds were excluded.

The army and the farmers of Sweden had different equine needs, which meant that the program was divided. Thoroughbred, Anglo-Norman, Hanoverian, and Trakehner stallions were imported to improve the military horse. To direct the breeding efforts and to consolidate the different breeds, the Swedish government began an examination system in 1874, which was to result in the production of the Swedish Warmblood. The Swedish Warmblood Association (SWA) was formed in 1928.

Olympic Medals

At the Olympic Games in 1912, Swedish Warmbloods won all three dressage medals. At the Rome Olympics in 1960, the Swedish Warmblood sire Drabant had six sons participating. At Seoul in 1988, 13 Swedish Warmbloods competed, and six won medals.

Today the Swedish Warmblood continues to be a superior riding horse, with tremendous rideability and intelligence. It is, like most warmblood breeds, pleasing to the eye, with a small, neat head, straight neck, compact body, straight back, rounded quarters, and strong legs with short cannons and good feet. It is adaptable to both the professional and the amateur rider.

LEFT

The Swedish Warmblood is another success story in the recent development of warmblood breeds and especially excels at dressage.

FINNISH UNIVERSAL

TEMPERAMENT: alert, reliable, easygoing

ORIGIN: Finland

SIMILAR BREEDS: light draft horses

HEIGHT: 15.2 hh

COLOR: chestnut, bay, brown, black

PERSONALITY TYPE: warm-blooded

TYPICAL USE: harness, riding

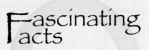

Its name describes it perfectly. The Finnish Universal, or Finnhorse, gets its name because it is said to be able to fulfill all needs for horses in Finland—from draft types to speedy trotters to leisure. In Finnish it is Suomenhevonen, or Suokki—a kind of pet name. It is thought to be around 1,000 years old and in Finland has been universal, being used as a warhorse by the military and then as a mode of transportation and more recently as a trotter. But it is becoming increasingly popular as a sport and leisure animal.

Mostly Trotters

The Finnish Universal is a sturdy creature standing about 15.2 hh and is of medium build. It is probably based on local stock—it is known there were horses in Finland from around the Bronze Age (3500–1100 B.C.) —crossed with native ponies from countries along the Baltic coastland and imported foreign breeds. So it is, essentially, a warmblood, although it does exhibit some coldblood characteristics, having an easygoing and docile nature. It is also kind and willing, with a fast-stepping, naturally active stride.

Coldblood Attributes

Although it has attributes of cold-blooded horses, the Finnish Universal is not unattractive. It has a well-shaped head that is not too large, a strong neck, and powerful shoulders and quarters. Its legs are clean and well muscled without much feather. It is most often chestnut, although bay, black, brown, and the occasional gray do occur. White markings are acceptable.

Fascinating Facts

Trotting is very popular in Finland, and most of the Finnhorse population is used as trotters—there are an estimated 19,000 Finnish Universals, of which around 2,000 are used as riding horses and around 1,000 as agricultural animals; the rest are trotters.

BELOW

Although not striking in appearance, the Finnish Universal is an extremely versatile breed and makes an excellent riding horse and light draft animal.

The Finnish Universal studbook was opened in 1907, and horses have to undergo quite stringent performance testing, which is designed to keep the breed clean.

ICELANDIC

HEIGHT: 12.3–13.2 hh

COLOR: all solid colors

PERSONALITY TYPE: warm-blooded

TYPICAL USE: riding, show, all-rounder

TEMPERAMENT: docile, gentle, lively

ORIGIN: Iceland

SIMILAR BREEDS: Exmoor

There is no word in Icelandic for "pony," so the country's little equine is always known as the Icelandic Horse. Its history dates back to the first settlers of Iceland in the late 800s, when the Vikings brought with them horses of various origins—claimed by some to be a breed called *Equus scandinavicus* that was in the peninsula and northern Europe at the time. Due to the isolation of Iceland from the rest of the world, this stock remained pure, while it was crossbred elsewhere and the original equine type was lost.

Norse Mythology

The Icelandic bears some resemblance to England's

little Exmoor—it has similar characteristics to the "toad eye," double-layered coat, and "snow chute" tail, attributes that would be almost essential to survival in the "land of fire and ice."

The Icelandic has played a vital role in its home country from the beginning. In heathen times the horse was highly regarded and renowned in Norse mythology—it played a big part in Norse mythological stories, as several Norse gods and their enemies, the giants, owned them. The most famous of all of these mythological horses was Sleipnir, the eight-footed pacer. The influence of the Norse myths is still visible, as many riding clubs bear names of mythical

horses, as do herds of horses in modern Iceland.

Useful Servant

More prosaically, to the people of Iceland the horse was the "most useful servant." It literally followed humans from birth to death—from collecting the doctor and midwife to pulling the coffin to the cemetery.

The first automobile arrived in Iceland in the year 1904, and almost immediately the horse became unneeded.

Fascinating Facts

The Icelandic is one of the five-gaited breeds, possessing the lateral *tölt*—a one-two-three-four beat gait that is fast and enormously comfortable for the rider. At shows, Icelandic Horses are often ridden at the *tölt*, while the rider holds a full glass of beer in one hand and the reins in the other without spilling a drop.

ABOVE LEFT

The ancient Icelandic horse breed is especially tough and willing and has a fast, smooth, running gait called the "tölt."

Enthusiastic individuals, however, kept breeding good horses, and Iceland's first horse breeding association was formed the same year the automobile arrived. Today there are about 80,000 horses in Iceland, no small number for a country with just 270,000 human inhabitants.

KLADRUBER

TEMPERAMENT: calm, kind, energetic

ORIGIN: former Czechoslovakia

SIMILAR BREEDS: Lipizzaner

HEIGHT: 16.2–17.2 hh

COLOR: gray, black

PERSONALITY TYPE: warm-blooded

TYPICAL USE: harness, riding

The Kladruber is an attractive breed that is always either black or gray. They make excellent driving horses and are popular as riding horses.

Emperors and kings were patrons of the old Kladruby stud, founded in 1579 by Rudolf II, Holy Roman Emperor (and King of Bohemia, now the Czech Republic), and located at the Perlstein stables, where Maximilian II (1527–76) had bred horses for the previous 20 years. The horses were based mainly on imported Spanish and Italian horses, crossed with Neapolitan, Danish, Holstein, Irish, heavier Czech, and Oldenburgs. All of the bloodlines used had some Andalusian breeding in their pedigree, and the breed was sometimes called *Equus bohemicus*.

Gray and Black

The Kladruber has many similarities to the Lipizzaner, which was bred along very similar lines. It was originally intended as a top-class carriage horse for the Imperial Court. The horse appeared in all coat colors, but from the mid-1700s it was based on three stallions—the gray Peopoli and two black stallions, both named Sacromoso—and from then on always appeared gray or black.

The gray Kladrubers are still bred at the Kladruby Stud in the Czech Republic, but the black herd was destroyed in the 1930s. A few of the black mares were rescued, and since then there have been stringent efforts to reestablish the line.

World-Class

An attractive breed, the Kladruber has a long head with a convex profile and a sensible, kind eye. Its mane and tail hair are abundant and beautiful; its neck muscular and well set with a nice arch from the withers to poll. It has sloping shoulders, a wide, deep chest, and a long back. Its hindquarters are muscular and strong, and the legs are clean and strong with good joints.

The Kladruber is a strong, long-lived, kind horse with a calm, energetic temperament. It makes an excellent competitive driving horse, possessing both speed and endurance, and it is frequently seen at world-class carriage trials. Crossed with lighter breeds, it also makes an excellent riding and competition horse.

WIELKOPOLSKI

HEIGHT: 15.3–16.2 hh

COLOR: all solid colors

PERSONALITY TYPE: warm-blooded

TYPICAL USE: competition, harness, riding

TEMPERAMENT: willing, even-tempered, kind

ORIGIN: Poland

SIMILAR BREEDS: all warmbloods

Perhaps the least known of all the warmbloods, Poland's version, the Wielkopolski, was developed in Central and Western Poland in 1964. It was based on two now extinct Polish breeds, the Pozan and the Masuren, or Marzury, and is also referred to as the Mazursko-Poznanski. The Pozan, which was a mix of Arabian, Thoroughbred, Trakehner, and Hanoverian blood, was a versatile middleweight, useful for riding and agricultural jobs. The Masuren was a quality riding horse, mainly Trakehner in origin.

Affinity for Dressage

Thoroughbred, Arabian, and Anglo-Arab blood were added to refine the breed. And the result is one of the best—if least publicized—European warmbloods, with the good looks, natural agility, and superb temperament of them all. The breed is versatile and talented. It is a natural athlete and is quick, probably due to the Thoroughbred blood, which makes it a superlative show jumper or event horse. Its natural balance and good movement also gives it an affinity for dressage. It is noted for its equable and willing nature and comfortable, long, free paces.

Presence

Today's Wielkopolski is bred along two lines: one lighter for leisure and competitive riding; and one heavier to make an excellent harness horse or middleweight riding horse. Most solid colors are seen, and it stands between 15.3 and 16.2 hh. Both have the Wielkopolski's quality and presence. It has a fine

head with a straight profile and an intelligent eye—the Thoroughbred influence, and to a lesser degree the Arabian's, are especially noticeable in its head and in its long, elegant neck. It has the sloping shoulders necessary for a long, flowing stride, and its chest is deep and wide, with plenty of heart room. Its legs are long and slender but with good joints and well-defined tendons. It has a compact body and the muscular quarters of the equine powerhouse that it is.

LEFT

The Wielkopolski is perhaps Poland's best-kept secret. It is amongst the most talented warmblood breeds and also the least publicized.

SHAGYA ARABIAN

TEMPERAMENT: intelligent, good-natured, willing

ORIGIN: Hungary

SIMILAR BREEDS: Arabian, Anglo-Arab

HEIGHT: 15–16 hh

COLOR: mostly gray, bay, chestnut, black

PERSONALITY TYPE: warm-blooded

TYPICAL USE: riding, harness, competition

If the Arabian is the "diamond" of all horse breeds, the Shagya Arabian is that diamond, cut and polished to equine perfection. It was created on the famous Austro-Hungarian military stud farms in the 1780s, primarily in Hungary in Babolna, Radautz, and Piber. Later, stud farms in Topolcianky (Czechoslovakia), Mangalia (Romania), and Kabijuk (Bulgaria) also bred Shagyas. The purpose was to develop a breed of superior cavalry and carriage horses, as well as prepotent sires to be used to improve other breeds.

More Substance

The Shagya combines the best components of the desert Arabian—elegance, toughness, endurance, and an inborn affinity with humans —with the desirable qualities of a riding horse—substance, trainability, athleticism, and excellent movement. It served as a cavalry mount and was displayed in parades for Europe's royalty.

It is bigger than the purebred Arabian, with a larger frame and more substance, although the Arab influence is clear in its concave profile. Most Shagya Arabians are gray, although bay, chestnut, and black also appear.

Outstanding Sire

The oldest damline recorded is that of Moldvai, foaled in 1781; another famous line is that of Tine, born in 1810. The breed was further developed by carefully breeding back over and over to desert-bred and purebred Arabians, combined with rigorous culling and selection. This long-term process can be traced in an unbroken line from the Shagyas of today all the way back to the beginning of the breed. Many Shagyas have pedigrees more than 20 generations long.

The most important stallion is the dapple gray Shagya, born in 1810. He was bred by the Bani Saher tribe of Bedouins and came to the stud at Babotna, around 36 miles (58 km) from Budapest in 1836. He was such an outstanding sire that he appears in almost all Shagya pedigrees. He not only left his mark on the breed but also gave it his name.

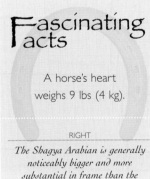

Fascinating Facts

A horse's heart weighs 9 lbs (4 kg).

RIGHT

The Shagya Arabian is generally noticeably bigger and more substantial in frame than the purebred Arab and is renowned for its equable temperament.

GIDRAN ARABIAN

HEIGHT: 16–17 hh

COLOR: chestnut

PERSONALITY TYPE: warm-blooded

TYPICAL USE: riding, harness

TEMPERAMENT: intelligent, unpredictable

ORIGIN: Hungary

SIMILAR BREEDS: Arabian

A rare breed, the Gidran Arabian, or the Hungarian Anglo-Arab, originated at the Hungarian stud in Mezohegyes, founded in 1785. The breed can be traced back to the stallion Siglavy Gidran (from which it gets its name), which was imported from Arabia in 1816. Gidran was from the noted Siglavy Arab strain and was an imposing chestnut. Put to a Spanish mare called Arrogante, he produced a colt foal called Gidran II, which was the foundation sire of the Gidran Arabian.

Cavalry Horse

During the 1800s the breed was developed further, primarily for use as cavalry horses. A number of mares were used, some local and some Spanish; later, infusions of Thoroughbred and further Arabian blood were added. The Gidran Arab developed along two basic lines: a heavier type more adapted to light farm and draft work and a lighter, faster, saddle horse.

The breed sustained substantial losses during the First World War, and after further Arab blood and some Kisber blood were introduced. Later, two Bulgarian stallions were introduced to bring in fresh blood.

LEFT

Following the First World War, blood from the Kisber stud was introduced to the Gidran in an effort to increase the numbers of the breed. Kisber Felvers are pictured here.

Upstanding

The Gidran Arabian is a large, upstanding horse, solidly built and exhibiting quality and class. It is almost always chestnut, with the refined head of the Arab, but not as delicate. Its neck is well-proportioned in relation to its body and is muscular and well set. It has a nice slope to its shoulders, which allows for freedom of movement, and its chest is deep and wide. Deep through the barrel, it has a strong, sometimes long back. Its quarters are also muscular, and the legs are strong with short, dense, cannon bones and well-formed feet. It generally stands between 16 and 16.2 hh, although it can be as big as 17 hh.

Fascinating Facts

It is believed that there are only around 200 Gidran Arabians in existence.

BELOW

The Gidran Arabian is now, sadly, a rare breed that was originally developed from Arab, Spanish, and Thoroughbred influences.

FURIOSO

HEIGHT: 15.3–16.2 hh

COLOR: brown, bay, chestnut, black

PERSONALITY TYPE: warm-blooded

TYPICAL USE: riding, competition, harness

TEMPERAMENT: calm, energetic, honest

ORIGIN: Hungary

SIMILAR BREEDS: Thoroughbred, Nonius

An English Thoroughbred gave its name to this Hungarian breed, based on the local Nonius mares at the Mezohegyes Stud, which had a formidable reputation as a horse-breeding center. Furioso was imported in 1841 and sired 95 stallions that were to form the basis of the breed. Another line was based on North Star, imported in 1844, which had some Norfolk Roadster blood. He was the grandson of Touchstone, winner of the 1834 St. Leger, and was related to Eclipse.

Dominant Characteristics

The Furioso and North Star were originally developed along entirely separate lines; however, by the end of the 1800s the progeny were crossbred, and the Furioso characteristics began to dominate. For a period the breed was known as the Furioso-North Star. Today's Furioso bears little resemblance to its Nonius roots and is now bred in Apajpuszta, Hungary, and also widely across Central Europe. A versatile riding horse, it is capable of competing in all major disciplines. It is strong and tough and has a calm but energetic temperament.

Steeplechaser

The Furioso has a correctly proportioned, refined head—more Thoroughbred-looking than that of the Nonius. Its neck is in proportion to the body and is muscular, with a prolific mane. It is often described as having basic workmanlike conformation, for which it is indebted to the Nonius. It tends to be a little long through the back but with a compact body,

muscular quarters, strong legs, and well let-down hocks. Its feet are generally good. It is wide through the chest, with sloping shoulders and deep through the girth. Conformational faults that may occur are pigeon toes in front and cow hocks behind.

Hardy and enduring, the Furioso also makes a good steeplechaser—a testament to its Thoroughbred forefathers.

NONIUS

HEIGHT: 14.3–16.2 hh

COLOR: bay, brown

PERSONALITY TYPE: warm-blooded

TYPICAL USE: competition, riding

TEMPERAMENT: easygoing, calm

ORIGIN: Hungary

SIMILAR BREEDS: all warmbloods

Like the Furioso, the Nonius has its roots in the Mezohegyes Stud in Hungary and is based on one sire—Nonius Senior. He was foaled in Normandy in 1810 and was taken by the Hungarian cavalry in 1813 after the defeat of Napoleon in Leipzig. He stood at stud for 22 years, during which time the breed that took his name was established. Nonius Senior was by a stallion called Orion, an English half-bred with some Norfolk Roadster blood, and out of a Norman mare.

Conformational Faults

Records show that Nonius was a light bay five-year-old, standing just under 17 hh. He had a large and heavy head with small eyes and long ears, short neck, high prominent withers, a long back, narrow and low hindquarters, and low-set tail. He had short and steep shoulder blades. He was narrow at the knees in the front and at the hocks behind. His conformational faults meant that initially Nonius was used very little for breeding in Mezohegyes. Only when it was noticed that his offspring did not inherit his looks and that they had excellent endurance and more correct conformation was he began to be bred.

Useful All-Rounder

He was then put to mostly Spanish, Lipizzaner, and Kladruber mares. When he died in 1838, he left behind 79 stallions and 137 mares. His son, Nonius IX, was also used to fix the breed type. Thoroughbred blood was later added for refinement.

The Nonius is strong and tough, with an amenable temperament. It makes a useful all-round riding horse and is generally well built and sound, with good solid legs. It is almost always bay or brown. Nonius mares have been put to English Thoroughbred stallions to produce first-rate competition and sporting horses.

Fascinating Facts

It is documented that Nonius Senior was not especially well conformed or attractive, although fortunately he did not pass on these traits to his progeny. It does seem strange, however, that such a poor stallion was used as a primary sire in Mezohegyes.

LEFT

The Nonius, with its muscular frame and good proportions, makes a top riding horse and an excellent driving horse.

KISBER FELVER

TEMPERAMENT: alert, willing, docile

ORIGIN: Hungary

SIMILAR BREEDS: all warmbloods

HEIGHT: 15.2–17 hh

COLOR: any solid color

PERSONALITY TYPE: warm-blooded

TYPICAL USE: competition, riding, harness

A relatively young breed, the Kisber Felver was developed at the Kisber Stud in Hungary, which was founded in 1853 primarily to breed Thoroughbreds. The stud produced such racing talents as Kisber, winner of the Epsom Derby, and Kincsem, which made its way into the *Guinness Book of Records* for an unbeaten 54 races. The Kisber Stud not only made its mark on Thoroughbred racing history but also developed a half-bred that was regarded as the world's most beautiful sporting horse.

Quality Warmblood

The Kisber Felver evolved from crosses of Thoroughbred, Furioso, Trakehner, Arabian, Anglo-Arab, and Selle Français. It was originally developed to be a useful sporting horse, with more substance than the Thoroughbred, and as a harness horse. Once the Kisber Felver had developed its fixed characteristics, it was commonly used on local stock to improve the progeny.

RIGHT

The Kisber Felver is a tough and talented young warmblood breed that is, however, not well-known outside of its native Hungary.

Those fixed characteristics add up to an attractive, quality warmblood, with a distinctly Thoroughbred look. It has a refined head with alert ears, well-proportioned neck that curves gently from the withers to the poll, sloping shoulders, a deep chest, and well-sprung ribs. Its back tends to be long, and its legs are muscular.

Not Well-Known

The Kisber Felver has a tough, sound constitution and is energetic and lively, qualities that made it adaptable to military purposes. Breed numbers were greatly reduced during the First and Second World Wars, and in 1945 over half the breeding stock was taken as war damages. In 1961 the remaining breeding stock was moved to the Dalmand Stud Farm, where the Kisber Felver is still bred today.

The Kisber Felver is not well-known, which contradicts its merits and worth as a competition horse. It is naturally athletic and makes a good jumping and eventing prospect.

LIPIZZANER

HEIGHT: 15.1–16.2 hh

COLOR: gray

PERSONALITY TYPE: warm-blooded

TYPICAL USE: High School, riding, show, harness

TEMPERAMENT: intelligent, spirited, kind

ORIGIN: Slovenia

SIMILAR BREEDS: Andalusian, Lusitano

Holy Roman Emperor Maximilian II (1527–76) brought Spanish horses to Austria in 1562 and founded the court stud Kladruby, in what is now the Czech Republic. His brother, Archduke Charles, established a similar stud with Spanish stock in 1580 in Lipica, Slovenia, near the Adriatic Sea. The Kladruby stud became known for its heavy carriage horses, while the Lipica stud produced riding and light carriage types. The two studs sometimes exchanged breeding stock—Kladruby produced Maestoso and Favory, two of the foundation sires of today's Lipizzaner.

Riding School

The aim was to produce a showy, predominantly gray horse for the ducal stables in Graz and the court stables in Vienna. The famed Spanish Riding School of Vienna was founded in 1572 to teach the nobility, and got its name from the fact that it used Spanish horses. There have also been infusions of Neapolitan, Arabian, Danish, and German blood. An

attempt to introduce Thoroughbred lines to the breed was not successful.

Interest in the art of classical riding revived during the Renaissance period, when the Spanish horse was considered the most adaptable mount because of its exceptional sturdiness, beauty, and intelligence. The athletic Lipizzaner was supremely adapted to the movements of the *haute école*, or High School.

RIGHT

The beautiful Lipizzaner horse is perhaps best known for the magical performances it gives with the Spanish Riding School in Vienna.

Six Stallions

The Lipizzaner breed is based on six foundation sires, the lines of which still exist today. These stallions were Pluto, a gray Spanish stallion, foaled in 1765 and bought from the Royal Danish Stud;

Conversano, a black Neopolitan stallion (1767); Neapolitano, a brown Neopolitan stallion (1790); Favory, a dun stallion, foaled at the Kladruby stud in 1779; Maestoso, a gray stallion foaled in 1819 at the Hungarian stud of Mezohegyes; and Siglavy, a gray Arabian (1810). Although the Lipizzaner is assumed to be only gray, until the 1700s there were Lipizzaners with various coat colors, including dun, spotted, and bay. The royal family preferred the light gray horses, however, so breeding was concentrated on this color.

Mare Lines

The six foundation sires produced distinctive lines of

Lipizzaner. Conversano stock have strong, ramlike heads and short backs with broad hocks. The Arabian influence is more obvious in Favory horses, which tend to be of

Lipizzaner. Conversano stock have strong, ramlike heads and short backs with broad hocks. The Arabian influence is more obvious in Favory horses, which tend to be of

Fascinating Facts

Lipizzaners are born dark brown or black, and their coats lighten as they grow older, through from gray to white—the long-lived Lipizzaner can survive long into its twenties. At the Spanish Riding School of Vienna, there is always a brown or black Lipizzaner for good luck.

BELOW
This magnificent breed was on the verge of being wiped out during the Second World War but was rescued and has since been reestablished.

lighter build, while Maestosos are powerful, with a long back and heavier heads. Neapolitano's progeny are taller, more rangy in appearance, with a high action. Pluto stock is sturdy and has a rectangular build, while Siglavy's is aristocratic, with an elegant head and a relatively short back.

As well as the foundation stallions, there are 18 mare family lines. Each stallion has two names—that of the sire and that of the dam—so horses would have names such as Pluto Theodorosta.

Edge of Extinction

The history of the Lipizzaner is somewhat stormy, and the breed was almost lost—at the beginning of the 1900s there were only 208 purebred

Lipizzaners left. The breed was brought to the very edge of extinction during the Second World War, when the stud was forced to leave its premises by the German High Command. It was saved, however, by the Spanish Riding School's then director, Colonel Alois Podhajsky (1898–1973). The stud is now located in Piber in the Austrian mountains, having been established there in 1920.

Today's Lipizzaner is a magnificent equine, with an attractive head that can show some Arabian influence, but

more usually it has typically Spanish characteristics. Its neck is short and muscular, with flattish withers, a deep chest, sloping shoulders that are conformed for riding or harness, a long back, and rounded hindquarters with a well-set tail. Its legs are short and muscular, and they usually have good bone.

Vienna's dancing white horses are a joy to watch, especially in the opulent splendor of the Spanish Riding School, and their suppleness and athleticism make them specially adapted to dressage.

UKRAINIAN RIDING HORSE

HEIGHT: 15.1–16.1 hh

COLOR: bay, brown, chestnut, black

PERSONALITY TYPE: warm-blooded

TYPICAL USE: competition, riding

TEMPERAMENT: calm, sensible, intelligent

ORIGIN: Ukraine

SIMILAR BREEDS: all warmbloods

Fascinating Facts

The Ukrainian Riding Horse Ikhor, ridden by Ivan Kizimov, won the dressage gold medal at the 1968 Olympic Games in Mexico.

RIGHT

This breed has only been established since the end of the Second World War but has already proven to be a useful and talented sporting horse.

A relatively new breed, the Ukrainian Riding Horse—sometimes also known as the Russian Riding, or Russian Saddle, Horse—was developed after the Second World War to meet the increasing demand for sporting horses. It was first developed at the Dnepropetrovsk Stud in the Ukraine. Today it is bred at the studs of Derkulsk, Yagonitsk, and Aleksandriisk. Despite its brief history the breed is well established in its characteristics because of the highly selective breeding process that is used.

Hanoverian Blood

The Ukrainian Riding Horse was based on local mare stock crossed with Trakehner, Hanoverian, and Thoroughbred stallions. Some Furioso and Gidran Arabian mares from Hungary were also used. The progeny was then interbred to establish the Ukrainian Riding Horse type. More Hanoverian blood was added to those considered too fine, while further infusions of Thoroughbred blood refined those that were too heavy. Since the original type was fixed, only Hanoverian and Thoroughbred blood has been used to refine and improve the breed.

Competition Bound

The horse has an attractive head set on a long, muscular neck, with sloping shoulders and a deep chest, although its back has a tendency to be long and hollow. Its croup is long and sloping. The horses are usually bay, chestnut, or black in color and stand 15.1–16.1 hh.

The horses are kept in a regulated environment. They begin training just before the age of two and are required to participate in a performance testing as two- and three-year-olds, which includes racing on the track, jumping, and dressage. Only the best are allowed to stand at stud. The most successful have competed at the highest level, including the Olympics.

PLEVEN

TEMPERAMENT: calm, obedient, willing

ORIGIN: Bulgaria

SIMILAR BREEDS: Anglo Arab

HEIGHT: 15.2–16 hh

COLOR: chestnut

PERSONALITY TYPE: warm-blooded

TYPICAL USE: riding, competition

Bulgaria's warmblood breed was developed at the former state stud called Klementina—now the Georgi Dimitrov Agricultural Center—in 1898. It was the result of crossing local stock with Arabian, Russian Anglo-Arab, and Gidran lines. The breed was officially recognized in 1951, and some Thoroughbred blood was introduced for refinement and quality and to increase the size. The result was a handsome horse with excellent, free-flowing paces and a natural jumping ability.

Sound Constitution

The Pleven has the calm warmblood temperament and is willing and obedient, economical to keep, and easy to train. It generally has a sound constitution and is tough and enduring. It has a pleasing head with a straight profile, a long, muscular neck, and well-formed, nicely sloping shoulders, which give it its very correct action and attractive way of going. It is broad and deep through the chest and has muscular quarters with slightly sloping croup. Its legs are well formed, with good bone and excellent feet.

SYRIAN

TEMPERAMENT: spirited, lively, intelligent

ORIGIN: Syria

SIMILAR BREEDS: Arabian

HEIGHT: 14.2–15.1 hh

COLOR: chestnut, gray

PERSONALITY TYPE: hot-blooded

TYPICAL USE: riding

Closely related to the Arabian, the Syrian Horse originates from Syria (now the Syrian Arab Republic) in Southwest Asia, bordering on Lebanon. Although very rarely standing more than 14.2 hh, the Syrian is regarded as a horse rather than a pony, and some reach 15.1 hh. Tough and frugal, having had to

adapt and thrive in its harsh natural climate, it bears a close resemblance to the Arabian and is thought to be a variation of the breed that developed its own distinctive characteristics because of its isolated homeland.

A Desert Survivor

Like the Arabian, the Syrian is supremely well equipped to survive in desert conditions, being able to withstand high temperatures during the day, as well as the cold of the desert night. It is generally considered less attractive than the Arabian, although it does possess the grace and presence of its close cousin. It is a good keeper, able to thrive on meager rations. Although it has a tendency to be "hot," the Syrian is trainable and makes a good riding horse.

CASPIAN

HEIGHT: 10–12.2 hh

COLOR: bay, brown, chestnut, gray

PERSONALITY TYPE: hot-blooded

TYPICAL USE: show, driving, riding

TEMPERAMENT: intelligent, lively, brave

ORIGIN: Persia (now Iran)

SIMILAR BREEDS: Arabian

In the 1960s an American named Louise Firouz discovered around 50 small horses living along the coast of the Caspian Sea, and she wrote: " . . . that they are so distinctively peculiar to one small region leads one to believe that they were systematically bred for a purpose at one time. Their remarkable characteristics come through so clearly that they are probably throwbacks to a strongly dominant breed." Ms. Firouz is credited with saving the Caspian Horse from the brink of extinction.

Ancient Lineage

Research into the history and origin of this beguiling little horse proved the ancient lineage of the Caspian. It was identified as a royal breed previously thought to be long extinct. Through examination and research of ancient Persian archaeological remains along with blood type, bone structure, and genetic testing, the Caspian was found to be the forerunner of Persia's native wild horses.

It is believed that the Mesopotamians used the Caspian to develop the

LEFT

These extraordinary tiny horses are an ancient breed of enormous quality, and display typical 'desert' features, being tough, fine-skinned and highly intelligent.

Arabian in 3,000 B.C., and the elegant Caspian does actually look like a miniature Arabian. Identification of the Caspian was aided by several of its unique features, such as its blood hemoglobin composition and its skeletal structure. It is a fine creature with an attractive head and "desert" characteristics, but it stands less than 12.2 hh.

Isolated Horses

Small, wild horses roamed the district of Persia around Kermanshah, now known as Bakhatran, in west central Iran. The most common theory of the horse's presence around Kermanshah is that many species were swept south ahead of glaciers, retreating to warmer climates. After the glaciers melted, many species returned to their former northern habitats, but some remained within fixed geographical areas, forming isolated breeding groups with distinctive genetic character-istics. This would account for the very early isolated pocket of Caspians in ancient Persia in the Zabras near Kermanshah.

Evidence that a Caspian-type horse existed as early as 3,000 B.C. can be found in ancient writings and artifacts.

A terracotta plaque from second-millennium Mesopotamia, showing a small horse ridden with a nose ring, can be seen at the British Museum.

Fascinating Facts

The Persian kings Ardashir I (ruled A.D. 226–241) and Shapur I (ruled A.D. 241–272) were depicted on stone reliefs with small horses that stood no more than waist-high.

PERSIAN ARAB

Persian

TEMPERAMENT: spirited, trainable, intelligent

ORIGIN: Persia

SIMILAR BREEDS: Arabian

HEIGHT: 14.2–15.2 hh

COLOR: gray, bay, chestnut

PERSONALITY TYPE: hot-blooded

TYPICAL USE: riding, racing

Horses are believed to have existed in Persia from around 2,000 B.C., which means that the Persian Arab predates the Arabian by around 1,500 years. Although the name "Persian Arab" is given to all horses from what is now Iran, there is a vast number of different regional strains throughout the country, named after the families that bred them. But they are all of the classical Arabian type, with its refined head with wide forehead and dished profile and small, alert ears.

Wiped Out

The southwestern region of Khuzestan produces some notable strains of the Persian Arab. There are also very set rules on the selective breeding process in place here, which has helped keep the strains pure. The Persian Arab is now greatly reduced in numbers, partly due to African horse sickness, which affected Iran in the 1950s and wiped out a vast number of the breed.

The Persian Arab is similar to the Arabian in conformation and characteristics, although it is slightly heavier in build. It is an attractive horse, with great presence and natural carriage and bearing. Compact and muscular through the body, it has the Arabian's elegantly arched neck, a broad, deep chest, rounded quarters, and a tail that is set and carried high. Generally it is gray, bay, or chestnut in color and stands between 14.2 and 15.2 hh. It makes a very good riding horse and is quick and agile, with enormous stamina and spirit.

New Breeds

Two breeds in Iran have developed from the Persian Arab: the Jaf from Kurdistan and the Darashouri from the Fars region. Both have predominantly Arabian characteristics and are spirited, quick, and have good stamina. The Jaf is considered to have better stamina than the Darashouri and is more able to cope in the extreme desert conditions. The Darashouri is deemed the more attractive and elegant of the two.

LEFT

The Persian Arab exhibits strong Arab characteristics, although it is generally slightly heavier in build and often bigger than its relative.

ARABIAN

HEIGHT: 14.2–15 hh

COLOR: all solid colors, except palomino

PERSONALITY TYPE: hot-blooded

TYPICAL USE: riding, racing, endurance

TEMPERAMENT: spirited, brave, affectionate

ORIGIN: Middle East

SIMILAR BREEDS: Akhal-Teke, Barb, Persian Arab

Centuries ago, in the inhospitable deserts of the Middle East, there emerged a breed of horse that would influence the equine world beyond all imagination. In the sweet grass oases along the Euphrates and Tigris rivers, in the countries that are now known as Syria, Iraq, and Iran, this desert survivor developed into today's glorious Arabian. The Arabian is considered to be the fountainhead of modern horse breeds, as there are very few that do not have some Arabian blood in their history.

LEFT

The Arabian is one of the most prepotent horse breeds and has influenced the development of the majority of other horse breeds at some stage.

Mark of Glory

The Arabian's past was inextricably bound with that of the Bedouins— their religious beliefs, their superstitions, and their traditions. To those desert people, the horse was a gift from Allah to be revered, cherished, and almost worshipped.

They believed that their magnificent horse was created by Allah, who said: "I call you horse; I make you Arabian, and I give you the chestnut color of the ant.

I have hung happiness from your forelock that hangs between your eyes; you shall be the lord of the other animals. Men will follow you wherever you go; you shall be as good for pursuit as for flight. Riches shall be made on your back, and fortune shall come through your mediation."

Allah then blessed the horse with the mark of glory—the white star in the center of its forehead.

Mythology and Romance

The Bedouins believed that the Arabian's unique traits were further gifts from Allah. The horse's *jibbah* (the shield-shaped bulge on its forehead) carried the blessings of Allah; the greater the *jibbah*, the greater the blessings. The horse's arched neck with the *mitbah* (the angle at which it joins the head), which makes it incredibly mobile, was a sign of courage. The high-set tail showed pride. All these traits, for which the horses were selectively bred, were held in high esteem and carefully kept *asil*, or pure.

The headmen of the tribes could relate verbally the full histories of each family of horse, and the mythology and romance of the breed grew with each passing century as

stories of courage, endurance, and wealth intermingled with the genealogies.

Enemy Raids

So revered was the Arabian that it would share the tent with its Bedouin owner, and it is thought that this is why the modern breed has such an affinity with humans. To its owner, the Arabian was primarily a weapon of war. Well mounted on a swift Arabian—usually a mare, as they did not whicker to other horses, thus giving away their position—the Bedouin could make a raid on an enemy settlement, capturing herds of camels, goats, sheep, and of course, more horses.

Universal Breed

The speed and endurance necessary for these raids remain Arabian strengths to this day. And the Arabian's beauty, with its exaggeratedly dished face, tiny, alert ears, and dark, liquid eye make it the most easily recognized of all horse breeds. As well as the *mitbah* and *jibbah*, the Arabian has other unique features: it has 17 ribs, 5 lumbar vertebrae, and 16 tailbones. All other equine breeds have 18 ribs, 6 lumbar vertebrae, and 18 tailbones.

Fine-boned and lean, the Arabian has the fine, silky hair of desert horses with a high sheen. Its mane and tail are long and abundant, with the tail carried gaily high. Its sloping shoulders give it the light, springy action for which it is so prized, and it has a short, compact back and long, slender limbs. The ancient Arabian was to provide the foundation for the horse of the sport of kings, the Thoroughbred.

AKHAL-TEKE

HEIGHT : 14.2–15.2 hh

COLOR : chestnut, bay, gray, palomino, black, dun

PERSONALITY TYPE: hot-blooded

TYPICAL USE: riding, competition, endurance, racing

TEMPERAMENT: lively, intelligent, stubborn

ORIGIN: Turkmenistan

SIMILAR BREEDS: Turkoman

Exotically beautiful, the Akhal-Teke is an ancient breed that gets its name from a Turkmenian tribe called Teke, which lived at the Akhal oasis in Turkmenistan. It was bred by the Turkmene warriors around 2,500 years ago, but horses very similar to the Akhal-Teke, probably the breed's ancestors, were bred in Ashkhabad as long ago as 1000 B.C. It has great endurance and stamina, as well as speed, and is able to cope easily with the extreme heat and intense cold of its Central Asian homeland.

Metallic Glow

As the chief mount of Turkoman warriors for centuries, the Akhal-Teke developed endless stamina, and with fresh forage available for only three months of the year in the arid desert, the Teke tribespeople

> LEFT
>
> *The Akhal-Teke is an elegant and unusual breed, distinguished by its high head and neck carriage.*

Tremendous Speed

Located away from the trade routes, bordered by the Kara Kum desert and Kopet Dag mountains, the Akhal oasis is in an area not subjected to continual conquest or occupation. The Teke tribespeople took great pleasure in their horses and produced a breed of ancient lineage and great purity. The Akhal-Teke is believed to be related to the Arabian and bears a distinct resemblance to the Munaghi Arabian—

> LEFT
>
> *These desert horses can cope with extreme temperatures and are tough and enduring. They are frequently raced and are incredibly fast.*

both were bred for racing and possessed tremendous speed. The similarities between these ancient breeds have raised the question as to which influenced the other and which one was developed first.

developed their own special methods of horse management. Kept in small bands, tied to stakes, and covered in blankets, the Akhal-Teke were fed pellets consisting of alfalfa, barley, and mutton fat. The result was a horse that can subsist on small amounts of food and water, becomes devoted to its master, and is suspicious of strangers.

The blankets also enhanced the metallic sheen of the horses' coat, which is a source of great pride for their owners—the Akhal-Teke's coat glows like pure gold. It has a unique hair structure that refracts light, producing colors from blazing palominos to electric black,

with a distinctive golden sheen. Today's Akhal-Teke retains every quality of endurance, speed, economy, intelligence, and beauty that was so prized throughout the centuries by so many different societies.

Royal Gift

It is widely believed that Bucephalus, the famous favored mount of Alexander the Great (356–323 B.C.), was of Turkmenian blood and therefore closely related to the Akhal-Teke. Also said to be fans of the Akhal-Teke were Roman emperors, Genghis Khan (c. 1162–1227), and the explorer Marco Polo (1254–1324). Queen Elizabeth II of England was presented with an Akhal-Teke in 1956. Her Majesty's grooms tried to wash off what they thought was polish but was the natural metallic sheen of the stallion's golden dun coat.

The horse is one of great beauty, with an elegant head and graceful neck, high withers, long back, and muscular hindquarters. It is very long in the leg and finely boned. It is highly intelligent and possesses a swift turn of foot; it is still used as a racehorse today.

It is also unrivaled in its powers of endurance—15 Akhal-Tekes traveled from Ashkhabad to Moscow in 1935, a distance of 2,700 miles (4,345 km), crossing 235 miles (378 km) of desert in three days with no water. This feat convinced breeders of the value of their glorious horse.

Dressage Medals

There is plenty of speculation about the role the Akhal-Teke played in the development of the Thoroughbred. Careful study of what is known of the Byerley Turk indicates that he was probably an Akhal-Teke and that the Darley Arabian was of the Munighi strain of Arabians and carried a large portion of Akhal-Teke blood.

The Akhal-Teke today is emerging as a sporting horse, having won Olympic medals in dressage and possessing a natural jumping ability. Although there are thought to be only around 3,000 left, it is hoped that this beautiful breed will continue to flourish.

TURKOMAN

HEIGHT: 15 hh

COLOR: most solid colors

PERSONALITY TYPE: hot-blooded

TYPICAL USE: riding, racing

TEMPERAMENT: intelligent, trainable, hardy

ORIGIN: Turkmenistan

SIMILAR BREEDS: Akhal-Teke

Bred in Iran, the Turkoman—sometimes also called Turkmene—is sometimes considered to be simply another strain of the Akhal-Teke breed. Whatever the case, it is now extinct in its original form, like the Yamud Horse, which was developed in the same region, although horses bred in the region are still called Turkoman. The original Turkoman had the Akhal-Teke's grayhound-like svelteness. It is also documented that some of these horses had the glowing metallic coat of the Akhal-Teke, giving credence to the suggestion that they became the same breed.

Nomadic Tribes

Modern Turkmenistan, with its population of roughly four million and its economy based largely on cotton and natural gas, was once among the republics of the Soviet Union. In older texts it is known as Turkmenia. For thousands of years before the 1879 Russian occupation, nomadic tribes and pastoral clans populated the territory, struggling interminably to

LEFT

The Turkoman horse is closely related to the Akhal-Teke and shares similar characteristics, including their gracefulness and speed.

graze their herds in the valley of the Amu Darya, Central Asia's longest river, and amid the foothills of the Kopet Mountains that now separate Turkmenistan from Afghanistan and Iran. Almost every Turkmene family owned at least one or two horses.

Bred to Race

The horses were bred to race and were raised in an unusual manner, with the mares kept in semi-wild herds that had to fend for themselves against the weather and predators, finding their own food. Colts were caught at six months and kept on long ropes, usually for life. The Turkoman horses were fed a special high-protein diet of chicken, barley, dates, raisins, and mutton fat.

Cherished by the nomads, the horses were called Argamaks by the occupying Russians, which meant "tall and refined." Swift and hardy, the horses had free-flowing movement and a good temperament, as well as great speed and stamina, characteristics that are seen in the Akhal-Teke today.

KARABAIR

TEMPERAMENT: brave, intelligent

ORIGIN: Uzbekistan

SIMILAR BREEDS: Arabian, Akhal-Teke, Karabakh

HEIGHT: 14.2–15 hh

COLOR: bay, chestnut, gray, black

PERSONALITY TYPE: warm-blooded

TYPICAL USE: riding, harness, mounted games

A Central Asian breed, the Karabair is an ancient equine based on stock that is documented as being in the Uzbekistan and northern Tajikistan regions for more than 2,000 years. It was probably a mix of Arabian and Mongolian blood, later influenced by other desert breeds such as the Turkoman and Akhal-Teke, as well as more Arabian infusions. It has similarities to the Arabian, such as innate toughness, stamina, and endurance, but physically it is less graceful.

Mounted Game

Uzbekistan is still populated by a vast number of nomadic people who have been, through the years, the principal breeders of the Karabair. Their lifestyle accounts for the number of different breeds that have influenced the development of the Karabair.

The horse is fairly central to the lives of the Uzbekistan people—it is used for riding and driving, as well as in the ridden game of kokpar. Kokpar is a ferocious contest which centers around gaining possession of the carcass of a dead goat. There are few rules and many injuries, and the Karabair is used almost exclusively in the game due to its bravery and speed.

LEFT

The Karabair is a desert breed that is central to the often-nomadic lives of the people of Uzbekistan. It is used for riding and driving and is surefooted, quick, and agile.

Clean-Cut Head

The Karabair had developed in three different types, all of a similar height. The first was a heavy type suitable for light draft, pack, and riding. The second was lighter and was mainly used for riding, while the third was better adapted to draft work. There is now less distinction between the three; the heavier type has almost disappeared, and the other two types have more or less converged.

The Karabair resembles the Arabian, Persian Arab, and Akhal-Teke. It has a medium-sized, clean-cut head with a straight or slightly convex profile, wide jaw, and high-set, medium-long neck. It has wide and well-muscled hindquarters and a sloping croup and shoulders, although the latter can sometimes be too upright. Its chest is well developed, and it has clean, strong legs with good feet.

KARABAKH

HEIGHT: 14–15 hh

COLOR: chestnut, bay, dun

PERSONALITY TYPE: warm-blooded

TYPICAL USE: riding, racing

TEMPERAMENT: spirited, courageous

ORIGIN: Azerbaijan

SIMILAR BREEDS: Karabair, Arabian, Akhal-Teke

Developed in Nagorny Karabakh between the Araks and Kura rivers in Azerbaijan, the Karabakh is another ancient mountain breed formed by crossing local equines with Persian Arabian, Arabian, and Turkmenian horses. The Arabian is the most pronounced, with the two breeds having many similarities, although the golden sheen of the Akhal-Teke is also sometimes seen in the Karabakh. The breed is thought to have been in existence since around the 400s.

Taken by Conquerors

Some historical sources mention that during the Arab invasion of Azerbaijan in the 700s and 800s, tens of thousands of horses with golden-chestnut coloring, which were characteristic colors for Karabakhs, were taken by the conquerors. There is some evidence that Karabakh ruler Ibrahim-Khalil Khan (1730–1806) possessed a horse herd numbering 3,000–4,000, mostly consisting of Karabakh.

The breed became increasingly popular in Europe in the 1800s; in 1823 an English company purchased 60 purebred Karabakh mares from Mehdi-Kulu Khan, the last ruler of the Karabakh khanate.

Salvaged

In the early 1900s the Karabakh numbers sharply decreased, mostly because of civil and ethnic wars in Azerbaijan.

In 1949 the breed was revived at Agdam Stud, but it suffered another setback during Armenian–Azeri conflict. In 1993 most of the Karabakhs were salvaged from the stud. These horses are currently bred in winter pastures in lowland Karabakh plains between the Barda and Agjabadi provinces.

Like most mountain breeds the Karabakh is tough and hardy, able to survive on little feed, a trait vital to the nomadic people of Azerbaijan. It is sure-footed and loyal but also possesses a good turn of foot.

Fascinating Facts

In 2004 a Karabakh horse named Kishmish from Agdam Stud in Azerbaijan set a speed record by running 3,280 ft. (1,000 m) in 1 min. 9 seconds and 5,249 ft. (1,600 m) in 1 min. 52 seconds.

RIGHT

This ancient mountain breed shares similarities with the Arab and horses of Turkmenistan, both of which influenced its development.

LOKAI

TEMPERAMENT: quiet, willing, obedient

ORIGIN: Tajikistan

SIMILAR BREEDS: Akhal-Teke, Karabair

HEIGHT: 14.3 hh

COLOR: chestnut, bay, gray, black, palomino

PERSONALITY TYPE: warm-blooded

TYPICAL USE: riding, pack

Despite its diminutive size, the Lokai—found in the region of Tajikistan—is much more of a horse than a pony. It is believed to date back to the 1500s and was bred by the Uzbek-Lokai people mainly in the Tajikistan and Kunguz mountains and in the valleys of their rivers. The terrain is rocky, and there is little fresh water—even the rivers, for the most part, have salt water. The horses are kept in herds out at pasture all year round, which makes them extremely tough and enduring.

Extreme Hardiness

The Lokai is characterized by good action and extreme hardiness. It has great endurance under saddle and pack and in national games (especially in the hair-raising kokpar, which demands an agile equine). It reaches maturity late but responds well to improved feeding and management, and it has an excellent temperament. A new breed of saddle horse is being bred in Tajikistan by mating Lokai mares to Arabian and Thoroughbred stallions to improve their size and refine their appearance, and Tersk blood has been introduced.

Fascinating **F**acts

Some Lokais have a curly coat, which can be traced back to the stallion Farfor, a curly-coated sorrel that was used for breeding from 1955–70. There are currently experimental breeding projects going on to find out more about the curly coat gene.

BELOW

Lokai horses are generally small in height but extremely hardy. Often they are plain in the head and can be prone to cow hocks.

Remarkably Agile

The Lokai tends to have a plain head with a straight profile set on a short, muscular neck. Its shoulders are reasonably sloping, and it has a deep, broad chest, wide withers, a short, compact back, and muscular quarters. Its legs are generally strong with well-defined tendons, although sometimes the breed does display conformational defects such as cow hocks and splayed front feet. These defects do not seem to have any adverse effect on the horse's agility or way of going.

NOVOKIRGHIZ

HEIGHT: 14–15 hh

COLOR: bay, brown, gray, chestnut

PERSONALITY TYPE: warm-blooded

TYPICAL USE: riding, harness, pack, agriculture

TEMPERAMENT: energetic, tough, honest

ORIGIN: Kyrgyzstan

SIMILAR BREEDS: Don

Mongolian stock was used to create a relatively new breed of horse developed in the 1930s in Kirghizia, or Kyrgyzstan, a country in Central Asia bounded to the north by Kazakhstan, to the east by China, to the west by Uzbekistan, and to the south by Tajikistan. The new breed was to replace the Old Kirghiz, which was a mountain breed from the high altitudes of Kirghizia and Kazakhstan mainly developed from Mongolian stock. The Novokirghiz is tough and adaptable to harness, riding, or agricultural work

Russian Don

The Novokirghiz is faster and more refined than the Old Kirghiz, mainly due to the infusions of Thoroughbred, Russian Don, and Budyonny crossed with the older breed. By 1918, 48 Thoroughbreds had been imported to the Issyk-Kul Stud and put to

Old Kirghiz mares. The breed became fixed in the 1930s and 1940s due to the repeated crossings between the Old Kirghiz, Thoroughbred, and Don and interbreeding of the progeny.

The new breed developed into three types: the saddle, the massive, and the basic. The

LEFT
The Novokirghiz breed is a refinement of the old Kirghiz horse. The breed was systematically improved at the Issyk-Kul Stud farm in Kirghizia.

massive type was the most successful of the three, being the most versatile and well adapted to the environment. The Novokirghiz is strong and frequently used as a packhorse in the mountains. The saddle and basic types were less adapted to the mountain climate and lacked stamina.

Improved Type

More latterly, less of a distinction was made between the three types, with

Fascinating Facts

Novokirghiz mares are used for milk, which is fermented and turned into koumiss, a mildly alcoholic drink that is a major staple of the local people's diet and similar to other fermented dairy products found across Central Asia.

a single, improved type now in existence. It can cope with any type of terrain and is tough and strong, with great endurance and an energetic temperament.

The Novokirghiz has a small, neat head, muscular neck, sloping shoulders, pronounced withers, longish back, and sloping hindquarters. Its legs are usually short and strong and muscular, although sickle hocks are frequently seen.

LEFT
The Kirghiz horses are well adapted to the mountainous environment, being surefooted and tough, and are used for riding and packing.

TERSKY

HEIGHT: 14.3–15.2 hh

COLOR: predominantly gray, bay, chestnut

PERSONALITY TYPE: warm-blooded

TYPICAL USE: competition, racing, endurance

TEMPERAMENT: easygoing, trainable, gentle

ORIGIN: Russia

SIMILAR BREEDS: Arabian, Streletsky (extinct)

With its distinguishing silver gray coloring and aristocratic pedigree, it is not surprising that, even for a relatively new breed, the Tersky, or Tersk, has so quickly become popular. The Tersky's immediate ancestor was the Streletsky Horse, a favorite among Russian officers for parades and dressage. The Streletsky was developed by crossing Arabian and Anglo-Arab horses with Karabakh, Orlov, Rostopchin, Persian, and Turkmenian blood and named after the Ukrainian farm where it began.

Fateful Popularity

Unfortunately for the Streletsky, its popularity as a cavalry mount also meant the extinction of the breed, as so many perished in the bloody civil war that followed the 1917 Russian Revolution. But two elegant silver Streletsky stallions remained: Tsenitel, foaled in 1910, and Tsilindr (1911). While just these two horses were not enough to resurrect the Streletsky breed, they would found another, equally successful one, the Tersk.

Both Tsilindr and Tsenitel lived long lives—the former, who died at the age of 27, produced several first-class stallions; daughters of the latter, who died at 23, were among the best breeding mares in the new herd.

Remarkable Journey

Some purebred Streletsky mares were also located, and they, as well as mares of complementary breeds such as Don, Kabardin, Arabian, and Lipizzaner, were used to expand the breeding herd. This new breed came to be named Tersky after the farm that received the remnants of the Streletsky herd in 1925. The breed is noted for its cheerful and easy disposition, trainability, longevity, fertility, and its stunning color—described by one devotee as "silver in the sun."

A versatile sporting horse, it can be found in dressage and endurance and has achieved success on the world stage in

Fascinating Facts

During the Second World War and under the threat of invasion by Germany in 1941, the Tersky herd was removed to western Kazakhstan for protection, a journey that took 21 days over a distance of 560 miles (900 km). By 1945 and the end of the war, the entire herd was brought back to the Stavropol Farm in the Northern Caucasus, where it remains to this day.

ABOVE LEFT

With its muscular, athletic frame and powerful hindquarters, the young Tersk breed has rapidly become very popular.

competition. Another "stage" on which Tersky can be found is the circus, where its color is prized.

KABARDIN

HEIGHT: 15–15.2 hh

COLOR: brown, bay, black

PERSONALITY TYPE: warm-blooded

TYPICAL USE: riding, harness, pack

TEMPERAMENT: brave, tractable

ORIGIN: Russia

SIMILAR BREEDS: Karabakh, Karabair

It is called the world's best mountain breed and was developed by the tribespeople of the Northern Caucasus. Like many Russian breeds, it is a product of centuries of primitive selective breeding for survival under the harshest conditions and is derived from the horses of the people of the steppes, crossed with Karabakh, Persian, and Turkmenian strains. Reliable and sure-footed as well as economical to keep, it has been used to improve native stock in Armenia, Azerbaijan, and Georgia.

Homing Device

The breed has exceptional stamina—in 1935 a group of Kabardins became famous for traveling 1,860 miles (2,993 km) through the Caucasian mountains in bad weather in only 37 days. The Kabardin has an extraordinary built-in "homing device," which helps them find their way both in darkness and bad weather.

During the 1917 Russian Revolution and ensuing civil war, numbers of the Kabardin were drastically reduced. Since the 1920s efforts have been made to reestablish this valuable breed using infusions of Turkmene, Karabakh, Persian, and Arabian blood to improve the breed and increase its size.

Fascinating Facts

In 1946 a major test of the performance of various Soviet breeds was organized in Moscow. It was a 155-mile (250-km) ride, with the last mile covered in a gallop. The winner was the Kabardin stallion Ali-Kadym; his time was 25 hours.

BELOW

The Kabardin does not always have the best conformation but is virtually unequaled as a mountain horse.

Sure-footed

The best Kabardins are raised at the Karachai and Malka farms—it is sometimes called the Karachai Horse. Since its development in the 1500s the breed has become at home in the mountains and has developed characteristics that are adapted to the terrain and the demands of the climate. It is very sure-footed over rugged ground and can easily cross the treacherous, steep mountain passes, negotiating river crossings and deep mountain snow. It rarely stumbles, even when trotting or even cantering downhill, and is impervious to cold, mountain showers, and hail.

KUSTANAIR

HEIGHT: 15–15.2 hh

TEMPERAMENT: calm, quiet, alert

COLOR: chestnut, gray, bay, brown, black, roan

ORIGIN: former U.S.S.R.

PERSONALITY TYPE: warm-blooded

SIMILAR BREEDS: Karabakh, Karabin

TYPICAL USE: riding, harness, light draft

The Kazakh (pictured here), along with native steppe horses, the Don, Streletsky, and some Thoroughbred blood all influenced the Kustanair breed.

When the former U.S.S.R. wanted a new breed of horse with two distinct types, the program began at three state studs—Kustanai, Turgai, and Orenburg—which were formally established in 1888, 1887, and 1890 respectively. However, it was the Kustanai Stud that had the earliest and best results and can be credited with establishing the breed, which was officially recognized in 1951, as well as giving it its name. The Kustanair was not selectively bred into two types until the 1920s.

Steppe Horses

The foundations for the Kustanair were the native steppe horses crossed with Don, Kazakh, the now-extinct Streletsky, and the Thoroughbred. Early crosses were largely unsuccessful; however, by using improved native mares and further infusions of Thoroughbred blood, the fixed characteristics of the Kustanair started to emerge.

Two groups of Kustanair were then taken and raised under different conditions. The first group was stabled, corn-fed, and selectively bred, while the second group were kept at pasture all year round and allowed to breed freely. The results were the formation of a distinct saddle horse type with quality and presence, adaptable to all riding purposes, and a hardier, tougher creature adaptable to both saddle and harness work. By the 1980s there were more than 40,000 registered Kustanairs.

Calm and Energetic

Both types of Kustanairs are extremely tough, with great stamina and endurance combined with a calm, quiet, and energetic disposition. This consequently makes them highly versatile saddle or harness horses. The Kustanair is an attractive equine, with some being more Thoroughbred in appearance. It has a fine, light head set on a long, muscular neck that is often set low. Its withers can be prominent, the shoulders sloping, the back straight and wide, and the croup sloping. It is deep and broad through the chest and has long, muscular legs, which have good joints and hard hooves.

The Kustanair often has prominent withers with the neck set low and an elegant and refined head.

LATVIAN

HEIGHT: 15–16 hh

COLOR: bay, brown, black, chestnut

PERSONALITY TYPE: warm-blooded

TYPICAL USE: competition, riding, harness

TEMPERAMENT: calm, willing, honest

ORIGIN: Latvia

SIMILAR BREEDS: all warmbloods

Probably the best-known example of a Latvian Horse—not to be confused with the Latvian Heavy Draft—is Ulla Salzgeber's dressage World Cup winner Rusty. He was foaled on April 2, 1988, at the Latvian stud farm Burtnieki and was originally named Rotors. In 1990 the horse was sold to Belarus and later to Germany. Rotors (Rusty) is by Rebuss out of Akra and three-quarters Hanoverian. He was on the winning German dressage teams at the 1998 World and 1999 European Championships.

regulated, with proper registration of stock and selective breeding. There was a shortage of horses in Latvia after the First World War, and at a congress of Latvian horse breeders in 1922, it was decided to breed middle-weight, warmblood types, adaptable to pleasure and competition riding, using Oldenburg, Hanoverian, and Holstein blood. Thorough-bred blood was also used, although to a lesser degree. The new Latvian Horse was recognized as a breed in 1952.

Warmblood Type

Latvia had her own heavy horse breed, which was very successful, and after the foundation of the Republic of Latvia in 1918, horse breeding became more

Competition Horse

The modern Latvian is a successful combination of the features of the utility and saddle horses. Tall, heavy muscled, and bony, it has a well-proportioned and solid build, although the joints are sometimes coarse. Muscles are well developed, bone

structure solid, chest broad, withers moderately pronounced or high and long, and with a normal slope; its legs are properly set with well-developed knee joints and hocks. Defects include short and ring-boned pasterns and cow

ABOVE

The beautifully proportioned and athletic build of the modern Latvian horse makes it ideally adapted to competitive work, especially dressage.

hocks. The most common colors are bay, brown, and black, but chestnut does sometimes occur.

The exploits of Rusty, as well as the show jumper Kasting Horses Vento, ridden by Helena Weinberg, are putting Latvia's warm-blood firmly on the competition horse map.

RUSSIAN TROTTER

TEMPERAMENT: quiet, trainable, energetic

ORIGIN: Russia

SIMILAR BREEDS: Orlov Trotter

HEIGHT: 15.3–16 hh

COLOR: bay, black, chestnut, gray

PERSONALITY TYPE: warm-blooded

TYPICAL USE: harness

Following the phenomenal success of the American Standardbred on Russia's harness racing tracks, prize money was restricted to Russian-bred horses—in effect, the Orlov Trotter. The result of the restriction was that competitors began to run "ringers." In early 1900s the American-bred William C.K. began racing with false papers as the Orlov Trotter Rassvet. Within a few months the steel-gray stallion—a color characteristic in the Orlov but rare in the Standardbred—had won 20,000 rubles.

Fascinating Facts

The most outstanding example of the Russian Trotter breed is the bay stallion Zhest, foaled in 1947 at the Kul'tura Stud. At the age of six he became the first trotter on the European continent to break the two-minute mark.

Superlative Speed

Russian breeders responded to racing prohibitions against foreign-bred horses by crossing imported American stallions with Orlov Trotters. The result was a horse of superlative speed but lacking the quality and refinement of the Russian breed. Further breeding produced a larger trotter of better quality, and Standardbred and Orlov Trotter blood were then added to the best offspring. Periodic infusions of both breeds are still added. The Russian Trotter—sometimes also called the Metis Trotter—became a recognized breed in 1950, and certain standards were set, including a height of no less than 15.3 hh for mares and 16 hh for stallions, to help improve the overall picture.

Record-Breaker

The modern Russian Trotter is a typical harness horse, generally clean and proportionally built, with well-developed muscles and tendons. Its head is light with a straight profile, its neck long, its back and quarters straight and well muscled, and its croup flat, long, and broad. The speed of the Russian Trotter is high. The 5,249-ft. (1,600-m) trot record is 1 min. 56.9 seconds. Today there are thought to be around 27,000 purebred Russian Trotters produced from 27 studs, the best of them being Elan, Smolensk, Zlynsk, Alexandrov, and Dubrovski.

LEFT
The Russian Trotter was developed from Orlov Trotter and American Standardbred crosses and is a quality and fast-trotting horse.

ORLOV TROTTER

HEIGHT: 16 hh

COLOR: gray, bay, black

PERSONALITY TYPE: warm-blooded

TYPICAL USE: harness, riding

TEMPERAMENT: quiet, intelligent, lively

ORIGIN: Russia

SIMILAR BREEDS: Don, all warmbloods

Russia's most famous horse breed is named after Count Alexei Orlov, credited with developing the Orlov Trotter at his Khrenov Stud, established in 1788. In recognition of his services to Catherine the Great (1729–96), he was made Commander of the Russian Fleet, and on winning a major battle was presented with a gray Arabian stallion, Smetanka. Smetanka was the grandsire of a stallion named Bars I, foaled in 1784, foundation stallion of the Orlov Trotter.

Fascinating Facts

The Orlov Trotter's robust constitution and high adaptability result in a long life span—the outstanding stallion Kvadrat was used as a sire up to the age of 32.

ABOVE RIGHT

The magnificent Orlov Trotter is Russia's best-known breed and is a classy, well-conformed trotting horse.

Superlative

Moved to the Khrenov Stud, Bars was crossed with mares of Arabian, Dutch, Danish, English, and Mecklenburg lines, and the best of the progeny were interbred until fixed characteristics were established. These were to be the Orlov Trotter, a quality carriage horse and a superlative trotter.

The best Orlov Trotters are bred at the Khrenov Stud, Dubrovski, Novotomnikov, and Perm, although horses from the different studs tend to have different traits, with the Orlov type being the most popular.

Distinct and Massive

Significant damage to the breed was caused by

uncontrolled crossing with the American Standardbred during 1885–1913, as well as by the First World War and the Russian Revolution, after which the breed had to be reestablished.

The modern Orlov Trotter is a giant horse of some distinction. Its head is refined and clean cut, its neck long and muscular and often high-set. Its withers are medium in height and length; its back is long and flat and sometimes slightly dipped. It has good legs with well-formed feet. It has a quiet but energetic temperament.

The Orlov Trotter is very fertile. At the studs there are 80–85 live births per 100 mares, and the survival rate to one year of age is 78–83 percent.

BUDYONNY

TEMPERAMENT: kind, brave, intelligent

ORIGIN: Russia

SIMILAR BREEDS: Don, Russian Trotter

HEIGHT: 15.1–16 hh

COLOR: chestnut

PERSONALITY TYPE: warm-blooded

TYPICAL USE: competition, endurance, racing

A Russian hero gave his name to this superb warmblood, created as a cavalry mount to replace horses lost in the First World War and bred by putting Russian Don and Chernomer mares to English Thoroughbreds. The Budyonny breed—sometimes called Budenny or Budyonovsky—was originally known as the Anglo-Don and was generally chestnut, often with the metallic sheen seen in the Don and in the Akhal-Teke. Arabian blood was later added, and the progeny bred back to the Thoroughbred to create a quality horse with stamina and endurance.

Three Foundation Sires

The Chernomer mares were similar to the Don, but they were slightly smaller and lighter. Other breeds, especially the Kazakh and Kirgiz from Mongolia, were not as successful. The required horse from these unions was one with stamina, toughness, and endurance, as well as courage, speed, and athleticism combined with an equable temperament.

At the military stud farm in Rostov, Marshal Budyonny experimented with about 70 Thoroughbreds to perfect his equine breed, but only three stallions were accepted into

the studbook as foundation sires: Simpatyaga, Inferno, and Kokas. Three sons of Simpatyaga, named Sagib, Saksagan, and Sagar; two of Inferno, Imam and Islam; and Kokas's son Kagul were to be crucial to the development of the Budyonny.

Progeny of fixed type and characteristics were soon being bred, and the Budyonny was recognized as a breed in 1948—ironically

the Russian cavalry was officially disbanded a handful of years later in 1954.

Mostly Chestnut

The same faults sometimes seen in the Don's conformation also occur, although to a somewhat lesser extent, in the Budyonny. The Budyonny's head reveals its Thoroughbred ancestry; it has bold, generous eyes and a straight or slightly concave profile. Most Budyonnys are chestnut, and although other colors occur, they are rare. The breed makes an excellent all-round competition horse.

DON

HEIGHT: 15.2–16.2 hh

COLOR: chestnut, brown

PERSONALITY TYPE: warm-blooded

TYPICAL USE: riding, competition, harness

TEMPERAMENT: willing, placid

ORIGIN: Russia

SIMILAR BREEDS: Budyonny

Originating from the Russian steppes in the area between the rivers Don and Olga, the Don Horse is a hardy breed that probably descended from crosses between the steppe-bred Mongolian and Turkoman, Karabakh, Akhal-Teke, and Orlovs. It was able to survive where lesser horses might have perished—the Cossack Cavalry, which contributed to Napoleon's defeat in Russia (1812), pursued the French all the way to Paris mounted on Dons. Many of the French horses died, unable to withstand the extreme cold.

choppy stride, and its quarters can be weak, with a straight croup and low-set tail. It sometimes has "calf" knees and sickle hocks. It has an Oriental-type head of average size, and the neck is generally well formed and muscular. It has a broad, deep chest and long, straight back, and hard, tough hooves.

Despite its shortcomings in conformation, it is very tough with great stamina. In 1951 a stallion named Zenith covered 193 miles (312 km) in 24 hours, resting for only four hours.

Selective Breeding

It was partly the fame garnered by the Don during these military campaigns that led to a concerted breeding campaign, and selective breeding began in full force in the 1830s. The Don was bred primarily for the cavalry, for both riding and harness, and was also used in developing and enhancing other breeds, such as the Budyonny.

At the beginning of the 1900s Thoroughbred and Arabian blood were added for refinement, but no more outcrosses have been introduced since then.

Great Stamina

The Don does still have conformational faults, despite efforts to breed them out. Its shoulders tend to be straight, giving it a

Fascinating facts

The Don is still used in harness, often in the traditional *tachanka*, a type of open cart or wagon in which four horses are harnessed side by side.

RIGHT

The Don is prone to some conformational problems, especially in the hindquarters and shoulders, but it is a willing and hardy animal.

PRZEWALSKI'S HORSE

TEMPERAMENT: aggressive when
threatened, sensitive

ORIGIN: Mongolia

SIMILAR BREEDS: Fjord, Exmoor

HEIGHT: 12–14 hh

COLOR: dun

PERSONALITY TYPE:
cold-blooded (arguable)

TYPICAL USE: wild

*This ancient breed,
with its primitive conformation
and dun coloring, is
considered the last true wild
horse breed in existence.*

Mongolia's national symbol, Przewalski's Horse, or Przewalski—or the Takh, in its native homeland—is the last surviving genuine wild horse in the world. Sometimes called the Asiatic Wild Horse, it is a dweller of the steppe; until some 15,000 years ago this immense belt of grasslands stretched away from Manchuria in the East to the Iberian Peninsula in the West. The 30,000-year-old cave drawings found in France and Spain depict a small, stout, wild horse with Przewalski-like features.

Earlier Discovery

It was originally believed that the Przewalski horse was "discovered" by the Russian explorer Colonel Przhevalsky, for whom it is named after, in 1881. More recent information indicates a much earlier encounter. A Scottish doctor who was

sent on an embassy to China by Peter the Great (1672–1725) wrote of his experiences in *Journey from St. Petersburg to Peking, 1719–1723*, and included an accurate description of this Asiatic Wild Horse.

Fascinating Facts

At the end of the 1900s and the beginning of the 2000s, small herds of Przewalski's Horse were returned to their native habitat as part of a project to save the wild breed. The Przewalski was previously found only in captivity.

Even earlier Hans Schiltberger, a Bavarian nobleman, was taken prisoner by the Turks and sold to the famous Tamerlane of the Golden Horde, who in turn gave Schiltberger to a Mongol prince named Egedi. Schiltberger spent several years in the Tien Shan mountains. He wrote of the

wild horses he observed in his memoirs *Journey into Heathen Parts*, written in 1427.

Chromosome Difference

The Przewalski differs from other horses in that it has 66 chromosomes, while all other breeds have 64. The horse is the size of a stocky pony, with dun coloring, black points, dorsal stripe, and zebra stripes on its legs. It has a short, bristly mane that stands up and is shed in the summer, so the Przewalski does not grow a long mane and does not have a forelock. Przewalskis are among the most threatened wildlife species in the world. The entire world population consists of no more than 1,500 individual animals.

ALTAI

HEIGHT: 13–14 hh

COLOR: chestnut, bay, black, gray, spotted

PERSONALITY TYPE: warm-blooded

TYPICAL USE: pack, meat, trekking

TEMPERAMENT: tough, calm, willing

ORIGIN: Central Asia

SIMILAR BREEDS: none

Conformational Defects

A sure-footed horse is essential to the tribespeople of this remote area because they must often travel over steep mountain trails cut out of the rock and cross fast-moving streams without slipping. The Altai is a very hardy animal that is indispensable to the people who depend on it.

Supremely adapted to year-round pasture grazing, it is an economical keeper and fairly even-tempered. It is not the most attractive creature. Its head is large and coarse, and its neck has a tendency to be fleshy rather than muscular. Its back is long and slightly dipped, although its croup is well developed. Its legs are short and sturdy, but conformation defects such as sloping pasterns and bowed hocks do occur. Still it has excellent feet and a strong constitution. It is most often seen in chestnut, bay, black, and gray, although spotted horses sometimes appear.

Packhorse

Altai Horses cross well with other breeds, such as the Thoroughbred, to make a good performance horse, retaining the Altai's hardy constitution but being larger and losing some of the conformation defects. The breed has also been crossed with some of the heavy draft breeds to produce animals for meat. The purebred Altai makes a good pack animal, too, due to its endurance and sensible nature.

Today the Altai is used for trekking in the steppes and in the Altai Mountains.

A mountain breed, the Altai evolved over a long period of time and has been sculpted by the harsh climate and conditions of its home in the Altai Mountains in southwest Siberia, where Russia, Mongolia, China, and Kazakhstan come together. The word Altai comes from *Al* (gold) and *tau* (mount)—so the horse comes from the "Mountains of Gold." Horses have always been important to the tribespeople and nomads in the region, who rely on them for transportation and pack.

MARWARI

TEMPERAMENT: docile, calm, brave

ORIGIN: India

SIMILAR BREEDS: Kathiawari

HEIGHT: up to 14.3 hh

COLOR: all colors

PERSONALITY TYPE: warm-blooded

TYPICAL USE: riding, military, police

India's Marwari descended from the splendid warhorses that served the ruling families and warriors of feudal India from the beginning of that country's long history. The status of these horses was unparalleled; they were deemed superior to men. Thus only the Rajput families and the Kshatriyas—a warrior caste—were permitted to ride the Marwari. It was said that, if injured during battle, the Marwari would not fall down until it had carried its rider to safety and would stand guard over its rider if he were injured.

Cavalry Mount

The exact origins of the Marwari are not known, although it is believed to have evolved in the state of Marwari and possibly in northwest India near Afghanistan. It developed along similar lines to its neighbor, the Kathiawari, which it resembles, and probably has a high percentage of Arabian blood.

The breed was renowned for its bravery. During the reign of the Mogul Emperor Akbar (1542–1605), the Rajput warriors formed the Imperial Cavalry, employing more than 50,000 horses, most of them Marwari.

Curling Ears

The Marwari remained popular for many years—it was even used in the First World War—but went into decline in the early 1900s and was almost extinct by the 1930s. It was saved by the Maharaja Umaid Singhji, who bought some Marwari stallions to breed with the best Marwari mares he could find. There is an ongoing effort by the Indian government to preserve the breed.

It is a noble equine, with tiny ears that curl in toward each other so that they touch—a hallmark also seen in the Kathiawari. Its elegant head is set on a muscular neck of

good length, with sloping shoulders and deep chest. Its back is compact, and its legs are very strong, with dense bone and hard feet.

RIGHT

The noble Marwari, with its tipped ears and majestic bearing, is one of India's best-loved horse breeds, along with the Kathiawari.

KATHIAWARI

HEIGHT: 14.2–15 hh

COLOR: predominantly chestnut

PERSONALITY TYPE: warm-blooded

TYPICAL USE: riding, police, polo

TEMPERAMENT: intelligent, affectionate

ORIGIN: India

SIMILAR BREEDS: Marwari, Indian Half-Bred

Although very similar in appearance and characteristics to the Marwari—not least in those tiny, curly ears—the Kathiawari is considered a separate breed. It is thought to date back to the 1300s, having evolved from native stock crossed with the Arabian. It gets its name from the Kathiawar peninsula of western Gujarat on the northwest coast of India. Like the Marwari, the Kathiawari was highly regarded, each royal household having its own horse, which was treated as a favored pet.

a shipwreck off the west coast of India and then bred at will with the local pony breeds. It is more likely that Arabians and other Oriental stock were shipped to India during the period of the Mogul emperors, and that these were crossbred with the indigenous breed, from which evolved the Kathiawari.

It certainly has Arabian characteristics, possessing great endurance and stamina. These abilities made it popular as a warhorse; in the 1800s it was used by both the British and the Mahratta cavalries.

Arabian Legend

Legend has it that some Arabians swam ashore from

Police Mount

The Kathiawari has the Marwari's elegant head and

graceful neck and the exaggeratedly turned-in ears. It is narrow and wiry in build, with sloping shoulders, deep chest, long back, and sloping croup. Its tail is set and carried high. Its legs are slender but strong, with tough feet, although many Kathiawaris have cow hocks. The horse is hardy and frugal.

Most Kathiawaris are chestnut, although all solid colors appear except black and some paints. The Kathiawari is a natural pacer, as is the Marwari.

Once bred by wealthy families who would name a strain after the foundation

mare, the Kathiawari is now bred at the government-controlled stud at Junagadh. Today it is used by the mounted police of Gujarat and for mounted games such as tent pegging and polo.

Fascinating Facts

The curled ears of Mawaris and Kathiawaris are often known as the "sting of the scorpion."

LEFT

The Kathiawari has similarities with the Marwari, and both breeds exhibit Arabian characteristics in conformation and personality.

INDIAN HALF-BRED

TEMPERAMENT: intelligent, sensible

ORIGIN: India

SIMILAR BREEDS: Kathiawari, Marwari,
Australian Stock Horse

HEIGHT: 15–16 hh

COLOR: all colors

PERSONALITY TYPE:
warm-blooded

TYPICAL USE: riding, military, police

Wiry and enduring, the Indian Half-Bred was developed in the 1800s for the Indian military, which needed a tough and hardy horse that was larger than the country's native breeds, the Marwari and Kathiawari, and their close cousin, the Sindhi. To create the Indian Half-Bred, they used Australian Stock Horses, or Walers, to add bone and substance and Arabians for refinement. Later Thoroughbred blood was added, perhaps because the native stock already had a proportion of Arabian influence.

Substantial

Before the development of the Indian Half-Bred, the Indian cavalry used mostly Arabian or part-bred Arabian horses, but the Waler had been imported at the beginning of the 1900s because it was larger and more adaptable.

LEFT

The Indian Half-Bred was originally developed for the Indian cavalry and is an extremely hardy and sound animal.

Crossed with the native breeds, the Waler produced a much more substantial equine. The Indian Half-Bred is now produced all over India, especially at the army remount depot in Saharanpur and the army stud in

Babugarh. As well as being used in the army, the Indian Half-Bred is widely used by the police force in towns and especially in the rural areas. The Half-Bred can be any color and stands between 15 and 16 hh.

Thoroughbred Benefit

The addition of Thoroughbred blood was to prove a major benefit to the Indian Half-Bred, as it was already well adapted to a hot and unforgiving climate. One stallion, named Thomas Jefferson, produced especially good stock and was used for several years at both Babugarh and Saharanpur.

When the subcontinent was partitioned into India and Pakistan in 1947, India kept eight English and four French Thoroughbreds, which were to form the basis of future breeding stock. Since then other breeds have been used, including Anglo-Arabs, Bretons, and Polish Arabs. The enduring Indian Half-Bred has a plain head, but it is well formed and sound, with excellent feet.

BARB

HEIGHT: 14.2–15.2 hh

COLOR: chestnut, bay, gray, black

PERSONALITY TYPE: hot-blooded

TYPICAL USE: riding, show

TEMPERAMENT: intelligent, brave, fiery

ORIGIN: North Africa

SIMILAR BREEDS: Arabian, Akhal-Teke

There is considerable debate about whether the Arabian came before the Barb or whether it was the other way around. Certainly the Barb, or Barbary Horse as it was sometimes known, is an ancient breed, and like the Arabian has had a considerable influence on other horse breeds. It is likely that the Barb contains some Arabian blood, and it is a testament to the dominance of the Barb's genes that it has maintained its characteristics. The Barb is sometimes mistaken for an Arabian, but they are two separate breeds.

Barbarian Warriors

The Barb traces back through antiquity to the time of the Persians and Scythians, in the area of the Fertile Crescent northeast of the Mediterranean Sea between the Tigris and Euphrates rivers, then southeast to the Persian Gulf, encompassing

RIGHT

The Barb is an ancient breed that, like the Arabian, has had considerable influence on the development of many other horse breeds.

the countries that are now Egypt, Israel, and Lebanon, and parts of Turkey, Jordan, Syria, Iraq, and Iran.

King Solomon was given several Barbs in approximately 1950 B.C., which is how the Israelites came to own Barbs. The Barb, a desert equine that was extremely tough and enduring, made an excellent warhorse and was used in this capacity by the Israelites, the Ishmaelites, and the Berbers. Some believe the name "Barb" came from the Berber warriors, who were notoriously barbarian in nature, but it is more likely that the name came from the Barbary Coast of North Africa from where the Berbers came.

Spanish Breeds

The Barb is of great importance to the development of the Spanish horses, of which it is believed to be a direct ancestor. Barbs were introduced to

Spain during the Moorish invasions that began in the 700s and influenced the Andalusian and Lusitano breeds. Through them, many other breeds of horses in Europe and the Americas were established.

But perhaps the single most important effect of the Barb was in the development of the English Thoroughbred. One of the three founding stallions of the Thoroughbred was called the Godolphin Arabian, but it is widely believed to have been a Barb. The Godolphin Arabian was a small 15-hh bay with a beautiful head but unnaturally high crest, and was seen pulling a cart in

Paris by Edward Coke. Mr. Coke purchased the horse, took him to England, and gave him to a friend, who passed him on to the Earl of Godolphin.

In 1731 he was being used as a teaser on a mare called Roxana, who was to be mated with a stallion named Hobgoblin. It is said that the Godolphin Arabian fought Hobgoblin and covered the mare himself. The resulting foal, Lath, became one of the most famous racehorses of the day, second only to Flying Childers, and founded one of the most successful dynasties of racing.

Rare Breed

The history of the Barb in England, however, is one that far precedes the Godolphin Arabian, and it is a well-known fact that Barbs were being imported to England for use in the royal studs as long ago as the reign of Richard II (1377–1400).

Along with the Thorough-bred, the Barb is also credited with having had a profound influence on the development of the Camargue horse of

France, to which it bears a striking resemblance, the Irish Connemara, and various French breeds.

The Barb should not be confused with the Arabian, as it has very distinctive characteristics, such as a convex or Roman profile that is seen in many of the Iberian horses influenced by the Barb.

Today the number of pure Barb Horses is greatly decreased—the World Organization of the Barb Horse (Organisation Mondiale du Cheval Barbe) was founded in Algeria in 1987 to try to save the breed.

RIGHT

The Barb, unlike the Arabian, has a distinctly convex profile, and this is seen in many of the Spanish breeds that the Barb influenced.

Wise Words

"Never look a gift horse in the mouth." Saint Jerome (A.D. 374–419), on the Epistle to the Ephesians.

BRUMBY

HEIGHT: 14–15 hh

COLOR: all colors

PERSONALITY TYPE: warm-blooded

TYPICAL USE: feral

TEMPERAMENT: uncertain temper, unpredictable

ORIGIN: Australia

SIMILAR BREEDS: Australian Stock Horse (Waler)

Horses arrived in Australia with the First Fleet that sailed from England in 1788. The journey was long and arduous, for horses as well as humans, and only the toughest survived that horrible voyage. These horses were probably Thoroughbred and heavy draft breeds and adapted to the demands of their harsh new land. Some either escaped or were abandoned and became feral, forming into natural herds and surviving on what little grazing and fresh water they were able to find. These horses form the basis for what is now known as the Brumby.

Pest Species

There is some debate about how they received their name. One theory is that they were named after a farrier, an Englishman named James Brumby who moved to Tasmania in 1804 and left behind some horses.

LEFT

The Brumby is Australia's feral horse that lives in large herds across Australia's open spaces. Its conformation can be poor, but it is tough.

When asked who the horses belonged to, people would say: "They're Brumby's." The name may also have come from an Aboriginal word *baroomby*, meaning "wild" in the language of the Pitjara people on the Warrego and Nogoa rivers in southern Queensland.

The horses thrived in the vast open spaces of Australia but were quickly considered to be pests. The Brumby makes a poor riding horse; it often has conformational defects, is not especially attractive, and is just too wild to be tamed. Although the mane and tail hair of the Brumby is used for musical instruments, brushes, and upholstery, the horse is otherwise of little use to humans.

Protecting the Herd

In the 1960s a systematic and excessive culling was introduced using rifles from a helicopter. It was far from exact and often left the wild horses mortally wounded to die a slow, painful death. There was international outcry, and although Brumbies are still culled, it is now carried out far more humanely. This culling is necessary not only to reduce the horses' impact on cattle farming and the natural environment but also for the protection of the wild herd. In drought conditions, horses could die of starvation and thirst.

AUSTRALIAN STOCK HORSE

TEMPERAMENT: sensible, intelligent

ORIGIN: Australia

SIMILAR BREEDS: Thoroughbred, Brumby

HEIGHT: 15–16 hh

COLOR: bay, chestnut, black, brown, gray

PERSONALITY TYPE: warm-blooded

TYPICAL USE: endurance, competition, harness, ranching

As Australia developed rapidly with increasing exploration from the 1830s on, knowledgeable horse breeders imported a steady stream of Thoroughbreds to improve the local stock. The use of Thoroughbred stallions on the condition-hardened local mares produced the beautiful strain of tough but stylish equine exemplified by today's Australian Stock Horse, or Waler.

Working Horses

The horse was originally known as the New South Waler; this was quickly shortened simply to Waler. Early Walers were highly regarded both as working stockhorses and as cavalry mounts, although they were never registered as a breed (it was not until 1971 that the Australian Stock Horse

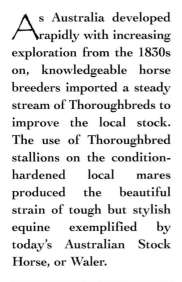

Society was established). Explorers, stockmen, troopers, settlers—all depended upon this reliable and versatile mount, whether they were exploring rough terrain, plowing land, herding sheep or cattle, or patrolling. The Indian cavalry used Walers extensively; later, during the First World War, Allied forces used them in huge numbers.

By the end of the 1800s the Waler was being exported to India alone at a rate of 5,000 a year, and Australia became the sole supplier of remounts to the British and Indian armies.

Great Demand

So many horses were exported that by the end of the Second World War, the Waler had almost disappeared. It was reestablished using Arabians and Thoroughbreds, and no further outcrossing has been used since the 1940s. The modern Waler has some similarities to the Thorough-

bred, especially noticeable in its fine head. Its neck is in proportion to its body and well set on good, sloping shoulders. It has a deep though not excessively wide chest and a strong back. Its quarters are muscular and very powerful and the legs strong and tough, with well-formed, hard hooves.

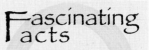

RIGHT
Also called Walers, these horses developed from Thoroughbreds and local stock and are known for their hardy constitution.

Fascinating Facts

Jousting is still practiced today; Foligno has an annual jousting tournament— the *Giostra della Quintana*— from a tradition dating back to the 1400s.

Heavy Horses

M ost draft horse breeds—the word "draft" comes from the Anglo-Saxon *ꝺragan*, meaning to draw or haul—are thought to have evolved from the ancient Forest Horse, a massive, slow-moving, primitive equine from northern Europe. Although now extinct, the Forest Horse was well adapted to its environment, developing broad, flat hooves that enabled it to live in the widespread swampy areas and a thick, wiry coat, which may have been dappled to provide camouflage.

Many of today's draft breeds display several characteristics this ancient equine is thought to have had: the blunt, heavy head, powerful build, and sturdy, short legs. Most are easy and economical keepers, requiring little feed or management, and almost all have a calm, equable nature. Although hot-blooded horses such as the Thoroughbred and the Arabian have often been used in the development of these drafts, the heavy breeds are considered cold-blooded like their primitive ancestor.

Long-standing Helpers

These horses have served humankind since time immemorial; they have accompanied us into war— carrying a knight in full armor or pulling heavy artillery in the 1900s—they have provided transportation, and they have plowed the fields and pulled wagons. Uncomplaining, they have worked hard and tirelessly side by side with us, pulling weights that we feeble humans could barely shift an inch for long distances and long hours.

Virtually all draft breeds combine the traits of strength, stamina, health, longevity, patience, and a docile temperament, which made them indispensable to generations of farmers before the age of mechanization. They have also provided humankind with sustenance—and even today, when many of us would cringe at the thought of eating horse flesh, some heavy horses are bred for their milk and their meat.

It is their committed endeavor and endearing nature, however, for which the world's heavy draft horses are most highly valued.

SUFFOLK PUNCH

TEMPERAMENT: docile, willing, hard-working

ORIGIN: England

SIMILAR BREEDS: Jutland, Brabant

HEIGHT: 16 hh plus

COLOR: "chesnut"

PERSONALITY TYPE: cold-blooded

TYPICAL USE: light draft, harness, riding, show

Now a rare breed, the Suffolk Punch was developed in Suffolk and Norfolk on the east coast of England. The area was bordered on the north, east, and south by the North Sea and on the west by the Fens. Isolated from their neighbors, the farmers of Suffolk developed a breed of horse to manage with their special way of life. To plow the heavy clay soil the horse had to possess not only power but also stamina, health, longevity, and docility. The mighty Suffolk Punch fulfilled all of these.

> **RIGHT**
> *Suffolks are described as having "the face of an angel, the body of a beer barrel, and the bottom of the farmer's daughter."*

Pure Breed

As the Suffolk farmer relied on his horses to work his land, he rarely sold them off. This kept the Suffolk Punch relatively unknown out of its fen homeland but also kept the breed pure. Of all the heavy draft breeds, the Suffolk Punch is thought to be the oldest, with references to the "Old Breed"—thought to be another name for the Suffolk Punch—dating back to 1506. Crisp's Horse of Ufford, deemed to be the foundation sire of the breed, was foaled in 1768. The first studbook was produced in 1880 by Herman Biddell, the first secretary of the Suffolk Horse Society.

Always Chesnut

The Suffolk Punch is always chesnut—and the color is correctly spelled without the middle "t"—of which there are seven recognized shades: bright, red, golden, yellow, light, dark, and dull dark. It has an intelligent head, which is fine for a heavy horse breed, with neat ears and a kind eye. Its neck is muscular with a pleasing arch, and it is compact and short-coupled. Its legs are short and its body appears to be too big for them—which has inspired the "Punch" part of the breed's name.

Those short legs are exceptionally strong and sound and do not have any feather—this would be a drawback in working the heavy clay soil of East Anglia.

SHIRE

HEIGHT: 17–18 hh

COLOR: black, bay, brown, gray

PERSONALITY TYPE: cold-blooded

TYPICAL USE: heavy draft, show

TEMPERAMENT: gentle, docile, willing

ORIGIN: England

SIMILAR BREEDS: Clydesdale, Brabant

W illiam the Conqueror is credited with bringing the "Great Horse"—a type of equine armored tank—to England in the 1000s after the Norman Conquest. Mighty and massive, this imposing creature could easily carry a knight in full armor. The modern breed gets its name from the counties of Derbyshire, Leicestershire, and Staffordshire where it developed. The original Great Horse was crossed with a mixture of Flanders and Friesian horses brought over to England by the Dutch.

Bakewell Black

Dutch contractors were working on the reclamation of land undertaken in the Fens. Their imported breeds were to have a profound effect on the development of the Shire. Interbreeding between the Great Horse, the Friesian, and finally the Flanders produced the English Black, named by Oliver Cromwell. It was much larger than the Great Horse, although it exhibited many of the features of the Flanders Horse and the predominantly black coloring passed down from the Friesian.

Dull in color, gross, and sluggish, it was greatly improved in the Midlands by the renowned breeder of the time, Robert Bakewell (1725–95) and his followers, and for a time it was popularly known as the Bakewell Black.

LEFT

Many of the large breweries used shire horses to pull their drays for advertising purposes and also to compete against each other at horse shows.

Gentle Giant

The Shire's foundation sire is believed to be Packington Blind, which sired the first Shires to appear in the studbook of 1878—the Shire Horse Society was formed in 1884. The breed was by then known as the English Cart Horse—infusions of different blood had largely bred out

For all its size, the Shire is an attractive horse with a charming, docile nature. It has a large head with a convex or Roman profile, wide forehead, and intelligent, kind eyes. Its long neck is arched and gives the animal a commanding appearance; its shoulders are deep and oblique, very able to support a collar. Its back is short and compact; its quarters long and sweeping and well muscled. It has long legs with plenty of hard, flat bone and exceptionally good feet, and it has lots of feather. Overall the Shire is a combination of considerable strength and noble beauty.

the predominantly black coloring, so Bakewell Black became a misnomer and changed to Shire with the founding of the breed society. The term "Shire" is thought to come from the Saxon word *schyran*, meaning "divide."

As news of this gentle giant spread, many stallions were exported, especially to the United States, where the American Shire Horse Association was founded in 1885.

Rent Payers

Meanwhile, in England ruthless veterinary examination at the London Shire Show virtually eliminated any conformation faults, such as unsound limbs and poor wind. The country's most powerful working horse increased greatly in value, so much that during the Great Depression of the 1930s, good Shire foals were nicknamed the "rent payers."

Mechanization at first had little effect on the fortunes of the Shire Horse; the first motorized vehicles for farmwork were inefficient and too expensive, way

Fascinating Facts

The Shire Horse holds the record for the world's biggest horse—Sampson, foaled in 1846 in Bedfordshire, England, stood 21.2½ hh, or 7 ft. 2½ in. (2.2 m) at the withers and weighed more than 1.5 tons.

beyond the means of many during the prolonged Depression. None could match the pulling power of the enormous Shire. It was the Second World War that was to have a devastating effect on the breed. It is thought that in its heyday, there were around one million Shire horses; by the

1960s numbers had dwindled to a few thousand.

Breed Revival

It is only in recent years that the breed has enjoyed a kind of a revival. Many London breweries used the Shire to pull their drays through the city, a wonderful and popular spectacle. Although still a draft horse, ridden classes for Shires have been introduced at British shows.

BELOW

The Shire horse is considered the largest of the draft breeds and has a huge pulling capacity. Plowing competitions such as this are not uncommon.

CLYDESDALE

HEIGHT: 17 hh and over

COLOR: bay, brown, chestnut, roan, black

PERSONALITY TYPE: cold-blooded

TYPICAL USE: draft, harness, riding, show

TEMPERAMENT: kind, docile, willing

ORIGIN: Scotland

SIMILAR BREEDS: Shire, Brabant

Scotland's pride was founded in Lanarkshire, a region formerly known as Clydesdale after the Clyde River, which runs through it. The history of the breed dates back to the middle of the 1700s, when native stock in Lanarkshire was bred to Flemish stallions in an effort to produce greater weight and substance. The first Flemish stallion, dark brown in color, was imported by the 6th Duke of Hamilton, and his tenants were granted its use free of charge.

Marked Improvement

After this a John Paterson of Lochlyloch brought a Flemish stallion from England—where these horses were also being used on native mares to produce what would later become the Shire Horse—which was also to prove successful. This stallion was black, with a white face and some white on its legs, and Lochlyloch blood soon became highly popular as a result of the marked improvement apparent in the region's youngstock.

This horse was followed by a 16.1 hh black stallion named Blaze, which belonged to Mr. Scott of Carstairs, and in 1782 it won first prize at the Edinburgh Show. Although nothing is known of the latter horse's pedigree, it is thought it was of coaching blood.

Breed Basis

All modern-day Clydesdales can trace their lineage back to a filly foal bought by Mr. Somerville of Lampits Farm,

LEFT
The Clydesdale breed originated in Scotland and along with the Shire horse is one of the most elegant draft breeds.

Fascinating Facts

The game horseshoes developed among Grecian soldiers, who could not afford a discus for the playing of quoits, so they modified the game and used old discarded horseshoes instead of a discus.

Carstairs, at a dispersing sale of stock belonging to Mr. Clarkson, who is thought to be a descendant of John Paterson—so it is likely this filly was in turn a descendant of the black Flemish stallion. The filly produced a black colt named Glancer—also

known as Thompson's Black Horse—which is to be found in the pedigrees of horses today.

The black Glancer had white on both hind legs and is described as "having a strong, neat body set on short, thick legs, the clean, sharp bones of which were fringed with nice, flowing, silken hair." His dam, known as the Lampits Mare, also foaled Farmers Fancy and Glancer I, and the frequent mating of descendants of these two is thought to have formed the basis of the Clydesdale.

Formidable

A daughter of Farmers Fancy, Jean, produced a filly foal by Samson in 1860, a powerful, dark bay that became the famous Keir Peggy. She produced Darnley, a rich bay with very little white. Among Darnley's most famous sons were MacGregor, Top Gallant, and Flashwood. Top Gallant's most prominent son was Sir Everard, which in turn was the sire of Baron's Pride.

Baron's Pride sired one of the breed's most famous sons, Baron of Buchlyvie. In 1911 he was sold for £9,500— the equivalent today would be around $500,000.

By this time the Clydesdale was firmly established as a formidable working horse, and between 1884 and 1945 more than 20,000 were exported to Australia, New Zealand, the Americas, Russia, Italy, and Austria.

Stylish Trot

After the Second World War, the agricultural industry in the United Kingdom largely replaced its working horses with mechanical power. Clydesdale numbers dwindled, and in 1975 the

horse was categorized by the Rare Breeds Survival Trust as "vulnerable"—in the years since and with the increase in breed numbers, it is now categorized as "at risk."

Despite its size, the Clydesdale oozes quality, with a straight head that is broad between the eyes, wide muzzle, large nostrils, and a bright, clear, and intelligent eye. It has a muscular neck (comparatively long for a draft breed), sloping shoulder and, deep body, with very sound, long legs and excellent feet. Like the Shire, it has plenty of fine, silky feather. It has a long, easy walk and a springy, stylish trot. A surprisingly active mover for such a large horse, the Clydesdale redefines the term "horsepower."

ARDENNAIS

HEIGHT: 14.3–16 hh

COLOR: bay, roan, chestnut

PERSONALITY TYPE: cold-blooded

TYPICAL USE: draft, meat

TEMPERAMENT: calm, tolerant, hardy

ORIGIN: France

SIMILAR BREEDS: Brabant, Auxois, Trait du Nord

modern horse and would have been used for riding as well as draft. It is known that they were widely used during the French Revolution (1789–99) and after by the French military. During the Napoleonic Wars, the Ardennais was renowned for its great stamina, endurance, and ability to survive under the harshest conditions.

Thoroughbred and Arabian in order to produce a strong, stocky horse with a kind but lively temperament. Despite the infusions of "hot" blood, however, the Ardennais is still considered cold-blooded rather than warm-blooded.

The Ardennais is handsome rather than beautiful, with a large head, compact body,

While there are also a Swedish Ardennes and a Belgian Ardennes, the original breed is from France and is the oldest of them all. It can be traced back to references made by Julius Caesar (100–44 B.C.) in his account of his conquest of Gaul, *De Bello Gallico*. It is thought that ancestors of this mighty draft horse were bred on the Ardennes—the mountainous region bordering France and Belgium—for more than 2,000 years and that the Ardennais has descended from the last of the Solutre.

Paleolithic Horse

The Solutre Horse (*Equus robustus*) was a prehistoric breed found in the area of the same name in the Burgundy region of France during the Paleolithic period in around 50,000 B.C. and probably formed the basis for many modern horse breeds.

The old type of Ardennais was probably somewhat lighter than the massive

Russia's heavy draft breeds probably evolved from the numbers of Ardennais left behind during the French retreat of 1812.

Handsome

Today's Ardennais was developed during the 1800s by crossing the original with the Boulonnais, Percheron,

ABOVE

The French Ardennais is an ancient breed that is especially noted for its stamina, toughness, and calm temperament.

stocky legs, and a short mane and tail. It is sure-footed enough to cope with rough and hilly terrain, and it is an economical feeder. Still used for draft work, it is also raised for its meat.

BRABANT (Belgian Heavy Draft)

TEMPERAMENT: generous, willing, placid

ORIGIN: Belgium

SIMILAR BREEDS: Shire, Clydesdale, Suffolk Punch

HEIGHT: 16–18 hh

COLOR: roan, chestnut

PERSONALITY TYPE: cold-blooded

TYPICAL USE: draft, meat

This breed was originally a warhorse, a Goliath among the heavy draft horse breeds, and owes its sound constitution and robust good health to the lush little corner of Europe where it was developed. Its nearest ancestor was the Flanders, or Flemish Horse, a huge, black powerhouse of an equine prized by the knights of the day, whom it could carry in their full armor with minimal effort, like a man lifting a kitten. Its fame spread— Richard I (1157–99) imported several Belgian horses to England.

Colossal Horse

Those British imports were to subsequently influence the Shire, Clydesdale, and Suffolk Punch. As demand for a lighter type of cavalry horse grew, however, the Belgian people resisted the temptation to scale down their massive equine and instead used it for agriculture, its great stature adapting well to the heavy soil and climate.

Until the beginning of the 1900s there were three different types of Brabants. The first was the Colossal

Fascinating Facts

In 1866 Dr A. G. van Hoorebeck of Illinois imported the first Brabant into the United States. This breed is now the most popular workhorse in the United States.

Horse of Mahaigne, for which the stallion Jean I was responsible; the second was the Big Horse of the Dendre, which was founded by the stallion Orange I; and the last was the Gray Horse of Nivelles, based on the stock produced by the stallion Bayard.

Good Walk

By the 1900s the three groups had become indistinguishable. The modern Brabant has a small head on a thick, muscular neck and huge, powerful shoulders. Its upright shoulders give it the short, choppy stride often seen in the draft breeds. It does, however, have a good walk. It also has an extremely willing and generous temperament, which combined with its incredible strength makes it an ideal heavy workhorse.

The Brabant is popular in the United States, where it is simply known as the Belgian Horse and has become much more refined.

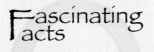

LEFT

The Brabant generally has an excellent walk, which combined with its biddable temperament, makes it a good workhorse.

COMTOIS

HEIGHT: 14.1–15.1 hh

COLOR: chestnut

PERSONALITY TYPE: cold-blooded

TYPICAL USE: light draft, meat

TEMPERAMENT: good-natured, trainable, willing

ORIGIN: France

SIMILAR BREEDS: Ardennais

This ancient breed is thought to have existed in France since the 300s, descending from horses brought to the area by the Burgundians, a people from northern Germany. The Franche-Comté and the Jura Mountains on the border of France and Switzerland are thought to be the original breeding ground of the breed. The Comtois was comparatively small for a draft breed, but its small, stocky stature, with short, hard-boned legs, was ideally adapted to its homeland's rough and rocky terrain.

"Cobby" Characteristics

In the 1500s the Comtois was used to improve the horses of Burgundy and became famous as a cavalry and artillery horse—Louis XIV (1638–1715) used this breed in his armies for both cavalry and artillery, as did Napoleon on his disastrous campaign into Russia in 1812. Subsequently, during the

LEFT

These versatile horses were used extensively by Louis XIV for his cavalry and artillery and by Napoleon during his Russian campaign.

1800s other draft breeds, such as the Norman, the Boulonnais, and the Percheron, were used to improve the Comtois, and since 1905 the use of Ardennais stallions has given the breed greater strength and better legs.

minimal feather and good, strong joints.

Long-lived

Good-natured, hardy, and easy to train, the Comtois is also long-lived. It is now bred in the mountainous regions of the Massif Central, the Pyrenees Mountains, and the Alps, for which it is perfectly adapted. It is still widely used for hauling wood in the high pine forests of the Jura and for work in the hilly

Today's Comtois is a lightly built draft horse with "cobby" characteristics. It has a large head set on a short, muscular neck, a broad, deep chest, and powerful hindquarters. It has short, strong legs with

vineyards of the Arbois area, and it is second only to the Breton Horse in numbers in France. Those bred for the meat industry, however, tend to be poorer specimens, as the emphasis is placed on producing bulk.

BRETON

TEMPERAMENT: sociable, easygoing, willing

ORIGIN: France

SIMILAR BREEDS: Ardennais

HEIGHT: 14.3–16.2 hh

COLOR: bay, gray, chestnut, roan

PERSONALITY TYPE: cold-blooded

TYPICAL USE: draft

A demanding climate and unforgiving landscape has made the mighty Breton France's premier draft breed. It originated in the province of Bretagne, also known as Brittany, in the northwest of France. Brittany has a history of breeding superb equines, dating back to the Middle Ages, and the Breton is the result of evolution over hundreds of years, culminating in a horse of great strength and durability. The Breton became sought after by military leaders around the time of the Crusades (1096–1270).

Comfortable gait

It is not known how horses first came to the mountains of Breton, although it is known that they have been there for thousands of years. The original Breton Horse was thought to be small, standing perhaps only about 14 hh, but it had a supremely comfortable gait—which was why it was so popular. During the 1600s Breton Horses were sent to New France (now Canada) by the French king Louis XIV, where it went on to influence the Canadian Horse, or Cheval Canadien.

A Dished Face

There are three types of Bretons, which come from different districts of Brittany. The Corlay Breton, or Central Mountain Breton, contains Arabian and Thoroughbred blood and stands between 14.3 and 15.1 hh. Considered the true descendant of the original, the Corlay Breton is the smallest of the breed and has a dished face.

The Postier Breton is the result of breeding with Norfolk Trotters and Hackneys during the 1800s and has those breeds'

Fascinating Facts

The Canadian Horse, or Cheval Canadien, is descended from Breton Horses sent from the stables of Louis XIV between 1665 and 1670. It also has Barb, Andalusian, and Norman blood and is today recognized as a true breed inherent only to Canada.

attractive gaits. It stands around 15.1 hh and makes a good coach horse. The Heavy Draft Breton was derived using Ardennais and Percheron blood and is very strong in relation to its size. It can stand up to 16.2 hh and has short but muscular legs.

ABOVE
The Breton horse is predominantly chestnut or roan in color and generally has a quality head and amenable nature.

All three types are easygoing, willing workers, and usually very sociable creatures.

AUXOIS

HEIGHT: 16.3 hh and over

COLOR: bay, roan, chestnut

PERSONALITY TYPE: cold-blooded

TYPICAL USE: draft, meat

TEMPERAMENT: gentle, willing, biddable

ORIGIN: France

SIMILAR BREEDS: Ardennais, Trait du Nord

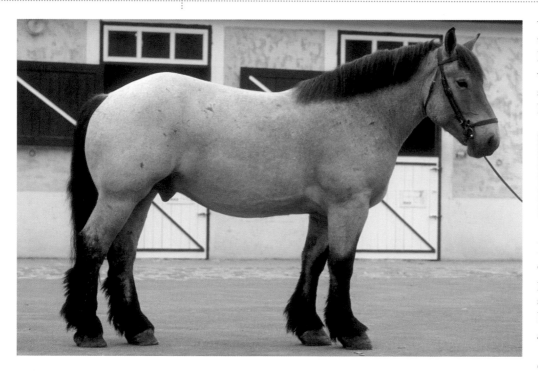

wide chest. It is broad through the back and has a long, sloping, muscular croup with a low-set tail. Although slender for its size, the Auxois has particularly powerful legs.

LEFT

Unlike many draft breeds, the Auxois often has a good slope to its shoulder, allowing it to move freely and quickly.

Its kind, biddable nature combines with its superb pulling power to produce a strong, durable equine. Its bulk means that the Auxois is also bred for its meat.

Today very few of these excellent equines remain, although efforts are being made to maintain the breed, especially around the Cluny Stud and the fertile areas of Yonne and Saône-et-Loire.

The Auxois is a descendant of the old Burgundian Horse that at one time existed side by side with the Ardennais, to which it is closely related. Compact and powerful, it is known to have been around since the Middle Ages and is therefore probably a distant descendant of the prehistoric Solutre Horse. It was originally from the Côte d'Or and Yonne regions in Burgundy, France, and has the hardiness, strength, stamina, and amiable nature of most heavy draft breeds.

is considerably larger than its close cousin, it is finer in the legs and has smaller quarters.

Despite its bulk, the Auxois can move surprisingly freely and quickly, due to its well-sloped shoulder.

Free and Fast

In the 1800s infusions of Boulonnais and Percheron blood, as well as Ardennais and Trait du Nord, were added to the Auxois to add height and substance. It most closely resembles the latter two, and selective breeding has resulted in the predominance of bay or red roan coloring. Since the 1900s only Ardennais blood has been added, and although the Auxois

Breed Revival

The Auxois has a relatively light head for a draft breed, with a broad forehead and small, alert ears. It is stoutly built, with a short, thick neck, flattish withers, and a deep,

TRAIT DU NORD

TEMPERAMENT: kind, gentle, easygoing

ORIGIN: France

SIMILAR BREEDS: Ardennais, Auxois

HEIGHT: 15.2–16.2 hh

COLOR: bay, roan

PERSONALITY TYPE: cold-blooded

TYPICAL USE: draft, agriculture, harness, meat

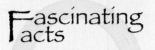

Considered, incorrectly, by many to be a "branch" of the Ardennais, the Trait du Nord is a fairly new breed—the studbook was opened in 1903. *Trait* is the French word for "draft," and *nord* refers to "north," which is the region in France from where this horse comes. The Trait du Nord is the result of crossbreeding Ardennais and Flemish horses with the Belgian Brabant. Constitutionally strong, calm, and enduring, it was formerly used in the vast cereal and sugarbeet farms in the north of France.

Briefly Popular

The horse is still bred in the areas around Lille, the Sommes, the Aisne, and the Pas-de-Calais, although its numbers are declining—the breed enjoyed a brief period of popularity after the studbook was established in the early 1900s, but it has since gone into decline. This is a shame because it possesses the vigor and energy necessary to enable it to trot at a remarkable pace, while at walking speed it has proved to be a well-balanced draft horse with the mass and thrust to create the maximum of power and ease of work. It also has great pulling power and hardiness combined with a calm disposition.

Energetic Trot

The Trait du Nord has a heavy head with a straight profile set on a short, muscular neck, flat withers,

BELOW

The short coupled and massive frame of this horse is typical of the Trait du Nord, a hardy, useful, draft breed whose numbers are sadly declining.

and a broad, deep chest. Its sloping shoulders give it the energetic trot, and it has a short, straight back. It has broad loins and a wide, muscular croup, which is nicely sloping. It legs are short and strong, well muscled, and feathered below the knee and hock, with broad, well-formed joints. It is ideally adapted to heavy draft work and for agricultural work in hilly and rough terrains, which it can easily cross. It makes a good harness horse, but it is also bred for its meat.

Fascinating Facts

The word "chivalry" comes from the French word for horse, *cheval*; the term became associated with the knights who gallantly rode on horseback and the ideal standard of behavior for such noblemen.

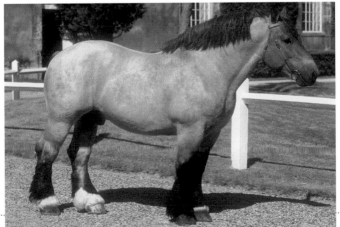

NORMANDY COB

HEIGHT: 15.2–16.3 hh

COLOR: chestnut, bay

PERSONALITY TYPE: warm-blooded

TYPICAL USE: light draft, riding, harness

TEMPERAMENT: docile, gentle, lively

ORIGIN: France

SIMILAR BREEDS: warmbloods

This light draft breed has a long history, dating back to the small but tough Bidet Horse that existed before the Roman Empire around 2,000 years ago. During Roman rule the Romans crossed the Bidet with their heavyweight pack mares to produce a strong horse of more quality that was equipped for military use. The Bidet was a tough and enduring creature, probably brought to France from Asia by the Celts, and as well as Mongolian influences, it likely contained Eastern blood.

Fascinating Facts

The phrase "straight from the horse's mouth" is actually misquoted from the Bible. In the book of Numbers (22:28), God speaks a prophecy through the mouth of a donkey, which would have made the original phrase "straight from the donkey's mouth."

Warm-blooded

Later, in the 1500s and 1600s some Arabian and Barb blood was added, followed by that of Thoroughbred and Norfolk Roadster. This means that, although a draft breed, the Normandy Cob is essentially a warmblood.

During the 1700s and 1800s two royal studs were established in France—in Le Pin in 1728 and in Saint-Lô in 1806, the latter becoming the center of breeding for the Normandy Cob. By 1976 the Saint-Lô stud was standing 60 Normandy Cob stallions. By the 1900s two distinct types of Cobs had developed: a lighter version equipped for riding and a heavier type for light draft, carriage, and farmwork. The second type is most common today.

Classy Horse

The modern Normandy Cob is a classy equine, with great presence and an energetic, extravagant gait. While docile and gentle, it has tremendous presence and activity. It has a plain but still attractive head, a shortish neck set on good shoulders, and a wide, deep chest. It has a short back and compact body, with a round croup and excellent legs with minimal feather. Although the breed was traditionally docked, the practice is now prohibited in some countries, so its tail is now braided and bound.

There is no studbook for the Normandy Cob, although its breeding is documented, and in some cases performance testing is carried out.

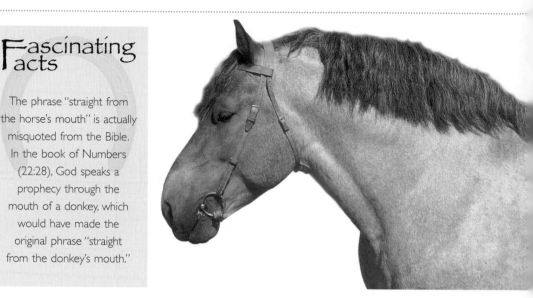

LEFT

The Norman Cob is one of the classiest of draft breeds, due to the influence of Thoroughbred and Arab blood, and it is extremely versatile.

POITEVIN

HEIGHT: 16–16.2hh

COLOR: dun, gray, bay, black, palomino

TEMPERAMENT: placid, docile

PERSONALITY TYPE: cold-blooded

ORIGIN: France

TYPICAL USE: donkey/mule production, meat

SIMILAR BREEDS: Auxois

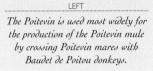

LEFT

The Poitevin is used most widely for the production of the Poitevin mule by crossing Poitevin mares with Baudet de Poitou donkeys.

Sometimes also known as the Mulassier, the Poitevin Horse originates in the Poitou region of France and is believed to be related to the ancient primitive Forest Horse of Northern Europe, a huge creature also known as *Equus ferus silvaticus,* or the Diluvial Horse. The Poitevin itself is a rather unprepossessing creature, unpleasing to the eye, with poor conformation and poor performance. It is the least known of the nine heavy French breeds and the most endangered.

Primitive Roots

The Poitevin is believed to have descended from various Danish and Norwegian heavy breeds that were probably imported to the regions during the land reclamation work of the seventeenth century. It was used as a draft horse and for working the land.

In appearance, the Poitevin has a coarse, heavy head with a straight or convex profile, set on a rather stumpy, muscular neck. Its shoulders are quite straight and are poorly conformed, and it is long through the body, with a straight back and sloping croup. Its legs are short in comparison to its body and somewhat thick, with coarse feathering. Its feet are large and flat, and its body hair coarse. Most Poitevins are dun—a throwback to its primitive roots—but gray, bay, black and palomino also occur.

Enduring

The Poitevin's biggest claim to fame is as a producer of the Baudet de Poitou, a donkey breed that can stand up to 16 hh. Hardy and tough, the latter has an amazingly quick, energetic stride for a donkey and shares its studbook with that of the Poitevin, which was started in 1885. Breeding Baudet de Poitou jackasses to Poitevin mares produces the Poitevin mule, a strong, tough and enduring animal with a long working life and a good disposition and constitution. Although the demand for mules has declined, they are enjoying greater popularity once again. The Poitevin itself is also bred for meat.

PERCHERON

HEIGHT: 15.2–17 hh

COLOR: gray, black

PERSONALITY TYPE: cold-blooded

TYPICAL USE: draft, agriculture, harness, riding

TEMPERAMENT: sensible, gentle, willing

ORIGIN: France

SIMILAR BREEDS: Boulonnais

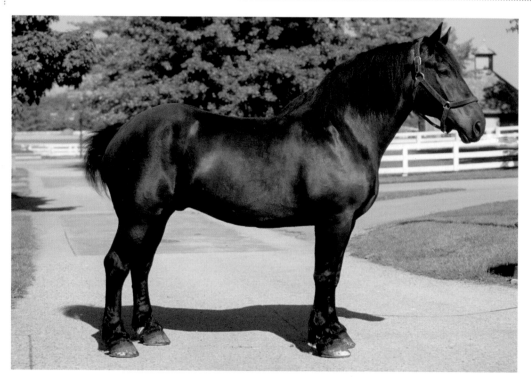

Perhaps the best known of all of France's heavy breeds, the Percheron gets its name from the La Perche district of northern France, but it can be found worldwide. It is a breed of great antiquity; evidence has been recovered of a type of horse, very similar to the Percheron, having existed in the La Perche area since the Ice Age, although its exact roots are unknown. It is thought to be distantly related to the Boulonnais, with which it shares its elegance and considerable beauty.

Free-flowing Stride

Arabian blood was crossed with the native mares of La Perche following the invasion of the Moors, who were defeated at the Battle of Tours in 732. Their abandoned, hot-blooded horses were bred to existing, heavy, Flemish stock. The influence of the Arabian blood is indicated especially in the unusually free-flowing and active stride of the Percheron.

Further infusions of Arabian blood were introduced during the Middle Ages. By the time of the Crusades the Percheron was widely recognized as outstanding for its substance and soundness, as well as for its beauty and grace.

Amazing Stamina

The renowned stud in Le Pin was a central breeding area for the Percheron, and in 1760 it imported an Arabian stallion named Gallipoli. He went on to sire one of the most famous Percheron stallions, Jean le Blanc, in 1830, and modern Percheron

bloodlines trace back to him. The Percheron was first imported to the United States in 1839, by an Edward Harris

Fascinating Facts

W. C. Fields, American comedian and actor, once joked and admired that: "Horse sense is the thing a horse has which keeps it from betting on people."

RIGHT

There is a high margin of Arab blood in the popular French Percheron, which is reflected in its versatility as a riding and draft animal.

from Moorestown, New Jersey. Just over 20 years later, two stallions, Normandy and Louis Napoleon, were imported to Ohio. The latter was sold to Illinois and into the ownership of the Dunham family, who were later instrumental in forming the breed society.

French Imports

During the 1870s and 1880s thousands of heavy draft horses were imported to the United States from Europe, especially stallions from France and Great Britain. Once the importers found the province of La Perche—and noted the superiority of its heavy horses—it became the primary source of imports.

During the winter of 1875–76 the National Association of

Importers and Breeders of Norman Horses was launched in Chicago, Illinois. The name was soon changed to Percheron-Norman, and within a few years had been shortened simply to "Percheron."

American Favorite

The financial downturn of 1893 halted the importations; between 1894 and 1898 there were virtually none, and the breeding of stock was greatly lessened. The former association went bust.

But recovery was quick. Importations were resumed in 1898, and between that

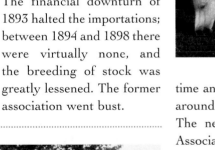

time and 1905 they averaged around 700 head a year. The new Percheron Horse Association of America was formed in 1902, and by 1906 there were 13,000 stallions registered. By 1930 the Percheron had become so popular that there were three times as many registered Percherons as other draft breeds combined.

Following the Second World War the breed was badly affected by mechanization, as

the tractor surpassed the horse. A handful of farmers—including Amish, who were great supporters of the breed—kept the Percheron alive over the next 20 years, and it continues to thrive as a breed in the United States today.

Fine Head

The Percheron has an exceptionally fine head, which is attributed to the Arabian blood, a well-made neck set onto good withers, deep chest, strong back, and muscled quarters. It has short, clean legs with minimal feathering and good, hard bone. The Percheron has been used to improve other breeds.

For a heavy horse the Percheron has grace, freedom of movement, and amazing stamina—it is able to travel at a trot for an incredible 35 miles (57 km) a day.

BOULONNAIS

HEIGHT: 15–15.3 hh

COLOR: mostly gray, chestnut, black, bay

PERSONALITY TYPE: cold-blooded

TYPICAL USE: draft, meat

TEMPERAMENT: gentle, kind

ORIGIN: France

SIMILAR BREEDS: Percheron

Called the Thorough-bred of draft breeds," the Boulonnais combines the elegance of the hotblood with the strength of the cold. One of the most beautiful of all of the drafts, the "White Marble Horse" can be traced back to the native stock of the Numidian army occupation of Boulogne in northern France in 55–54 B.C. During the Crusades two breeders concentrated on creating a warhorse that would be fast and agile, yet still strong enough to carry a knight in full armor through a rigorous battle.

Horse of the Tide

Eustache, Comte de Boulogne, and Robert, Comte d'Artois, crossed the heavy Northern stallions with German Mecklenberg mares, similar to modern Hanoverians, in order to create the base warhorse. The Spanish occupation of nearby Flanders during the 1600s brought in Spanish Barb, Andalusian, and Arabian horses, and the distinctive Boulonnais emerged, of which there were two types.

Fascinating Facts

Today the annual race still known as the Route du Poisson commemorates the now-extinct *mareyeur* type of Boulonnais, in recognition of the horse's role in bringing fresh seafood to Paris.

The smaller *mareyeur* variety—the name means "Horse of the Tide"—was used to pull heavy carts of fish from Boulogne to Paris, a distance of almost 200 miles (340 km). The Route du Poisson was crossed in under 18 hours, allowing Parisians to have fresh fish on their dinner tables.

Mostly Gray

With better roads and rail transportation, the *mareyeur* type was allowed to die out. The larger Boulonnais, a direct heir to the warhorse bloodlines, is still

bred in small numbers, but two world wars almost destroyed the breed. In the early 1900s there were thought to be 600,000 Boulonnais in France. There are now only an estimated 700 Boulonnais in France, 150 in Germany, and fewer than 75 in Belgium. Most Boulonnais today are gray—around 15 percent are chestnut, black, or bay. It is said to resemble a small, "wide-awake" Percheron.

RIGHT

The Boulonnais, like the Percheron, contains Arab blood and is noted for its especially attractive head and great stamina.

ITALIAN HEAVY DRAFT
(Tiro Pesante Rapido)

TEMPERAMENT: quiet, biddable, sociable

ORIGIN: Italy

SIMILAR BREEDS: Breton

HEIGHT: 15–16 hh
COLOR: mostly chestnut, bay, roan
PERSONALITY TYPE: cold-blooded
TYPICAL USE: draft, agriculture, meat

Experimental breeding led to the development of the Italian Heavy Draft—known in Italian as the Tiro Pesante Rapido, which means "quick heavy draft." It originated in the northern regions of Italy but was popular throughout the country. The breed began with native stock being crossed with Brabant, Percheron, and Boulonnais; many of these early experiments were unsuccessful. When the Breton was bred with the local mares, however, the Italian Heavy Draft was born.

A Distinctive Brand

Originally, Neapolitan, Arabian, and Hackney horses were crossed with the native mares of Ferrara in northern Italy to produce a lightweight, active workhorse. But a need arose for a heavier farm and heavy artillery breed. The earlier crossings with the Boulonnais produced what came to be known as the Agricultural Heavy Horse, but then the Breton was added and the new name was coined, and the studbook was opened in 1926. Horses that are accepted to the studbook are branded with a five-runged ladder with a shield on the near side of their hindquarters.

> **RIGHT**
>
> *These predominantly chestnut horses are versatile, useful agricultural animals known for their especially good trot.*

Popular Breed

The Breton passed to the Italian Heavy Draft its fast, active trot, which influenced the latter's nickname, and it closely resembles the Breton in appearance. It is almost always chestnut with flaxen mane and tail, although bays and roans also appear.

It is a highly attractive, cobby little horse, with a quality head for a draft breed, a powerful neck, excellent shoulders, and compact, muscular body. Its legs are sometimes weak and considerably light in bone, but the overall picture is of a pleasing horse. It is an economical and easy keeper and matures quickly.

The Italian Heavy Draft is still used in its homeland for farmwork and remains popular—one third of all breeding stallions in modern Italy are her native heavy horse.

FREIBERGER (Franches-Montagne)

HEIGHT: 14.3–15.3 hh

COLOR: chestnut, bay

PERSONALITY TYPE: cold-blooded

TYPICAL USE: farm, pack, military, light draft, riding

TEMPERAMENT: kind, calm, willing

ORIGIN: Switzerland

SIMILAR BREEDS: none

Also known as the Franches-Montagne, the Freiberger was developed in the Jura Mountains of Switzerland—this small range, north of the Alps, is sometimes called the Freiberger Mountains—at the end of the 1800s. It was created by crossing the native Bernese Jura Horse with the English Thoroughbred and the Anglo-Norman, with some influences from the Ardennais and the Arabian. It is highly versatile, being used for light draft, farmwork, riding, and competition.

Upland Farmers

As a mountain breed, the Freiberger is naturally sure-footed and tough and far more equipped to work in the hilly mountainous areas than a tractor. It is still widely used by the upland farmers of Jura and by the Swiss army, which favors it as a pack and patrol animal. The Freiberger is also found all over Europe.

There are two distinct types within the Freiberger breed: a broader, heavier stamp with greater muscle development, and a lighter, finer type. Today the continuing demands for a competition horse as well as a leisure riding animal mean that there is a trend toward breeding the lighter type.

Founding Sire

Many modern Freibergers trace back to one stallion called Vaillant, foaled in 1891, which was a mix of Norfolk Roadster, Anglo-Norman, and English hunter blood. Valliant was a great-grandson of a half-bred English hunter stallion named Leo H., which had some Norfolk Roadster blood and was imported to Switzerland in 1865. Poulette, Vaillant's grandam on both sides, was thought to be of Thoroughbred and Anglo-Norman stock. Imprévu, an Anglo-Norman imported in 1889, produced a second important line through his great-grandson, Chasseur.

Other outcrosses to French, English, and Belgian horses had no lasting effect, and it was not until after the Second World War that a new bloodline emerged from Urus, another stallion with Norman blood. Since then further outcrosses have been carefully monitored. Anglo-

Normans are usually selected, but Arabian blood has also been added.

Fascinating Facts

Horse enthusiast Winston Churchill once proclaimed: "No hour of life is wasted that is spent in the saddle ... There is something about the outside of a horse that is good for the inside of a man."

Swiss Cross

The Freiberger today is bred at the federal Swiss stud in Avenches, where breeding is strictly regulated experiments have begun with crossing the Freiberger with the Swiss Half-Blood, or Schweizer Halbblut, to make a lighter, more elegant competition horse. It has an

Ponylike

The pure Freiberger has a small, almost ponylike head that can be a little heavy, with a pronounced jawline and a broad forehead. Its neck is muscular and arching, with a good sloping shoulder, broad and pronounced withers, and a straight and powerful back. The Freiberger does not, like so many draft breeds, suffer conformational faults in its legs, which in this breed are invariably good and clean, with strong joints, plenty of bone, and good, hard feet. It sometimes has a small amount of feathering, although modern breeding has largely bred this out. Sometimes a finer head is seen, with an almost Arabian outlook, although this is not necessarily desirable.

The Freiberger is always bay or chestnut, but variations of shades do occur, and it stands between 14.3 and 15.3 hh. Sure-footed, agile, and good-natured, the Freiberger is an energetic, little horse with power, sweet temper, endurance, and agility. Overall it is a triumph for its breeders, who continue to produce this excellent mountain draft. Although the lighter type is still more popular, it is more of a draft breed than a light horse.

and highly selective. A Freiberger that has been bred in Avenches is branded with a Swiss cross.

The Freiberger matures quickly into a well-balanced, active, and calm equine that is a willing and easy worker with equable temperament. Over the past few years

active stride that makes it successful in dressage and natural athleticism that allows it to stand its ground in the show-jumping arena.

RIGHT
Freiberger horses tend to have small, attractive, and almost ponylike heads set onto a heavily muscled neck.

NORIKER

HEIGHT: 16–17 hh

COLOR: chestnut, bay, roan, dun

PERSONALITY TYPE: cold-blooded

TYPICAL USE: draft, harness, riding, agriculture

TEMPERAMENT: calm, placid, willing

ORIGIN: Austria

SIMILAR BREEDS: Brabant, Black Forest Chestnut, Haflinger

The name of this breed comes from the ancient Roman state of Noricum, high in the Alpine regions of Austria. The Romans constructed an extensive road system in Noricum, and as old relics show, horses closely resembling the Noriker—also known as the Norisches Kaltbult, or Pinzgauer—were used to pull wagons and were also pack animals. The breed is renowned for being sure-footed as well as tough and constitutionally sound, and it is capable of pulling considerable loads over long distances.

Strict Guidelines

The Romans established studs, and it is likely that the Noriker developed from the heavy warhorse that was being selectively bred in the Salzburg region. During the Middle Ages the Noriker continued to be bred but by then in studs attached to monasteries. Today it is widely bred throughout southern Germany, where it is known as the South German Coldblood, as well as in Austria. It is likely that Haflinger and also Spanish, Neapolitan, and Burgundian horses feature in its history.

RIGHT
These attractive horses are predominantly liver chestnut in color, with a striking flaxen mane and tail.

The Prince-Archbishop of Salzburg is credited with forming the Noriker studbook around 400 years ago, and strict guidelines were drawn up to which the breed had to conform.

All-rounder

The breeding of the Noriker is currently based on five bloodlines: Volcano, Nero, Diamand, Schaunitz, and Elmar. The aim was to breed a sturdy, amiable, enduring type of horse, one that was sound and sure-footed—in other words, an ideal all-round workhorse for a mountainous terrain. Half of these horses were bay, although chestnut also appeared. The leopard spot markings displayed on early Norikers—the Pinzgauer strain of Noriker, once considered a separate breed, was seen—became increasingly rare. Today the most common color is liver chestnut with flaxen mane and tail, which contributes to the breed's overall good looks.

Noriker breeding stallions are required to pass demanding tests that are used to measure their strength and speed.

SCHWARZWÄLDER FÜCHSE
(Black Forest Chestnut)

TEMPERAMENT: good-natured, gentle, lively

ORIGIN: Germany

SIMILAR BREEDS: Noriker, Breton

HEIGHT: 14.3–15hh

COLOR: sorrel to dark chestnut, occasionally gray

PERSONALITY TYPE: cold-blooded

TYPICAL USE: agriculture, forestry, harness, riding

In its German homeland, the Schwarzwälder Füchse, Black Forest Chestnut is known as the "Pearl of the Black Forest," and this active, lively, little horse is one of the most attractive of the draft breeds. It comes from the Black Forest in Baden-Wurttemberg in southern Germany and is small and hardy, able to cope with the long winters of the region, and sure-footed enough to cross the hilly regions of its woodland home with ease. The farmers of the region have used it for hundreds of years.

Forged Papers

Horses existed in the Black Forest as long ago as the Middle Ages, and more recently the Noriker draft has had a major influence on the Schwarzwälder Füchse. The Schwarzwälder Füchse does resemble a small Noriker or a larger Haflinger. Infusions of Breton blood have, later on, also had some impact on the breed, but attempts to use the Brabant, or Belgian Heavy Draft, to increase size have been mainly unsuccessful.

When the breed association was formed in 1896 and a studbook was established, breeders were instructed to use only Belgian stallions.

The traditional farmers secretly used native stallions, however, and forged the resulting foals' identity papers. By the First World War the authorities finally realized that the Belgians were not equipped for the Schwarzwäld farmers, and they lifted the restrictions.

Striking Color

Lively and agile, long-lived and fertile, the Schwarzwälder Füchse stands around 15 hh. It has a refined head for a draft breed, with a wide forehead and tapering muzzle. Its neck is strong and its shoulders muscular and powerful. Its legs are fine but strong, with little feathering, and it has good feet. Its color varies from sorrel to dark chestnut, usually with flaxen mane and tail, although a striking dark silver dapple—known in Germany as Kohlfuchs—sometimes appears.

Fascinating Facts

The name Schwarzwälder Füchse translates as "Black Forest Sorrel," but the last word has become "Chestnut." The breed is sometimes called Schwarzwälder Kaltblut, which means "Black Forest Coldblood."

ABOVE

This relatively small draft breed is highly attractive and especially hardy. It is sure-footed and well-adapted to hilly terrain.

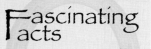

SCHLESWIG HEAVY DRAFT

HEIGHT: 15.2–16 hh

COLOR: chestnut

PERSONALITY TYPE: cold-blooded

TYPICAL USE: agriculture, harness, riding

TEMPERAMENT: willing, kind, active

ORIGIN: Germany

SIMILAR BREEDS: Jutland

Fascinating Facts

Barbara Jo Rubin was the first female jockey to win a race in 1969.

The Schleswig Heavy Draft gets its name from the Schleswig-Holstein region of northern Germany, which borders on Denmark and at times has been a part of that country. It is therefore not surprising that the Schleswig resembles the Jutland, the Danish heavy horse to which it is closely related. A relatively new

breed, the Schleswig Heavy Draft was developed during the second half of the 1800s as a draft breed of a medium stature; the breed society was established in 1891.

Severely Depleted

The breed is based on the Jutland and can be traced back to one stallion, Aldrup Munkedal, and his descendants, Hovding and Prins af Jylland. Infusions of lighter blood, including Yorkshire Coach Horse and Thoroughbred, are thought to have had little lasting effect. Later a Suffolk Punch stallion named Oppenheim LXII was used, and traces of his influence remain.

By the end of the 1800s the Schleswig was in demand for pulling trams and buses and to work the land. The breed survived the First World War—during which its homeland was under Danish rule—although numbers were severely depleted. Breton and Boulonnais blood was introduced with great success.

Ten Stallions Left

The Second World War had a more devastating impact, and the surviving Schleswig horses were bred back to Jutlands to reestablish the breed. Still it is believed that there are only around 10 purebred stallions left today.

The Schleswig is an attractive, cobby type of draft horse, with a good-looking head, short, crested neck, powerful shoulders, a body that tends to be long but with good depth through the girth, and strong limbs with a fair amount of feather. It is most often chestnut with flaxen mane and tail. A second type of Schleswig has been developed that is lighter and makes a good riding horse.

RHINELAND HEAVY DRAFT

TEMPERAMENT: quiet, willing, docile

ORIGIN: Germany

SIMILAR BREEDS: Brabant

HEIGHT: 16–17 hh

COLOR: chestnut, sorrel, roan

PERSONALITY TYPE: cold-blooded

TYPICAL USE: agriculture, draft, harness

Known variously as the Rhenisch-Deutsches Kaltblut, Rhenish-Belgian, Rhenish-German, or German Coldblood, the Rhineland Heavy Draft is also called different things in different regions of its homeland, such as Westphalian Draft, Altmarker Draft, Saxon-Thuringian Draft, Renish Draft, and Mecklenburg Draft. It was developed during the second half of the 1800s for agricultural and draft purposes, and it enjoyed a relatively brief period of popularity.

Highly Efficient

The breed was once the most common horse in Germany—the studbook was opened in 1876—but it is now rare, with

LEFT

Percheron blood, such as the horse pictured, was also used to refine and improve the Rhineland Heavy Draft.

a total population of around 2,000. Since the age of mechanization, especially, the numbers of the Rhineland Heavy Draft have dramatically decreased, and now only around 2 percent of the German horse population are draft breeds.

LEFT

The Rhineland Heavy Draft breed developed from the Ardennes breed, like the horse pictured, crossed with other draft breeds.

The Rhineland Heavy Draft was developed largely from the Brabant (Belgian Heavy Draft), with infusions from the Ardennais, Clydesdale, Percheron, and Boulonnais, to produce a heavyweight but attractive animal of great power. It made an excellent farm and draft horse and was highly efficient in both roles.

Low to the Ground

For its size it has a small but well-shaped head with a heavy jaw, set on an extremely powerful, well-arched neck with a pronounced crest. It generally has low withers, but its shoulders are likely to

be huge, and it has a broad, deep chest. Its back is short and wide, its quarters rounded and muscular, its legs short and strong, with good joints and very hard feet. It stands between 16 and 17 hh and is most usually sorrel, chestnut, or roan in color, although occasionally bay and black do occur.

The Rhineland appears low to the ground due to the shortness of its leg in comparison to the bulk of the body, but it is not unattractive. It has an excellent temperament, being quiet yet willing and energetic when it is asked to be.

DUTCH HEAVY DRAFT

HEIGHT: 16–17 hh

COLOR: chestnut, bay, gray

PERSONALITY TYPE: cold-blooded

TYPICAL USE: agriculture, draft

TEMPERAMENT: intelligent, gentle, willing

ORIGIN: The Netherlands

SIMILAR BREEDS: Brabant

Developed in the Netherlands after 1918, the Dutch Heavy Draft is a relatively new breed and the heaviest of all the country's horses. It was developed by crossbreeding the Belgian Brabant, Zeeland-type Dutch mares, and the Ardennais and still bears a resemblance to the Brabant. The aim was to produce a massive, powerful horse of strong and solid build. It was most popular in the provinces of Zeeland and North Brabant, where it worked the large, arable farms in the heavy, marine clay.

Long Working Life

Although the Dutch Draft is a huge, solid horse, it is surprisingly active and generally has a long working life. Before mechanization it was invaluable to the Dutch farmer, and it was found extensively throughout Gelderland, North Brabant, and Limburg due to its phenomenal strength and gentle temperament. It was also found on the large farms in the clay areas of the Groningen, but it did not succeed in ousting the

ABOVE

These powerful horses with their huge frame are capable of pulling huge loads and are well equipped to deal with the heavy clay ground of their homelands.

region's eponymous breed. When the Royal Dutch Heavy Draft Society was formed on December 22, 1914, its aim was to produce a handsome, strong horse with power, especially equipped for prolonged and heavy haulage or traction.

Free and Easy

The Dutch Heavy Draft is a gigantic creature, but its head is far from coarse, with

a straight instead of convex profile, short, lively ears, and a kind, intelligent eye. It has a short neck, often set on loaded shoulders, good well-formed withers, muscular chest and hindquarters, and a wide, strong back. It has a sloping croup and low-set tail, strong legs with plenty of muscle, and good, hard

bone and excellent feet. Despite its size, its movement should be free and easy. It is generally intelligent, a good doer, and economical to keep.

Since mechanization, numbers have suffered serious decline, but a few good breeding animals still exist.

JUTLAND

TEMPERAMENT: quiet, willing, biddable

ORIGIN: Denmark

SIMILAR BREEDS: Schleswig, Suffolk Punch

HEIGHT: 15.3 hh

COLOR: generally chestnut

PERSONALITY TYPE: cold-blooded

TYPICAL USE: draft, parade

Pictures from the 800s of Danish warriors show them riding horses that appear similar to the modern Jutland, although the breed is believed to have started out in the 1100s. The Jutland was used not only as a draft horse but also as a popular mount of the knights of medieval times, having both the strength and stamina to carry a knight in full armor. The modern version of the breed is not used for riding, however, and is believed to have been developed in around 1850.

Suffolk Connection

It is generally accepted that one stallion, Oppenheim LXII, had a major influence on the Jutland. He was imported to the region in 1860 by the well-known horse trader Oppenheimer of Hamburg, who specialized in Suffolk Punches— Oppenheim is thought to be a Shire–Suffolk Punch cross. Six generations after Oppenheim came the stallion Aldrup Menkedal, which is considered the foundation sire of the breed. Almost all Jutland breeding can now be traced back to Hovding and Prins af Jylland, two of his sons. These horses also appear in the pedigree of the Schleswig Heavy Draft, which is closely related to the Jutland.

There is a theory that the Vikings took Danish horses into Britain and that the Suffolk Punch developed from these, and there are certainly similarities between the modern Jutland and the Suffolk Punch.

Cleveland Bay

The Jutland is a compact, heavy horse with short, stocky legs and some feathering, although breeders are trying to eliminate this. In the past the breed has been criticized as having weak joints, which once again breeders have been trying to improve. Its head is generally plain but not unattractive. It is believed to have some Cleveland Bay and Yorkshire Coach Horse blood in its lineage, which has added some refinement, and Frederiksborg blood was added to improve its paces.

LEFT
The impressive Jutland breed was used both as a draft animal and for riding, and it was one of the favorite mounts of the medieval knights.

DOLE GUDBRANDSDAL

HEIGHT: 14–15 hh

COLOR: black, bay, brown

PERSONALITY TYPE: cold-blooded

TYPICAL USE: pack, light draft, harness

TEMPERAMENT: gentle, honest, calm

ORIGIN: Norway

SIMILAR BREEDS: Friesian, Fell, Dales

The Gudbrandsdal has the luxuriant mane and tail seen in the Fell, Dales, and Friesian horses and is a powerful horse with strong legs and feet. It undergoes testing and grading, being

Luxuriant Mane

Two types of Doles were developed—the heavy draft Gudbrandsdal and the Dole Trotter. Despite the fact that the first cross of warmblood and Dole produced good riding animals, the practice of crossbreeding with Dole has more or less ceased and use of the Thoroughbred has been restricted.

Fascinating Facts

Before the Gudbrandsdal may be used for breeding purposes, its lower legs and feet are routinely X-rayed to ensure that there are no weaknesses.

judged on its pulling power and trot. Trotters used for racing must have a good performance record to be allowed to be used for breeding.

Although the National Dolehorse Association was not established until 1967, the Dole Gudbrandsdal is actually an ancient breed, originating in the great central valley of Gudbrandsdal that connects the Oslo region of Norway to the North Sea coast. It is one of the smallest coldbloods, and in appearance it greatly resembles Britain's Fell and Dales ponies. The strong similarity is hardly surprising, as all three breeds would have derived from the same prehistoric, wild stock.

Trade Routes

Between the years 300 and 700 Friesian merchants from the Netherlands introduced their own black horses to both Norway and the British Isles. Later, between the years 800 and 1066, there was a great amount of influence back and forth between western Norway and the north of England.

The Dole Gudbrandsdal was developed as a pack animal, carrying goods along Norway's overland trade routes. But in the 1800s experiments were made with the breed, crossing the Dole with Swedish Warmbloods and English Thoroughbreds to produce a lighter type of riding horse. One stallion in particular, Odin, thought to be a Thoroughbred–Norfolk Trotter cross imported in 1834, was to have a great amount of influence. The Dole Gudbrundsdal went on to be influenced by the stallion Brimen 825.

NORTH SWEDISH

TEMPERAMENT: willing, calm, biddable

ORIGIN: Sweden

SIMILAR BREEDS: Dole Gudbrandsdal, Swedish Ardennes

HEIGHT: 15–15.3 hh

COLOR: most solid colors

PERSONALITY TYPE: cold-blooded

TYPICAL USE: forestry, draft

A lighter type of draft horse, the North Swedish is ideally equipped to the forest and lumber work in the Swedish woodlands for which it was principally bred and at which it is more efficient than machinery. It is related to the Dole Gudbrandsdal, having both developed from the ancient native horses of Sweden and Norway. It is a smallish, stocky creature, with incredible strength, draft capability, stamina, and endurance and is notably long-lived, appearing immune to many equine diseases.

Young Breed

As a breed the North Swedish is still young, its studbook having been established in 1909. Infusions of Friesian and Oldenburg, as well as some of the heavier European draft breeds, have been introduced. Since 1903 however, there have been stringent breeding regulations in an effort to stabilize its type and retain its admirable characteristics. Leading this has been the Stallion Rearing Institute of Wangen in Jamtland, which is now one of the major North Swedish studs.

Rigorously Tested

This is probably one of the most rigorously tested breeds in the world, having to undergo testing on its pulling power, action, and fertility. Its lower legs are X-rayed to ensure no defects are bred on.

County Horse Days events are held annually, where stallions and mares are examined in a number of different situations, and special attention is paid to the horse's temperament.

The North Swedish Horse is willing and cooperative. It has a ponylike head (which can be a little heavy), muscular and crested

ABOVE
This is a relatively young and very versatile draft breed, whose qualities have been maintained through rigorous breed standards.

neck, and sloping shoulders that give it a long, springy stride. Recognized colors are brown, black, chestnut, buckskin, palomino, smoky, and gray. The final color, however, is acceptable only where descent is verifiable back to the Norwegian "blue horse."

A lighter version of the breed, the Swedish Trotter, has also been developed.

SWEDISH ARDENNES

HEIGHT: 15.2–16 hh

COLOR: black, brown, bay, chestnut

PERSONALITY TYPE: cold-blooded

TYPICAL USE: agriculture, draft, forestry

TEMPERAMENT: kind, gentle, calm

ORIGIN: Sweden

SIMILAR BREEDS: Ardennais

In the late 1800s it was felt that existing Swedish native breeds were not well-equipped to manage the heavy agricultural work required. The large Ardennais was therefore introduced to Sweden in 1872; by 1880 most

ABOVE/RIGHT

The Swedish Ardennes developed from the French Ardennes, pictured, and are popular agricultural horses, especially in the timber industry.

of south and central Sweden had imported or crossed Ardennais.

These heavier horses were bred with native stock, and conformation was now given priority. By 1874 examinations were required before a Swedish Warmblood, Swedish Ardennes, or North Swedish Horse could be entered into the studbook. The Swedish Ardennes studbook was opened in 1901.

Frugal Rations

The Swedish Ardennes remains popular as a carthorse and is also used for hauling timber in inaccessible mountain areas. It can withstand extreme variations in climate, is a strong and exceptionally eager worker, and can survive on frugal rations. A muscular, compact horse known for its longevity and overall good health, it has a heavy head, short, thick

neck, wide chest, well-muscled shoulders, and short back. Its short legs have a little feathering.

SOKOLSKY

HEIGHT: 15–16 hh

COLOR: chestnut, bay, brown

PERSONALITY TYPE: cold-blooded

TYPICAL USE: draft, agricultural, pack, trek

TEMPERAMENT: kind, willing, even-tempered

ORIGIN: Poland

SIMILAR BREEDS: Dole Gudbrandsdal, Brabant

Developed in the 1900s the Sokolsky was produced using crosses of Brabant, Belgian Ardennes, Norfolk, Dole Gudbrandsdal, and Anglo-Norman stock. The result is a versatile draft horse of great strength that is not excessively heavy. Tough and hardy, with free, active gaits, it is an excellent worker and economical feeder.

These traits have led to the Sokolsky's popularity. Its home, Sokolka in northeast Poland, is on the edge of the Knyszyn Primeval Forest, bordering Belarus. The area

includes both river valleys and glacial hills, and the Sokolsky is also used as a pack animal and for trekking.

Growing reputation

The Sokolsky has a slightly heavy head, straight profile, large, kind eyes, and alert ears. Its neck is long but very

muscular and broad at the base. Its well-constructed shoulders are reasonably sloping. It has a deep chest and pronounced withers, and a short, straight back, with a sloping, muscular croup. Its legs are strong with well-formed, hard hooves. The Sokolsky's reputation has spread, and it is now also bred in parts of Russia.

LATVIAN HARNESS HORSE

TEMPERAMENT: patient, kind, willing

ORIGIN: Latvia

SIMILAR BREEDS: Dole Gudbrandsdal, Oldenburg

HEIGHT: 15–16 hh

COLOR: bay, black, chestnut

PERSONALITY TYPE: cold-blooded

TYPICAL USE: light draft, riding

Three types of horses were developed in Latvia, which was then a part of the Soviet Union, in the 1800s. These were the Latvian Light Harness Horse, the lightweight Latvian, and the heavier version of the harness type. This last is believed to have descended from the old Forest Horse, a primitive creature considered the root of most cold-blooded draft breeds in the world today. The Latvian Harness Horse was established in 1952.

Influential Infusion

It is thought that continuing infusions of Dole Gudbrandsdal, North Swedish, Zemaituka, Finnish Universal, and Oldenburg, as well as other heavy European breeds, were added. The most influential infusions—in all versions of the Latvian horse—were those from the Oldenburg, Hanoverian, and Holstein. During the first

RIGHT

There are three types of the Latvian Harness Horse, with the lightest strain, pictured, making a useful riding and light draft horse.

half of the 1900s, 65 Oldenburg stallions and 42 Oldenburg mares were imported from the Netherlands, which became the base for developing the breed. Further crosses were made using Hanoverian, Norfolk Roadster, East Friesian, and Ardennais.

Patient and Willing

The resulting equine was a plain but good-looking animal with a slightly large but pleasing head, expressive eyes, and small, neat ears. It has a long muscular neck set on high withers—a trait not often seen in a draft breed—desirably sloping shoulders, and a deep, broad chest. Its back can often be straight, and other conformational defects are a tendency toward cow hocks and a predisposition to ring bone. That being said, the Latvian Harness Horse is generally well structured and muscular, with good legs and hard joints, plenty of stamina and endurance, as well as a patient and willing disposition.

Today the riding version of the Latvian is most common, as pleasure and competition riding continue to grow in popularity, and the heavier type is rarely seen.

Fascinating Facts

Horses cannot vomit. Therefore, whatever a horse consumes must pass through the digestive system. This inability to vomit is the most common reason for colic, a big problem for horses.

LITHUANIAN HEAVY DRAFT

HEIGHT: 15–16 hh

COLOR: chestnut, bay, black, gray, roan

PERSONALITY TYPE: cold-blooded

TYPICAL USE: draft

TEMPERAMENT: gentle, quiet, willing

ORIGIN: Lithuania

SIMILAR BREEDS: Latvian Harness Horse

Although the Lithuanian Heavy Draft originated in Lithuania at the end of the 1800s, the breed has been registered only since 1963 (when Lithuania was still a part of the Soviet Union). But there is no denying its popularity—by 1964 there were an estimated 62,000 Lithuanian Heavy Drafts in the breed's homeland, a testament to its versatility, its demand, and its fertility. The breed was developed by crossing the Zemaituka, or Zhumd, ponies with the Swedish Ardennes and the Finnish Universal Horse.

Highly Fertile

To ensure the breed is preserved, potential stallions

have to pass a series of rigorous performance tests before being allowed to be used as breeding stock. The Lithuanian enjoys considerable longevity and is also highly fertile—at the best studs, such as Nyamun, Sudav and Zhagar, the foal crop is 80 percent, with a

survival rate up to one year of age of 76–79 percent.

Immensely strong and enduring with a quiet temperament, the Lithuanian is equipped for heavy draft and agricultural work. It thrives in harsh and extreme landscapes and seems unaffected by the cold.

Fascinating Facts

Horse whisperers are said to be able to communicate with the horse in its own language. Some have used this ability to train horses, while others use it to "heal" with their hands.

Setting Records

The Lithuanian Heavy Draft is renowned for its excellent walk and trot—relatively rare in draft horses—and has set several records. It can pull a

LEFT

This draft breed has a especially good walk and trot, which combined with its extreme hardiness, has made it an extremely popular horse in its home country.

weight of 330 lbs (150 kg) for a distance of 6,561 ft. (2,000 m) in 13 minutes 20 seconds, and it can trot the same distance pulling 110 lbs (50 kg) in 4 minutes 45 seconds.

It is a nicely proportioned horse, with a large head that is clean-cut but sometimes a little coarse. It has a short and well-muscled neck, reasonably pronounced withers, and a wide, deep chest. Its back is short and powerful, with a rounded croup and a high-set tail. The legs are short with well-formed feet. Similarities can be found between the Lithuanian Heavy Draft and the heavier Latvian Harness Horse in both conformation and paces.

TORIC

TEMPERAMENT: calm, sensible

ORIGIN: Estonia

SIMILAR BREEDS: Postier Breton

HEIGHT: 15–15.2 hh

COLOR: chestnut, bay, brown, gray

PERSONALITY TYPE: cold-blooded

TYPICAL USE: all-round utility

An all-purpose utility breed, the Toric, also known as Tori, was developed in Estonia at the Tori Stud between 1890 and 1950. To develop the breed, native Estonian mares, thought to be Klepper, were crossed with European warmblood stallions. A draft horse of great quality, the Toric is also sometimes referred to as the Estonian Klepper or Double Klepper.

Taking Shape

The Toric's founding stallion was named Hetman and was a son of a sire called Stewart. Stewart—it is possible this name was that of the horse's owner—was known to be a cross between a Norfolk Trotter and an Anglo-Norman mare. He bred Hetman from an undocumented hunter mare.

The Tori Stud was established in 1856 in Estonia's Pärnu county, largely because the horses of the region were near extinction. There followed various experimental crossings—the stud had been established with 47 mares and 7 stallions, plus imported Finnish horses, three Arabian stallions, and two trotters. But it was not until the arrival of Hetman, foaled in 1886, that the new breed began to take shape.

Valuable Nucleus

Using Hetman and then his sons, a valuable nucleus was formed, but by 1930 detrimental signs of inbreeding were recorded. In 1937 the number of lines was increased with the

ABOVE

The modern Toric is a light draft horse of extreme elegance and refinement, and it is surprisingly athletic, with an aptitude for jumping.

introduction of imported Postier Breton stallions.

The modern Toric is a light draft and harness type with a clean, solid build. It has a large or medium-sized head, with a straight profile, a long, muscular neck, massive shoulders, and a broad, deep chest. Its back has a tendency to be long but is wide, with muscular quarters and a well-set tail. The legs are short and strong, with good joints and strong tendons. Recently emphasis has been on producing a good, all-round, sporting horse.

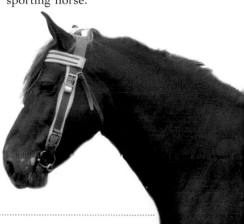

MURÄKOZI

HEIGHT: up to 16 hh

COLOR: chestnut with flaxen mane and tail, brown, bay, black, gray

PERSONALITY TYPE: cold-blooded

TYPICAL USE: draft, agriculture

TEMPERAMENT: willing, honest, biddable

ORIGIN: Hungary

SIMILAR BREEDS: Ardennais

Hungary's heavy draft horse was developed in the area of the Mura River in the southern part of the country and continues to be bred there today, as well as in Poland and in the countries of the former Yugoslavia. It was developed by putting native Hungarian mares called Mur-Insulan—which translates as "from the Mura region"—to Ardennais, Noriker, and Percheron stallions. Some Thoroughbred and Arabian blood was added, although the Murakozi is considered a coldblood.

Great Demand

This combination has produced a useful, quality, draft horse that is extremely strong, good-looking, and quick for such a heavy breed. In the years between the two world wars, the Muräkozi was extremely popular in Hungary and was extensively used on farms. Arable farming in Hungary increased after the First World War, and the Muräkozi was in great demand—by the 1920s it made up about 20 percent of the country's entire equine population.

By the end of the Second World War, however, the breeding stock of the Muräkozi was severely depleted, and outside blood was introduced to reestablish the horse. Between 1947 and 1949, 17 Ardennais stallions from France and 59 from Belgian were imported.

Farmer's Friend

The Muräkozi is an economical keeper, able to thrive on frugal pickings, and generally matures early, so it is capable of going into work at the age of two. It is hard-

ABOVE

The Murakozi typically has very little feathering on its legs, and its legs are generally relatively fine in comparison to the bulk of its frame.

working and biddable, a boon to the farmers of Hungary.

It has the plain head of many of the draft breeds, with a convex profile and large, kindly eye. It has generally good conformation, with a short, muscular neck, low, broad withers, and powerful sloping shoulders. Its chest is

deep and wide and its body compact, with a well-sprung rib cage. Its legs can be light for its frame, and there is little feather.

RUSSIAN HEAVY DRAFT

TEMPERAMENT: willing, trainable, calm

ORIGIN: former Soviet Union

SIMILAR BREEDS: Ardennais,
Soviet Heavy Draft

HEIGHT: about 14.3 hh

COLOR: chestnut, roan, bay

PERSONALITY TYPE: cold-blooded

TYPICAL USE:
light draft, agriculture

Systematic breeding of a small draft horse that was strong, fast, easy to handle, and economic to feed began in Russia in the 1860s using Ardennais, Brabant, and Orlov lines on native Ukrainian mares. The two main breeding centers were the state studs in Khrenov and Derkul, as well as Chesma, Kochubei, and Chaplits. In 1875 there were nine Ardennais stallions in Russia; by 1915 there were almost 600. Once there was a small nucleus of the new breed, they were backbred to fix type.

Active Stride

The Orlov Trotter blood was thought to give the Russian Heavy Draft its swift, active stride, but the Ardennais blood was so influential that for some time, the breed was known as the Russian Ardennes. During this period the breeding centers in Chesma and the Dubrovsk, and subsequently the Pershino and Khrenov studs, played a major role in developing the new draft.

The Russian Heavy Draft was introduced to the world's zoo-technical public at the Paris Exhibition of 1900. But the First World War, followed by the Russian Revolution, nearly wiped the breed out.

Longevity and Fertility

Efforts were made to reestablish the breed, even though in 1924 only 92 Ardennais stallions could be located. The year before breeding stock in Dubrovsk was moved to the Novoalexandrov Stud in the Voroshilovgrad region, while the Khrenov stock was moved first to Pershino and subsequently to Uralsk and Kuedin studs. By 1937 the stock of purebreds was reconstituted, and the Russian Heavy Draft was registered as a breed in 1952. It is small for a draft horse, standing only about 14.3 hh,

LEFT
The Russian Heavy Draft is an attractive, small, draft horse that is typically highly fertile and long-lived.

but it enjoys both longevity and continued fertility. The stallion Kolodnik, foaled in 1952, was still being used for breeding up to 1978, while the mare Logika, foaled in 1962, produced 18 foals in as many years and was still going strong in 1989.

Fascinating Facts

Horses and ponies can rest and even sleep standing up because of a fixed apparatus in their patella, or kneecap.

SOVIET HEAVY DRAFT

HEIGHT: 15–16 hh

COLOR: chestnut, brown, bay

PERSONALITY TYPE: cold-blooded

TYPICAL USE: draft, meat

TEMPERAMENT: gentle, willing, honest

ORIGIN: former Soviet Union

SIMILAR BREEDS: Brabant

Percheron and Brabant stallions used on the native mares were to produce the Soviet Heavy Draft at the end of the 1800s. The breeding area was very extensive, including Yaroslavl, Vladimir, Gorki, Penza, Ryazan, Tula, Tambov, Voronezh and Orel regions, and Mordovia. These regions had a developed agricultural industry, requiring strong and sufficiently fast horses of ample size, muscle, and power. The Soviet Heavy Draft fulfilled every need.

Breeding Centers

Three state breeding centers —Pochinkovsk, Mordovian, and Gavrilovo-Posad—were established in 1936 in what was then the Soviet Union. Alexandroz farm in Vladimir region and Yaroslavl farm branched off from Gavrilovo-Posadsk, and subsequently the Pochinkovsk and the Mordovian facilities were transformed into studs. These last two are still the two leading breeding areas.

In the Baltic zone, new breeds—the Lithuanian and the Estonian Heavy Draft— began to be formed on a different local mare basis.

Solid Build

The Soviet Heavy Draft is a huge horse of solid build that matures quickly, but it is less resistant to equine diseases than some other draft breeds. Despite their substantial size, they have surprisingly free movement at both the walk and trot.

The horse has a well-proportioned head, with a pronounced jaw and straight or slightly convex profile. Its neck is muscular with a tendency to be short, and its shoulders are straight and strong—this straightness does not seem to have an adverse effect on the horse's action. It has low withers and a long back, sometimes occasionally dipped—again this conformational fault does not appear to be detrimental to the breed, nor do its often pigeon-toed front legs and sickle-hocked hind. The Soviet Heavy Draft is a good milk and meat producer, and a new line is being developed that will hopefully eliminate the conformational defects.

VLADIMIR HEAVY DRAFT

TEMPERAMENT: willing, gentle, kind

ORIGIN: former Soviet Union

SIMILAR BREEDS: Clydesdale

HEIGHT: up to 16 hh

COLOR: most solid colors

PERSONALITY TYPE: cold-blooded

TYPICAL USE: light draft, harness

is muscular but longer than in other draft breeds, and powerful shoulders. Its chest is broad and more developed than that of the Clydesdale; it has pronounced withers and is tremendously deep in the girth. Its back can be long and sometimes weak, but it has sloping muscular quarters. Its legs are long like those of the Clydesdale, with plenty of feathering.

LEFT

The influence of Shire and Clydesdale blood on the development of the Vladimir Heavy Draft is clearly displayed in this photograph.

This breed, officially recognized only since 1946, was developed at the collective and state breeding establishments in the Vladimir and Ivanovo regions of Russia; the state stables of Gavrilovo-Posadsk—instrumental in the development of the Russian Heavy Draft—also played a role. The Vladimir Heavy Draft was established primarily through crosses between Clydesdale and Shire sires with local mares, with the aim of producing a middleweight draft breed with good pulling power and speed.

Clydesdale Sires

The foundation sires can be traced back to three Clydesdales: Lord James and Border Brand, both foaled in 1910, and Glen Albin, born in 1923. Infusions of Cleveland Bay, Percheron, and Suffolk Punch blood were also added, as well as some from the Ardennais. From 1925, however, no additional outcrosses were permitted, and the breed was further evolved by taking the best of the progeny and interbreeding to produce the standard Vladimir of today. There are currently four lines of Vladimir Heavy Draft, with modern breeding being carried out at the Yuryev-Polski stud.

Quality and Presence

The Vladimir Heavy Draft owes much to its Clydesdale roots, with the Shire influence being less apparent. It has a large head with a straight or convex profile, a well-proportioned neck that

The breed has considerable quality and presence, as well as possessing the typical gentle and willing temperament found in other draft breeds, making it easy to handle. It is used to pull the traditional Russian "troika," or horse-drawn sled.

Useful Addresses

American Horse Council
1616 H Street NW
7th Floor
Washington, DC 20006
USA
Tel: +1 202 296 1970
www.horsecouncil.org

**American Youth
Horse Council**
6660 D-451 Delmonico
Colorado Springs
Colorado 80919
USA
Tel: +1 800 TRY AYHC
www.ayhc.com

**American Association of
Equine Practitioners**
4075 Iron Works Parkway
Lexington
Kentucky 40511
USA
Tel: +1 859 233 0147
www.aaep.org

American Equestrian Alliance
P.O. Box 6230
Scottsdale
Arizona 85261
USA
Tel: +1 602 992 1570
www.americanequestrian.com

**United States
Equestrian Federation**
4047 Iron Works Parkway
Lexington
Kentucky 40511
USA
Tel: +1 859 258 2472
www.usef.org

**American Association of
Riding Schools**
8375 Coldwater Road
Davison
Michigan 48423-8966
USA
Tel: +1 810 496 0360
www.ucanride.com

United States Dressage Federation
4047 Iron Works Parkway
Lexington
Kentucky 40511
USA
Tel: +1 859 971 7722
www.usdf.org

**United States Equestrian
Team Foundation**
1040 Pottersville Road
P.O. Box 355
Gladstone
New Jersey 07934
USA
Tel: +1 908 234 1251
www.uset.org

United States Eventing Association
525 Old Waterford Road, NW
Leesburg
Virginia 20176
USA
Tel: +1 703 779 0440
www.useventing.com

National Reining Horse Association
3000 NW 10th Street
Oklahoma City
Oklahoma 73107
USA
Tel: +1 405 946 7400
www.nrha.com

**The United States Equine
Rescue League**
1851 W. Erhinghaus St. Suite 146
Elizabeth City, NC 27909
USA
Tel: +1 800 650 8549
www.userl.org

**National Horse
Protection League**
P.O. Box 318
Chappaqua
New York 10514
USA
Tel: +1 202 293 0570
www.horse-protection.org

**The Humane Society of the
United States**
2100 L Street, NW
Washington, DC 20037
USA
Tel: +1 202 452 1100
www.hsus.org

British Horse Society
Stoneleigh Park
Kenilworth
Warwickshire, CV8 2XZ
UK
Tel: +44 (0) 8701 202 244
www.bhs.org.uk

Horse & Hound
9th Floor Blue Fin Building
110 Southwark Street
London, SE1 0SU
UK
Tel: +44 (0)20 3148 4562
www.horseandhound.co.uk

Further Reading

Baskett, John, *The Horse in Art*, Yale University Press (New Haven, Conneticut), 2006

Bowen, Edward, *Horse Racing's Greatest Moments*, Eclipse Press (Lexington, Kentucky), 2001

Burn, D. and Fitzsimons, C., *Identification Guide: Horses & Ponies*, Flame Tree Publishing (London, U.K.), 2008

Draper, Judith, *The Ultimate Encyclopedia of Horse Breeds and Horse Care*, Hermes House (London, U.K.), 2003

Draper, Judith, *The Book of Horses: An Encyclopedia of Horse Breeds of the World*, Southwater Publishing (London, UK), 2003

Johns, Catherine, *Horses: History, Myth, Art*, Harvard University Press (Cambridge, Massachusetts), 2007

Frape, David, *Equine Nutrition and Feeding*, Wiley-Blackwell (Hoboken, New Jersey), 2004

Giffin, James M. and Gore, Tom, *Horse Owner's Veterinary Handbook*, Howell Book House (Hoboken, New Jersey), 1997

Green, John, *Horse Anatomy*, Dover Publications (Mineola, `New Jersey), 2006

Hakola, Susan E., *The Equus Illustrated Handbook of Equine Anatomy*, Primedia Equine Network (Gaithersburg, Maryland), 2006

Harris, Susan E., *Horse Gaits, Balance, and Movement*, Howell Book House (Hoboken, New Jersey), 2005

Harris, Susan E., *Grooming to Win: How to Groom, Trim, Braid, and Prepare Your Horse for Show*, Howell Book House (Hoboken, New Jersey), 1991

Hausman, Gerald and Hausman, Loretta, *The Mythology of Horses: Horse Legend and Lore Throughout the Ages*, Three Rivers Press (New York, New York), 2003

Hedge, Juliet and Wagoner, Don (Ed.s), *Horse Conformation: Structure, Soundness,` and Performance*, The Lyons Press (Guilford, Conneticut), 2004

Hendricks, Bonnie L., *International Encyclopedia of Horse Breeds*, University of Oklahoma Press (Norman, Oklahoma), 2007

Hill, Cherry, *Horse Handling & Grooming*, Storey Publishing (North Adams, Massachusetts), 1997

Jahiel, Jessica, *The Rider's Problem Solver*, Storey Publishing (North Adams, Massachusetts), 2006

Lewis, Lon D.; Knight, Anthony; Lewis, Bart; and Lewis, Corey, *Feeding and Care of the Horse*, Wiley-Blackwell (Hoboken, New Jersey), 1996

Lucas, Sharon, *The New Encyclopedia of the Horse*, Dorling Kindersley (London, U.K.``), 2001

McBane, Susan, *The Illustrated Encyclopedia of Horse Breeds*, Wellfleet Press (Seacaucus, New Jersey), 1997

Micklem, William, *Complete Horse Riding Manual*, Dorling Kindersley (London, U.K.), 2003

Murdoch, Wendy, *Simplify Your Riding*, Carriage House Publishing (Middleton, New Hampshire), 2004

Pavord, Tony and Pavord, Marcy, *The Complete Equine Veterinary Manual*, David & Charles Publishers (Newton Abbot, Devon, U.K.), 2004

Pickeral, Tamsin, *The Horse: 30,000 Years of the Horse in Art*, Merrell Publishers (London, U.K.), 2006

Self-Bucklin, Gincy, *How Your Horse Wants You to Ride*, Howell Book House (Hoboken, New Jersey), 2006

Sly, Debby, *The Ultimate Book of the Horse and Rider*, Hermes House (London, U.K.), 2004

Smith, Mike, *Getting the Most from Riding Lessons*, Storey Publishing (North Adams, Massachusetts), 1998

Swinney, Nicola Jane, *Horse Breeds of the World*, The Lyons Press (Guilford, Conneticut), 2006

Vogel, Colin, *Complete Horse Care Manual*, Dorling Kindersley (London, U.K.), 2003

Glossary

action
The way a horse moves at various gaits, also reflected in head, neck, and tail carriage.

aids
Signals from the rider or handler to the horse that imparts to the animal what the rider / handler wants it to do. They can be natural (such as mind, seat, weight, body) or artificial (such as whips and spurs).

airs
Movements of the High School (*Haute École*), associated with advanced or classical equitation, such as "airs above the ground," where the horse leaves the ground.

appendicular skeleton
Bones in horse's legs, shoulders, and hindquarters.

axial skeleton
Skull, backbone, and ribcage.

back at the knee
A conformational fault in which the forelegs curve back below the knee. Opposite of over at the knee.

bay
Brown horse with black points.

brand
Marks put on horse's coat for identification.

breed (n.)
Subspecies of horses' that has a defined set of distinguishing characteristics, which may have been encouraged and developed by man.

blaze
Wide white mark on horse's face.

bone
Measured around the circumference of the horse's leg, just below the knee. Dictates how much weight the horse can carry. Hard bone is desirable, as it enables horses to carry heavier weights.

bowed hocks
Hocks turn out, with feet turning in. *See also* "cow hocks;" "sickle hocks."

buckskin
Color similar to dun but generally brighter and darker; the color of a tanned hide.

bull neck
Short, thick neck.

calf knees
Also known as "back at the knee."

canines
Four teeth in the interdental space, usually found only in male horses (called "tushes").

cardiac sphincter
Muscle at entrance to horse's stomach.

carriage driving
Driving a two- or four-wheeled carriage using one, two, or four horses. Modern carriage driving trials are three-day events.

carriage horse
Horse used to pull carriages—usually relatively light and elegant and used in carriage driving competition.

carthorse
Large, strong, cold-blooded, draft horse used to pull carts or other heavy loads.

chestnut
Horse with an orange or reddish brown coat of varying shades.

coach horse
Horse used to pull a coach or carriage, usually powerfully built for fairly heavy loads.

cob
Small, stocky horses with compact bodies, short legs, and steady dispositions. A type, rather than a breed, usually of unknown or mixed breeding.

coffin joint
Between pedal bone and short pastern in horse's foot.

coldblood (n.), cold-blooded (adj.)
Large horse with calm, gentle disposition; equipped for slow, hard work. Draft horses are considered coldbloods.

colt
Uncastrated male horse or pony under the age of four.

conformation
A horses' shape and "composition;" especially determined by the body parts' proportion and relationship to one another.

coronet band
At the top of horse's foot.

cow hocks
Hocks turn in, with feet turning out. *See also* "bowed hocks;" "sickle hocks."

croup
Topline of a horse measured from the point of the hip to the point of the buttock.

dam
The horse's female parent.

depth of girth
The measurement from the horse's withers to the elbow.

dental star
Black mark found on front of tables of teeth.

destrier
This word described the finest and strongest medieval warhorse ridden by knights. A type of horse and not a breed of horse.

digital cushion
Large piece of tissue at back of horse's foot (also called "plantar cushion").

dished face
A concave profile, such as that of the Arabian.

dock
The part of the horse's tail on which the hair grows.

dorsal stripe
A line of darker hair extending from the horse's neck to the tail, seen in the "primitive" breeds. Also called "eel stripe."

draft
Heavy horse, or a term applied to a horse drawing any vehicle.

dressage
Training a horse to the highest possible level so that it accurately performs a number of movements at different paces in a relaxed way in response to the rider's subtle aids.

dun
Horse with a yellowy brown coat and black points, often with a dorsal stripe.

endocrine system
Releases hormones into horse's body.

English saddle
Saddle with a steel cantle and pommel and no horn (unlike a Western saddle), designed to allow freedom of movement.

ermine marks
Patches of color in horse's white socks or stockings.

eventing
Eventing is a complete competition combining dressage, show jumping, and cross-country. Events take place over one, two, or three days.

ewe neck
Well-developed muscle underneath the neck and weak topline.

feather
Long hair on the lower legs and fetlocks, common in heavy draft breeds.

flaxen
White mane and tail on chestnut.

filly
Female horse or pony under the age of four.

five-gaited
A horse that can demonstrate five gaits—three natural (walk, trot, canter) and two "man-made" (slow and rack).

freezemark
White numbers on horse's coat, put on with chilled markers, for identification.

frog
Horny, V-shaped part of bottom of horse's foot.

gait
The horse's action, such as walk, trot, or canter; also applied to the American gaited horses.

gaited horse
Horse that performs a foot fall pattern outside the normal walk, trot, canter sequence.

Galvayne's Groove
Develops down the outside of upper corner incisors; can be used to help judge a horse's age.

gelding
Castrated male horse.

goose-rump
When the quarters slope sharply from croup to dock.

hack
General riding horse. Show quality hacks have flawless manners and looks.

hand
Traditional unit of measurement for horses. One hand equals 4 in. (10.16cm). The symbol for this unit is "hh" (standing for "hands high").

harness horse
Horse used for pulling vehicles.

Haute École
High School, the classical art of advanced riding, seen, for example, in the Spanish Riding School of Vienna.

heavy horse
Any large draft breed.

herring-gutted
When the underside of the body slopes steeply up toward the stifle.

hindquarters
The back quarters of a horse from the flank to the tail.

hollow back
Dipped back; can develop with age. Also called "sway back."

hotblood (n.), hot-blooded (adj.)
Light saddle horse, such as the Thoroughbred and the Arabian, with highly-strung, fiery-tempered nature.

hunter
Horse bred and trained to be ridden for hunting. Can either be show hunters or working / field hunters.

incisors
The 12 biting teeth at the front of a horse's mouth.

infundibulum
Large, dark hole found in center of tables of teeth.

interdental space
Gap between the incisors and premolars.

jibbah
A shield-shaped bulge on the forehead, unique to the Arabian.

Isabella
Another term for palomino.

jumper's bump
When the horse has a pronounced croup.

laminae
Leaves of tissue between hoof wall and pedal bone.

light horse
Any equine over 15 hh that is not one of the heavy draft breeds.

light of bone
A conformation fault where the amount of bone below the knee is too small in comparison to the size of the horse.

loaded shoulder
Excessive muscle formation; a conformational fault.

lunging
(Also called "lungeing" or "longeing"). Where a horse is held on a long rope and told to circle around its trainer for training and exercise.

lymphatic system
Drains excess fluid and helps horse's body fight infection.

mare
Adult female horse or pony.

mealy muzzle
Oatmeal-colored muzzle seen on the Exmoor Pony.

mitbah
The angle at which the Arabian's head meets the neck; unique to the breed.

molars
The 12 chewing teeth at the back of a horse's mouth.

navicular bone
Small bone in horse's foot.

over at the knee
A conformational fault; the opposite of back at the knee.

pacer
A horse that performs a lateral action rather than diagonal, like the trot.

palomino
Horse with a yellowy gold coat and white mane and tail.

pastern bone
Extends from horse's lower leg into top of the foot.

pedal bone
Large bone in horse's foot.

perlino
Cream-colored horse with blue eyes.

piebald
Horse with black-and-white patches.

pigeon toes
When the toes turn in.

plantar cushion
Large piece of tissue at back of horse's foot (also called "digital cushion").

points of the horse
Specific external parts of the horse. In relation to color, the points of the horse refer to the mane, tail, muzzle, tips of the ears, and lower legs.

polo pony
Fast, agile, and quick-thinking horse used to play the game of polo, even if it is taller then the maximum height for a pony (14.2 hands).

pony
Small horse, usually under 14.2 hands. However, ponies are not necessarily simply a small or miniature horse, as they tend to differ from horses in other ways. For example, they may have thicker manes, tails, and coat; proportionally shorter legs, wider barrels, shorter and thicker necks; and sometimes calmer temperaments.

posting
In rising trot, when the rider rises from the saddle for one beat and sits in the saddle for the alternate beat.

premolars
The 12 chewing teeth at the back of a horse's mouth.

prepotency
The ability to pass on characteristics to the progeny.

presence
The "sparkle" seen in show horses and competition horses that says: "Look at me."

primitive
The term used to describe early horse breeds, such as Tarpan, Przewalski's, and Solutre.

prophet's thumb mark
Muscular indentation, usually on neck or shoulder; considered lucky.

quarters
See hindquarters.

rack
A four-beat gait known as the fifth gait in some North American breeds. Also called "single-foot."

remount
A horse used for service in an army or the police force.

roach back
Back curves up toward and over the loins.

Roman nose
Nose that is convex in profile.

saddle horse
Horse bred or trained for riding.

sickle hocks
Hocks that are too bent and weak. See also "bowed hocks;" "cow hocks."

sire
The horse's male parent.

skewbald
Horse with patches of white and any color other than black.

snip
White on horse's nose.

sock
White on a horse's leg extending from the foot to the fetlock or below.

sole
Bottom of horse's foot.

sporting horse
Type of horse—purebred or crossbred—that is used for equestrian disciplines such as dressage, jumping, eventing,` or endurance.

stallion
Adult male horse that has not been castrated (gelded).

star
White mark on horse's forehead or between eyes.

stocking
White on horse's leg extending from the foot to between the fetlock and knee or hock (or sometimes higher, known as "white legs").

stripe
Narrow white mark on horse's face.

studbook
Book in which the pedigree of purebred stock are officially recorded.

swan neck
Long neck that is dipped in front of the withers and then arched, with the highest point farther back, then the poll.

sway back
Dipped back; can develop with age. Also called "hollow back."

tables
Top surface of lower incisors.

tack
The various saddles, bridles, and other equipment used in horse riding, driving, and management.

teaser
A substitute stallion used to test whether a mare is ready to be mated.

tölt
The lateral gait seen in the Icelandic Horse.

trotting horse; trotter
Horse that has been trained to trot, for example, in harness racing.

tushes
Four teeth in the interdental space, usually found only in male horses (also called "canines").

type
"Types" of horses are not breeds` but usually a group of breeds that share similar

characteristics or are used for a specific activity such as polo or hunting.

wall
Outside of horse's foot.

warmblood (n.),
warm-blooded (adj.)
Generally a half-bred or part-bred horse of an even temperament, usually crossed out from Arabian or Thoroughbred stock or the result of a cross between hot-blooded and cold-blooded breeds to create a sturdy, athletic horse.

Western pleasure
Western-style competition, specifically judging conformation and temperament, gait cadence, and speed.

Western saddle
Saddle used for western riding and for working on horse and cattle ranches, a distinctive feature of which is the horn.

withers
The highest part of a horse's back on the ridge behind the neck and between the shoulders.

white face
When the white on a horse's face covers the eyes, forehead, and large part of the muzzle.

whorls
Places where the hair swirls and grows in different directions.

wolf teeth
Remnants of defunct, first premolars; one or more found in some horses.

zebra stripes
Dark stripes on the horse's lower legs, a primitive feature.

Picture Credits

Illustrations by **Ann Biggs**.

All photographs are courtesy of **Bob Langrish** except:

Animal Photography: Venyamin Nikiforov: 179 (tr, ct), 288 (tl, b), 291 (tr, c), 336 (tl, c); Sally Anne Thompson: 179 (b, cr), 248, 267, 270 (c), 273, 285, (tr), 336 (b), 337

Ardea: Hans Dossenbach: 125 (bl), 127 (tl), 178 (tl, c), 183 (b); Chris Knights: 334 (cl, b)

Corbis: 24 (t), 29 (b), 182 (tl, cr); James L. Amos: 76 (c); Araldo de Luca: 23 (b); The Art Archive: 23 (c); Asian Art & Archaeology, Inc.: 23 (t); Bettmann: 12 (cl), 14 (bl), 24 (bl), 24 (cr), 28 (br), 29 (tr); Stefano Bianchetti: 24 (br); Bureau L.A. Collection: 5 (ctl), 28 (t); Burstein Collection: 22 (cl); Christie's Images: 26 (t, b); The Gallery Collection: 27 (tl); Gianni Dagli Orti: 12 (cl); Lindsay Hebberd: 182 (cl); Historical Picture Archive: 12 (b); John Noble: 19 (c); John Springer Collection: 28 (bl); Barry Lewis: 21 (t); Leo Mason: 17 (b); Stewart Mike: 16 (br); National Gallery, London: 27 (tl); Galen Rowell: 183 (tr); Skyscan: 22 (b); Stapleton Collection: 25 (t); The State Russian Museum: 22 (tl), 25 (b); Graham Tim: 8,

13 (tl, tr); Underwood & Underwood: 15 (tr); Patrick Ward: 13 (b); Nik Wheeler: 27 (b); Bo Zaunders: 74 (t); Jim Zuckerman: 21 (c)

FLPA: Mark Newman: 130 (t), 133 (b); Jurgen & Christine Sohns: 133 (t); Frank Stober: 131 (t); Zhinong Xi; 133 (c)

Foundry Arts: 180 (b), 184 (tl, cr), 277 (tr, cl), 291 (b), 328 (tl, bl), 329 (tr, br), 340 (tl, b)

Kit Houghton: 150, 167, 183 (cr), 184 (cl, br), 249 (tr, ctr), 270 (tl, b), 272 (tl, c, bl), 276 (tl, b)

Shutterstock: Terry Alexander: 88 (tl), 93 (b); Joy Brown: 85 (c); kyslynskahal 85 (t); melis 84 (b); Gabriel Moisa: 79 (b) Cheryl Ann Quigley: 103 (b); Virtuelle: 74 (bl);

TopFoto: 22 (cr), 29 (tl), 288 (c)

Every effort has been made to contact copyright holders, and we apologize in advance for any omissions. We will be pleased to insert appropriate acknowledgments in subsequent editions of this publication.

Index